Charles Whitehead

Lives and Exploits of English Highwaymen, Pirates, and Robbers

Charles Whitehead

Lives and Exploits of English Highwaymen, Pirates, and Robbers

ISBN/EAN: 9783337158828

Printed in Europe, USA, Canada, Australia, Japan

Cover: Foto ©ninafisch / pixelio.de

More available books at **www.hansebooks.com**

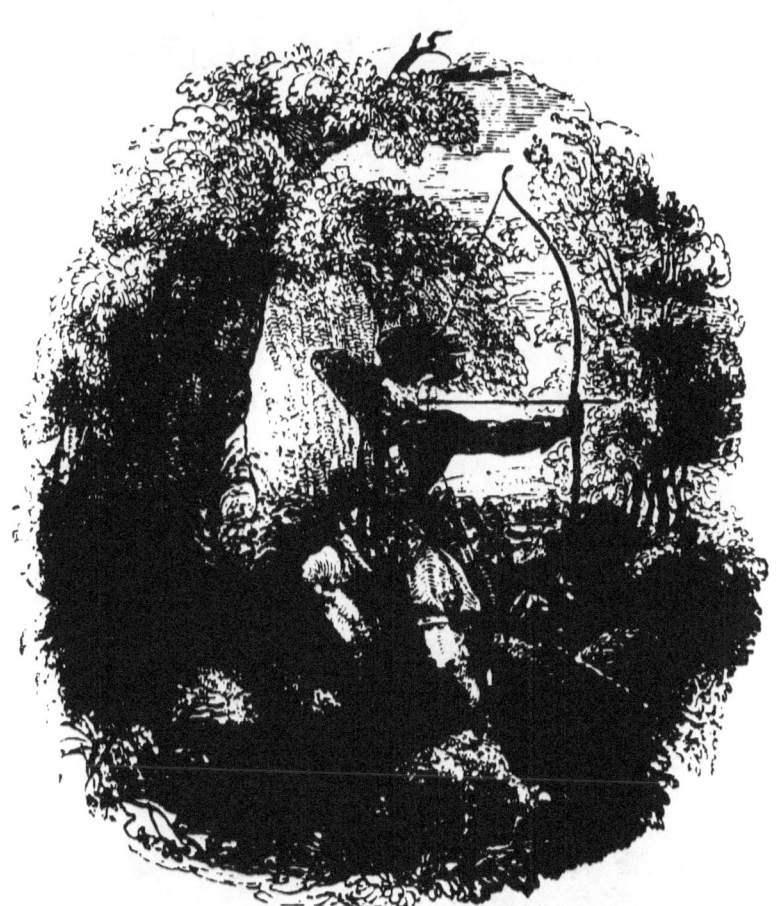

Page 1.

LIVES AND EXPLOITS

OF

ENGLISH HIGHWAYMEN,

PIRATES, AND ROBBERS;

DRAWN FROM THE MOST AUTHENTIC SOURCES,

By Capt. CHARLES JOHNSON,

WITH ADDITIONS

By C. WHITEHEAD, Esq.

Embellished with Twelve Spirited Engravings.

"Little villains oft submit to Fate,
That great ones may enjoy the world in state."

LONDON:
PRINTED FOR THE BOOKSELLERS.
1883.

PREFACE.

He alone is a truly brave man, who, being powerful, thinks it disgraceful to insult the feeble : many who pass for brave in the estimation of the world, are yet cowardly enough to commit base and barbarous actions : what else can be said of those, who possessing strength of mind and vigour of body, employ their faculties to rob and oppress the weak and ignorant? It is an easy matter to assume the semblance of fortitude and resolution; but few, very few, are the individuals who really possess those noble qualities: particularly such hardened villains whose lives and exploits are so faithfully recorded in the following work.

In presenting to the public a new edition of the " Lives of English Highwaymen, Pirates, and Robbers," the editor is tempted to indulge in a few more observations which, uncalled for, perhaps, by those who seek in a book of this nature for amusement alone, are nevertheless not misplaced or unimportant, when it is remembered that the utility of the work is to be vindicated, and its object to be approved.

It is incumbent on the Author or Editor of a book to indicate the aim and end of his performance; hence the necessity for a preface. It is the privilege of the reader (a privilege, we fear, confirmed by custom) to pass it over without perusal ;— hence its inutility.

It may be well, in the first place, to offer a short account of the literary fate of the various characters who figure in the succeeding pages. In the year 1711, Captain Alexander Smith put forth a small volume, containing the "Lives of Noted Highwaymen, Robbers, Thieves and Pickpockets," who had flourished during his own period of existence. The demand for this volume was so great as to induce the Captain to present his readers with a second, and subsequently with a third, volume. These latter volumes having been got together for the purpose of supplying the appetite of an excited public, were made up of the biographies of way-side heroes, and round-house rogues, upon whom justice has long since laid her inevitable fingers; together with a few of his own time, whom the Captain, during the preparation of his first volume, had either overlooked or had deemed unworthy of commemoration. The lives contained in the second and third volumes were, accordingly, disposed without the slightest regard to chronological arrangement or biographical propriety.

After the lapse of a few years, Captain Charles Johnson, having previously published "Lives of English Pirates," turned a magnetic eye towards the labours of Captain Alexander Smith; and, converting them to his proper use, introduced his own pirates to the highwaymen, thieves, and pickpockets of the other, and with very few additions of his own, and without any sensible or intelligible transposition of the order in which they had formerly appeared, published the whole in one folio volume.

From this performance, our object has been to select the best and the most important lives; excluding, for the most part, the meaner pickpocket, and the as yet uneducated thief, arranging them as nearly as possible in chronological succession, and adding such subsequent lives as bring down the work nearly to the present period.

We have, we confess, restricted ourselves, with a few exceptions, to a notice of English pirates and highwaymen. The former, by reason of the increased severity of our laws against piracy, have of late years almost disappeared from the face of the blue waters; and the latter, partly from the circumstance that highway robbery is no longer a profitable trade, in consequence of our paper currency and banking system, but chiefly from the establishment of an efficient patrole, have become altogether extinct.

We wish, therefore, the present work to be considered, not in the light of a mere calendar of crime, but as a collection of biographies of two distinct classes of persons, interesting in themselves, and displaying actions and adventures which are never likely to be performed in this country, or by the natives of this island again.

There is another reason (of itself a sufficient one) why we have left the undisciplined pickpocket and the common thief of former days to travel to oblivion without impaling them on our biographical pen; they are so completely outdone in ingenuity, skill, extent of resources, and fertility of invention, by the more accomplished professors of the present day. It may be both interesting and important to preserve the adventures of the bold and enterprising highwayman; but we conceive that the petty details of the mean and dastardly pickpocket, or the miserable minutiæ of wretched baseness on the part of our mothief, are more appropriately relinquished to the pages of the Newgate Calendar, and, perhaps, perused with the most intense interest in the instantaneous chronicle of the daily news paper.

It is maintained by a few well-disposed, but, we cannot help thinking, mistaken persons, that works of this nature, laying open, as they do, scenes of depravity and of almost unparalleled wickedness, are calculated, by rendering vice more visible, to weaken the abhorrence with which it should be regarded. They urge, or appear to do so, that while villainy is kept out of sight, it cannot very well enter into the mind; and yet, with a philosophical and religious faith in the inherent goodness of human nature, they also believe it so prone to evil that you have only to mention vice to endanger virtue, and that the former is never so irresistible as when she appears to us in her own person.

It may be true, although poetical, that "beauty unadorned is adorned the most," but we are not aware that vice is beautiful, or that she participates in the same dishabille advantages as beauty. On the contrary, it is more popularly believed, that—

> "Vice is a monster of such hideous mien,
> As, to be hated, needs but to be seen."

The verification of which, if true, cannot be better ascertained than through the effect produced by the perusal of the following work, in which her "hideous mien" is plainly enough to be discerned, even by the weakest optics or the most oblique vision. In truth, vice is never dangerous except when she comes disguised in the semblance of virtue; and the "false Duessa" ceases to be attractive immediately her disenchantment is completed. She is not loved or followed for her own sake, but for the sake of virtue, whom she, to the unpurged eye, resembles; and if we wanted one further evidence of the essential goodness of human nature, in spite of its weaknesses and its follies, we should find it in the universal execration and horrence with which confessed and open wickedness is denounced by mankind.

We contend, then, that not only is there nothing in the following pages that can for a moment be supposed to endanger the most elastic principle, but that a perusal of this work cannot fail to conduce to the service of morality, in the confirmation and strengthening of worthy and stable principles of integrity.

It is impossible to dwell upon recitals of this nature, involving the conduct and character of so many individuals, of all degrees of talent, from the highest to the lowest—some sinning, perhaps, through original and blindest ignorance—others committing crimes, in spite of their better knowledge, and in defiance of their own conscience,—and all (with very few exceptions) coming to a disgraceful and untimely end—without rising from the perusal with the conviction that, looking upon religion and morality with Dr. Paley's eye of expediency alone, not only is honesty the best, but it is the *sole* policy.

With these remarks, we leave this book to the indulgent consideration of our readers.

CONTENTS.

ENGLISH HIGHWAYMEN.

Robin Hood	1
Thomas Dun	17
Sir Gosselin Denville	21
Sawney Beane	23
Thomas Wynne	26
Thomas Witherington	28
James Batson	32
John Cottington, *called* " Mulled Sack"	42
Captain James Hind	45
Gilder Roy, *called* " The Bonnie Boy"	56
Captain Philip Stafford	62
Claude du Vall	67
Captain Dudley	73
Jonathan Simpson	83
William Davis, *called* " The Golden Farmer"	84
William Nevison	89
William Cady	95
Patrick O'Brian	100
Thomas Rumbold	102
Thomas Simpson, *called* " Old Mob"	115
John Bird	123
Thomas Cox	126
Colonel Jack	129
Captain Howard	156
Nathaniel Hawes	161
Tom Rowland and Frank Osborn	165
James Whitney	168
The Waltham Blacks	175
Timothy Buckeley	181
Thomas Jones	183
Arthur Chambers	185
John Ovet	190
Captain Evans	192
Thomas Dorbel	195
Dick Adams	197
William Gettings, *called* " the Hereford Boy"	201
Edward Bonnet	203
Richard Keele	208
Will Ogden and Tom Reynolds	210
John Price	212

	Page
Joseph Blake	215
Jack Shepherd	217
Jonathan Wild	221
Richard Turpin	223
Henry Cook	235
Henry Simms, *called* " Young Gentleman Harry"	237
James Maclaine	247
Eugene Aram	259
George Barrington	273

ENGLISH PIRATES.

Sir Henry Morgan	291
Captain Avery	303
Captain Martel	312
Captain Teach, *called* " Blackbeard"	314
Captain Charles Vane	323
Captain John Rackam	328
Captain Edward England	331
Captain Davis	346
Captain Roberts	354
Captain Kennedy	363
Captain Worley	366
Captain Lowther	368
Captain Spriggs	373
Captain Roche	375
Captain Gow	377
Captain Upton	379
Captain Edward Low	380
Paul Jones	385

AUTHENTIC MEMOIRS

OF THE

LIVES AND EXPLOITS

OF

ENGLISH HIGHWAYMEN,

PIRATES, AND ROBBERS.

Of the robbers and highwaymen of ancient times, history furnishes us with but few examples, and with fewer facts; we have however deemed it expedient, as a collection of biographical sketches, like the present, might be considered imperfect, without some notice of them, to present our readers with such accounts as we have been able to glean from authentic sources of those who appear to have been the " most celebrated in their vocation;" and by so doing form a perfect chronological biography of men, whose calling, in this country at least, is now happily extinct, and whose crimes and excesses, have been met with the universal execration and abhorrence of mankind, and now only serve " to point a moral or adorn a tale."

The earliest of these worthies who bore the enviable title, and of whom we have any authentic account, was the renowned outlaw of " merry Sherwood forest,"

ROBIN HOOD,

of whose predatory exertions of power,—enrichment of the poor by the plunder of the wealthy,—defiance of kings, magistrates, and judges, let the ballads of his own time speak.

It appears that he was born at Locksley, in Nottinghamshire, a place no longer in existence, about the year 1160, in the reign of King Henry II. and is reputed to have been Earl of Huntingdon, a title to which, it is said, he had no small pretension. There is no doubt but that his lineage was noble, and his true name Robert Fitzooth, which a pliant commentator conjectures was *easily* corrupted by vulgar pronunciation into Robin Hood.

In his youth he is stated to have been of an extravagant and lawless disposition, and, having dissipated his inheritance, insomuch that it had become forfeited, and being in the predicament of outlawry for debt, he sought an asylum in the woods, and levied contributions on the wealthy passenger who might chance to traverse his self-granted territories.

In these forests, of which he chiefly inclined to Barnsdale in Yorkshire, Sherwood in Nottinghamshire, and Plompton Park in Cumberland, he reigned for many years, with all the authority, if not in all the splendour, of a legitimate sovereign; and his subjects, in process of time, amounted to the number of a hundred archers, " men most skilful in battle, whom four times that number of the boldest fellows durst not attack."

The royal forests at that period abounded with deer, and, consequently, afforded to Robin Hood and his retainers a sufficient supply of provender during the year; and it is apparent that there could be no lack of fuel for the purpose of dressing their venison. Henry II., however, determining to punish him, for making such rueful havoc among his fat bucks, had him formally accused and summoned bold Robert to court, to answer the charge The Earl, however, preferred the company of his own good fellows, to that of the King's courtiers; and refused to obey the mandate. Upon this, Henry dispatched an armed force to bring him in, alive or dead. The Earl met his enemy most gallantly, and his archers galled the King's men so much with their first flight, that they fronted about towards London, and marched home as speedily as their wounds would allow them. This was deemed rank treason; and the Earl was forthwith declared an outlaw.

At this time, it was rumoured at court, that Huntingdon was about to lead to the altar, Matilda, the daughter of Lord Fitzwater—as brave a wench as ever brushed dew from green sward—who had been Robert's companion from her childhood; and, since she had been able to bend a bow, had shone by his side in the King's chases, outraging the forest laws with almost as great audacity as her favorite Fitz-Ooth himself. The King thought this would be an excellent opportunity of waylaying the Earl, and appointed young Sir Ralph Montfauçon, with a chosen troop, to perform the service.

The youthful Knight divided his men into equal numbers, and dispatching his Lieutenant with one half to seize upon the Castle of Locksley, which he knew would be but ill-guarded while the Earl was away at the wedding, with the remainder he proceeded, to the place where the ceremony was to be performed.

Robert and Matilda stood before the altar, and the sleek and rosy Abbot had already begun to officiate, when a thundering noise was heard at the gate, and the iron tread of a number of soldiers soon rung upon the marble floor. It was Sir Ralph and his troop. Striding up to the altar, the Knight placed his drawn sword between the youthful lovers, and exclaimed, " In the King's name, I forbid this marriage; and do attach thee, Robert Fitz-Ooth, as a false traitor!—Yield thee!" The Earl's sword was drawn in an instant; he struck down Sir Ralph's weapon, clasped Matilda in his arms, and after warmly kissing her lips, commended her to her father's care. " We must part awhile, my sweet Maud," said he, " but we shall meet again. Although the ceremony be incomplete, henceforth, I would have thee bear thyself as the bride of Fitz-Ooth." He then made a sign to his followers, and commenced a furious attack upon the soldiers, hoping to cut his way through them and escape. A desperate skirmish ensued. The King's men stood it bravely; but Robert, with the aid of his good sword, and backed by his bold adherents, fought forward to the chapel-door; then, retreating with his men to an eminence, he exchanged his sword for a bow and quiver, and did such execution among the pursuers that they soon thought proper to desist.

King Henry was sorely grieved at the Earl's having thus evaded him; and swore, in his wrath, that the castle and lands of Locksley, which Sir Ralph's Lieutenant had seized, should be the reward of that man who could bring in the Earl. Upon this, Sir Ralph, who had been suddenly smitten with the beauty of fair Matilda, and thought that the possession of Locksley castle would certainly be a passport to old Fitzwater's favor, which was one step towards that of his daughter, began to collect men again. He soon mustered a chosen band of followers, and started in high spirits towards the haunts of the outlaw. He beat up all the country round the Ouse and Trent, but without the least success. His followers fell off by degrees, and, at length, he was left with only a single squire to pursue his adventures.

The next morning they rode forth to the green to see the sports of Gamwell Feast. While the Knight was yet enjoying the delicious odour of the gathered flowers with which the place was bedecked, he perceived a flutter in the assembly, and every eye suddenly turned in one direction. He looked round and beheld a fair lady in green and gold, riding up under the trees, accompanied by a stout and strong Friar in grey, and several fair damsels and gay youths. The lady had a quiver by her side, and bore a bow and arrow in her hand. Her hair might vie with the glossy black of the raven's wing; it curled up like clusters of dark grapes under her round hat, which was surmounted by a plume of feathers that lay down as if habitually borne back by the wind, Sir Ralph, on their nearer approach, recognized the fair Matilda Fitzwater, and her ghostly adviser and companion, Friar Michael, whom he had seen at the Abbey, on the morning of the fray between his men and the followers of Fitz-Ooth.

A number of foresters, equipped in trim dresses of Lincoln green, came up in another direction, and hearty greetings ensued between the new comers and the Gamwells. Matilda was crowned Queen of May; a hogshead was set abroach, and the hot logs soon began to crackle under the buck haunches which the foresters had brought to regale themselves and their friends upon. The sports of the feast commenced, and after many games and pastimes, the trial of archery ensued. A golden arrow and the hand of the May Queen in the dance were to be the conqueror's rewards. Sir Ralph obtained a bow and arrows from young Gamwell, but was outshot by the whole of the foresters; and had the mortification to see one of them lodge his arrow's head in the golden circle, and receive the prize from the beautiful Matilda. The lady was then led forth by the successful archer and invited to try her skill. Sir Ralph could not but most deeply admire the surprising grace of her attitude, as, gently curving her fine figure and taking her station, she drew the arrow to its head, and, loosening it with a motion that gave a slight flutter to her plumes and ringlets, lodged it side by side in the circle with that of the forester. The youth then led her to the dance, and Sir Ralph gazed on her fascinating charms until he began to feel most severely the pangs of baffled love and jealousy. Turning his eyes for a moment on the forester's face, he discovered lineaments, with which he felt that he had been before acquainted. On perusing them more attentively, he was confirmed in his suspicions. Approaching young Gamwell, he asked him if he knew the forester who was dancing with the May Queen. "Yes," replied Gamwell, —" I do;—his name is Rob." "He is Huntingdon, the Outlaw, and would be a prize worth taking;" said Sir Ralph, " do you think your fellows would assist?"—" Aye—one side or the other."—" But which, think you?"—" That you will find, an' you try."—" I have the King's warrant to take this man—how should I act, think you?"

—" I would counsel thee as a friend, Sir Knight, to take thyself off as quietly as thou well canst; for wert thou better backed than thou hast ever yet been, here, in such a cause as the taking of yonder green forester, you would get nought but bruised ribs and broken skull. To say nought of old Sir Guy of Gamwell and his yeomen, nor the foresters yonder, there is the May Queen can fence, and draw the bow, and handle the stick and staff, all in most dainty perfection; that Friar is a match for as many men as there are feet in his oak staff, and, methinks, it's a full cloth yard above his sconce as it stands.''

Sir Ralph, on hearing this, deemed it prudent to keep himself quiet; and stealing off the first opportunity, he hurried to Nottingham, and there demanded an armed force of the Sheriff, charging him, nomine regis, to assist in capturing the Outlaw. After some little delay, a body of fifty picked men were accoutred for the enterprize, and with Sir Ralph and the Sheriff at their head, marched away towards Gamwell Hall.

" By the mass, Sir Knight," quoth the Sheriff as they rode along, " I'll wager an acre of the best land in my keeping, that this outlaw—this fellow that was once Earl of Huntingdon, is now the very rogue Robin—Robin Hood, as he is called, that abides here in Sherwood Forest, with a troop of forest blades in Lincoln Greens who take toll of all comers. I have fallen into perils, times not to be numbered, in striving to take him. Sir, he kills the King's deer, and robs all wealthy travellers on the road, with a grace and courtesy not to be surpassed. More especially delighteth he in spoiling those in authority; Abbots or Bishops are sweet prey to him; them he robs with infinite glee, and leaves their purses as lean as their bodies are usually fat. Why, Sir, the most grave and saintly Bishop of Hereford, passing hereby lately with his retinue and high selerer, after the collection of divers rents, lit upon a set of seeming peasantry, roasting buck haunches (most monstrous rogues!) on the King's way-side. Incensed at their disloyalty, in regaling their carrion carcases with that flesh which is, by statute limited to the maw of Kings, or their appointees, the Bishop seized the curs, and ordered them to be brought bound here before me at Nottingham. With that, up starts a tall and proper fellow, and with one wind of a bugle-horn, brings up from the green-glades and coverts, sixty fair bowmen, all arrayed in the grass-colored livery of Robin. The very nose of the Bishop waxed pale at first, but when they tied his holy person to a rough beech, it partook of the hue of his enemies' garments, and by degrees, wained again into a dim, but steadfast cerulean blue. Sore wrath was he, as you may guess, to be, by these rogues, enforced to say mass for their sins in the green aisles of the forest; but, strange to say, in despite of his fears, he gorged gloriously on their venison; which, he affirmeth to this day to have been gifted with a flavor surpassing all things he had heretofore tasted. After grace and good wine, they made him pay for his provision, with the full sum contained in his purse and that of his selerers, enforced him to make the stump of an oak his pallet for the night; and, on the morrow, sent him off with small comfort in his heart, and a rueful rheum in his ghostly eye. The Bishop soon raised the country upon Robin, and hunted the mad despoiler of other men's gold into a cot; whereupon the forester changed clothes with the old woman abiding therein, and the Bishop brought her arrayed in a pair of Sherwood breeches and green doublet to Nottingham in triumph. By the Lord, Sir, in despite of the reverence due to my Lord Bishop and my own shrieval gravity, I could not but crow right lustily at the discovery, and the mutual railing between the old woman and the Lord Bishop. Ha! ha! assure thyself of this, Sir Knight—the Earl of Huntingdon on being despoiled of his Castle, and outlawed, hath turned a gallant thief, as well as a gay forester; he is the Robin Hood who doeth such deeds hereabouts, as make honest men, who have more coin than courage, turn up their eyes, quiver in their hose, and double-bar their doors, which were passingly well bolted before."

The Sheriff had scarcely done narrating the adventure of the Lord Bishop with Robin, when he perceived a party approaching an old bridge upon which his nag had just set foot. This party consisted of sweet Maud Fitzwater, with her constant attendants, young William Gamwell, of Gamwell Hall, who, it may be as well to notice, was our hero's cousin and best friend, Robin Hood himself, and some half a score of forest lads in their usual array. The Shrieve looked at his fifty men, and thought them such good odds against fifteen, that he forthwith prepared to make an attack. The first arrow from the opposite party, found a home in Sir Ralph's arm, and he was obliged to fall back with an attendant to get it extracted. A flight from all the foresters' bows followed this, which had been aimed by Matilda herself. Friar Michael's staff, after making two or three eddies in the air, fell at last upon the centre of the vortex, which happened to be the Sheriff's pate, and dislodged him from his saddle in a twinkling. Right sturdy were the blows which ensued upon the ribs of Nottingham's sheriff; who, finding the operation unpleasant, roared lustily for reprieve. This, at length, was granted by the Friar, at Matilda's intercession, and the Sheriff found himself a prisoner fast locked in the gaunt grasp of a forester, whose iron fingers clutched his wrists like felon's manacles.

The staff of Michael did good service on the pates of many of the Sheriff's force; several flat noses, dislocated shoulders, and peeled sconces, bore testimony to its hardness, and the vigor with which it was handled. After a short fight, the Nottingham men clapped spurs to their horses, and such of them as were lucky enough to escape the sword of Robin, the cudgel of Midge the miller, the arrows of Maud and the foresters, and Michael's oaken toy, galloped off towards Nottingham, leaving both their leaders in the hands of those whose capture they had anticipated.

Matilda drew the arrow from Sir Ralph's arm—bound up the wound with her scarf—told him that she might have lodged the weapon in his heart, had she pleased—and, bidding him and the Shrieve never again molest her brave Robin, under pain of shafts more mortally directed, rode off with her party. On approaching Arlingford Castle, where her father dwelt, she made on towards the gateway, and Robin, with his friends, bent his course to the Greenwood.

The next day, a large civil power arrived at Arlingford Castle, and, in the king's name, demanded the body of Matilda Fitzwater, for wounding a Knight on the King's duty, and aiding an outlaw in the resistance and bruising of the Sheriff's power. "Sheriff's pease-pudding," cried the testy old Baron; "away with you for a set of false lying vagabonds! talk to me of my daughter's wounding —Go your ways, scoundrels, or my long-bows shall be made ready to welcome you." The Baron then brought out his followers: and the civil party, seeing the castle so well defended, deemed it prudent to retire, and journeyed to the neighbouring Abbey, there to demand the body of Friar Michael. The Abbot, however, refused to deliver him up, but promised to call a chapter of Monks, and pass such a sentence on him as he might be found to merit. "This will not do," said they. "But it shall do," quoth the Abbot; "and if it will not do, nothing shall be done. So, I pray you, Sirs, retire; or I shall be provoked and lay you under the bitter ban of Holy Mother Church." Terrified at this threat, the party rode off to Gamwell Hall; where, after a vigorous resistance on the part of Sir Guy and his yeomen, young William Gamwell was taken prisoner, carried to Nottingham, and condemned to gibbet and halter without mercy.

Meanwhile, the Friar was tried by his peers, the monks and sentenced to imprisonment and privation from buck's flesh and wine. This Michael could not endure; he roughly remonstrated; the Abbot was positive, and, on Michael's attempting to retire, the monks hemmed him in. Whereupon, Michael lifted up that staff which had done such mischief at the bridge, and beat his dearly beloved brethren most grievously. After mowing them down right and left, he finished by levelling the Lord Abbot, by a most orthodox and right clerkly punch in the paunch from the point of his sapling, and wishing them a hearty "Peace be with you," took his departure for the Greenwood; gave himself wholly up to Robin Hood; and, till the storm should blow over, determined to be a true forester. According to the custom of Sherwood, he was baptised on joining the outlaws with a flask of canary, and was thenceforth called Friar Tuck.

Little John, after having fought like a true yeoman in defence of young Gamwell, followed him aloof towards Nottingham. No sooner did he hear of his condemnation, than he started like a roebuck towards the wood, and brought the doleful tidings to the haunt of Robin Hood, just as the baptismal of Friar Michael had concluded. Robin resolved, if possible, to rescue his cousin from the noose intended for him by the Sheriff How he sped in his attempt so to do, we shall presently see.

The Sheriff of Nottingham, albeit still sore with the Friar's bruises, resolved to attend the execution of young Gamwell. William was led forth pinioned; his sister and father stood by him at the foot of the ladder in a most melancholy humor; he had refused the proffer of the Shrieve's priest, and tarried for the one whom Little John had promised to provide. After some delay, the holy man approached, under the conduct of John. No sooner had he gained the side of the youth, than, whispering in his ear, he drew forth a bugle and broad sword, threw off his cloak, and appeared a forester in green. With one hand he lifted the bugle to his mouth and blew a shrill blast; while, with the other, he cut the cords that bound his cousin. Gamwell instantly wrenched a sword from one of the sheriff's men, and he, with old Sir Guy, Little John, and the forester (who, it will be guessed, was Robin Hood himself), kept the sheriff's people at bay, until a hundred stout lads of the Greenwood, in obedience to the blast of their leader's bugle, ran up to their rescue. After putting to flight the civil power, they hastened towards the forest; and young Gamwell, deeming his transgression unpardonable, joined the outlaws, and was in his turn christened by the renowned name-of Scarlet. Little John abode with him in Sherwood, while old Sir Guy and his daughter removed for safety sake to a distant seat of the family in Yorkshire.

About this time, King Henry the Second observeth a most quaint and right dainty chronicler of the doings of Robin Hood, to whom we are somewhat indebted, went to make up his quarrel in the next world with Thomas-à-Becket. Richard ascended the throne, and while he waged war against the Saracens in Palestine, Robin Hood, with his adherents, feasted on his deer, and levied contributions on his lieges in Sherwood. Prince John was now paramount in England; and happening to see the young heiress of Arlingford, while sojourning in the vicinity of Nottingham, he became, according to tradition, desperately enamoured of her ; and, presuming that it would be taken as an honor to the house of Fitzwater to make its rose his concubine, he dispatched one of his courtiers to solicit the fair person of Matilda, as his leman. The bluff old Baron wanted to slay the messenger outright ; but fair Matilda interceded in his behalf, and he was only tossed in a blanket, and set in the stocks to allay the fever consequent on the pastime; then ducked most royally in the ditch, and set in the stocks again to dry.

Prince John took a freak into his head to be in a mighty passion about this; he vowed to chastise the old Baron's insolence, and to get the lady by force of arms. With this intent, he sat down before the Castle with a chosen band of troops. The first night of his encampment, he was awoke by a horrible clangour close to his tent. The besieged had sallied out, and were at work, pell-mell, among their enemies. A party of foresters had at the same moment attacked his rear. It was evident that the Baron and his people were intent on cutting through the camp, and escaping. Furious at the idea of losing the fairest heart in England, John sallied forth to the very centre of the moil. There he discovered two youths fighting side by side, the one wearing the colours of Arlingford, the other a bonny suit of Lincoln green. In the slenderest of the two, he recognized Matilda; and gathering some of his stoutest fellows together, he attacked and separated the lady from her companion. "Fair huntress,' said he, " yield thee to me—wilt thou?"—"Win me, if you can," was the reply—"attempt it, if you dare." The words were accompanied with a blow from her baldrick, which would have cleft the royal pate in twain, but for the helmet which protected it. Prince John was too courteous to try to harm his lady-love; but he soon found himself compelled to be on the alert in his own defence. Matilda had slightly tinged her blade in his blood twice or thrice, when her sword broke on the ridge of his nose or the edge of his buckler, history saith not which, and she was just on the point of seizure, when some unseen hand dealt the Prince a blow betwixt the shoulders that would have levelled a bullock.

To this uncivil salutation, John was indebted to that staff which was evermore found in the company of Friar Tuck. That worthy, having thus disposed of the Prince, knocked about his heroes like nine-pins, rescued the lady, and followed the Baron with his men, who were already trooping off with the foresters, a body of whom had, as we said, attacked the royal troops simultaneously with the besieged, towards the heart of Sherwood.

Thus ousted from her parental roof, Matilda, with her father's leave, agreed that the ceremony of marriage betwixt herself and the lord of her heart should be completed. Friar Tuck officiated, and Little John fulfilled very satisfactorily the grave function of Clerk. " Now," said Matilda, " I am thy bride, Robin: but though we be wedded, yet we will not bed; the laws of chastity enjoined in Sherwood, neither you nor I will infringe. Let us tarry in patience for awhile. King Richard will, it may be, soon return; I feel sure he will not only restore my father to Arlingford, but pardon thee, Robin, and make thee Earl of Huntingdon again. Meantime, let us submit to the accustomed change of name on joining the outlaws of Sherwood. I take no title: I will not be called by courtesy, Countess of Huntingdon until thou art its rightful Earl; neither shall you name me as heretofore, Matilda Fitzwater, nor fair Maud, nor aught else but Maid Marian; for maid will I be, albeit a bride, while thou art an outlaw." This was agreed to by all parties, and the Baron journied to old Sir Guy Gamwell's, to abide with him till the return of Cœur de Lion brought better days.

Little John, who was one of his old master's body guard on the journey, on his return to Sherwood, met with a stranger on the borders of the forest, riding along in the most melancholy mood. " Ho! Sir Rueful," cried the page, " turn thee hitherward, thou must go and dine with my master to-day." " And who is he?" asked the stranger. " Robin Hood." " Aye I have heard of him often, and will now see him; yesterday one of us would have had a broken skin rather than I would have budged a hair's-breadth for thee; to day, do as thou wilt with me." Little John felt interested with the youth's words and appearance, and by degrees wormed out the secret of his melancholy as they went along. He had been a favored wooer of a brave wench, until a rich old Knight entered love's lists with him; and to his rival did the girl's parents assign the prize.

Little John repeated this story to Robin and Marian, and the youth was presently brought before them and seated by the side of the forest Queen. "How art thou called, gentle youth?" inquired Marian, "Allan, fair lady," replied the youth. "'Tis Allan-a-dale," grunted sturdy Midge the miller. "I know him—a proper lad, and handles a quarter staff like a true yeoman's son. By the thumb of my grandfather, and draws the long bow right bravely: almost a match for Little John himself—by this cudgel." " Aye, sayest thou so, Midge?" quoth Robin, "and when is this Knight to be wedded to thy love, lad?" "To-morrow, at Edmistow Church." "Is she content, think you?" "Not so, indeed, or I would scarce sigh for her—she is enforced to the match." "Then mark thee, Allan, I will prevent it."

The next day Robin disguised himself as a harper, took little John with him, and went to the wedding. The Bishop and his train were waiting the arrival of the decrepid bridegroom in the church-porch, when Robin approached them. After he had played an air or two on his harp, to the Bishop's great entertainment, the Knight neared the Church with his intended bride and her friends. "Hark you, Bishop," said Robin, suddenly stopping his minstrelsy; this is not an equal match; the man is sixty and the maiden sixteen; I will not have it completed." "Thou wilt not have it," cried the enraged Knight, "stand by, or I'll break thy bones." "I shall not stand by nor budge unless the bride say you are her chosen one."

The girl attempted to speak, but her emotions overpowered her, and she burst into tears. "Mark you that, Bishop!" cried Robin, and he blew a blast that brought up Friar Tuck, Midge, Maid Marian, and Scarlet, and some three-score bowmen in green, with young Allan-a-dale at their head. The Bishop and Clerk were speedily stript of their robes, and Tuck and little John arrayed therein in their stead. The lovers were united with all befitting form; and leaving the old Knight to rue the loss of the precious jewels in which he had bedecked the bride, young Allan-a-dale tripped lightly away in the company of the foresters.

It would ill become us, who profess to be historians of Robin Hood, to omit narrating his rencounter with the Friar of Dunchurch, whom Robin met one day with a fat buck across his saddle. The Friar did not know Robin, who happened to be a-foot, and armed with a short quarter-staff only. "How now," quoth Robin, "Sir Priest, what is this the ensample of loyalty you set, to kill the King's deer thus by broad daylight; nay, and that too within the range of the Sherwood bowmen; who engross, by the old right of belt and shaft, all venison which fatteneth beneath the trees whereof they themselves make a canopy? Should Robin hear of this"—"A pish for Robin Hood," replied the ghostly brother of Dunchurch, " thinkst thou, churl, that one who has appetite for a haunch, and manhood and skill enough to kill the best buck in the range, would quail at the sound of Robin's name, or even the sight of his verdant doublet? Mass! I have lived long enough hereabout, to hear of that rogue's doings, and every bold trick of his sets my limbs itching to have a moil with him. He hides himself deeply in these coverts, or, by St. Botolph, I would have notched his head with cudgel ere this. I shall not die content until I bring down a buck under his nose. Would that I might find grace enough in the eyes of St. Dunstan to cast me in Robin's way, so that I might try if his skill at quarter-staff be such as men repute. By'r lady I would maul him." "Why thou vain churchman," quoth Robin, " hast thou so much self-love in thee as to think thyself a mate for him thou speakest of? Alight, I entreat thee, most reverend Friar, and I will teach thee, in some seconds, that I—even I whom thou dost now look upon so contemptuously, will score thy pate in such fashion. that thy own fraternity of Dunchurch shall not know thee again." "What hast thou to wage with me," replied the Friar, " provided I do condescend to open thy pipkin— what hast thou to wage with me on the event? For we of Dunchurch do not toil for nothing." "Here are thirty gold pieces," replied Robin, tossing a purse on the glade, "which I will place against thy horse and buck, that I despoil thee of the power of chewing venison or cygnet—that I ruin thy jaw-bone, encased as it is in fat, within less time than the emptying of a full flask." Upon this, the Friar alighted, and to it they went pell-mell; after a few blows, the Friar, whom Robin found much more expert at handling a staff than he had expected, was stretched on the grass, and bellowed aloud for quarter. Robin then made himself known, took the horse and buck, but in consideration of the address he had shewn in cudgel-playing, invited the Friar of Dunchurch to his haunt, where Tuck so well entertained him, that he abode three days in the Greenwood, and was so loath to depart, that it was not before Tuck who began to look upon him as an intruding rival, threatened him with the flavour of his eight-foot staff, that the Friar of Dunchurch returned to his home.

Another of Robin's mad freaks was to go in disguise to a shooting match, which was held near London, where, in the presence of Prince John himself, he bore off the prize of archery from the very flower of the Prince's bowmen; and although at that time large rewards were offered to any one that would take him, Robin returned safe to his Marian and merry men in the Greenwood. There it was not safe to attack him; for he had by this time, gathered so strong a force of stout archers, that he bade the royal power defiance within ten miles of Sherwood. Stow says there were not four hundred taller, braver, or better marksmen in the country; and thenceforth the Knights of Prince John's court, shewed no disposition to contend with them.

His old enemy the Sheriff of Nottingham, was now dead, and our hero longed for an opportunity to play some prank on his successor, who, before his elevation to the Shrieval dignity, had frequently endeavoured to do him an ill turn; and this, as it is said, was the way he contrived to effect his purpose.

One day, he met with a butcher going to market, and bought his whole cargo, and his mare with it, which came together to about twenty pounds. With these Robin immediately went to market, sold his bargain presently, making such good pennyworths, that all the people thought he had stolen the meat. He then put into an inn at Nottingham, and treated all his customers, to the value of five pounds; which coming to the Sheriff's ears, who was at the same time in the inn, and taking him to be some prodigal spark of whom he might make something, intruded into his company, and after some short discourse, asked him, if he had any more meat to sell. " Not ready killed," said Robin, " but I have two or three hundred head of cattle at home, and a hundred acres of land to keep them on, which if you will buy, I'll sell you them a pennyworth." The Sheriff snapped at the proffer, and took four hundred pounds in gold with him. Away they rode together; but he was very much surprised at the melancholy place the supposed prodigal had brought him to, feared they should meet with a man called Robin Hood, and began to wish himself back again; but it was too late; for Robin winding his horn, presently came Little John, with fifty of his companions, who were commanded by Robin, to take the Sheriff to dinner with them; assuring them, he had money enough to pay his share. Accordingly they got a collation ready for the Sheriff, and after dinner was over, led him into the forest, and there took all his gold from him, good part of which he had borrowed from the innkeeper, before he had joined Robin Hood.

Robin Hood and Maid Marian had reigned King and Queen of the forest glades for many a moon, when one afternoon a strong and sturdy-looking Knight was hailed on the borders of Sherwood by a young archer, who was leaning forest-fashion against a beech-tree, and boldly bidden to follow to Robin Hood's haunt. "And who is Robin Hood?" asked the Knight. "The Lord of these green woods," was the reply; "and he takes toll of all passers. Will you come with me and pay it, or shall I enforce you to make me my master's treasurer?" "Enforce me! thou insolent boy!" "Boy, I am not; neither am I man, and yet, methinks, if you will dismount, I should make you deem me more of the latter than you now seem to think I am!"

The Knight dismounted, and without very little ceremony, commenced the fight. Before, however, either was harmed, the staff of Tuck peered over the bushes. In a moment he was between the combatants. "What!" cried he, "assailing our Virgin Queen!" "Queen!" quoth the Knight, "if she be woman, never was wench like her." "That it were flat treason to deny—is she not Marian? Why! What sayest thou for bearing blade against her? Wilt thou, by way of change, have a little of my oak staff? Or wilt thou go and eat with us? Wilt fight, or wilt eat? Or wilt eat and fight, or fight and eat? I am thy man any way."

The Knight liked the humour of Tuck so well, that he grasped his hand in amity, knelt in homage to the forest Queen, and followed them to the wood. Robin welcomed him most courteously, and after finishing to despoil a monk, who was fast bound to a tree, he invited him to eat and be merry. Right jovial grew that knight, and deeply delighted seemed he with his green-vested host; so that when Robin asked him for his gold, he bid him search and take all with a free welcome. "And would it were more," quoth he, "for thy sake." "Say you so?" said Robin, "then I take no doit of it. Thou art a true man, and shalt fare freely, without a penny cost."

At this moment, a heavy tread of horses was heard, near at hand, on the greensward; Robin and his merry men seized their bows and stood on the defensive. Anon a party of horsemen rode up; and the leader of them sprang off his horse, embraced Robin, and exclaimed, "What hast thou forgotten me? I am Sir William Lee, to whom this day twelvemonth thou didst lend four hundred pounds, on the bare credit of his word. It saved my lands from the rapacious claw of the holy church; and here am I come, pursuant to my promise, to pay thee with grateful thanks." Sir William now turned to the stranger knight, and dropping on his knee, with doffed cap and joyful voice, exclaimed—" God save King Richard !"

The foresters all did the like, and the forest rang with shouts in honour of their royal visitor. " Up! up !" cried Cœur-de-Lion, for it was, indeed, the King himself, newly returned from the Holy Land; "Up! all of ye! I have heard your story, Robin, and thine too, fair lady. Your father shall sit in Arlingford again, and if Robin will quit the glades, and resume his title, he shall be a peer of Cœur-de-Lion : your followers shall be pardoned, and such of them as you part with, I will entertain; and if ever I hold with priest, or confess me to a cowl, thou Friar shalt be, if thou wilt, that priest, and thine that cowl."

" I thank thee, brave King," said Tuck, "and were it so, the only penance which I should ever enjoin for thy sins, would be the drinking of some extra flasks of right good canary wine, in which penance I would so mortify myself as to partake; but by the mass my liege, wert thou to command my poor attendance, I should be bold enough to say, that while these live (pointing to Robin and Marian) no Prince or peer shall seduce their Friar from them."

The foresters joyfully embraced the King's proposal, and the nuptials of the lovers were soon after formally celebrated in the presence of old Sir Guy, the Baron and even as some chronicles have it, of brave King Richard himself, at Locksley Castle, where Robert Fitz-Ooth was installed again as Lord of its broad lands, and rightful Earl of Huntingdon.

The Friar was domiciled in Locksley Castle, and lived as merrily there as he had in the forest; frequently breaking forth and slaughtering a deer in his former abiding place for his own present diversion and future-eating. The Earl of Huntingdon forsook all his former freaks and lived in good repute for many years; but his tranquillity was broken in upon soon after the death of his friend King Richard and the usurpation of the throne by his enemy John, and the Earl was compelled to quit Locksley Castle and take to the wood again. Dropping their titles of Earl and Countess of Huntingdon our hero and heroine resumed their old forest names of Robin Hood and Maid Marian; although, it has been quaintly observed, the latter appellation was then as much a misnomer as that of *Little* John. The Friar of course followed his friends to the woods and used his staff to as much purpose as ever. Many of Robin's former adherents soon flocked round him, and he reigned for several years as absolutely in Sherwood as he had done before he had received the pardon of Cœur-de-Lion.

occasioned by the circumstance of a gentleman running off from certain bailiffs who were conducting him to prison. Upon this, Wynne ran also out into the street, and hearing somebody behind him crying out, " Stop him! stop him!" his conscience instantly awoke, so that he stopped, and exclaimed, " I am the man!" " You the man!" cried the people; " What man?" " The man," replied Wynne, " that committed the murder in Honey-lane twenty years ago, for which a poor man was hanged wrongfully. Upon this confession, he was carried before a magistrate, to whom he repeated the same acknowledgement, and was committed to Newgate, tried, condemned, and executed before the house where he perpetrated the horrid deed. Justice also overtook his family, who were privy to his guilt. Upon the intelligence of his shameful end, his wife immediately became deranged, and continued so to her death. Two of his sons were hanged in Virginia for robbery, and the whole family were eventually reduced to beggary.

THOMAS WITHERINGTON

This man flourished in the time of James I. He was the son of a gentleman of Carlisle, who possessed a considerable estate, and brought up his children suitably to his condition. Young Witherington received a liberal education, as his father intended that he should live free from the toil and hazard of business, and the father dying, he came into possession of the estate, which soon procured him a rich wife, who afterwards proved the chief cause of his ruin. She was loose in her conduct, and violated her matrimonial obligations, which drove him from his house to seek happiness in the tavern, or in the company that frequented it. These by degrees perverted all the good qualities he possessed; nor was his estate less subject to ruin and decay; for the mortgages he made on it, in order to support his luxury and profusion, soon reduced his circumstances to the lowest ebb. Undisciplined in poverty, he was possessed of too independent a spirit to stoop either to relations or friends for a precarious subsistence, and to solicit the benevolence of his fellow-men was what his soul abhorred. Starve he could not, and only one way of living presented itself to his choice—that of levying contributions on the road. This he followed for six or seven years with tolerable success, and we shall now relate a few of his most remarkable adventures.

Upon his first outset he repaired to a friend, and lamenting his late irregularities, declared his determination to live by some honest means; and for this purpose he required a little money in establishing himself, hoping his friend would find it convenient to accommodate him. His friend was overjoyed at the prospect of his amendment and willingly lent him fifty pounds, with as many blessings and exhortations. But Witherington frustrated these kind intentions, for with the money he bought himself a horse and other necessaries fit for his future enterprises.

Stopping one night at Keswick in Cumberland, he met with the Dean of Carlisle. Being equally learned, they found each other's company very agreeable, and Witherington passed himself off for a gentleman who had just returned from the East Indies with a handsome competency, and was returning to his friends at Carlisle, among whom he had a rich uncle, who had lately died and left him sole heir to his estate. " True," said the Dean, " I have often heard of a relation of Mr. Witherington's being in the East Indies, but his family, I can assure you, received repeated information of his death, and what prejudice this may have done to your affairs at Carlisle, to-morrow will be the best witness." The Dean then told him his own history, and concluded with these words :—" And I am now informed that to support his extravagance, Mr. Witherington frequents the road, and takes a purse whenever he can extort it." Our adventurer seemed greatly hurt at this account of his cousin's conduct, and thanked the doctor for his information. The evening was afterwards spent very agreeably and they promised each other to travel together on the following day to Carlisle.

Accordingly, the next morning they sat out on their journey, and having arrived at a wood on the road, Witherington rode close up to the Dean, and whispering into his ear, " Sir, though the place at which we now are is private enough, yet willing that what I do should be still more private, I take the liberty to acquaint you that you have something about you that will do me an infinite piece of service."—" What's that?" answered the doctor, " you shall have it with all my heart."—" I thank you for your civility," said Witherington. " Well then, to be plain, the money in your breeches'-pocket will be very serviceable to me at the present moment."—" Money!" rejoined the Doctor; " Sir, you cannot want money ; your garb and person both tell me you are in no want."— " Ay, but I am; for the ship in which I came over happened to be wrecked, so that I have lost all that I brought from India ; and I would not enter Carlisle for the whole world without money in my

Little John, Scarlet, and Midge the miller, with young Allan-a-dale, now the forest minstrel, were still alive, and gloried in enrolling themselves under the gay banner of their former lord and lady, Robin Hood and Marian.

Robin levied toll as before upon fat Friars and portly Abbots, relieved the needy whenever he could, and killed and ate the King's deer, until he grew old. A volume might be filled with his exploits, but we have said enough to give our readers a sufficient idea of the character and doings of this forest hero.

Different accounts have been given of the manner of his death; but that which seems entitled to most credit, states that he who had so long dared bolt and baldrick at last fell a victim to the treachery of a Monk. In the olden days surgery was frequently practised by those in religious orders, and it is told in tale and sung in ballad that Robin having sent for a Friar to bleed him, the rogue contrived to kill instead of cure him. His death took place in the year 1247, when he was above sixty years of age. He was buried in Kirkley park, in the county of York, near two hillocks, called Robin Hood's butts, at which, tradition says, the Sherwood foresters used to shoot when Robin was lord of the Greenwood.

Upon the decease of their beloved leader, the band broke up, but what was the lot of Marian, or whether she survived Robin or no, it is not in our power to say. A monument was erected above his grave, bearing the following inscription, with which we shall conclude this brief outline of his life.

> ROBERT, Earl of Huntingdon,
> Lies underneath this little stone.
> No archer ever was so good,
> His name it was bold Robin Hood.
> Full thirty years, and something more,
> These northern parts he vexed sore;
> Such outlaws as he, in any reign,
> May England never see again.

THOMAS DUN.

This man lived in the time of Henry III., and of his sanguinary life and cruel death we have the following account:—

Thomas Dun was born in Bedfordshire, in the time of Henry III. Even in his childhood, he was noted for his pilfering propensities, and the cruelty of his disposition, and in after life his atrocities were so many, that our space will only enable us to find room for the recital of a few.

His first exploit was on the highway to Bedford, where he met a waggon full of corn going to market, drawn by a beautiful team of horses. He accosted the driver, and in the middle of the conversation stabbed him to the heart with a dagger which he always carried about his person. He buried the body and mounting the waggon, proceeded to the town, where he sold all off and decamped with the money. He continued to commit many petty thefts and assaults, but judging it safer to associate himself with others he repaired to a gang of thieves, who infested the country, leading from St. Alban's to Towcester, where they became such a terror that the king was obliged to build a town to check his power in the country, and which retains his name to this day,—Dunstable.

This precaution was, however of little avail, for he pursued his courses to a great extent. Among his gang were many artists who enabled him to pick locks, wrench bolts and use deaf files with great effect. One day having heard that some lawyers were to dine at a certain inn in Bedfordshire, about an hour before the appointed time, he came running to the inn, and desired the landlord to hurry the dinner, and to have enough ready for ten or twelve. The company soon arrived, and the lawyers thought Dun a servant of the house, while those of the house thought him an attendant of the lawyers. He bustled about, and the bill being called for he collected it, and having some change to return to the company they waited till his return, but growing weary, they rang the bell and enquired for their money when they discovered him to be an impostor. With the assistance of his associates, he made clear off with a considerable booty of cloaks, hats, silver spoons and every thing of value upon which he could lay his hands.

After this adventure Dun and his associates went and put up at another inn. They rose up in the night-time, insulted the landlord, did violence to the land'ady, then murdered them both and pillaged the house of every thing valuable. Dun had an animosity to lawyers and he determined to play a rich one a trick. He waited upon him, and very abruptly demanded payment of a bond which he produced, and the gentleman found his name so admirably forged, that he could not swear it was not his own handwriting. He assured Dun however that he had never borrowed the money, and would not pay the bond. He then left him, telling the lawyer that he would give him some employment. A law-suit was entered into, and several of his comrades came forward and swore as to the debt being just, and he was about getting a decision in his favour, when the lawyer produced a forged receipt for the debt which some of his clerks likewise swore to, upon which Dun was cast. He was in a great passion at being outwitted, and swore he never heard of such rogues as to swear they had paid him a sum which was never borrowed.

This was one of the few instances where he did not display that barbarity of disposition which is evinced in all his other adventures, and which makes us refrain from the enumeration of many of them. He became however such a terror to every one, that the Sheriff of Bedford sent a considerable force to attack him in his retreat. Finding that his strength was equal, if not superior to that of the Sheriff, he commenced the attack and completely routed them, taking eleven prisoners, whom he hung upon the trees round the wood to scare others by the example of their fate. The clothes served them to accomplish their next adventure, which was a design to rob a nobleman in the neighbourhood. They proceeded in the attire of the Sheriff's men and demanded entrance in the name of the king to make search for Dun. After searching every corner they asked for the keys of the trunks to examine them which when they received, they loaded themselves with booty and departed. The nobleman complained to parliament against the Sheriff, when upon investigation, the trick was discovered.

Nothing prevented Dun from accomplishing any object which he had in view, as he possessed the greatest temerity and cruelty that could fall to the lot of man. He would under the disguise of a gentleman wait upon rich people and upon being shewn into their rooms murder them and carry away their money.

There was a rich knight in the neighbourhood from whom Dun wished to have a little money. Accordingly he went and knocked at his door, which the servant opening, he enquired if her master was at home, and being answered in the affirmative, he instantly went up stairs and familiarly entered his room, some compliments having passed, he sat down in a chair and began a humorous discourse which attracted the attention of the knight; Dun then approached and demanded a word or two in his ears. Sir, says he, my necessities come pretty thick upon me at present, and I am obliged to keep even with my creditors, for fear of cracking my fame and fortune too. Now having been directed to you by some of the heads of the parish as a very considerable and liberal person, I am come to petition you in a modest manner, to lend me a thousand marks, which will answer all the demands upon me at present " A thousand marks !" answered the knight, " why, man, that's a capital sum; and where's the inducement to lend you so much money, who are a perfect stranger to me?"—" Sir, you must be mistaken, I am the honest grocer of Bedford, who has so often shared your favours." " Really, friend, I shall not part with my money but on a good security, and what security have you?" " Why, this dagger," says Dun, (pulling it out of his breast) " is my constant security; and unless you let me have a thousand marks instantly, I shall pierce your heart!" this threat produced the intended effect, and he instantly delivered the money.

Having lost his road in the country, he arrived at a house where ne enquired if they could accommodate a benighted traveller with a bed. The gentleman of the house politely told him that all his house was occupied with friends and relations, who had just arrived to be present at the celebration of his daughter's marriage, which was to take place the next day, otherwise, he should have been very welcome. When he was unwillingly departing, the gentleman informed him, if he was not superstitious, and had courage enough, there was one room unoccupied, in which he might sleep, but that it was haunted. Dun was above all silly apprehensious of that nature, and accepted the offer, and after being well entertained, retired to his room, the company all praying for his quiet rest. A good fire had been made in the room, and when all the house was at rest, he lay anxiously waiting for something to appear; when the door of his chamber opened, and in came the bride, of whom he had taken particular notice at supper. At first he was at a loss to know whether it was only a resemblance, but soon satisfied himself that it was the real lady, though, whether she was walking in her sleep or not, he could not say, he however resolved to watch her motions. She seemed to look stedfastly upon his countenance, and then going round the bed, gently turned up the clothes, and lay down by his side, where she had not lain long, before she drew a rich diamond ring from her finger, placed it on the pillow, and left the room with the same silent step as she had entered it. He did not wish to disturb her, as she had left so good a prize behind her. He soon fell asleep, dreamed that the lady again appeared, and said that she detested the person to whom she was going to be married, and entreated him to assist her in this conjuncture. Dun, however, had got what he wanted, and departed next morning, without satisfying the curiosity of the company, or thanking the gentleman for his kindness.

By this time Dun had become formidable to both rich and poor; but one melancholy circumstance attended his depredations, they were in almost every instance stained with blood. He however continued his infamous course twenty years, the vicinity of the river Ouse in Yorkshire being the usual scene of his exploits; and being attended by fifty armed men on horseback, the inhabitants of the country were afraid to seize him.

His last adventure was as remarkable as those of his former life. His infamy daily increasing, the people of that district at length determined no longer to suffer his depredations; and, he and his gang were so closely pursued, that they were constrained to divide themselves, each seeking for safety for himself. Dun having concealed himself in a small village, was at last discovered, and the house he was in surrounded. Two of the strongest courageously posted themselves at the door; Dun seized his dagger, laid them both dead, bridled his horse, and in the midst of the uproar escaped. He was, however, hotly pursued by one hundred and fifty men, armed with clubs, pitchforks, rakes, and whatever rustic weapons they could find, who coming up with him, dismounted him from his horse, but, to the astonishment of all, he again mounted and galloped off, cut his way through the crowd; and multitudes flocking from all quarters, the pursuit was renewed. He was, a second time, dismounted, and now employed his feet: he ran for the space of two miles; but when he halted to breathe a little, three hundred men were ready to oppose him, his courage and strength, however, still remaining unsubdued, he burst through them, fled over a valley, threw off his clothes, seized his sword in his teeth, and plunged into a river in order to gain the opposite bank.

To his sad surprise, however, he perceived it covered with new opponents; he swam down the river, but was pursued by several boats, until he took refuge on a small island. Determined to give him no time to recover from his fatigue, they attacked him there.

Thus closely pursued, he plunged again into the river with his sword in his teeth; he was pursued by the boats, repeatedly struck with their oars; and after having received several blows on the head, he was at last vanquished.

He was conducted to a surgeon to have his wounds dressed, then led before a magistrate, who sent him to Bedford gaol under a strong guard. Remaining there two weeks, until he was considered recovered, a scaffold was erected in the market place, and, without a formal trial, he was led forth to execution. When the two executioners approached him, he warned them of their danger if they should lay hands upon him; he accordingly grasped both, and nine times overthrew them upon the stage before his strength was exhausted, so that they could not perform their duty. His hands were first chopped off at the wrist; then his arms at the elbows; next, about an inch from the shoulders; his feet below the ancles; his legs at the knee; and his thighs about five inches from his trunk; the horrible scene was closed by severing his head from the body; and consuming it to ashes; the other parts of his body were fixed up in the principal parts of Bedfordshire, as a warning to his companions. The quantity of blood that was shed during his career, restrains even the tear of pity upon his miserable fate.

SIR GOSSELIN DENVILLE,

Who lived in the time of Edward II., was descended of very honourable parents at Northallerton, in the North Riding of Yorkshire. His family came into England with William the Conqueror, who assigned them lands for their services, where they lived in great repute, until the days of our hero. He was intended, by his father, for the priesthood, and for this purpose was sent to college, where he prosecuted his studies with great assiduity and seeming warmth. As he was naturally of a vicious disposition, he merely dissembled to please his father, until he should get possession of his fortune.

His natural habits however could not long be restrained, and he soon displayed his propensity to a luxurious and profligate life; and it appears that so vicious was his conduct, that he broke his father's heart; and his newly acquired wealth, he and his brother Robert contrived soon to dissipate in licentiousness and luxury.

The first enterprise of note which we find recorded of Sir Gosselin is one in which he was joined by Middleton and Selby, two robbers of that time, with a considerable force. Their design was to rob two Cardinals, sent into this kingdom by the Pope, which they accomplished with great success. Not only travellers, but monasteries, churches, nunneries, and houses, were the objects of their attacks, and they were not merely content with booty, but barbarously murdered all who made the least opposition.

A Dominican monk, of the name of Andrew Simpson, was once met by our knight and his associates, and obliged to surrender his purse; wishing, however, to make pastime of him, they compelled him to mount a tree and preach an extempore sermon.

The monk selected for his text these words: "A certain man went down from Jerusalem to Jericho, and fell among thieves, who, stripped him of his raiment and wounded him, and departed leaving him half dead;" and he commented thereon in a very learned manner, hoping to move the hearts of his hearers, but without success, they were too far plunged in iniquity to reform.

They continued their course, and every day became more formidable, and robbed with such boldness that country-seats were forsaken, and safety sought in fortified cities. They defeated forces sent out to suppress them, and were not deterred from any project, either by the magnitude of the danger, or the greatness of the individuals concerned. The king himself when on a tour through the north of England, was beset by the gang in priests' habits, and he and his nobles had to submit themselves to be rifled. This robbery was highly resented, and several proclamations offering great rewards were issued for the apprehension of any or every of them. The promise of the premium bred traitors among themselves, and in less than a month afterwards sixty were delivered up to justice.

The last recorded exploit of Sir Gosselin and his remaining associates was an attack which he made upon the Bishop of Durham. They rifled his palace of every thing valuable, and maltreated not only himself but his servants and family. But the fortune of our knight seemed now on the wane.

His amours were many, and among them was one with the wife of a publican whose house he used to frequent, not so much for the goodness of the ale as the beauty of the hostess. The husband, however, sought his revenge in due season, and betrayed the knight and his men one evening while they were carousing in his house. The sheriff and five hundred men surrounded the party, who fought desperately, but it was not before two hundred of the besiegers had fallen, and they were completely hemmed in that they surrendered. They were escorted under a strong guard to York, where, without the privilege of a trial, they were immediately executed to the joy of thousands, the satisfaction of the great, and the delight of the community, who waited upon them to the scaffold, triumphing in their ignominious exit.

SAWNEY BEANE,

"The Man Eater."

OUR next narrative presents such a picture of human barbarity, that, were it not attested by the most unquestionable historical evidence, it would be rejected as altogether fabulous and incredible, it is that of Sawney Beane.

This man was born in East Lothian, about eight miles east of Edinburgh, in the reign of James 1. of Scotland. His father was a hedger and ditcher, and brought up his son to the same laborious employment. Naturally idle and vicious, he abandoned that place in company with a young woman equally idle and profligate, and retired to the deserts of Galloway, where they took up their habitation by the sea-side. The place which they selected for their dwelling was a cave of about a mile in length, and of considerable breadth, so near the sea, that the tide often penetrated into the cave above two hundred yards. The entry had many intricate windings and turnings, leading to the extremity of the subterraneous dwelling, which was literally "the habitation of horrid cruelty."

In this cave they commenced their depredations, and to prevent the possibility of detection, they murdered every person they robbed. Destitute of the means of obtaining any other food, they resolved to live upon human flesh, and accordingly, when they had murdered any man, woman, or child, they carried them to their den, quartered them, salted the limbs, and dried them for food. In this manner they lived, carrying on their depredations and murder, until they had eight sons and six daughters, eighteen grandsons and fourteen granddaughters, all the offspring of incest.

But though they soon became numerous, yet such was the multitude which fell into their hands, that they had often superabundance of provisions, and would at a distance from their own habitation, throw legs and arms of dried human bodies into the sea by night.

These were often cast out by the tide, and taken up by the country people, to the great dismay of all the surrounding inhabitants. Nor could any one discover what had befallen the many friends, relations, and neighbours who had unfortunately fallen into the hand of these merciless cannibals.

In proportion as Sawney's family increased, every one that was able acted his part in these horrid assassinations. They would sometimes attack four or six men on foot, but never more than two upon horseback. To prevent the possibility of escape, they would lie in ambush in every direction, so that if they escaped the attack of the first, they might be assailed with renewed fury by second party, and inevitably murdered. By this means they always secured their prey, and prevented detection. At last, however, the vast number who were slain raised the inhabitants of the country, and all the woods and lurking-places were carefully searched; yet, though they often passed by the mouth of the horrible den, it was never once suspected that any human being resided there. In this state of uncertainty and suspense concerning the authors of such frequent massacres, several innocent travellers and inkeepers were taken up on suspicion, because the persons who were missing had been seen last in their company, or had last resided at their houses. The effect of this well-meant and severe justice constrained the greater part of the inkeepers in those parts to abandon such employments, to the great inconvenience of those who travelled through that district.

Meanwhile, the country became depopulated, and the whole nation was at a loss to account for the numerous and unheard-of villanies and cruelties that were perpetrated, without the slightest clue to the discovery of the abominable actors. At length the horrible scene was terminated in the following manner. One evening, a man and wife were riding home upon the same horse from a fair which had been held in the neighbourhood, and being attacked, the husband made the most vigorous resistance; his wife, however, was dragged from behind him, carried to a little distance, and her entrails instanlly taken out. Struck with horror the husband redoubled his efforts to escape, and even trod some of the assassins down under his horse's feet. Fortunately for him, and the inhabitants of that part of the country, in the mean time, twenty or thirty in a company came riding home from the fair, but upon their approach, Sawney and his bloody crew fled into a thick wood, and hastened to their infernal den.

This man. who was the first that had ever escaped out of their hands, related to his neighbours what had happened, and showed them the mangled body of his wife lying at a distance, the bloodthirsty wretches not having time to carry it along with them. They were all struck with astonishment and horror, took him with them to Glasgow, and reported the whole adventure to the chief magistrate of the city, who, upon this information, instantly wrote to the king, informing him of the matter. In a few days, his majesty in person, accompanied by four hundred men, went in quest of the perpetrators of these horrid cruelties. The man, whose wife had been murdered before his eyes, went as their guide, with a great number of blood-hounds, that no possible means might be left unattempted to discover the haunt of such execrable villains.

They searched the woods, and traversed and examined the seashore; but as they passed by the entrance into their cave, some of the blood-hounds entered it, and raising an uncommon barking and noise, gave indication that they were about to seize their prey. The king and his men returned, but could scarcely conceive how any human beings could reside in a place of utter darkness, and where the entrance was difficult and narrow; but, as the blood-hounds increased in their vociferation, and refused to return, it occurred to all that the cave ought to be explored to the extremity. Accordingly, a sufficient number of torches was provided; the hounds were permitted to pursue their course; a great number of men penetrated through all the intricacies of the path, and at length arrived at the private entrance of the cannibals.

They were followed by all the band, who were shocked to behold a sight unequalled in Scotland if not in any part of the universe. Legs, arms, thighs, hands, and feet, of men, women, and children, were suspended in rows like dried beef, some limbs and other members were soaked in pickle; while a great mass of money, both of gold and silver, watches, rings, pistols, clothes, both linen and woollen, with an immense quantity of other articles, were either thrown together in heaps, or suspended upon the sides of the cave.

The whole cruel, brutal family, to the number formerly mentioned, were seized; the human flesh buried in the sand of the sea-shore; the immense booty carried away, and the king marched to Edinburgh with the prisoners. This new and wretched spectacle attracted the attention of the inhabitants, who flocked from all quarters to see, as they passed along, so bloody and unnatural a family which had increased, in the space of twenty-five years, to the number of twenty-seven men and twenty-one women. Arrived in the capital, they were all confined in the Tolbooth under a strong guard, and were next day conducted to the common place of execution in Leith Walk, and executed without any formal trial, it being deemed unnecessary to try those who were avowed enemies of all mankind and of all social order.

The enormity of their crimes dictated the severity of their death. The men had their entrails thrown into the fire, their hands and legs were severed from their bodies, and they were permitted to bleed to death. The wretched mother of the whole crew, the daughters, and grandchildnen, after being spectators of the death of the men, were cast into three separate fires, and consumed to ashes. Nor, did they, in general, display any signs of repentance or regret but continued, with their last breath, to pour forth the most dreadful curses and imprecations upon all around.

THOMAS WYNNE.

This notorious criminal was born at Ipswich, in the reign of Queen Elizabeth, at which place he continued till he was between fifteen and sixteen, and then went to sea. Nine years after, coming to London, and associating with loose company, especially with females, he left no villainy undone for the support of himself and them in their extravagances, till at last he became so expert in house-breaking and all sorts of theft, that he was esteemed the most remarkable villain in his time; accordingly we find that he had the boldness to rob the royal lodgings at Whitehall Palace, of plate to the amount of £400, for which he was taken and committed to Newgate. But fortunately for him, her majesty's act of grace coming out, granting a free pardon for all offences except murder, treason, and other notorious crimes, he was allowed the benefit of that act, and thus obtained his liberty. But neither the Queen's clemency, nor the eminent danger to which he had been exposed, had any effect upon him; for, pursuing his villanies, he was soon constrained to hire himself as under servant in the kitchen, to the Earl of Salisbury, to avoid detection. While he was in this post, he had the audacity to make love to the Countess's attendant, who, astonished at such insolence in a man of his rank, returned his addresses with contempt, which exasperated him so much, that his love turned to hatred, and he vowed vengeance. He accordingly embraced an opportunity, and used her very brutally, until she was under the necessity of calling to the other servants for assistance, and from his treatment took to her bed, and remained very unwell for some time. The Earl, informed of his cruelty, ordered him to be whipped by the coachman, and the same to be repeated once a week during a month, but having satiated his vengeance upon the woman, he decamped from the house, after robbing the coachman of £9, borrowing £15 of the master-cook, carrying off a silver cup of the Earl's, and all the best clothes of the woman whom he had so greatly injured, and went in quest of new adventures.

After this, Wynne often dressed himself in the garb of a porter, and carried off parcels, consigned to carriers, and continued undetected in this practice, until he had acquired about two hundred pounds, for which the different carriers had to pay through their neglect. Taught by experience, however, they began to look better after the goods entrusted to their care, so that Wynne had to turn to a new employment.

After having reigned eight years in his villanies, he determined to rob a linen-draper, in Honey Lane, who, with his wife were living upon their industry, and accordingly one evening he broke into their house, cut both their throats while they were asleep, rifled the house to the amount of £2500; and, to prevent detection, sailed to Virginia, with his wife and four children.

Not appearing in the neighbourhood next day as usual, and the doors remaining locked, the neighbours were alarmed, sent for a constable, and burst open the doors, when they found them weltering in their blood, and their house pillaged. Enquiry was of course made, and a poor man, a beggar, was taken up on suspicion, because he had been seen sitting upon a bench before the house the previous day: and although nothing but circumstantial evidence appeared against him, he was tried, condemned, and executed in front of the dwelling, and his body hung in chains at Holloway.

In the meantime the murderer remained in a foreign land, where he prospered, and his riches greatly increased; but after he had resided about twenty years in Virginia where his family had become numerous, he resolved to visit England before his death, and then to return to deposit his bones in a foreign grave, this resolution was a fatal one to him, for during his stay in London, he happened one day to enter a goldsmith's shop in Cheapside, intending to purchase some plate to take with him on his return, and while he was in treaty for the same, an uproar took place in the street, pocket."—" Friend, I may urge the same plea, and say I would not go into that city without money for the world; but what then? If you are Mr. Witherington's nephew, as you have told me you are, you would not thus peremptorily demand money of me, for at Carlisle your friends will supply you; and if you have none now, I will bear your expenses to that place."—" Sir," said Witherington, " the question is not whether I have money or not, but concerning that which is in your pocket; for, as you say, my cousin is obliged to take purses on the road, and so am I; so that if I take your's, you may ride to Carlisle, and say that Mr. Witherington met you and demanded your charity." After a good deal of expostulation, the Dean, terrified at the sight of a pistol, delivered to Witherington a purse containing fifty guineas, before he pursued his journey to Carlisle, and our adventurer set off in search of more prey.

Soon after this event Witherington went to Newcastle, and put up at an inn where some commissioners were to meet that day, to make choice of a schoolmaster for a neighbouring parish. The salary being very handsome, many young clergymen and students appeared as competitors: and being possessed of sufficient qualifications, Witherington bethought him of standing a candidate, for which purpose he borrowed coarse plain clothes from the landlord, to make his appearance correspond with the conduct he meant to pursue. Repairing to the kitchen, and sitting down by the fire, he called for a mug of ale, putting on a dejected countenance. One of the freeholders who came to vote, observing him as he stood warming himself by the fire, was taken with his countenance, and entered into conversation with him. He very modestly let the freeholder know that he had come with the intention of standing as a candidate, but when he saw so many gay young men as competitors, and fearing that every thing would be carried by interest, he resolved to return home. " Nay," replied the honest freeholder, " as long as I have a vote, justice shall be done; and never fear, for egad, I say, merit shall have the place, and if you be found the best scholar, you shall certainly have it; and to show you I am sincere, I now, though you are a stranger to me, promise you my vote, and my interest likewise." Witherington thanked him for his civility, and consented to wait for the trial. A keen contest took place between two of the most successful candidates, when our adventurer was introduced as a man who had so much modesty as to make him fearful of appearing before so great an assembly, but who nevertheless wished to be examined. He con fronted the two opponents, and exposed their ignorance to the trustees, who were all astonished at the stranger. He showed it was not a number of Greek and Latin sentences that constituted a good scholar, but a thorough knowledge of the nature of the book which he read, and the ability to discover the design of the author. Suffice it to say, that Witherington was installed into the office with all the usual formalities.

Conducting himself with much moderation and humility, the churchwardens of the parish took a great fancy to him, and made him overseer and tax-gatherer to the parish; and the rector likewise committed to his care the collection of his rents and tithes. The friendly disposition towards Witherington extended itself over the parish, and never was a man believed to be more honest or industrious. Of the latter qualification, we must say, in this instance, he showed himself possessed; but of the former he had never any notion. His opinion had great weight with the heads of the parish, and he proposed the erection of a new school-house, and for this purpose offered, himself, to sink a year's salary towards a subscription. It was willingly agreed to, and contributions came in from all quarters, and a sum exceeding £700 was speedily raised. The mind of Witherington was now big with hope, but, being discovered by two gentlemen, who had come from Carlisle, he made off with all the subscriptions and funds in his possession, leaving the parish to reflect upon the honesty of their schoolmaster and their own credulity.

He afterwards went to Buckinghamshire, and being at an inn in the county town, fell into the company of some farmers, who, he discovered, were come to meet their landlord with their rents. They were all tenants of the same proprietor, and poured out many complaints against him for his harshness and injustice, in not allowing some deduction from their rents, or time after quarter-day, when they met with severe losses from bad weather or other causes; and learning that this landlord was very rich, and so miserly that he denied himself even the necessaries of life; he determined, if possible, to rifle him before he parted.

The landlord soon arrived, and the company were shown into a private room; Witherington, upon pretence of being a friend of one of the farmers, and a lawyer, accompanied them. He requested a sight of the last receipts, and examined them with great care. and then addressing the landlord, " Sir," said he, " These honest men, my friends, have been your tenants for a long time. and have paid their rents very regularly; but why they should be so fond of your farms at so high a rent I am unable to comprehend, when they may get other lands much cheaper; and that you should be so unreasonable as not to allow a reduction in their rents in a season like this, when they must lose instead of gaining by their farms. It is your duty, Sir, to encourage them, and not to grind them so unmercifully, else they will soon be obliged to leave your farms altogether." The landlord endeavoured to argue the point; and the farmers seeing the drift of Witherington, refrained from interfering. "It is unnecessary," resumed Witherington, "to have more parley about it; I insist on behalf of my friends here, that you remit them a hundred and fifty pounds of the three hundred you expect them to pay you, for I am told you have more than enough to support yourself and family." "Not a sous," replied the landlord. "We'll try that presently. But pray, Sir, take your pen, ink and paper, in the mean time, and write out their receipts, and the money shall be forthcoming immediately." "Not a letter, till the money is in my hands." "It must be so then," answered Witherington; "you will force a good-natured man to use extremities with you;" and so saying, he laid a brace of loaded pistols on the table. In a moment the landlord was on his knees, crying, "Oh! dear Sir, sweet Sir, kind Sir, merciful Sir, for God of Heaven's sake, Sir, don't take away the life of an innocent man, Sir, who never intended harm to any one. Sir." "Why, what harm do I intend you, friend? Cannot I lay the pistols I travel with on the table, but you must throw yourself into this unnecessary fear? Pray, proceed to the receipts, and write them in full of all demands to this time, or else,"—" Oh, God, Sir! oh, dear Sir! you have an intention—pray, dear Sir, have no intention against my life." "To the receipts then, or by Jupiter Ammon! I'll—"—" O yes, I will, Sir." With this the old landlord wrote full receipts, and delivered them to the respective farmers.

"Come," said Witherington, "this is honest, and to show you that you have to deal with honest people, here is a hundred and fifty pounds; and I promise you, in the name of these honest men, that if things succeed well, you shall have the other half next quarter-day." The farmers paid the money, and departed astonished, and not a little afraid, at the consequences of this proceeding. Witherington ordered his horse, and enquired of the ostler the road the old gentleman had to travel, and presently took his departure.

He chose the road which the old gentleman had to travel, and soon observed him jogging away in sullen silence, with a servant behind him. When he observed our hero he would have fled, but Witherington seized the bridle of his horse, and forced him to proceed, bantering him upon the folly of hoarding up wealth, without enjoying it himself, merely for some spendthrift son to squander after his death. "For," he continued, "money is a blessing sent from Heaven, in order that, by its circulation, it may afford nourishment to the body politic; and if such wretches as you, by laying up thousands in your coffers to no advantage, cause a stagnation, there are thousands in the world that must feel the consequences, and I am to acquaint you of them; so that a better deed cannot be done, than to bestow what you have about you upon me; for, to be plain with you, I am not to be refused;" and hereupon he presented his pistol. The old gentleman, in trepidation for his life, resigned his purse, containing more than three hundred and fifty guineas; and Witherington, unbuckling the portmanteau from behind the servant, placed it on his own horse, and left the old landlord with an admonition, to be in future affable and generous to his tenants, for they were the persons who supported him, adding, that, if he ever again heard complaints from them, he would visit his house, and partake liberally of what he most coveted.

The county, after this adventure, was up in pursuit of Witherington, and he retired to Cheshire with great expedition, where he committed numberless depredations; but at last being obliged to leave this part of the country, he took to the London road, where he perpetrated a robbery between Acton and Uxbridge; after which he was detected and committed to Newgate, where he led a most profligate life till the day of his execution.

He was executed with Jonathan Woodward and James Philpot, two most notorious housebreakers, who had once before received mercy from King James I. upon his accession to the throne.

JAMES BATSON.

OF this famous robber, who was born in the first year of James the First, we have no other history than what is given in his own words, and we are therefore compelled, in default of other particulars, to lay his auto-biography before our readers.

"I suppose," says he, "that according to custom, the reader will expect some relation of my genealogy, and as I am a great admirer of fashion, I shall gratify his curiosity. My grandfather had the good fortune to marry a woman well skilled in vaulting and rope-dancing, and who could act her part uncommonly well. Though above fifty years of age, and affected with the phthisic, she died in the air. To avoid seeing other women fly as she had done, her husband would not marry again; but diverted himself with keeping a puppet-show in Moorfields, deemed the most remarkable that ever had been seen in that place. My grandfather was also so little, that the only difference between him and his puppets was, that they spoke through a trunk, and he without one. He was, however, so eloquent, and made such lively speeches, that his audience were never rendered drowsy. All the apple-women, hawkers, and fish women, were so charmed by his wit, that they would run to hear him, and leave their goods without any guard but their own straw-hats.

"My father had two trades, or two strings to his bow; he was a painter and a gamester, and master much alike to both; for his painting could scarcely rise so high as a sign-post, and his hand at play was of such an ancient date, that it could scarcely pass He had one misfortune, which, like original sin, he entailed upon all his children; and that was his being borne a gentleman, which is as bad as being a poet, few of whom escape eternal poverty.

"My mother had the misfortune to die longing for mushrooms. Besides myself she left two daughters, both very handsome and very young; and though I was then young myself, yet I was much better skilled in sharping than my age seemed to promise. When the funeral sermon was preached, the funeral rites performed, and our tears dried up, my father returned to his daubing, my sisters to their stitching, and I was despatched to school. I had such an excellent memory, that though my dispositions were then what they have continued to be, yet I soon learned as much as might have been applied to better purposes than I have done. My tricks upon my master and my companions were so numerous, that I obtained the honourable appellation of the Little Judas. My avaricious disposition soon appeared, and if my covetous eyes once beheld any thing, my invention soon put it into my possession. These, however, I could not obtain gratis, for they cost me many a boxing bout every day. The reports of my conduct were conveyed home, and my eldest sister would frequently spend her white hands upon the side of my pate; and even sometimes carried her admonitions so far, as politely to inform me, that I should prove a disgrace to the family.

"It was my good fortune, however, not to be greatly agitated by her remonstrances, which went in at one ear and out at the other. It happened, however, that my adventures were so numerous, and daily increasing in their magnitude, that I was dismissed the school with as much solemnity as if it had been by beat of drum. After giving me a complete drubbing, my father carried me to a barber, in order to be bound as his apprentice. I was first sent to the kitchen, where my mistress soon provided me with employment, by showing me a parcel of dirty clothes, informing me, that it made part of the apprentice's work to clean them: "Jemmy," says she, "mind your heels, there's a good boy!" I hung down my head, tumbled all the clouts into a trough, and washed them as well as I could. I so managed the matter, that I was soon discarded from my office, which was very fortunate for me, for it would have put an end to poor Jemmy in less than a fortnight.

"The third day of my apprenticeship, my master having just given me a note to receive money, there came into the shop a cavalier with a large pair of whiskers, and told my master he would have them turned up. The journeyman not being at hand, my master began to turn them up himself, and desired me to heat the irons. I complied, and just as he had turned up one whisker, there happened a quarrel in the street, and my master ran out to learn the cause. The scuffle lasting long, and my master desirous to see the end as well as the beginning of the bustle, the spark was all the time detained in the shop, with the one whisker ornamented, and the other hanging down like an aspin leaf. In a harsh tone he asked me, if I understood my trade; and I, thinking it derogatory to my understanding to be ignorant, boldly replied, that I did; 'Why, then,' said he, 'turn up this whisker for me, or I shall go into the street as I am, and kick your master.' I was unwilling to be detected in a lie, and deeming it no difficult matter to turn up a whisker, never showed the least concern, but took up one of the irons, that had been in the fire ever since the commencement of the street bustle, and having nothing to try it on, and willing to appear expeditious, I took a comb, stuck it into his bristly bush, and clapped the iron to it; no sooner did they meet, than there arose a smoke, as if it had been out of a chimney, with a whizzing noise, and in a moment all the hair vanished. He exclaimed furiously, 'Thou son of a thousand! dost thou take me for St. Lawrence, that thou burnest me alive! with that he let fly such a bang at me, that the comb dropped out of my hand, and I could not avoid, in the fright, laying the hot iron close along his cheek: this made him give such a shriek as shook the whole house, and he, at the same time, drew his sword to send me to the other world. I, however, recollecting the proverb, 'That one pair of heels is worth two pair of hands,' ran so nimbly into the street, and fled so quickly from that part of the town, that though I was a good runner, I was amazed when I found myself about a mile from home, with the iron in my hand, and the remainder of the whisker sticking to it. As fortune would have it, I was near the dwelling of the person who was to pay the note my master gave me: I went and received the money, but deemed it proper to detain it in lieu of my three days' wages.

'This money was all exhausted in one month, when I was under the necessity of returning to my father's house. Before arriving there, I was informed, that he was gone to the country to receive a large sum of money which was due to him, and therefore went boldly in, as if the house had been my own. My grave sisters received me very coldly, and severely blamed me for the money which my father paid for my pranks. Maintaining, however, the honour of my birthright, I kept them at considerable distance, and the domestic war being thus prolonged, I one day lost temper, and was resolved to make them feel the consequences of giving me sour beer; and, though the dinner was upon the table, I threw the dish at my eldest sister, and the beer at the younger, overthrew the table, and marched out of doors on a ramble. Fortunately, however, I was interrupted in my flight by one who informed me, that my father was dead, and in his testament had very wisely left me sole heir and executor. Upon this I returned, and soon found the tones and tempers of my sisters changed, in consequence of the recent news. I sold the goods, collected the debts, and feasted all the rakes in town, until not one farthing remained.

"One evening, a party of my companions carried me along with them, and, opening the door of a certain house, conveyed from thence some trunks, which a faithful dog perceiving, he gave the alarm. The people of the house attacked the robbers, who threw down their burdens to defend themselves: meanwhile, I skulked into a corner all trembling. The watch made their appearance, and seeing three trunks in the street, two men dangerously wounded, and myself standing at a small distance, they seized me as one concerned in the robbery. Next day I was ordered to a place of confinement, and could find no friend to bail me from thence. In ten days I was tried, and my defences being frivolous and unsatisfactory, I was about to be hoisted up by the neck, and sent out of the world in a swinging manner, when a reprieve came, and in two months a full pardon.

"After this horrid fright, (for I was not much disposed to visit the dwelling of my grandfather,) I commenced travelling merchant, and, according to my finances, purchased a quantity of wash-balls, tooth-picks, and tooth-powders. Pretending that they came from Japan, Peru, or Tartary, and extolling them to the skies, I had a good sale, particularly among the gentry of the playhouse. Upon a certain day, one of the actresses, a beautiful woman of eighteen, and married to one of the actors, addressed me, saying, 'She had taken a liking to me, because I was a confident, sharp, forward youth; and therefore, if I would serve her, she would entertain me with all her heart; and that, when the company were strolling, I might beat the drum and stick up the bills.' Deeming it an easier mode of moving through the world, I readily consented, only requesting two days to dispose of my stock, and to settle all my accounts.

"In my new profession my employments were various, some of which, though not very pleasant, I endeavoured to reconcile myself to, inasmuch as they were comparatively better than my former. In a little time I became more acquainted with the tempers of my master and mistress, and became so great a favourite, that fees and bribes replenished my coffers from all expectants and authors who courted their favour. Unfortunately, however, one day, in their absence, I was invited by some of the party to take a walk, and, going into a tavern, commenced playing at cards, till my last farthing was lost. Determined, if possible, to be revenged of my antagonist, I requested time to run home for more money: it was readily granted. I ran and seized an article belonging to my mistress, and pawned it for a small sum, which soon followed my other stores. But evils seldom come alone: I was in this situation not only deprived of my money, but also obliged to decamp."

The next adventure of Batson was to enlist as a soldier. It happened, however, that his captain cheating him out of his pay, a grievous quarrel arose. Batson soon found that it was dangerous to reside in Rome and strive with the Pope. His captain, upon some pretence of improper conduct had him apprehended, tried, and condemned to be hanged. The cause of this harsh treatment was a very simple one: "For," says Batson, "I was one day drinking with a soldier, and happened to fall out about a lie given.

My sword unluckily running into his throat, he kicked up his heels, through his own fault, for he ran upon my point, so that he may thank his own hastiness." Upon this our hero says, " as if it had been a thing of nothing, or as a matter of pastime, they gave sentence that I should be led in state along the streets, then mounted upon a ladder, kick up my heels before all the people, and take a swing in the open air, as if I had another life in my knapsack. A notary informed me of this sentence, who was so generous that he requested no fee, nor any expenses for his trouble during the trial. The unfeeling gaoler desired me to make my peace with my Maker, without giving me one drop to cheer my desponding heart. Informed of my melancholy condition, a compassionate friar came to prepare me for another world, since the inhabitants of this were so ready to bid me farewell. When he arrived, he enquired for the condemned person, I answered, ' Father, I am the man, though you do not know me.' He said, ' Dear child, it is now time for you to think of another world, since sentence is passed, and, therefore, you must employ the short time allowed you in confessing your sins, and asking forgiveness of your offences.' I answered, ' Reverend father, in obedience to the commands of the church, I confess but once in the year, and that is in Lent; but if, according to human laws, I must atone with my life for the crime I have committed, your reverence, being so learned, must be truly sensible that there is no divine precept which says, ' Thou shalt not eat or drink;' and therefore, since it is not contrary to the law of God, I desire that I may have meat and drink, and then we will discourse of what is best for us both; for I am in a Christian country, and plead the privilege of sanctuary.'

" The good friar was much moved at finding me so jocular when I ought to be so serious, and began to preach to me a loud and a long sermon upon the parable of the lost sheep, and the repentance of the good thief. But the charity bells that ring when criminals are executed knolling in my ears, made a deeper impression upon my heart than the loud and impressive voice of the friar. I therefore kneeled down before my ghostly father, and cleared the store-house of my sins, and poured forth a dreadful budget of iniquity. He then gave me his blessing, and poor Batson seemed prepared to take his flight from a world of misfortunes and insults.

" But having previously presented a petition to the Marquis D Este, then commanding officer, he at that critical moment called me before him. He being a merciful man, respited my sentence, and sent me to the gallies for ten years. Some friends farther interfered, and informed the Marquis, that the accusation and sentence against me were effected by the malice of the captain, who was offended because I had insisted for the whole of my listing money. The result was, that he ordered me to be set at liberty, to the disappointment of my captain, together with that of the multitude and the executioner.

"The deadly fright being over, and my mind restored to tranquility, I went forth to walk, and to meditate upon what plans I should pursue in the rugged journey of life. Every man has his own fortune, and, as good luck would have it, I again met with a recruiting officer, who enlisted me, and, from partiality, took me home to his own quarters. The cook taking leave of the family, I was interrogated if I understood any thing in that line. To this I replied, as usual, in the affirmative, and was accordingly installed in the important office of cook.

"In the course of a military life, my master took up his winter residence at Bavaria, in the house of one of the richest men in those parts. To save his property, however, the Bavarian pretended to be very poor, drove away all his cattle, and removed all his stores to another quarter. Informed of this, I waited upon him, and acquainted him, that, as he had a person of quality in his house, it would be necessary for him to provide liberally for him and his servants. He replied, that I had only to inform him what provisions I wanted, and he would order them immediately. I then informed him, that my master always kept three tables, one for the gentlemen and pages, a second for the butler and under officers, a third for the footmen, grooms, and other liveries; that for these tables he must supply one ox, two calves, four sheep, twelve pullets, six capons, two dozen of pigeons, six pounds of bacon, four pounds of sugar, two of all sorts of spice; a hundred eggs, half a dozen dishes of fish, a pot of wine to every plate, and six hogsheads to stand by. He blessed himself, and exclaimed, 'If all you speak of be only for the servants' tables, the village will not be able to furnish the master's.' To this I replied, that my master was such a good-natured man, that, if he saw his servants and attendants well provided, he was indifferent to his own table; a dish of imperial stuffed meat, with an egg in it, would be sufficient for him. He asked me of what that same imperial stuffed meat was composed? I desired him to send for a grave-digger and a cobbler, and while they were at work, I would inform him what there was wanting. They were instantly called. I then took an egg, and putting it into the body of a pigeon, which I had already gutted with my knife, said to him, 'Now, sir, take notice; this egg is in the pigeon, the pigeon is to be put into a partridge, the partridge into a pheasant, the pheasant into a pullet, the pullet into a turkey, the turkey into a kid, the kid into a sheep, the sheep into a calf, and the calf into a cow; all these creatures are to be pulled, fleed, and larded, except the cow, which is to have her hide on; and as they are through one into another, like a nest of boxes, the cobbler is to sew every one of them that they may not slip out; and the grave-digger is t throw up a deep trench, into which one load of coals is to be cas and the cow laid on the top of it, and another load above her,—the fuel set on fire, to burn about four hours, more or less, when the meat being taken out, is incorporated, and becomes such a delicious dish, that formerly the emperors used to dine upon it on their coronation-day; for which reason, and because an egg is the foundation of all that curious mass, it is named the 'imperial egg-stuffed meat.' The landlord was not a little astonished, but after some conversation we understood each other, and the master left the matter to my care.

"In the course of my negociations with the landlord, I incurred the displeasure of my master, who, discovering my policy, came into the kitchen, seized the first convenient instrument, and belaboured me most unmercifully. He was, however, punished for his rashness, by the want of a cook for two weeks.

"The French scoundrels were audacious enough to pay us a visit while we remained here. I was ordered out with the rest, but I kept at the greatest distance, lest any bullet should have mistaken me for some other person. No sooner did I receive the intelligence that the French were conquered than I ran to the field of battle, brandishing my sword, and cutting and splashing among the dead men. It unfortunately happened, however, that as I stuck one of them with my sword, he uttered a mournful groan, and, apprehensive that he was about to revenge the injury done to him, I ran off with full speed, leaving my sword in his body. In passing along, I met with another sword, which saved my honour, as I vaunted that I had seized it from one in the field of battle.

"While thus rambling through the field of blood and danger, my master was carried home mortally wounded, who called me a scoundrel, and cried, 'Why did you not obey me?' 'Lest, Sir,' replied I, 'I should have been as you now are.' The good man soon breathed his last, leaving me a horse and fifty ducats.

"Being again emancipated from bonds of servitude I began to

enjoy life, and continued to treat all my acquaintance so long as my money would permit. The return of poverty, however, made me again enlist under the banners of servitude.

"About this time a singular occurrence happened to me. I chanced to go out into the street, when my eyesight was so affected that I could not discern black from green, nor white from grey Observing the candles suspended in a candle maker's shop, and taking them for radishes, I thought there was no great harm if I tasted one of them. Accordingly, laying hold of one, down fell the whole row, and being dashed to pieces upon the floor, a scuffle ensued; I was taken into custody, and made to pay the damage, which operated to restore my sight to its natural state.

"Not long after this adventure, I was assailed with love for the fair sex, and, after some sighs and presents, I was bound to a woman for better or for worse, and continued with her until the charms of the marriage state and the pleasures of domestic life began to pall upon me, and an ardent desire to return to my old course of adventure took possession of my mind. Towards the attainment of this desirable end, I one day kicked my wife out of doors, dressed myself, and prepared to sally forth. I had no sooner effected this liberation, than a tavern was my first resting place to recruit my spirits and to redeem lost time.

"I at last formed the resolution of returning to my native home, and there spending the evening of my bustling life in calm repose. After travelling many a tedious mile, I got to London. Arrived in the capital, I went directly to my father's house but found it in the possession of another, and my sisters departed this life. As both of them had been married, and had left children, there was no hope of any legacy by their death: I was therefore under the necessity of doing something for a living. Finding the gout increasing upon me, I, by the advice of an acquaintance, took a public-house; and, as I understood several languages, I thought I might have many customers from among foreigners."

Batson then gravely concludes his own narrative in these words:—

"I intend to leave off my foolish pranks, and, as I have spent my juvenile years and money in keeping company, hope to find some fools as bad as myself, who delight in throwing away their estates and impairing their health."

He accordingly took the Ram Inn, in Smithfield, and acquired a considerable sum. But, being desirous to make a fortune with one dash, he hastened his end. Among others who put up at his house was a gentleman who had purchased a large estate in the country, and was going to deliver the cash. The ostler observed to his master, that the bags belonging to the gentleman were uncommonly heavy when he carried them into the house. They mutually agreed to rob, and afterwards to murder him; and the ostler accomplished the horrid deed. But, differing about the division of the spoil, the ostler got drunk, and disclosed the whole matter. The house was searched, the body of the gentleman found and both the murderers were seized, tried, and condemned. The ostler died before the fatal day, but Batson was executed, and according to the Catholic faith, died a penitent, a year before the restoration of King Charles II.

JOHN COTTINGTON,
CALLED
"MULLED SACK."

The father of this man was a haberdasher in Cheapside, but, living above his income, he died so poor that he was interred by the parish. He had eighteen children, fifteen daughters and three sons. Our hero was the youngest of the family, and at the age of eight, was bound apprentice to a chimney-sweeper. In his first year, deeming himself as expert at his profession as his master, he left him, and, acting for himself, soon acquired a great run of business.

Money now coming in upon him, he frequented tne tavern, and, disdaining to taste of any thing but mulled sack, he acquired that appellation. One evening he there met with a young woman, with whom he was so enamoured, that he "took her for better for worse." But, not enjoying that degree of comfort in this union which his imagination had painted to him, he frequented the company of other women, until it became necessary to make public contributions to supply their pressing necessities. His first trials were in picking pockets of watches, and any small sums he could find. Among others, he robbed a lady famous among the usurers, of a gold watch set with diamonds, and another lady of a similar piece of luxury, as she was entering the church to hear a celebrated preacher. By the aid of his accomplices, the pin was taken out of the axle of her coach, which fell down at the church door, and in the crowd, Mulled Sack, being dressed as a gentleman, gave her his hand, while he seized her watch. The pious lady did not discover her loss, until she wished to know the length of the sermon, when her devout meditations, excited by the consoling exhortation of the pious preacher, were sadly interrupted by the loss of her timepiece. It is related, that, upon a certain occasion, he had the coldness to attempt the pocket of Oliver Cromwell, and that the danger to which he was then exposed determined him to leave that sneaking trade, and in a genteel manner to enter upon the honourable profession of public collector on the highway.

He entered into partnership with Tom Cheney. Their first adventure was attacking Colonel Hewson, who had raised himself by his merit from a cobbler to a colonel. He was riding at some distance from his regiment upon Hounslow-heath, and, even there, in sight of some of his men, these two rogues robbed him. The pursuit was keen: Tom's horse failing him, he was apprehended, but Mulled Sack escaped. The prisoner, being severely wounded, intreated that his trial might be postponed on that account. But, on the contrary, lest he should die of his wounds, he was condemned at two o'clock, and executed that evening.

One Horne was the next accomplice of Mulled Sack. His companions were, however, generally unfortunate. Upon their first attempt, Horne was pursued, taken and executed.

Thus, twice bereft of his associates, he acted alone, but generally committed his depredations upon the republican party, who then had the wealth of the nation in their possession. Informed that the sum of four thousand pounds was on its way from London, to pay the regiments of Oxford and Gloucester, he concealed himself behind a hedge which the waggon had to pass, presented his pistols, and the guard supposing that many more were concealed, fled, and left him the immense prize.

There were a few passengers in the waggon, who were greatly affrighted. He, however, consoled them, assuring them that he would not injure them, saying, "This which I have taken is as much mine as theirs who own it, being all extorted from the public by the rapacious members of our commonwealth, to enrich themselves, maintain their janizaries, and keep honest people in subjection, the most effectual way to do which is to keep them very poor."

When not employed as a chimney-sweep, which profession he still occasionally pursued, he dressed in high style, and is said to have received more money by robbery than any man in that age. One day, being informed that the receiver-general was to send up to London six thousand pounds, he entered his house the night before, and rendered that trouble unnecessary. Upon the noise which this notorious robbery occasioned, Mulled Sack was apprehended; but through cunning, baffling the evidence, or corrupting the jury, he was acquitted.

In a little time after, he robbed and murdered a gentleman, and, for fear of detection, went to the Continent, and was introduced into the Court of Charles the Second. Upon pretence of giving information, he came home again, and applied to Cromwell, confessed his crime, but proposed to purchase his life by important information. But whether he failed in his promise, or whether Cromwell thought that such a notorious offender was unworthy to live, cannot be ascertained; one thing is certain, that he was tried and executed in the forty-fifth year of his age, in the month of April, 1659.

His portrait (which is now excessively rare,) has been engraved—and Granger, in his " Biographical History of England," says that he never saw the print, but in a very curious and valuable volume of English portraits by the old engravers, collected in the reign of Charles I. in the possession of John Delebere, Esq. of Cheltenham in Glocestershire. The editor of this work has seen upwards of £50 given for an impression of this engraving at a public sale—the print represents him in a fantastic and humorous chimney-sweeper's dress, with a cap and feather, and laced band, his clothes tucked up, and coat ragged; he has a scarf on his arm; on his left leg is a fashionable boot with a spur; on his right foot a shoe with a rose; he has a sword by his side, and a hollybush and pole on his shoulder; in his left hand is another pole with a horn on it; a pipe, out of which issues smoke is in his right hand, and at the bottom are the following lines—

"I walke the Strande and Westminster, and scorne
To march i' the Cittie, though I bear the horne,
My feather and my *yellow* band accorde
To prove me courtier; my boote, spur and sword,
My smoking pipe, scarf, garter, rose on shoe,
Shew my brave mind, t' affect what gallants do.
I dance, sing, drink, and merrilye pass the day.
And like a chimney, sweepe all care away."•

• This medley of the dress of the man of fashion, and the chimney-sweeper is not unlike that which Lassels mentions in his " Voyage of Italy" where he describes a carnival at Rome; " but never," says the author, " did any mascarade please, like that speculative Italian, who mocked both the French and the Spaniards at once, by walking up and down the street, clad half like a Don, and half like a Mounsier," &c.
Part 11, *p.* 190, *&c.*

CAPTAIN JAMES HIND.

The father of Hind was an industrious saddler, a cheerful companion, and a good Christian. He was a native of Cnipping Norton, Oxfordshire, where James was born. As our hero was his only son, he received a good education, and remained at school, until he was fifteen years of age.

He was then sent as an apprentice to a butcher in that place, and continued in that employment during two years. Upon leaving his master's service, he applied to his mother for money to bear his expenses to London, complaining bitterly of the rough and quarrelsome temper of his master. The complying mother yielded, and, giving him three pounds, she, with a sorrowful heart, took farewell of her beloved son.

Arrived in the capital, he soon contracted a relish for the pleasures of the town. His bottle and a female companion became his principal delight, and occupied the greater part of his time. He was unfortunately detected one evening with a woman of the town who had just robbed a gentleman, and along with her confined until the morning. He was acquitted because no evidence appeared against him, but his fair companion was committed to Newgate.

Captain Hind, soon after this accident, became acquainted with one Allan, a famous highwayman. While partaking of a bottle, their conversation became mutually so agreeable that they consented to unite their fortunes.

Their measures being concerted, they set out in quest of plunder. They fortunately met a gentleman and his servant travelling along the road. Hind being raw and inexperienced, Allan was desirous to have a proof of his courage and address; he, therefore, remained at a distance, while Hind boldly rode up to them and took from them fifteen pounds, at the same time returning one to bear their expenses home. This he did with so much grace and pleasantry, that the gentleman vowed that he would not injure a hair of his head though it were in his power.

About this period, the unfortunate Charles I. suffered death for his political principles. Captain Hind conceived an inveterate enmity to all those who had stained their hands with their sovereign's blood, and gladly embraced every opportunity to wreak his vengeance upon them. In a short time, Allan and Hind met with the usurper, Oliver Cromwell, riding from Huntingdon to London. They attacked the coach, but Oliver, being attended by seven servants, Allan was apprehended, and it was with no small difficulty that Hind made his escape. The unfortunate Allan was soon after tried, and suffered death for his audacity. The only effect which this produced upon Hind was to render him more cautious in his future depredations. He could not, however, think of abandoning a course on which he had just entered, and which promised so many advantages.

The captain had ridden so hard to escape from Cromwell and his train that he killed his horse, and, having no money to purchase a substitute, he was under the necessity of trying his fortune upon foot, until he should find means to procure another. It was not long before he espied a horse tied to a hedge with a saddle on and a brace of pistols attached to it. He looked round and observed a gentleman on the other side of the hedge. "This is my horse," exclaimed the captain, and immediately vaulted into the saddle. The gentleman called out to him that the horse was his. "Sir, said Hind, "you may think yourself well off that I have left you all the money in your pocket to buy another, which you had best lay out before I meet you again, lest you should be worse used." So saying, he rode off in search of new booty.

There is another story of Hind's ingenious method of supplying himself with a horse upon a similar occasion. It appears that, being upon a second extremity reduced to the humble station of a footpad, he hired a sorry nag, and proceeded on his journey. He was overtaken by a gentleman mounted on a fine hunter, with a portmanteau behind him. They entered into conversation upon such topics as are common to travellers, and Hind was very eloquent in the praise of the gentleman's horse, which inclined the other to descant upon the qualifications of the animal. There was upon one side of the road a wall, which the gentleman said his horse would leap over. Hind offered to risk a bottle on it, to which the gentleman agreed, and quickly made his horse leap over. The captain acknowledged that he had lost his wager, but requested the gentleman to let him try if he could do the same; to which he consented, and the captain, being seated in the saddle of his companion, rode off at full speed and left him to return the other miserable animal to its owner.

At another time the captain met the regicide Hugh Peters in Enfield chace, and commanded him to deliver his money. Hugh, who was not deficient in confidence, began to combat Hind with texts of scripture, and to cudgel our bold robber with the eighth commandment: " It is written in the law," said he, that " Thou shalt not steal;" and furthermore, Solomon, who was surely a very wise man, spoke in this manner; " Rob not the poor, because he is poor." Hind was desirous to answer him in his own strain, and for that purpose began to rub up his memory for some of the texts he had learned when at school. " Verily," said Hind, " if thou hadst regarded the divine precepts as thou oughtest to have done, thou wouldst not have wrested them to such an abominable and wicked sense as thou didst the words of the prophet, when he said, 'Bind their kings with chains, and their nobles with fetters of iron.' Didst thou not then, detestable hypocrite, endeavour, from these words, to aggravate the misfortunes of thy royal master, whom thy cursed republican party unjustly murdered by the gate of his own palace?" Here Hugh Peters began to extenuate that proceeding, and to allege other parts of the scripture in his own defence. "Pray, Sir," replied Hind, " make no reflections against men of my profession, for Solomon plainly said, 'do not despise a thief.' But it is to little purpose for us to dispute, the substance of what I have to say is this, deliver thy money presently, or else I shall send thee out of the world to thy master, the devil, in an instant." These terrible words of the captain's so terrified the old Presbyterian, that he forthwith gave him thirty broad pieces of gold and then departed.

But Hind was not satisfied with allowing so bitter an enemy to the royal cause to depart in such a manner. He accordingly rode after him at full speed, and, overtaking him, addressed him in the following language —" Sir, now I think of it, I am convinced this misfortune has happened to you because you did not obey the words of the scripture, which expressly says, ' provide neither gold, nor silver, nor brass in your purses, for your journey,' whereas it is evident that you had provided a pretty decent quantity of gold. However, as it is now in my power to make you fulfil another commandment, I would by no means slip the opportunity; therefore pray give me thy cloak." Peters was so surprised that he neither stood still to dispute nor to examine what was the drift of Hind's demand. But he soon made him understand his meaning, when he added, " You know, Sir, our Saviour has commanded, that if any man take away thy cloak, thou must not refuse thy coat also; therefore I cannot suppose that you will act in direct contradiction to such an express command, especially as you cannot pretend you have forgot it, seeing I now remind you of that duty." The old Puritan shrugged his shoulders some time before he preceeded to uncase them; but Hind told him that his delay would be of no service to him, for he would be implicitly obeyed, because he was sure that what he requested was entirely consonant with the scripture. He accordingly surrendered, and Hind carried off the cloak.

The following sabbath, when Hugh ascended the pulpit, he was inclined to pour forth an invective against stealing, and selected for his subject these words. " I have put off my coat, how shall I put it on?" an honest plain man, who was present, and knew how he had been treated by the robber, promptly cried out, "Upon my word, Sir, I believe there is nobody here can tell you, unless Captain Hind were here." Which ready answer to Hugh's scriptural question put the congregation into such an outrageous fit of laughter, that the parson was made to blush, and descended from his pulpit, without prosecuting the subject farther.

The captain as before mentioned, indulged a rooted hatred against all those who were concerned in the murder of the late king; and frequently these men fell in his way. He was one day riding on the road, when President Bradshaw, who had sat as judge upon the king, and passed the sentence of death upon him, met with the captain. The place where they came into collision was on the road between Sherbourne and Shaftesbury. Hind rode up to the coach, and demanded Bradshaw's money, who, supposing that his very name would convey terror along with it, informed him who he was. "Marry," cried Hind, "I neither fear you nor any king-killing villain alive. I have now as much power over you, as you lately had over the king, and I should do God and my country good service, if I made the same use of it; but live, villain, to suffer the pangs of thine own conscience, till justice shall lay her iron hand upon thee, and require an answer for thy crimes, in a way more proper for such a monster, who art unworthy to die by any hands but those of the common hangman, or at any other place than Tyburn. Nevertheless, though I spare thy life as a regicide, be assured, that unless thy money is delivered up immediately, thou shalt die for thy obstinacy."

Bradshaw began to perceive that the case was not now with him as it was when he sat at Westminster Hall, supported by all the strength of the rebellion. Fear took possession of his soul, and discovered itself in his countenance. He put his trembling hand into his pocket, and pulled out about forty shillings in silver, which he presented to the captain, who swore he would that minute shoot him through the heart, unless he found coin of another species

To save his life, the sergeant pulled out that which he valued next to it, and presented the captain with a purse full of Jacobuses.

But though Hind had got possession of the cash, he was inclined to detain the sergeant a little longer, and began the following eulogium upon the value of money:—

"This, sir, is the metal that wins my heart for ever! O precious gold! I admire and adore thee, as much as either Bradshaw, Prynne, or any other villain of the same stamp, who, for the sake of thee, would sell his Redeemer again, were he upon earth. This is that incomparable medicament, which the republican physicians call the wonder-working plaster; it is truly catholic in operation, and somewhat of kin to the Jesuit's powder, but more effectual. The virtues of it are strange and various: it maketh justice deaf, as well as blind; and takes out spots of the deepest treasons as easily as Castile soap does common stains; it alters a man's constitution in two or three days, more than the virtuoso's transfusion of blood can do in seven years. It is a great alexipharmic, and helps poisonous principles of rebellion, and those that use them; it miraculously exalts and purifies the eye-sight, and makes traitors behold nothing but innocence in the blackest malefactors; it is a mighty cordial for a declining cause; it stifles faction and schism as certainly as rats are destroyed by common arsenic; in a word, it makes fools wise men, and wise men fools, and both of them knaves. The very colour of this precious balm is bright and dazzling. If it be properly applied to the fist, that is in a decent manner, and in a competent dose, it infallibly performs all the above-mentioned cures, and many others too numerous to be here mentioned."

The captain having finished his panegyric upon the virtues of the glittering metal, pulled out his pistol, and again addressed the sergeant, saying, "You and your infernal crew have a long while run on, like Jehu, in a career of blood and impiety, falsely pretending that zeal for the Lord of Hosts has been your only motive. How long you may be suffered to continue in the same course, God only knows. I will, however, for this time, stop your race in a literal sense of the word." And without farther delay, he shot all the six horses that were in the carriage, and left Bradshaw to ponder on the lesson he had received.

Hind's next adventure was with a company of ladies, in a coach upon the road between Petersfield and Portsmouth. He accosted them in a polite manner, and informed them that he was a protector of the fair sex, and it was purely to win the favour of a hard-hearted mistress that he had travelled the country. "But, ladies," added no, " I am at this time reduced to the necessity of asking rel.ef having nothing to carry me on in the intended prosecution of my adventures." The young ladies who had read many romances, could not help concluding that they had met with some Quixote or Amadis de Gaul, who was saluting them in the strains of knight-errantry. "Sir knight," said one of the most jocular of the company, " we heartily commiserate your condition, and are very much troubled that we cannot contribute towards your support; for we have nothing about us but a sacred *depositum*, which the laws of your order will not suffer you to violate." The captain was much pleased at having met with such a pleasant lady, and was much inclined to have permitted them to proceed; but his necessities were at this time very urgent. " May I, bright ladies, be favoured with the knowledge of what this sacred depositum, which you speak of, is, that so I may employ my utmost abilities in its defence, as the laws of knight-errantry require." The lady who had spoken before told him, that the depositum she had spoken of was £3000, the portion of one of the company, who was going to bestow it upon the knight who had won her good-will by his many past services. " Present my humble duty to the knight," said he, "and be pleased to tell him that my name is Captain Hind; that out of mere necessity I have made bold to borrow part of what, for his sake, I wish were twice as much; that I promise to expend the sum in defence of injured lovers, and in the support of gentlemen who profess knight-errantry." Upon the name of Captain Hind, the fair ones were sufficiently alarmed, as his name was well known all over England. He, however, requested them not to be affrighted, for he would not do them the least injury, and only requested £1000 of the £3000. As the money was bound up in several parcels, the request was instantly complied with, and our adventurer wished them a prosperous journey, and many happy days to the bride.

Taking leave of the captain for a little, we shall inform our readers of the consequences of this extorted loan of the captain's. When the bride arrived at the dwelling of her intended husband, she faithfully recounted to him her adventures upon the road. The avaricious lover refused to accept her hand until her father should agree to make up the loss. Partly because he detested the request, and partly because he had sufficiently exhausted his funds, the father refused to comply. Her hand was therefore declined, because it was emp ied of the third part of her fortune; and the affectionate and high-spi ited lady died of a broken heart. Hind often declared that this adventure cost him great uneasiness, while it filled him with detestation at the dishonourable and base conduct of the mercenary lover.

The transactions of Hind were now become so numerous, and made him so well known, that he was forced to conceal himself in the country. During this cessation from his usual industrious labours, his funds became so exhausted, that even his horse was sold to maintain his own life. Impelled by necessity, he often resolved to hazard a few movements upon the highway; but he had trafficked so long in that quarter, that he dared not risk any adventure of that kind. Fortune however commiserated the condition of the captain, and provided relief. He was informed that a doctor, who resided in the neighbourhood, had gone to receive a handsome fee for a cure which he had effected. The captain then lived in a small house which he had hired upon the side of a common, and which the doctor had to pass in his journey home. Hind, having long and impatiently waited his arrival, ran up to him, and in the most piteous tone and suppliant language, told the doctor his wife was suddenly seized with illness, that unless she got some assistance, she would certainly perish, and entreated him just to tarry for a minute or two, and lend her his medical assistance, and he would gratefully pay him for his trouble as soon as it was in his power.

The tender-hearted doctor, moved with compassion, alighted and accompanied him into his house, assuring him that he should be very happy to be of any service in restoring his wife to health. Hind showed the doctor up-stairs; but they had no sooner entered the door, than he locked it, presented a pistol, showing, at the same time, his empty purse, saying:—" This is my wife; she has so long been unwell, that there is now nothing at all within her. I know, Sir, that you have a golden remedy in your pocket for her distemper, and if you do not apply it without a word, this pistol shall make the day shine into your body!" The doctor would have been content to have lost his fee, upon condition of being delivered from the importunities of his patient; but it required only a small degree of the knowledge of symptoms to be convinced, that obedience was the only thing which remained for him to observe: he therefore emptied his own purse of forty guineas into that of the captain, and thus left our hero's wife in a convalescent state. Hind then informed the doctor, that he would leave him in possession of his whole house, to reimburse him for the money which he had taken from him. So saying, he locked the door upon the doctor, mounted that gentleman's horse, and went in quest of another county, because the one he was in would, in consequence of this adventure, become too dangerous for him.

Hind has been often celebrated for his generosity to the poor; and the following is a remarkable instance of his virtue in that particular. He was upon one occasion extremely destitute of cash, and had waited long upon the road without receiving any supply. An old man, jogging along upon an ass, at length appeared. He rode up to him, and very politely inquired where he was going. " To the market, at Wantage," said the old man, " to buy me a cow, that I may have some milk for my children." " How many children have you?" The old man answered, " Ten." " And how much do you mean to give for a cow ?" said Hind. " I have but forty shillings, master, and that I have been scraping together these two years." Hind's heart ached for the poor man's condition; at the same time he could not help admiring his simplicity; but, being in absolute want himself, he thought of an expedient which would serve both himself and the poor old man. " Father," said he, " the money which you have is necessary for me at this time; but I will not wrong your children of their milk. My name is Hind, and if you will give me your forty shillings quietly, and meet me again this day se'nnight at this place, I promise to make the sum double." The old man reluctantly consented, and Hind enjoined him " to be cautious not to mention a word of the matter to any body between this and that time." The old man came at the appointed time, and received as much as would purchase two cows, and twenty shillings more, that he might thereby have the best in the market.

Though Hind had long frequented the road, yet he carefully avoided shedding blood; and the following is the only instance of this nature related of him. He had one morning committed several robberies, and among others, had taken more than £70 from Colonel Harrison, the celebrated Parliamentary general. As the Roundheads were Hind's inveterate foes, the colonel immediately raised the hue-and-cry after him, which was circulated in that part of the country before the captain was aware of it. At last, however, he received intelligence at one of the inns upon the road, and made every possible haste to fly the scene of danger. In this situation the captain was apprehensive of every person he met upon the road. He had reached the place called Knowl Hill, when the servant of a gentleman, who was following his master, came riding at full speed behind him. Hind, supposing that it was one in pursuit of himself, upon his coming up, turned about, and shot him through the head, when the unfortunate man fell dead upon the spot. Fortune favoured the captain at this time, and he got off in safety. The following adventure closes the narrative of Hind's busy life.

After Charles I. was beheaded, the Scots remained loyal, proclaimed his son Charles II., and resolved to maintain his right against the usurper. They suddenly raised an army, and, entering England, proceeded as far as Worcester. Multitudes of the English joined the royal army, and among these Captain Hind, who was loyal from principle, and brave by nature. Cromwell was sent by Parliament with an army to intercept the march of the royalists. Both armies met at Worcester, and a desperate and bloody battle ensued. The king's army was routed. Captain Hind had the good fortune to escape, and reaching London, lived in a retired situation. Here, however, he had not remained long, when he was betrayed by one of his intimate acquaintances. It will readily be granted that his actions merited death by the laws of his country, but the mind recoils with horror from the thought of treachery in an intimate friend.

Hind was carried before the Speaker of the House of Commons, and, after a long examination, was committed to Newgate and loaded with irons; nor was any person allowed to converse with him without a special permission. He was brought to the bar of the Session-house at the Old Baily, indicted for several crimes, but, for want of sufficient evidence, nothing worthy of death could be proved against him. Not long after this, he was sent down to Reading under a strong guard, and, being arraigned before Judge Warburton, for killing George Symson at Knowl Hill, as formerly mentioned, he was convicted of wilful murder. An act of indemnity for all past offences was issued at this time, and he hoped to have been included; but an order of council removed him to Worcester gaol, where he was condemned for high treason, and hanged, drawn and quartered, on the 24th September, 1652, aged thirty-four years. His head was stuck upon the top of the bridge over the Severn, and the other parts of his body placed upon the gates of the city. The head was privately taken down and interred, but the remaining parts of his body remained until consumed by the influence of the weather.

In his last moments he declared that his principal depredations had been committed against the republican party, and that nothing grieved him so much as not living to see his royal master restored. In his confession which he made previous to his death, he merely declares that he departed from England and went to the Hague; but after three days went to Ireland, and landed at Galloway, and became corporal to the Marquis of Ormond's life-guard; was wounded at Youghal, in the right arm and hand; made an escape to Duncannon, thence to Sicily, and the Isle of Man; went to Scotland, sent a letter to his majesty, and represented my services, &c. which was favourably accepted; for no sooner had the king notice of my coming, but immediately had admittance and kissed his hand, and commended me to the Duke of Buckingham, then present; came to England, was in the engagements of Warrington and Worcester, where I kept the field till the king fled; and in the evening, the gates being full of flying persons, I leaped over the wall by myself only, travelled the country, and lay three days under bushes and hedges, because of the soldiery, till I came to Sir John Packington's woods, where I lay five days; and afterward came on foot to London, by the name of James Brown; lodged five weeks in London, and was taken November 9th, 1651, at Dowry the barber's, near Dunstan's church, in Fleet-street. This is all that was declared by him, who remains captived in close prison in the gaol of Newgate.—JAMES HIND.

The following are a few verses to his memory, which, if not remarkable for poetical merit, are interesting, and not without ingenuity.

TO THE MEMORY OF CAPTAIN HIND.

BY A POET OF HIS OWN TIME

Whenever death attacks a throne
Nature through all her parts must groan,
The mighty monarch to bemoan.

He must be wise, and just, and good,
Though not the state he understood,
Nor ever spar'd a subject's blood.

And shall no friendly poet find
A monumental verse for Hind,—
In fortune less, as great in mind?

Hind made our wealth one common store,
He robb'd the rich to feed the poor,—
What did immortal Cæsar more?

Nay, 'twere not difficult to prove
That meaner views did Cæsar move:
His was ambition, Hind's was love,

Our English hero sought no crown,
Nor that more pleasing bait, renown:
But just to keep off fortune's frown.

Yet when his country's cause invites,
See him assert a nation's rights!
A robber for a monarch fights!

If in due light his deeds we scan,
As nature points us out the plan,
Hind was an honourable man.

Honour, the virtue of the brave,
To Hind that turn of genius gave,
Which made him scorn to be a slave.

Thus, had his stars conspir'd to raise
His natal hour, this virtue's praise
Had shown with an uncommon blaze.

Some new epocha had begun
From every action he had done;
A city built, a battle won.

If one's a subject, one at helm,
'Tis the same vi'lence, says Anselm
To rob a house or waste a realm.

Be henceforth, then, for ever join'd,
The names of Cæsar and of Hind;
In fortune different, one in mind.

The only portrait of this singular man extant is that which is prefixed to his confession, and which is now very scarce; a copy from this was made by Richardson, in his collection, which is readily to be met with. There is also an engraving of a man in armour on horseback, bearing the name of Captain John Hind, but it is not authentic, being a portrait of Charles II. altered.—*See Granger's Biographical History of England, vol. 4.*

GILDER ROY,
CALLED
"THE BONNIE BOY."

This hero, who, with his merry men, ravaged the Scottish country and pillaged the inhabitants, was descended of a very good family, and born in Perthshire, in the Highlands of Scotland; his father died just as he was of age, when leaving him an estate of about 80 marks a year, he thought himself fully capable to the management of it, without the advice of his friends: by which means he, in short managed it all away, and run through it in about a year and a half; upon which he soon became very needy, and a fit subject to be moulded into any shape that had an appearance of profit. Having thus, by his irregularities, reduced himself to a very poor condition, he was very burthensome to his mother, who often supplied him with money out of her jointure, which he always quickly consumed; but she perceiving that no good admonitions would reclaim his extravagancy, withheld her hand, and would not answer his expectation; whereupon, lying at her house one night, he arose, entered his mother's bed-chamber, cut her throat with a razor, and then plundered and burnt the house to the ground.

This unparalleled piece of villainy filled the whole country with horror, and a proclamation was issued out for his apprehension, with a considerable reward to them that should bring him to justice. He then fled into France, where being on a solemn day at the church of St. Denis, in Paris, whilst Cardinal Richlieu was celebrating high mass, at which the king was present, Gilder Roy had his hand in the Cardinal's purse, which was hanging at his side, while he was officiating at the altar; his majesty perceiving the transaction, Gilder Roy, who was dressed like a gentleman, seeing himself discovered, held up his finger to the king, making a sign to take no notice, and he should see good sport. The king, glad of such an occasion of mirth, let him alone; and a little while after, coming to the Cardinal, he took occasion, in discourse, to oblige him to look into his purse for money, which he missing, began to wonder. The king knowing which way it went, was more than ordinarily merry; until, being tired with laughter, he was willing that the Cardinal might have again what was taken from him. The king thought that he who took the money was an honest gentleman, and of some account, as he kept his countenance so well; but Gilder Roy had more wit than to come near them, for he acted not in jest, but in good earnest. Then the Cardinal turned all the laughter against the king, who using his common oath, swore by the faith of a gentleman. it was the first time that ever a thief had made him his companion.

He went from France into Spain, and being one day at Madrid, he went into the Duke of Medina-Celi's house, when that grandee had made a great entertainment for several foreign ministers. Several pieces of plate were locked in a trunk, and stood in a little room next to a hall where the feast was, in which room many servants were waiting for their masters. Gilder Roy went in a Spanish habit, accoutred in all respects like the steward of the house, and going to those that sat on the trunk, desired them to rise, because he was going to use it: which they having done, he caused it to be taken up by some porters that followed him in, and got clear off with it.

Gilder Roy having been about three years out of his own country, and thinking the villainy which he had perpetrated there was forgotten, returned to Scotland again, where he soon became a most notable highwayman; and the first person on whom he exercised this unlawful calling, was the Earl of Linlithgow, whom he robbed of a gold watch, a diamond ring, and eighty pieces of gold. In a little time his name became so dreaded through the whole country, that travellers were afraid to pass the roads without a great many in company; and when money was short with him, he would enter into Athol, Lochaber, Anguis, Mar, Baquehan, Murray, Sutherland, and other shires in the north of Scotland, and drive away the people's cattle, unless they paid him contribution, which they did quarterly, and had his protection; which was safeguard enough for their own persons, or goods, from receiving damage by him, or any of his gang.

When Oliver Cromwell embarked at Donaghadey, in the north of Ireland, and landed at Port-Patrick in Scotland, the news thereof came to Gilder Roy, who was then lurking in the Shire of Galloway, accordingly he met him on the road towards Glasgow, Cromwell having only two servants with him, he commanded him to stand and deliver, but the former, thinking three to one was odds, refused to obey; they then came to an engagement, and several pistols were discharged on both sides for nearly a quarter of an hour; when the bold robber pretended to yield his antagonists the day, by running as fast as he could from them; they pursued him very closely for near half an hour, and then suddenly turning upon them, the first mischief he did was shooting Oliver's horse, which, falling on his side as soon as wounded, broke the Protector's leg; as for his servants, he shot one of them through the head, and the other, begging quarter, it was granted; but Oliver being disabled, he had the civility to put him on an ass, and, tying his legs under his belly, sent them both to seek their fortunes.

Three of his roguish companions being apprehended and sent to the Tolbooth, a prison in Edinburgh, they broke out, but were soon retaken, and committed to Glasgow gaol; and soon after they were executed without the gates of the city, and left hanging on the gallows, until their carcases should rot and fall away by piece-meal. Gilder Roy highly resenting the indignity thus offered to his comrades in iniquity, vowed revenge; and it not being long before he met the judge who passed the sentence upon them, in the road going to Aberdeen, he attacked his coach, first stripping his coachman and two footmen, and tying their hands and feet, threw them into a deep pond; he then robbed the judge of all he had valuable about him, cut the coach to pieces, and shot the four horses that were in it dead. But not being satisfied with this barbarity, he drove the judge into a wood, and bound him to a tree; at night he went with some of his accomplices, and putting him on a horse behind one of them, brought him to the gallows where his three comrades were still hanging; which gallows was made like a turnstile, only the beams, on each end of which is nailed a strong iron hook, to which the rope is fastened, has no motion. " Now," said Gilder Roy to the judge, " by my soul, mon, as this unlucky structure, erected to break people's craigs, is not uniform without a fourth person taking his lodging here too, I must e'en hang you upon the vacant beam." Accordingly he was as good as his word, and for fear the government should not know who was the hangman, he sent a letter to the ministers of state, to acquaint them with his proceedings. This insolence caused the legislature to contrive ways and means to suppress the audaciousness of Gilder Roy, and his companions, who were dreaded far and near; and among them one Jennet, a lawyer, promoted the law for hanging a highwayman first, and judging him afterwards; which law being approved of, it received the sanction of the Government, without any contradiction, and was often put in force against many gentlemen of the road.

Gilder Roy being thus successful in his villanies, grew so intolerably wicked, that it was his delight, not only to rob on the highway, but also to murder those who refused to give him what they had, and burn houses and barns where the least affront was offered him. But at last a second proclamation being issued for his apprehension, with a reward of one thousand marks for any one that should take him, dead or alive, one Margaret Cunningham, with whom he kept company, betrayed him when he came next to her house; which being surrounded by about fifty men, and he sensible by whom he was trepanned, ran into her bed-chamber, and murdered her; he then returned to the room from whence he came, and defended himself with such undaunted bravery, that before they could take him, he killed eight of them; but then he was overpowered and put into a dismal dungeon, in the castle of Edinburgh, where he had heavy shackles put on his legs, strong chains about his middle, and his hands fastened behind him; in that state he was kept three days and nights, without any allowance of victuals or drink; when, without any trial, he was conveyed by a strong guard to the market-cross in Edinburgh, and was there hanged on a gibbet, thirty feet high, in April, 1658, aged 34 years. He was afterwards hung in chains on another gibbet, erected ten feet higher, between that city and Leith.

If traditional report be true, it would seem that Gilder Roy belonged to the proscribed " clan Gregor ;" and in these traditions many other romantic exploits are told of him. The ancient ballad recording his fall was composed not long after his death by a young woman who unfortunately was attached to him. That the ballad was popular in England before 1650 is evident from a black-letter copy of it, printed at least as early as that date. Another copy occurs, with some few variations, in Playford's " Wit and Mirth," Vol. III. 1702. The sentiments and language of the olden time are not always in strict accordance with the modern prudery: we are no less prurient, but we are infinitely more precise. Certain freedoms have been skillfully pruned away by the judicious hand of Miss Halket, of Pitferran, who afterwards married Sir Henry Wardlaw, of Pitreavie, in Fifeshire This amiable and accomplished lady, whose talent is well known as the authoress of " Hardiknute," has softened, expunged, and added, as necessity might require; and the result of her labours we now present to the public:—

ENGLISH HIGHWAYMEN.

BALLAD.

Gilder Roy was a bonnie boy,
  Had roses tull his shoone,
His stockings were of silken soy,
  Wi garters hanging doune:
It was, I weene, a comelie sight
  To see sae trim a boy;
He was my jo and heart's delight,
  My handsome Gilder Roy.

Oh, sike twa charming een he had,
  A breath as sweet as rose;
He never ware a Highland plaid,
  But costly silken cloathes:
He gain'd the luve of ladies gay,
  Nanc e'er tull him was coy;
Ah, wae is mee! I mourn the day
  For my dear Gilder Roy.

My Gilder Roy and I were born
  Baith in one toun together;
We scant were seven years beforn
  We gan to luve each other.
Our dadies and our mammies they
  Were filled wi mickle joy,
To think upon the bridal day
  'Twixt me and Gilder Roy.

For Gilder Roy, that luve of mine
  Gude faith, I freely bought
A wedding sark of Holland fine,
  Wi silken flowers wrought;
And he gied me a wedding ring
  Which I receiv'd wi joy;
Nae lad nor lassie eir could sing
  Like me and Gilder Roy.

Wi mickle joy we spent our prim
  Till we were baith sixteen,
And aft we past the langsome time
  Amang the leaves sae green:

GILDER ROY.

Aft on the banks we'd sit us thair,
   And sweetly kiss and toy;
Wi garlands gay wad deck my hair
   My handsome Gilder Roy.

Oh, that he still had been content
   Wi me to lead his life.
But, ah! his manfu' heart was bent
   To stir in feates of strife.
And he in many a venturous deed
   His courage bauld wad try;
And now this gars mine heart to bleed
   For my dear Gilder Roy.

And when of me his leave he tuik,
   The tears they wat mine ee:
I gave tull him a parting luik,
   " My benison gang wi thee:
God speed thee well, mine ain dear heart!
   For gane is all my joy;
My heart is rent sith we maun part,
   My handsome Gilder Roy!"

My Gilder Roy, baith far and near,
   Was fear'd in every toun,
And bauldly bare away the gear
   Of money a lowland loun.
Nane e'ir durst meet him man to man,
   He was sae brave a boy;
At length with numbers he was ta'en,
   My winsome Gilder Roy.

Wae worth the loun that made the laws
   To hang a man for gear;
To reave of life for ox or ass,
   For sheep, or horse, or mare!
Had not their laws been made sae strict,
   I neir had lost my joy;
Wi sorrow neir had wat my cheek
   For my dear Gilder Roy.

Giff Gilder Roy had done amisse,
  He maught hae banished been;
Ah! what sair cruelty is this,
  To hang sike handsome men!
To hang the flower o' Scottish land,
  Sae sweet and fair a boy!
Nae lady had sae white a hand
  As thee, my Gilder Roy.

Of Gilder Roy sae fraid they were,
  They bound him mickle strong;
Tull Edenburrow they led him thair,
  And on a gallows hung:
They hung him high aboon the rest,
  That was sae trim a boy;
Thair dyed the youth whom I lued best,
  My handsome Gilder Roy.

Thus having yielded up his breath,
  I bore his corpse away;
Wi tears, that trickled for his death,
  I wash't his comelye clay;
And siker in a grave sae deep
  I laid the dear lued boy;
And now for ever maun I weep
  My winsome Gilder Roy!

CAPTAIN PHILIP STAFFORD.

This singular character was a native of Berkshire, and born about the year 1622. His father had a small estate, with which, by cultivating it himself, he rendered his family comfortable. Philip was an only child, and therefore received such an education as the place and circumstances of his father could afford. But while at school, he was more distinguished for boxing and wrestling, than for the exercise of his mental faculties.

When the time generally allotted to young men of a moderate fortune at school was expired, Philip was taken home, and destined by his father to follow the plough. In his youthful years he imbibed the principles of religion and of loyalty which were current in that eventful period; when war commenced between Charles I. and his subjects, Stafford was one of the first who joined the royal standard. He continued in the army during that successful rebellion, but his actions are involved in the obscurity of the times. It is obvious, however, that he signalized himself, as he received the name of captain during that war.

Upon the death of Charles, the opposite party were invested with all power, and the loyalists were constrained to conceal themselves from the fury of their adversaries. The small estate of Stafford was, among many others, sequestrated, and he was thereby deprived of all means of subsistence. In these desperate circumstances he formed the resolution of making depredations upon the enemies of his late king, and he considered that it was just to levy contributions upon those who had taken away the life of his prince and had deprived him of his paternal inheritance.

He first cast his eyes upon an old republican, who had drunk deep in the troubled stream of the times, and had married a young lady in order to obtain her fortune. In the character of a servant, and assuming the dress and the language of the party, he succeeded in hiring himself as a servant into that family. By his insinuating address and engaging manners, he won the affections of his master, and was soon admitted to enter into conversation with him and his mistress, and in the most dexterous manner imitated the religious phrases and sentiments of the Puritans. But he soon employed language of a different kind to his mistress; alienated her affections from her lawful husband, and so grossly imposed upon him, that, when he would sometimes unexpectedly find them alone and in close conversation, he would conclude that religion was the subject of their earnest conversation. Under the disguise of religion, and emboldened by the credulity of the old husband, Stafford remained with increasing favour in the family, until an heir was born to enjoy the fortune of the good old republican.

Indifferent to all the ties of honour and of religion, Stafford and the lady carried on their criminal correspondence: and often amused themselves with the credulity of the husband and his unabated attachment to Stafford. In the moments of wanton levity, the lady had made him a present of a ring and also of some jewels, and had not only informed him of a quantity of jewels which her husband had collected, but actually showed him the place where they were deposited. The violent passion of avarice now assumed its dominion over him, and he formed the resolution to seize the cabinet of jewels, and even to abandon his favourite mistress in quest of new adventures.

But his plan could not be effected without the aid of some other person, and he was long doubtful whom he could trust in so delicate and important a matter. At last he fixed upon one named Tom Perry, the son of a French refugee, whom he had formerly known at school, and with whose temper and disposition he was thoroughly acquainted. He, accordingly, provided a key to the door of the place where the jewels were deposited, took care to have the window so broken and injured that it appeared to have suffered violence from without, had a ladder brought and laid at the foot of the window, and such noise made as might be heard by some of the servants. Stafford, always attentive to his duty and his master's interest, was the first to give the alarm in the morning. The rest of the servants were called, they remembered to have heard the noise, they saw the ladder, and suspicion could rest upon none of them, far less upon the faithful Stafford.

Perry was successful in disposing of the jewels at a good price, and received such a gratuity as was sufficient to retain him in the service of his new employer, who remained for some time in his station to prevent the shadow of guilt staining the fair character which he had so dexterously maintained.

Fully convinced that he could always render the females subservient to the accomplishment of his plans, Stafford next directed his attack upon a very handsome lady who had been two years married. To his no small mortification, however, he found that she estimated her favours at the sum of one hundred guineas. When all his attempts to alter her first proposal were unsuccessful, his inventive mind devised the following scheme to effect his purpose. Being upon friendly terms with the husband, and frequently visiting in the family, he one day took an opportunity to borrow a hundred guineas, under the pretence that he stood in need of that sum to complete a £500 purchase, in the meantime showing him £400 which he had in reserve from the late sale of the jewels. He readily obtained his request, and, having arranged matters with the lady, he came according to appointment, one day to her house, when several persons were at dinner and the husband absent. He immediately pulled out his purse, and addressed her, saying, " I have borrowed one hundred guineas from your husband, and as he is not here, I will leave the money with you, and the parties here present will be witnesses to the payment." The good lady, unac-

Page 67.

quainted with the fact that he had borrowed that sum from her husband, only supposed that this was a dexterous manœuvre to prevent suspicion of his intentions towards her and received the money with all good humour. It is unnecessary to relate the sequel of the adventure.

A few days after, Stafford took an opportunity, when the husband was present, to inform him, in the presence of several guests at his table, that he had repaid the hundred guineas to his wife that he had lately borrowed of him. The lady changed colour, but could not deny the fact, and the husband was satisfied with the punctual repayment of his money. Nor was Stafford contented with the success of his adventure, but took care to have the same whispered all over the neighbourhood.

One day, when Stafford was on his way to his native country, with a design only to see his relations, and not to rob any one, as at that time he was flush of money, fortune threw in his way a considerable prize, which he could not refuse. At Maidenhead Thicket he overtook an old gentleman, whom, from his appearance, he immediately supposed to be what was then quaintly termed "one of the godly." He accosted the traveller in his usual polite manner, and, soon discovering the turn of the old gentleman to be that of a puritanical fanatic, he so ordered his behaviour as to be in perfect harmony and accordance with his neighbour. The brethren were delighted with the good fortune which had thrown them together; and the old gentleman in particular expatiated upon the goodness of Providence in sending him such a companion: "but," said he, "we must ascribe every thing that befalls us to a wise Providence, and, for my part, I am always content with my lot, as being assured in myself that all things are for the best, and work together for the good of the elect," of whom (as Stafford soon discovered by his conversation,) he considered himself one. Being arrived however, at the thickest part of the forest, Stafford addressed him in his real character, saying, that "as he was a man who could be content with any thing, and considered every thing as ordered for the best, he had no occasion for so much money as he carried with him;" and presenting a pistol to his breast, demanded his purse, and told him he would pray that a good supper and a warm bed might be waiting him at the next inn. He received the old gentleman's purse with forty guineas in it, and, after leading him into the middle of the thicket, tied him to a tree, and galloped off through byeways into Buckinghamshire.

He was overtaken by darkness before he had gained the high

road, but observing a light at some distance, he rode up to it, and found it to proceed from a neat, comfortable country lodging. He knocked at the door, and said that, having lost his way, and being benighted, if he could be favoured with a lodging for the night, he would thankfully pay for it. The mistress of the house had been expecting her husband from London; and thinking it was he, she came to the door, when, hearing his story, and believing him, from his appearance to be a gentleman, she ordered his horse to the stable, and invited him to partake of a comfortable supper she had prepared for her husband, who seemed to have been detained longer than she expected. Stafford wondering at his good fortune, was resolved to make the best of his golden opportunity. But the vicious habits in which he had now become a proficient, had gained such an ascendancy over his natural disposition, that in this instance he was guilty of more than common felony: he, with very little gratitude for the favours he had received, tied the lady to her bed, and forced her to discover to him where he should find the money and plate belonging to her husband. Having secured about £300 worth of booty, he went to the stable, mounted his horse, and proceeded to London by the most private way he could find, to avoid detection.

By success in his profession, Stafford amassed a considerable sum of money: in order, therefore, to avoid discovery, as he was now well known all over the country, he retired to a little village in the north of England, and there lived in the most retired and frugal manner. The more to avoid suspicion, he assumed the appearance of sanctity, attended the church and the private meetings; and, exercising his talents, soon acquired great popularity as a speaker among the simple country people. After he had continued there about a year, the minister of the congregation dying, he, in a little time after, was called to the charge, and with seeming reluctance commenced preacher, with the annual income of £40. In this station, Stafford acquitted himself to the entire satisfaction of the congregation, until his predilection for the fair sex rendered it necessary for him secretly to retire from that place. Upon his departure, however, he took care to carry off the plate and linen of the church, to a considerable amount.

The Captain now assumed his proper character. About four miles from Reading he overtook a wealthy farmer, who was returning from selling some wheat, and entered into conversation with him, and, learning that he was possessed of a certain sum of money, he presented a pistol to his breast, threatening him with instant death unless he delivered up his purse. The terrified farmer instantly complied, and gave Stafford £33. But he had scarcely taken leave of the farmer, when two gentlemen, well mounted, came up to him, and being informed of what had happened, rode after Stafford, and in the space of an hour overtook and dismounted him, seized the money, and carried him before a justice of the peace, who committed him to prison. At the ensuing assizes he was tried and condemned. During his confinement he lived in a sumptuous manner, was visited by many of his own profession, who formed a plan for his deliverance, and agreed to make him their leader. The matter, however, transpiring, the day of his execution was changed, and Stafford miserably disappointed.

The Captain was dressed in a fine light coloured suit of clothes, with a nosegay in his breast, and appeared perfectly unconcerned. In passing a tavern, he called for a pint of wine, and drank it off, informing the landlord that he would pay him when he returned. Arrived at the place of execution, he looked wistfully around, and endeavoured to prolong the time; but when he saw none coming to his assistance, he became pale and trembled greatly. When about to be turned off, he presented the Sheriff with a paper, containing a short statement of his adventures, and the causes which led him to embrace the mode of life which brought him to such a fatal end.

CLAUDE DU VALL.

Some of our readers may object to the introduction into this work of the life of any highwayman, however celebrated, whose fortune it was to have been born in France; but, without insisting upon the celebrity of the person whose life we are about to narrate, it will be sufficient in reply to say, that many of the adventures achieved by Claude du Vall were performed in this country, and that he is accordingly, to all intents and purposes, although a Frenchman by birth, an English highwayman by profession.

This noted person was born at Domfront, in Normandy.* His

---

* We find, by reference to an old life of Du Vall, published in 1670, that Domfront was a place by no means unlikely to have produced our adventurer. Indeed, it appears that common honesty was a most uncommon ingredient in the moral economy of the place, as the following curious extract from the work in question will abundantly testify:—

" In the days of Charles IX. the Curate of Domfront, out of his own father was a miller, and brought up his son in the Catholic faith, giving him an education suited to the profession, for which he was intended,—namely, that of a footman. But, although his father was careful to train up his son in the religion of his ancestors, he was himself utterly without religion. He talked more of good cheer than of the church; of sumptuous feasts than of ardent faith; of good wine than of good works.

Du Vall's parents were exempted from the trouble and expense of rearing their son at the age of thirteen. We first find him at Rouen, the principal city of Normandy, in the character of a stable-boy. Here he fortunately found retour horses going to Paris; upon one of these he was permitted to ride, on condition of assisting to dress them at night. His expenses were likewise defrayed by some English travellers whom he met upon the road.

Arrived at Paris, he continued at the same inn where the Englishmen put up, and, by running on messages, or performing the meanest offices, subsisted for a while. He continued in this humble station until the restoration of Charles II., when multitudes from the Continent returned to England. In the character of a footman to a person of quality, Du Vall also repaired to this country. The universal joy which seized the nation upon that happy event contaminated the morals of all: riot, dissipation, and every species of profligacy abounded. The young and sprightly French footman

---

head began a strange innovation and oppression in that parish; that is, he absolutely refused to baptize any of their children, if they would not, at the same time, pay him his funeral fees: and what was worse, he would give them no reason for this alteration, but only promised to enter bond for himself and successors, that hereafter, all persons paying so at their christening shall be buried *gratis*. What think ye the poor people did in this case? They did not pull his surplice over his ears, nor tear his mass-book, nor throw crickets at his head: no, they humbly desired him to alter his resolutions, and amicably reasoned with him; but he, being a capricious fellow, gave them no other answer, but ' What I have done, I have done; take your remedy where you can find it; it is not for men of my coat to give an account of my actions to the laity:' which was a surly and quarrelsome answer, and unbefitting a priest. Yet this did not provoke his parishioners to speak one ill word against his person or function, or to do any illegal act. They only took the regular way of complaining of him to his ordinary, the Archbishop of Rouen. Upon summons, he appears; the Archbishop takes him up roundly, tells him he deserves deprivation, if that can be proved which is objected against him, and asked him, what he had to say for himself? After his due reverence, he answers, that he acknowledges the fact, to save the time of examining

entered keenly into these amusements. His funds, however, being soon exhausted, he deemed it no great crime for a Frenchman to exact contributions from the English. In a short time, he became so dexterous in his new employment, that he had the honour of being first named in an advertisement issued for the apprehending of some notorious robbers.

One day, Du Vall and some others espied a knight and his lady travelling along in their coach. Seeing themselves in danger of being attacked, the lady resorted to a flageolet, and commenced playing, which she did very dexterously. Du Vall taking the hint, pulled one out of his pocket, began to play, and in this posture approached the coach. "Sir," said he to the knight, "your lady performs excellently, and I make no doubt she dances well; will you step out of the coach, and let us have the honour to dance a courant with her upon the heath!" "I dare not deny any thing, sir," replied the knight readily, "to a gentleman of your quality and good behaviour; you seem a man of generosity, and your request is perfectly reasonable." Immediately the footman opened the door, and the knight out. Du Vall leapt lightly off his horse, and handed the lady down. It was surprising to see how gracefully he moved upon the grass; scarcely a dancing master in London but would have been proud to have shown such agility in a pair of pumps, as Du Vall evinced in a pair of French riding boots. As

---

witnesses; but desires his grace to hear his reasons, and then to do unto him as he shall see cause. 'I have,' says he, been curate of this parish seven years; in that time I have, one year with another, baptized a hundred children, and not buried one. At first I rejoiced at my good fortune to be placed in so good an air; but, looking into the register-book, I found, for a hundred years back, near the same number yearly baptized, and no one above five years old buried; and which did more amaze me, I find the number of communicants to be no greater *now* than they were *then*. This seemed to me a great mystery; but, upon farther enquiry, I found out the true cause of it; for all that were *born* at Domfront were *hanged* at Rouen. I did this to keep my parishoners from hanging, encouraging them to die at home, the burial duties being already paid.'

"The Archbishop demanded of the parishioners, whether this was true or not? They answered, that too many of them came to that unlucky end at Rouen. 'Well, then,' says he, 'I approve of what the curate has done, and will cause my secretary, in *perpetuam rei memoriam*, to make an act of it;' which act the curate carried home with him, and the parish cheerfully submitted to it, and have found much good by it; for within less than twenty years, there died *fifteen* of natural deaths, and now there die three or four yearly."

soon as the dance was over, he handed the lady to the coach, but just as the knight was stepping in, "Sir," said he, "you forget to pay the music." His worship replied, that he never forgot such things, and instantly put his hand under the seat of the coach, pulled out £100 in a bag, which he delivered to Du Vall, who received it with a very good grace, and courteously answered, "Sir, you are liberal, and shall have no cause to regret your generosity; this £100, given so handsomely, is better than ten times the sum taken by force. Your noble behaviour has excused you the other £300 which you have with you." After this, he gave him his word that he might pass undisturbed, if he met any other of his crew, and then wished them a good journey.

At another time, Du Vall and some of his associates met a coach upon Blackheath, full of ladies, and a child with them. One of the gang rode up to the coach, and in a rude manner robbed the ladies of their watches and rings, and even seized a silver sucking-bottle of the child's. The infant cried bitterly for its bottle, and the ladies earnestly entreated he would only return that article to the child, which he barbarously refused. Du Vall went forward to discover what detained his accomplice, and, the ladies renewing their entreaties to him, he instantly threatened to shoot his companion, unless he returned that article, saying, "Sirrah, can't you behave like a gentleman, and raise a contribution without stripping people; but, perhaps, you had occasion for the sucking-bottle yourself, for, by your actions, one would imagine you were hardly weaned." This smart reproof had the desired effect, and Du Vall, in a courteous manner, took his leave of the ladies.

One day Du Vall met Roper, master of the hounds to Charles II., who was hunting in Windsor Forest; and, taking the advantage of a thicket, demanded his money, or he would instantly take his life. Roper, without hesitation, gave him his purse, containing at least fifty guineas: in return for which, Du Vall bound him neck and heel, tied his horse to a tree beside him, and rode across the country.

It was a considerable time before the huntsmen discovered their master. The squire, being at length released, made all possible haste to Windsor, unwilling to venture himself into any more thickets for that day, whatever might be the fortune of the hunt. Entering the town, he was accosted by Sir Stephen Fox, who inquired if he had had any sport. "Sport!" replied Roper, in a great passion, "yes, sir, I have had sport enough from a villain who made me pay full dear for it; he bound me neck and heels, contrary to my des're, and then took fifty guineas from me to pay him for his labour, which I had much rather he had omitted."

England now became too contracted a sphere for the talents of our adventurer; and, in consequence of a proclamation issued for his detection, and his notoriety in the kingdom, Du Vall retired to his native country. At Paris he lived in a very extravagant style, and carried on war with rich travellers and fair ladies, and proudly boasted that he was equally successful with both; but his warfare with the latter was infinitely more agreeable, though much less profitable, than with the former.

There is one adventure of Du Vall at Paris, which we shall lay before our readers. There was in that city a learned Jesuit, confessor to the French King, who had rendered himself eminent, both by his politics and his avarice. His thirst for money was insatiable, and increased with his riches. Du Vall devised the following plan to obtain a share of the immense wealth of this pious father.

To facilitate his admittance into the Jesuit's company, he dressed himself as a scholar, and, waiting a favourable opportunity, he went up to him very confidently, and addressed him as follows: "May it please your reverence, I am a poor scholar, who have been several years travelling over strange countries, to learn experience in the sciences, principally to serve my country, for whose especial advantage I am determined to apply my knowledge, if I may be favoured with the patronage of a man so eminent as yourself." "And what may this knowledge of yours be ?" replied the father, very much pleased, " if you will communicate any thing to me that may be beneficial to France, I assure you, no proper encouragement shall be wanting on my side." Du Vall, upon this growing bolder, proceeded: " Sir, I have spent most of my time in the study of alchemy, or the transmutation of metals, and have profited so much at Rome and Venice, from great men learned in that science, that 1 can change several metals into gold, by the help of a philosophical powder which I can prepare very speedily."

The father confessor was more elated with this communication than all the discoveries he had obtained in the way of his profession, and his knowledge even of his royal penitent's most private secrets gave him less delight than the prospect of immense riches which now burst upon his avaricious mind. " Friend," said he, " such a thing as this will be serviceable to the whole state, and particularly grateful to the king, who, as his affairs go at present, stands in need of such a curious invention. But you must let me see some proof of your skill, before I credit what you say, so far as to communicate it to his majesty, who will sufficiently reward you, if what you promise be demonstrated. Upon this, the confessor conducted Du Vall to his house, and furnished him with money to erect a laboratory, and to purchase such other materials as were requisite, in order to proceed in this invaluable operation, charging him to keep the secret from every living soul. Utensils being fixed, and every thing in readiness, the Jesuit came to witness the wonderful operation. Du Vall took several metals and minerals of the basest sort, and put them in a crucible, his reverence viewing every one as he put them in. Our alchymist had prepared a hollow tube, into which he conveyed several sprigs of real gold; with this seeming stick he stirred the operation, which, with its heat, melted the gold, and the tube at the same time, so that it sank imperceptibly into the vessel. When the excessive fire had consumed all the different materials which he had put in, the gold remained pure to the quantity of an ounce and a half. This the Jesuit ordered to be examined, and, ascertaining that it was actually pure gold, he became devoted to Du Vall, and, blinded with the prospect of future advantage, credited everything our impostor said, furnishing him with whatever he demanded, in hopes of being made master of this extraordinary secret. Thus were our alchymist and Jesuit, according to the old saying, as " great as two pickpockets." Du Vall was a professed robber; and what is a court favourite but a picker of the people's pockets? So that it was two sharpers endeavouring to outsharp one another. The confessor was as candid as Du Vall could wish; he showed him all his treasures, and several rich jewels which he had received from the king, hoping, by these obligations, to incline him to discover his wonderful secrets with more alacrity. In short, he became so importunate, that Du Vall was apprehensive of too minute an enquiry, if he denied the request any longer; he therefore appointed a day when the whole was to be disclosed. In the mean time, he took an opportunity of stealing into the chamber where the riches were deposited, and where his reverence generally slept after dinner; finding him in deep repose, he gently bound him, then took his keys, and unhoarded as much of his wealth as he could carry off unsuspected; after which, he quickly took leave of him and France.

It is uncertain how long Du Vall continued his depredations after his return to England; but we are informed, that in a fit of intoxication he was detected at the Hole-in-the-Wall, in Chandosstreet, committed to Newgate, convicted, condemned, and executed at Tyburn, in the twenty-seventh year of his age, on the 1st of January, 1669: and so much had his gallantries and handsome figure rendered him the favourite of the fair sex, than many a bright eye was dimmed at his funeral; his corpse was bedewed with the tears of beauty, and his actions and death were celebrated by the immortal author of the inimitable Hudibras. He was buried with many flambeaux, amidst a numerous train of mourners, (most of them ladies,) in Covent Garden Church; a white marble stone was laid over him, and the following epitaph engraven on it

> Here lies Du Vall, reader, if male thou art,
> Look to thy purse, if female, to thy heart;
> Much havoc has he made of both, for all
> Men he made stand, and women he made fall.
>
> The second Conqueror of the Norman race,
> Knights to his arms did yield, and ladies to his face.
> Old Tyburn's glory, England's bravest thief,
> Du Vall, the ladies' joy—Du Vall, the ladies' grief.'

There is no authentic portrait of this "lady killer" in existence that we are aware of.

CAPTAIN RICHARD DUDLEY

WAS born at Swepston in Leicestershire. His father once possessed a considerable estate, but through extravagance lost the whole except about sixty pounds per annum. In these reduced circumstances he went to London, intending to live in obscurity, corresponding to the state of his finances.

Our young hero had a promising genius, and received a liberal education at St. Paul's school. But a naturally vicious disposition baffled all restraints. When only nine years old he showed his covetous disposition, by robbing his sister of thirty shillings, and absconding with it. In a few days, however, he was found, brought home, and sent to school, where his vicious propensities were only strengthened by indulgence. Impatient of the confinement of a school, he next robbed his father of a considerable sum of money, and absconded. His father, however, discovered his retreat, and, despairing of his settling at home, sent him on board a man-of-war, in which he sailed up the straits, and behaved gallantly in several actions. Upon his arrival in England, he left the ship, under the pretence that a young officer had been preferred before him, upon the death of one of the lieutenants. In a short time he joined a band of thieves, assisted them in robbing the country-house of admiral Carter, and escaped detection. Having at length commenced robber, the first remarkable affair in which he was engaged, was that of breaking into the house of a lady at Blackheath, and carrying off a large quantity of plate.

He and his associates were successful in selling the plate to a refiner; but in a short time he was apprehended for the robbery, and committed to Newgate While there, he sent for the refiner, and severely reproached him in the following manner: " It is," said he, " a hard thing to find an honest man and a fair dealer: for, you cursed rogue, among the plate you bought, there was a cup with a cover, which you told us was but silver gilt, buying it at the same price with the rest; but it plainly appeared, by the advertisement in the gazette, that it was a gold cup and cover; I see you are a rogue, and that there is no trusting anybody." Dudley was tried, convicted for this robbery, and sentenced to death: but his youth, and the interest of his friends, procured him a royal pardon.

For two years he conducted himself to the satisfaction of his father, so that he purchased for him a commission in the army. In that situation he also acquitted himself honourably, and married a young lady of a respectable family, with whom he received an estate of a hundred and forty pounds a-year. This, with his commission, enabled them to live in a genteel manner. Delighting however, in company, and having become security for one of his companions for a debt, and that person being arrested for it, one of the bailiffs was killed in the scuffle, and Dudley was suspected of being the murderer. What strengthened this suspicion was, that Dudley was the avowed enemy of all that class of society.

Having banished every virtuous feeling, being more inclined to live upon the ruins of his country than the fruits of industry, and more disposed to fight than to work, he abandoned his own house, joined a band of robbers; and soon became so expert in the business, that there was scarcely any robbery committed but he acted a principal part in it. Pleased with this easy way of obtaining money, and of supporting an extravagant expenditure, he prevailed upon his brother William, to join him in his employment. It happened, however, that Will had not been long in his new occupation, when the captain was apprehended for robbing a gentleman of a watch, a sword, a whip, and nine shillings. But, fortunately for him, the evidence was defective, and he escaped death a second time.

Being fully hardened in vice, he immediately recurred to his old trade, robbed on the highway, broke into houses, picked pockets, or performed any act of violence or cunning by which he could procure money. Fortune favoured him long, and he went on with impunity, but was at last apprehended for robbing Sir John Friend's house. Upon trial the evidence was decisive, and he received sentence of death. His friends again interposed, and through their influence his sentence was changed for that of banishment. Accordingly, he and several other convicts were put on board a ship bound for Barbadoes. But they had scarcely reached the Isle of Wight, when he excited his companions to a conspiracy, and, having concerted their measures while the ship's company were under hatches, they went off with the long boat.

No sooner had he reached the shore than he abandoned his companions, and travelled through woods and by-paths. Being in a very mean dress, he begged when he had no opportunity to steal. Arriving, however, at Hounslow-heath, he met with a farmer, robbed him, seized his horse, and, having mounted, set forward in quest of new spoils. This was a fortunate day, for Dudley had not proceeded far on the heath when a gentleman well dressed, and better mounted than the farmer, made his appearance. He was commanded to halt and to surrender. Dudley led him into a retired thicket, exchanged clothes and horse, rifled his pockets, then addressed him, saying, "That he ought never to accuse him of robbing him, for according to the old proverb, exchange is no robbery;" so bidding him good day he marched off for London. Arrived there, he went in search of his old associates, who were glad to see their friend; and who, in consequence of his fortunate adventures and high reputation among them, conferred upon him the title of captain, all agreeing to be subject to his commands. Thus, at the head of such an experienced and desperate band, no part of the country was secure from his rapine, nor any house sufficiently strong to keep him out. The natural consequences were, that he soon became known and dreaded all over the country.

To avoid capture, and to prevent all inquiries, he paid a visit to the north of England, and, being one day in search of plunder, he robbed a Dutch colonel of his horse, arms, and fine laced coat. Thus equipped, he committed several other robberies. At length, however, he laid aside the colonel's habit, only using his horse, which soon became dexterous at his new employment. But one day meeting a gentleman near Epsom, the latter resisted the captain's demands, and discharged his pistol at Dudley. In the combat, however, he was victorious, wounded the gentleman in the leg, and, having stripped him of his money, conveyed him to the next village, that he might receive medical assistance, and then rode off in search of new adventures. The captain and his men were very successful in this quarter. No stage, nor coach, nor passenger, of which they had intelligence, could escape their depredations, and scarcely a day passed without the commission of some notorious villainy.

Captain Dudley and his men went on in a continued course of good fortune, acquiring much wealth, but amassing little, as their extravagance was equal to their gains. On one ill-fated day, however, having attacked and robbed the Southampton coach, they were keenly pursued, and several of them taken, but Dudley escaped. Deprived of the chief part of his own forces, he now attached himself to some housebreakers, and with them continued to commit many robberies; in particular, with three others, he entered the house of an old woman in Spitalfields, gagged her, bound her to a chair, and rifled the house of a considerable sum of money, which the good woman had been long scraping together. Hearing the money clink that was to be taken from her, she struggled in her chair, fell down upon her face, and was stifled to death, while the captain and his companions went off with impunity. But when the old woman came to be interred, a grandson of her's, who had been one of the robbers, when about to be fitted with a pair of mourning gloves, changed countenance, was strongly agitated, and began to tremble. He was suspected, charged with the murder, confessed the crime, and informing upon the rest, two of them were taken, tried, and condemned, and the three hanged in chains.

Yet, though Dudley's name was published as accessary to the murder, he long escaped detection. At length, however, he was apprehended, and charged with several robberies, of which he, by dexterous management, evaded the deserved punishment. He was also called upon to take his trial for the murder of the old woman; but the principal evidence, upon whose testimony the other three were chiefly condemned, being absent, he escaped suffering for that crime. The dexterous manner in which he managed that trial, the witnesses whom he had suborned, and the manner in which he maintained his innocence before the jury, were often the cause of his boast and amusement.

The profligate Dudley was no sooner relieved from prison than he hastened to join his old companions in vice. Exulting to see their captain again at their head, they redoubled their activity, and committed all manner of depredations. Among other adventures, they robbed a nobleman on Hounslow-heath of fifteen hundred pounds, after a severe engagement with his servants, three of whom were wounded, and two had their horses shot under them. They next directed their course along the west country road, and having robbed a parson, enjoined him, under the most terrific threats, to preach a sermon in praise of thieving. He was forced to comply and the sermon being ended, they returned his money, and gave him four shillings to drink their health and success.

After this adventure, they left off infesting the highways, and rode for London. Arrived in the capital, the captain's brother employed his dexterity about town in several adventures, which go far to show how well the brother profited by the example and instructions of the captain. He first dressed himself as a countryman, with a pair of dirty boots on, and a whip in his hand, and went to Bartholomew Fair, where he wandered all the forenoon without meeting any prey. But as he was returning, he accosted a plain countryman, saying, "Have a care, honest friend, of your money, for we are going into a cursed place, full of thieves, rogues, and pickpockets. I am almost ruined by them, and I am glad that they have not taken the teeth out of my head. Let one take ever so good care, they will be sure of his money; the devil certainly helps them."

The face of the countryman glowed with courage as he replied, "I defy all the devils to rob me of any thing I value. I have a round piece which I'll secure;" and thrusting it into his mouth, he rushed confidently into the fair. Will was only desirous to ascertain the fact that he had money about him; therefore, giving his instructions with a few sixpences and groats to a hopeful boy, he immediately run after the countryman, while Will followed at a distance. The boy coming up with the countryman, fell down before him, scattering the money all around; then starting up, he raised the most hideous noise, crying that he was undone, that he must run away from his apprenticeship, that his master was a furious man, and that he would certainly be killed. The countryman and others flocked around, and endeavoured to assist the boy in gathering up the lost money. Then one of them said, "Have you found all?" "Yes, all the silver, but that is of no avail; there is a broad piece of gold which I was carrying to my master for a token sent from the country, and for the loss of it I shall be killed. Alas! I am undone! what will become of me?" Will now advanced among the crowd, and was equally concerned for the unhappy boy; and seeing the countryman standing by, he gravely observed that he had seen him put a piece of gold into his mouth. The mob instantly seized him, and while one opened his mouth by force, another extracted the broad piece of gold; and when he attempted to speak in his own defence, he was kicked, pinched, and so tossed about, that he was glad to escape with his life. Meanwhile, the boy slipped away among the crowd, and at an appointed place met Will to surrender to him his booty.

Having changed his clothes, Will went into the market, and mingling with the crowd, learned that the countryman was gone to an inn, where he had sent for his master, a knight of a large estate, and some other respectable persons, to attest his character. Will knew this person well, and hastened to the exchange, in full hopes of meeting him. Having reconnoitered the gentleman, and followed him until he perceived an opportunity, he robbed him of every guinea he had, except one, which he considerately left him to pay for his dinner. The knight, repairing to the inn, laughed heartily when the poor countryman informed him that he had been robbed, while he told him that he also had, in like manner, been just fleeced upon the Exchange. The countryman laughed in his turn, and said, " Sir, let us make our escape from this roguish place;" adding, with a shrug of the shoulders, " Sir, they'll steal our small guts to make fiddle-strings of them."

The gentleman, having recruited his purse, went out the next day to the Exchange. Will paid him the same compliment the second day. The knight was surprised how it was possible for any man to rob him when he was so forewarned, and so much upon his guard; but, looking hastily about, his eye fixed upon Will, whom he suspected to be the delinquent. He went up to him, and, taking him by the button, informed him that he strongly suspected that he was the person who had robbed him; but, as he was a gentleman of a large fortune, he did not regard the money, and would freely pardon him, and give him all the money, upon condition that he would inform him by what means he had done so. " This," said he, " I promise upon my honour." " Your word of honour," said Will, " is sufficient; I know the greatness of your fortune; I am the man. I will wait on your worship at the tavern, and there show you some of my art more freely than I would do to my fellow rogues." In their way to the inn, the gentleman informed Will, that as he wished to make a frolic of the matter, he would send for some other gentlemen to be present, assuring him, at the same time, that he should sustain no damage from any discovery that he might make to them. " I know you're a gentleman," said Will, " and men of honour scorn to keep base company. Call as many as you please; I'll take their word, and I know that I am safe."

When the gentlemen arrived, Will told them many things which greatly astonished and pleased them; and when he pulled out the piece of gold, and informed them how he had used Roger, the gentleman's tenant, he was immediately sent for to increase the amusement. " What would you say," cried the knight, as he entered, " if you saw your gold again?" " Oh:" said he, " I wish I could; but if my mouth can't keep it, where shall I put it? 'Sblood! I'd rather see the rogue; I'd make a jelly of his bones!" " There he is," said the knight, " and there's your broad piece." As Roger began to heave and to bully, his master commanded him to take his piece of gold, and sit down by him: upon which, the pacified Roger, seeing how things went, drank to his new acquaintance.

One of the gentlemen pulling out a curious watch, said, he wondered how it was possible to take a watch out of a fob; that it certainly must be carelessness on the part of the owner. " No," said Will, " if the gentleman will take a turn in Moorfields, I'll wager a guinea I'll have the watch before he returns, let him take what care he pleases, and I shan't stir out of the room." " Done," cried the gentleman; and every gentleman in the room laid down his guinea, while Roger staked his broad piece. The gentleman went out, and was careful that he would not suffer man, woman, nor child to come near him. When the time approached that he should return, a boy came pretty near him, but, to avoid suspicion, ran past him, and at the same time looking on his back, informed the gentleman that it swarmed with vermin. The gentleman observing them, and loathing the sight, said, " Good boy, take them off, and I'll give you a shilling." The boy did so, at the same time stealing his watch; and having received his shilling, ran off. The gentleman returned to the tavern, wondering how he could possibly come by such vermin, and taking the greatest care that no person should approach him.

Upon his return to the tavern, Will asked him what o'clock it was? He attempted to pull out his watch, but to his utter astonishment and confusion, it was gone. Upon this, Will produced it, and asked the gentleman if that were his! The gentleman was struck dumb, casting up his hands and eyes, and, full of amazement, addressed Will, saying, "You must have had the assistance of the devil." "Of a boy," said Will. "Did not a boy pick you clean?" "There's the devil," said the gentleman; "and he threw them on, too, I suppose." "Ay, through a quill," said the other.

All present were astonished at the ingenuity of the trick, but particularly plain Roger, who could not, at times, restrain his laughter. "Oh!" said Will, " this trick is not worth talking about: it is only one of those we commit to our boys. There is a nobleman just passing the window, with a very rich coat upon his back; I'll wager, as before, to steal it from him, before all his followers, and bring it here on my own back. The gentlemen all staked their guineas, and were seconded by Roger. "Come, now," said Will, "this matter must not be entrusted to a boy; you will give me leave to go myself, nor must you restrict me to any particular time to return." So out he ran, and followed the nobleman from street to street, until he saw him enter a tavern.

The nobleman was conducted up-stairs. Will bustling in after him, hastened to the bar-keeper, and desired him to lend him an apron, as his master would be served only by his own footman. "He is a very good customer, and expects the very best wine: I must go to the cellar and taste it for him." The apron being given, he went to the cellar, and returned with some of the best of each wine for his pretended master. He ran so quickly up and down stairs, and was so alert at his work, that none of the other servants could equal him. Meanwhile, the company up-stairs taking him for the servant of the house, were highly satisfied with his attendance. Will was also careful to give full cups to the servant who should have served in his place, with some money, which the other was very glad to receive for doing nothing. He seldom also went into the room without passing some merry jest to amuse the company. They were so highly pleased with him, that they said one to another, "This is a merry, witty fellow; such a man as he is fit to make a house; he deserves double wages." When Will saw his plan ripe for execution, he came into the room with some wine, and by the aid of his knife, made a slit in my lord's coat. Returning with a bottle in one hand, and his other hand full of glasses, before he approached his lordship, he started and stared, saying, "What fellows are those who have made that coat?" with other imprecations against the tailor. Then some of the company rising up, saw the rent in my lord's coat, and cried. "My lord, the tailor has cheated you." Will, drawing near, said, "Such things may happen; but give me the coat, and I'll carry it privately under my master's cloak to an acquaintance of mine, who will presently make it as good as if it had not been torn." Borrowing a great coat of a gentleman present, the nobleman gave Will his coat to carry to the tailor, who, coming down stairs informed the landlord of the disaster, received his cloak, and, putting the rent coat below it, seized a good beaver hat off one of the cloak-pins, and hastened from the tavern. Arriving at the inn where the gentlemen were anxiously waiting his return, he went into another room dressed himself, and entered with the cloak and beaver on. "What!" said one of them, "instead of a coat, you come with a cloak, and great need for it; for," he added, "there's a deal of knavery under it." Will then opened the cloak, and showed them the coat, saying, that he had received the cloak and beaver into the bargain; and gave an account of the whole adventure.

Meanwhile, my lord and his company had waited long in expectation of the servant, whom they supposed to have been one of the waiters of the house. The landlord also wondering that they were so long in calling for more wine, one of the servants was sent upstairs to force trade. He entered the room, saying, "Call here, call here, gentlemen?" "Yes," said one of them, "where is your fellow-servant that waited upon us?"—"my fellow-servant!" exclaimed the other; "he said he was my lord's servant, and that his master would be served by none but himself." My lord replied, "How can that be? I have only one gentleman of my own retinue; the rest are with my lady. He that served us came in with an apron, and in the character of one of the servants of the house:—call up the landlord!" Boniface instantly waited upon them, when one of the gentlemen asked him, if he kept sharpers in his house, to affront gentlemen and to rob them? "Nay," replied the vintner, who was a choleric man, "do you bring sharpers along with you, to affront me and rob my house? I am sure I have lost a new cloak and beaver; and, for aught I know, though you look like gentlemen, you may be sharpers yourselves; and I expect to be paid by you for my losses, as well as for the reckoning." One of them instantly drew upon him, enraged at his insolent language; but the landlord ran down stairs in affright, and armed the whole house, entreating them not to suffer such rogues to escape. In the mean time, he seized a sword, the servants armed themselves with spits, pokers, and such other weapons as the house afforded. A great uproar was soon raised: and the nobleman coming first out to penetrate through the crowd, made a thrust at the landlord, but was beaten back with a fire-shovel in the hand of one of the waiters, and narrowly escaped being run through with a long spit in the hands of a cook maid. His lordship, seeing the door so completely guarded, shut himself up in the room, and began to consult with the rest of the company what was best to be done. Fortunately, however, the gentleman who was in the other tavern with Will, conjecturing that a quarrel might ensue between the nobleman and the vintner, who had lost his cloak and beaver, sent his own landlord to inform him, that the rogue was caught, and in safe custody. He was admitted up stairs, waited on his lordship, and communicated to him the whole affair. A cessation of arms took place. They drank to the health of the landlord, assuring him, that in future they would be friendly to his house; but, in the mean time, they attended their peace-maker to the tavern, where Will was exhibiting his dexterity. The vintner went along with them, and, after common compliments, Will restored the coat, the cloak, and the beaver, and continued to amuse them during the remainder of the evening with the relation of his adventures.

But to return, at length, to the captain his brother. He had, along with his companions, committed so many robberies upon the highway, that a proclamation was issued against them, offering a reward to those who should bring them, either dead or alive. This occasioned their detection, for having committed a robbery, and being closely pursued to Westminster ferry, the wherryman refused to carry any more that night. Two of them then rode off, and the other four gave their horses to a waterman to lead to the next inn. The horses foaming with sweat, the waterman began to suspect that they were robbers who had been keenly pursued, and communicated his suspicions to the constable, who secured the horses, and went in search of the men.

He was not long in seizing one of them, who confessed; and the constable, hastening to the inn, secured the rest, and, having placed a strong guard upon them, rode to Lambeth, and making sure of the other two, led them before a justice of the peace, who committed them to Newgate.

At the next sessions, captain Dudley, his brother, and three other accomplices, were tried, and condemned to suffer death.

After sentence, Captain Dudley was brought to Newgate, where he conducted himself agreeably to his sad situation. He was conveyed from Newgate with six other prisoners. He appeared pretty cheerful, but his brother lay all the time sick in the cart. The ceremonies of religion being performed, they were launched into another world on the 22nd of February, 1681, to answer for the numerous crimes of their guilty lives.

The bodies of the captain and his brother, having been cut down, were put into separate coffins, to be conveyed to their disconsolate father, who at the sight, was so overwhelmed, that he fell dead upon them, and was buried at the same time and in the same grave with his two sons.

JONATHAN SIMPSON.

THIS man was the son of a respectable gentleman in Launceston, in Cornwall, and put an apprentice to a linen-draper. After serving his time with great approbation, his father gave him £1500 to commence business for himself.

He had not been a year in business, when he married a merchant's daughter, and received with her £200 as a portion. Such an accession to his wealth enabled him to extend his business, and to conduct it with ease. But money cannot procure happiness. The affections of the young lady had been gained by a man of less fortune, and, to please her father, she had given her hand where she could not bestow her heart; and, though married to another, she continued in a degree of familiarity with her former lover that excited her husband's jealousy, the most violent of all passions.

In a short time, after having lived in a very unhappy manner, Simpson took the opportunity to sell all off, and having shut up shop, went away with what money he could raise, determined no longer to remain in Bristol. He was now possessed of about £5000, but his expenses were so extravagant, that this large sum was soon exhausted. He then went to the highway, committed a robbery, was apprehended, and would certainly have been hanged, had not some of his rich relations procured a reprieve. The difficulty of obtaining it may be guessed from the fact, that it arrived at Tyburn just when the rope was about his neck. Such was his obduracy, that, when returning to Newgate behind one of the Sheriff's men, the latter asked him, what he thought of a reprieve when he was come to the gallows? " No more than I thought of my dying day.'

When he came to the prison-door, the turnkey refused to receive him, saying, he was sent to be executed, and that he was discharged of aim, and would not permit him to enter without a new warrant

Upon which Simpson exclaimed, " What an unhappy cast-off dog am I, that both Tyburn and Newgate should in one day refuse to entertain me! Well, I'll mend my manners for the future, and try whether I can't merit a reception at them both, next time I am brought thither."

He immediately recommenced his operations, and one day robbed a gentleman of a purse full of counters, which he supposed were gold. He kept them in his pockets, always anxiously looking out for his benefactor. About four months after, he met him upon Bagshot Heath, riding in a coach: " Sir," said he, " I believe you made a mistake the last time I had the happiness of seeing you, in giving these pieces. I have been troubled ever since, lest you should have wanted them at cards, and am glad of this opportunity to return them; only, for my care, I require you to come this moment out of your coach, and give me your breeches, that I may search them at leisure, and not trust any more to your generosity, lest you should mistake again." A pistol enforced his demand, and Simpson found a gold watch, a gold snuff-box, and ninety-eight guineas, with five jacobuses.

At another time he robbed Lord Delamere of three hundred and fifty guineas. He was almost unequalled in his depredations; in one day he robbed nineteen different people, and took above £200; and, in the space of six weeks, committed forty robberies in the county of Middlesex. He even ventured to attack the Duke of Berwick, and took from him articles to a very great value.

But wickedness has a boundary, over which it cannot pass. Simpson attacked two captains of the guards: a strong struggle ensued: his horse was shot under him, and he was wounded in both arms and one of his legs before he was taken. He was sent to Newgate, and now found that he was not refused entrance; and he soon also discovered, that Tyburn was equally ready to receive him. His execution took place on the 8th September, 1686.

WILLIAM DAVIS,

CALLED

"THE GOLDEN FARMER."

THIS man was a native of North Wales, and he obtained the title of *The Golden Farmer* from his custom of paying any considerable sum in gold. He was born in the year 1626. At an early period of life he removed to Sudbury, in Glocestershire, where he took a farm, married the daughter of a wealthy innkeeper, by whom he had eighteen children, and followed that industrious employment merely to disguise the real character of a robber, which he sustained without suspicion for the space of forty-two years. He usually robbed alone. One day, meeting some stage coaches, he stopped one of them, full of ladies, all of whom complied with his demands, except a Quaker, who vowed she had no money, nor any thing valuable about her: upon which, fearing lest he should lose the booty of the other coaches, he told her, he would go and see what they could afford him, and return to her again. Having rifled the other three coaches, he was as good as his word; and the Quaker, persisting in her former statement, enraged the Farmer to such a degree, that, seizing her by the shoulder, and employing language which it would be hardly proper here to set down, he so scared the poor Quaker, as to cause her to produce a purse of guineas, a gold watch, and a diamond ring. Whereupon, they parted as good friends as when they were first introduced to each other.

Upon another occasion, our desperado met the Duchess of Albemarle in her coach, as she was riding over Salisbury Plain; but he encountered greater difficulty in this case than he had contemplated. Before he could attack the lady, he was compelled to engage a postillion, the coachman, and two footmen; but, having disabled them all by discharging several pistols, he approached his prey, whom he found more refractory than the female Quaker. Perceiving another person of quality's coach approaching, with a retinue of servants, he contented himself by pulling three diamond rings from her fingers by force, snatching a rich gold watch from her side, and venting a portion of abuse upon her obstinate ladyship.

It was not very long after this exploit, that our adventurer met with Sir Thomas Day, a justice of the peace, living at Bristol. They fell into discourse together, and, riding along, the Golden Farmer informed his new acquaintance, that a little while before, he had narrowly escaped being robbed by a couple of highwaymen, but, luckily, his horse having better heels than theirs, he had got clear of them. "Truly," said Sir Thomas, " that had been very hard; but, nevertheless, as you would have been robbed between sun and sun, the county, upon suing it, would have been obliged to make your loss good." Thus, chatting together, and coming to a convenient place, the Golden Farmer shot Sir Thomas's man's horse under him, and, compelling him to retire to a distance, presented a pistol to the knight's heart, and demanded his money. "I thought, sir," said Sir Thomas, "that you had been an honest man." "Your worship is mistaken," cried the Farmer, "and if you had had any skill in physiogonomy, you might have perceived that my countenance is the very picture of necessity; so deliver presently, for I'm in haste." Sir Thomas, therefore, being constrained to give him the money he had about him, which was about 60*l.* in gold and silver, the other humbly thanked his worship, and told him, that what he had parted with was not lost, because he had been robbed between sun and sun, and could therefore come upon the county.

One Mr. Hart, a young gentleman of Enfield, who, it appears, possessed a good estate, but was not overburdened with brains, riding one day over Finchley Common, where the Golden Farmer had been for some months hunting for prey, was met by him, and saluted with a smart slap with the flat of his drawn hanger upon his shoulders : " A plague on you !" said the farmer; " how slow you are, to make a man wait upon you all the morning: come, deliver what you have, and go to the devil for orders!" The young gentleman, rather surprised at this novel greeting, began to make several excuses, saying, he had no money about him: but his incredulous antagonist took the liberty of searching him, and, finding about him above a hundred guineas, he bestowed upon him two or three farther slaps on the shoulders, telling him at the same time, not to give his mind to lying in future, when an honest gentleman required a small gratuity from him.

Another time, this notorious robber having paid his landlord about 80*l.* for rent, the latter, going home with it, was accosted by his goodly tenant in disguise, who bidding him stand, said:— " Come, Mr. Gravity, deliver what you have in a trice !" The old gentleman, fetching a deep sigh, to the hazard of displacing several buttons from his waistcoat, told him, that he had not above two shillings about him, and hoped, therefore, he was more a gentleman than to take so small a matter from a poor man. " I have no faith," replied the Farmer; " for you seem, by your habit, to be a man of better circumstances than you pretend; therefore, open your budget, or I shall fall foul of you." " Dear sir," cried the landlord, " you can't be so barbarous to an old man ? What! have you no religion, pity, or compassion in you? Have you no conscience ? Have you no respect for your body or soul ?" " Don't talk of age or barbarity to me," said the tenant, " for I show neither pity or compassion to any body. Talk of conscience to me! I have no more of that dull commodity than you have; therefore, deliver every thing you have about you, before this pistol makes you repent your obstinacy." The landlord being thus threatened, delivered his money, without receiving a receipt for it, although he had given one to the Farmer.

An old grazier at Putney Heath was the next victim to the avaricious farmer. Having accosted him on the road, he informed him, that there were some suspicious persons behind them, whom he suspected to be highwaymen; and, if that should be the case, he begged that he would conceal ten guineas for him, which would be safer with him, from the meanness of his apparel. He accepted the charge, and said, that as he himself had fifty guineas bound in the lappet of his shirt, he would deposit them along with his own. In a short time, the Farmer said:—" It does not appear that any person will run the risk of his neck by robbing you to-day; it will, therefore, be as well that I do so myself." Without any farther preamble, therefore, he demanded of him, instead of delivering up his purse, to cut off the lappet of his shirt, but, declining to comply with his request, the Farmer put himself to the trouble of lightening the fore-garment of the grazier.

Squire Broughton, a gentleman of the Middle Temple, was the succeeding prey of the Golden Farmer. Happening to meet at an inn upon the road, the Farmer pretended to be on his way to the capital, concerning an offence that a neighbouring farmer had committed against him, by allowing his cattle to break into his grounds. Meanwhile, he requested that Squire Broughton would recommend him to an expert and faithful agent to conduct his cause. Like every other lawyer, Broughton was desirous to have him for a client, and proceeded to explain the nature of his cause. Having spent the night at the inn, they proceeded next morning on their journey, when the Farmer addressed the counsellor, saying, " Pray, sir, what is meant by trover and conversion in the law of England?" He replied, that it signified, in our common law, an action which one man has against another, who, having found any of his goods, refuses to deliver them up on demand, and perhaps converts them to his own use.

The Golden Farmer, being now at a place convenient for his purpose, " Very well, then, sir," said he, " should I find any money about you, and convert it to my use, it is only actionable, I find." " That is a robbery," said the barrister, " which requires no less a satisfaction than a man's life." " A robbery!" replied the Golden Farmer; " why, then, I must commit *one* in my time:" and presenting his pistol, he instantly demanded his money or his life. Surprised at his client's rough behaviour, the lawyer began to remonstrate in strong terms upon the impropriety of his conduct, urging, that it was both contrary to law and to conscience. His eloquent pleading, however, made no impression upon the mind of the Farmer, who, putting a pistol to his breast, compelled the lawyer to deliver his money, amounting to 40*l.* some large pieces of gold, and a gold watch.

One day, accosting a tinker upon the road, whom he knew to have 7*l.* or 8*l.* upon him, he said, " Well, brother tinker, you seem to be very decent, for your life is a continual pilgrimage, and, in humility, you go almost bare-footed, making necessity a virtue." " Ay, master," replied the tinker, necessity compels when the devil drives, and, had you no more than I, you would do the same." " That might be," replied the Farmer, " and I suppose you march all over England." " Yes," said the tinker," I go over a great deal of ground, but not so much as you ride." " Be this as it will, I suppose your conversation is unblameable, because you are continually mending." " I wish," replied the tinker, " that as much could be said in commendation of your character." The Farmer replied, that he was not like him, who would rather steal than beg, in defiance of whips and imprisonment. Determined to have the last word of the Farmer, the tinker rejoined, " I would have you to know, that I take a great deal of pains for a livelihood." The Farmer, equally loquacious, replied, " I know that you are such an enemy to idleness, that, rather than want work, you will make three holes in mending one." " That may be," said the honest tinker, " but I begin to wish that there were a greater distance between us, as I do neither love your conversation nor appearance." " I am equally ready to say the same of you; for, though you are entertained in every place, yet you are seldom permitted to enter the door of any dwelling." The tinker repeated his strong suspicions of the Farmer. " Nor shall it be without cause!" exclaimed he ; " therefore, open your wallet, and deliver the money that is there." Here their dialogue being about to close, the tinker entreated, that he would not rob him, as he was above a hundred miles from home; but the Golden Farmer, being indifferent to all the consequences of the loss of the other's property, seized both his wallet and his money, and left the poor tinker to renew his journey and his toils.

This famous highwayman had only a few more acts of violence to perform. His actions and character being now universally known, many a hue-and-cry was sent after him, and conspired to his overthrow. He was seized and imprisoned, tried and condemned. He spent his life in prison in the same merry way in which his former life had been passed, and a violent death terminated his wicked course, on the 20th December, 1689.

WILLIAM NEVISON.

The advancement of the arts and sciences is not more rapid than the progress of folly and vice. In the following memoir it will be demonstrated, that the best education may be perverted by vicious dispositions.

William Nevison was born at Pomfret, in Yorkshire, in 1639, and his parents, being in good circumstances, conferred upon him a decent education. He remained at school until he was about thirteen years of age. During that period, his expanding talents promised a luxuriant harvest; but the general bent of his future character, and the ruling motive of all his actions were exhibited at that period. He commenced his depredations by stealing a silver spoon from his own father. The too indulgent parent, instead of chastising him for the crime, transferred the unpleasant work to the schoolmaster. The father who resigns authority over his own children may expect either to lose them altogether, or to have his heart grieved and his family dishonoured by their conduct. The schoolmaster having punished young Nevison for his theft, he spent a sleepless night in meditating revenge. He knew that the pedagogue had a favourite horse, which grazed in an adjacent paddock. William rose early in the morning, moved quietly into his father's closet, stole his keys, and supplied himself with cash to the amount of 10l.; then, taking a saddle and bridle from his father's stable, he hastened to the paddock in which the schoolmaster's horse was accustomed to feed; and, having saddled and bridled the animal, with all haste rode towards London. About a mile or two from the capital, he cut the throat of the poor horse, for fear of detection. Arrived in London, he changed his name and clothes, and then hired himself to a brewer. Although circumstances compelled him to be for a while industrious, in order to obtain the necessaries of life, his mind was always upon the stretch to invent some more expeditious mode of acquiring money than the slow return of annual pay; accordingly, he often ineffectually, attempted to rob his master. One evening, however, the clerk happening to use his bottle too freely, Nevison followed him into the counting-house, and, while he was enjoying a recruiting nap, stole the keys of the desks, and relieved them of their burden, to the amount of about 200*l*. Without waiting to discover whether the clerk or the servant would be blamed for the deficiency of the cash, he sailed for Holland.

But change of climate had no effect in changing his nature. Through his instigation, the daughter of a respectable citizen robbed her father of a large sum of money, and a quantity of jewels, and eloped with the Englishman. They were pursued, taken, and committed to prison. Thus detected, Nevison would certainly have finished a short but villainous career in a foreign land, had he not fortunately effected his escape.

With no small difficulty he arrived in Flanders, and enlisted into a regiment of English volunteers, under the command of the Duke of York. In that station he behaved with considerable reputation, and even acquired some money; but his restless temper and disposition to acquire riches, by whatever means, did not permit him to remain in a situation of industry and sobriety. He deserted, went over to England, with his money purchased a horse, together with all other necessaries, and commenced his depredations in a systematic form. His success was uncommon, and he every day found means to replenish his coffers, and to nourish his extravagance. Nor would he unite his fortune with any one, who, from selfish motives, might feel disposed to participate in his lucrative employment.

One day Nevison, who went otherwise by the name of Johnson, travelling on the road, and scouring about in search of a prize, met two countrymen, who, coming up towards him, informed him, that it was very dangerous travelling forward, for that the way was set, and they had been robbed by three highwaymen, about half a mile off; and if he had any charge of money about him, it were his safest course to turn back. Nevison, asking them what they lost, they told him 40*l*.; upon which he replied, " Turn back with me, and shew me the way they took, and my life to a farthing, I'll make them return you your money again." They rode along with him till they came in sight of the highwaymen, when Nevison, ordering the countrymen to stay behind him at some distance, rode up, and spoke to the foremost of them, saying, " Sir, by your garb and the colour of your horse, you should be one of those I have been looking after; and if so, I must tell you, that you have borrowed of two friends of mine 40*l.*, which they desire me to demand of you, and which, before we part, you must restore." "How!" cried the highwayman, "forty pounds! What! is the fellow mad?" "So mad," replied Nevison, "that your life shall answer me, if you do not give me better satisfaction." Upon this, he drew his pistol, and suddenly clapped it to the other's breast, who finding that Nevison had also his reign, and that he could not get his sword or pistols, yielded, telling him, his life was at his mercy. "No," said Nevison, "it is not that I seek, but the money you robbed these two men of, who are riding up to me, which you must refund."

The thief was forced to consent, and readily to deliver such part as he had, saying, his companions were in possession of the rest; so that Nevison, having made him dismount, and taking away his pistols, which he gave to the countryman, ordered them to secure him, and hold his own, whilst he took the thief's horse, and pursued the other two, whom he soon overtook; for they, thinking him their companion, stopped as soon as they saw him; so that he came up to them in the midst of a common. "How now, Jack," said one of them, "what made you engage with yon fellow?" "No, gentlemen," replied Nevison, "you are mistaken in your man: yon fellow, as you are pleased to term him, is a prisoner in the custody of my friends and hath sent me to you for the ransom of his life, amounting to no less than the prize of the day, which if you presently surrender, you may go about your business; if not, I must have a little dispute with you at sword and pistol!" At which, one of them fired at him, but, missing his aim, received Nevison's bullet in his right shoulder; and being thereby disabled, Nevison was about to discharge at the other, when he called for quarter, and came to a parley, which in short, was made up, with Nevison's promise to send their friend, and their delivering him all the ready money they had, amounting to 150*l.* Having obtained his booty, he rode back to the two countrymen, and released their prisoner, giving them their whole 40*l.*, with a caution, for the future, to look better after it, and not like cowards, as they were, to surrender on such easy terms again.

In all his exploits, Nevison was tender of the fair sex, and bountiful to the poor. He was also a true loyalist, and never levied any contributions upon the Royalists. One day, fortunately encountering a rich usurer, he stopped his coach, and demanded that he would deliver the money which he had extorted from poor widows and orphans. The pistol presented to his breast, and the reproaches of the highwayman, filled his guilty mind with inexpressible terror, and he began to expostulate for his life. "That shall be granted," replied Nevison, " upon condition of your surrendering your gold." The other reluctantly drew out sixty broad pieces of gold; but this sum not being adequate to the necessities of Nevison, he constrained the usurer to mount upon the postilion's horse, and allowed the coach with the three ladies in it to proceed. The poor Jew, now thinking the hour was verily nigh at hand when he would be bereft of life and separated from his treasures, experienced all the violent emotions of terror, chagrin, and despair. Nevison compelled him to draw a note upon sight for 500*l.* upon a scrivener in London. He then permitted him to ride after his friends to acquaint them with his misfortunes, while he himself rode all night, that he might have the money drawn before advice could be forwarded to stop the payment.

After several adventures of a similar nature, Nevison one day robbed a rich grazier of 450*l* and then proposed to himself to retire with the spoil. Accordingly, he returned home, and, like the prodigal son, was joyfully received by his father, who, not having heard of him during seven or eight years, supposed that he had been dead. He remained with his father until the day of the old man's death, living as soberly and honestly as if no act of violence had ever sullied his reputation. Upon the death of his father, however, he returned to his former courses, and his name became a terror to every traveller upon the road. To such an extent did he carry his plans, that the carriers and drovers who frequented the road willingly agreed to leave certain sums at such places as he appointed, to prevent their being stripped of their all.

Continuing his wicked course, he was at last apprehended, thrown into Leicester gaol, put in irons, and strictly guarded: but, in spite of all the precautions of the county, he effected his escape. One day, two or three of his trusty friends visited him, one of whom, being a physician, gave out that he was infected with the plague, and that, unless he was removed to a larger room, where he might enjoy the free air, he would not only himself perish, but communicate the infection to all the inhabitants of the goal. He was instantly removed, and the gaoler's wife would not allow her husband to go farther than the door of his room, for fear of the infection, which afforded Nevison and his friends time to perfect their scheme. The physician came twice or thrice every day to see him, and continued to declare his case hopeless At last a painter was brought in who painted his body all over with spots, similar to those that appear upon a person infected with the pestilence. In a few days after, he received a sleeping draught, and was declared to be dead. The inquest who sat upon his body were afraid to approach in order to make minute inspection, and thus a verdict was returned that he had died of the plague. His friends now demanded his body, and he was carried out of prison in a coffin.

This insertion into a coffin only rendered him more callous and daring in vice. He, with redoubled vigour, renewed his depredations, and, meeting his carriers and drovers, informed them, that it was necessary to increase their rents, in order to refund his expenses while in gaol and his loss of time. It was at first supposed, that it was his ghost, who carried on the same pranks that he had done in his life-time. The truth of this, however, came to be suspected, and a reward of 20*l.* was offered to any person who would restore him to his former domicile.

Resolved to visit the capital, he upon his journey met a company of canting beggars, pilgrims, and idle vagabonds. Continuing in their company for some time, and observing the merry life that they pursued, he took an opportunity to propose himself as a candidate for admission into their honourable fraternity. Their leader applauded his resolution, and addressed him in these words:—" Do not we come into the world beggars, without a rag upon us? And do we not all go out of the world like beggars, saving only an old sheet over us? Shall we, then, be ashamed to walk up and down the world, like beggars, with old blankets pinned about us? No! no! that would be a shame to us, indeed. Have we not the whole kingdom to walk in at our pleasure? Are we afraid of the approach of quarter day? Do we walk in fear of sheriffs, bailiffs, and catchpoles? Who ever knew an arrant beggar arrested for debt? Is not our meat dressed in every man's kitchen? Does not every man's cellar afford us beer and the best men's purses keep a penny for us to spend?" Having, by these words, as he thought, fully fixed him in love with begging, he then acquainted the company with Nevison's desire, in consequence of which they were all very joyful, being as glad to add one to their society, as a Mussulman to obtain a proselyte. The first question they asked him was, if he had any "*loure*" in his "*bung?*" Nevison stared at them, not knowing what they meant; till at last, one informed him it was money in his purse. He told them he had but eighteen-pence, which he gave them freely. This, by a general vote, was condemned to be spent in a booze for his initiation. They then commanded him to kneel down, which being done, one of the chief of them took a "*gage* of *booze*," which is a quart of drink, and poured the same on his head, saying, "I do by virtue of the sovereign liquor, install thee in the Roage, and make thee a free denizen of our ragged regiment. So that henceforth it shall be lawful for thee to cant only observing these rules —First, that thou art not to wander up and down all countries, but to keep to that quarter that is allotted thee; and, secondly, thou art to give way to any of us that have borne all the offices of the wallet before; and, upon holdding up a finger, to avoid any town or country village, where thou seest we are foraging for victuals for our army that march along with us. Observing these two rules, we take thee into our protection, and adopt thee a brother of our numerous society."

The leader having ended his oration, Nevison rose up, and was congratulated by all the company's hanging about him, like so many dogs about a bear, and making such a hideous noise, that the chief, commanding silence, addressed him as follows:—"Now that thou art entered into our fraternity, thou must not scruple to act any villanies, whether it be to cut a purse, steal a cloak-bag, or portmanteau, convey all manner of things, whether a chicken, sucking-pig, duck, goose, or hen, or to steal a shirt from the hedge; for he that will be a "*quier cove*," (a professed rogue,) must observe these rules. And because thou art a novice in begging, and understandest not the mysteries of the canting language, thou shalt have a wife to be thy companion, by whom thou mayest receive instructions." And thereupon, he singled out a girl of about seventeen years of age, which tickled his fancy very much: but he must presently be married to her after the fashion of their "*patrico*," who, amongst the beggars of this period was their priest. Whereupon the ceremony was performed after this manner:—

They took a hen, and, having cut off the head of it, laid the dead body on the ground, placing Nevison on one side, and his intended on the other; this being done, the priest, standing by, with a loud voice bade them live together till death did them part; then shaking hands, and kissing each other, the ceremony of the wedding was over, and the whole group appeared intoxicated with joy. Night approaching, and all their money being spent, they betook themselves to a barn not far off, where they broached a hogshead, and went to sleep.

Nevison, having met with this odd piece of diversion in his journey, slipped out of the barn when all was asleep, took a horse, and posted directly away. But, coming to London he found there was too much noise about him to permit him to tarry there: ne therefore returned into the country, and fell to his old pranks again. Several who had been formerly robbed by him, happening to meet him, imagined that his ghost walked abroad, having heard the report of his pestilential death in Leicester gaol. In short, his crimes became so notorious, that a reward was offered to any that would apprehend him: this made many waylay him, especially two brothers, named Fletcher, one of whom Nevison shot dead; but, going into a little village about thirteen miles from York, he was taken by Captain Hardcastle, and sent to York gaol, where, on the 15th March, 1684, he was tried, condemned, and executed, aged forty-five.

WILLIAM CADY.

This gentleman was a native of Norfolk county, and the son of an eminent surgeon. After the preparatory steps of education, William went to the University of Cambridge, and was tutor to Lord Townsend. He was during that time made Bachelor of Arts, and continued to pursue his studies until deprived of his father, by death.

The loss of a prudent father to a young man, forms a remarkable era in his life. If he is left with an ample fortune, he has then the means of gratifying his wishes, whether in the field of benevolence or in that of dissipation: and though left with no fortune, yet he is then at full liberty to follow his ruling inclination. Upon the intelligence of his father's death, William went to London and began to practise medicine. His first patient was his own uncle, who, being dangerously affected with an imposthume, was cured by him in the following manner:—

When he entered his uncle's bedchamber, his first care was to examine the state of the old gentleman's stomach: for this purpose he ranged about the room, overturning every plate and dish, to discover what had been given him to eat. He at last discovered an old saddle, which he thought would answer for the intended experiment. Upon seeing this he cried out, " Uncle, your case is very desperate!"—" Not so bad, I hope," said the uncle, " as to make me past remedy."—" Heaven knows that," cried Cady; " but a surfeit is a terrible thing, and I perceive that you have got a violent one."—" A surfeit!" said the old gentleman: " you mistake, nephew; it is an imposthume that I am affected with."—" The deuce it is!" replied Cady; " why, I could have sworn it had been a surfeit, for I perceive you have ate a whole horse, and left us only the saddle; at this he held up the saddle; and the old gentleman fell into such a fit of laughter as instantly broke his imposthume, so that he became quite well in less than a fortnight.

This is not the only instance of a disease of this nature being cured by a fit of laughter; and it is certainly an agreeable mode of being relieved of a painful and dangerous malady.

For this speedy and unexpected cure, his uncle gave him fifty guineas, which supplied his extravagances for one month, but his purse soon becoming empty, he took his leave of the healing art, in which he had been so successful, and commenced robber. His first adventure was with a captain of the guards and another gentleman, of whom he enquired the way to Staines, as he was a stranger. They informed him that they were going to that place, and that they would be glad of his company. When he arrived at a convenient place, Cady shot the gentleman through the head, and, turning to the officer, told him that " if he did not deliver, he should share the same fate." The other replied that as he was a captain of the guards, Cady must fight if he expected to get anything from him. " If you are a soldier," cried Cady, " you ought to obey the word of command, otherwise you know your sentence: I have nothing to do but to tie you neck and heel." " You are an unconscionable rogue," said the captain, " to demand money of me who never owed you any." " Sir," replied Cady, " there is not a man that travels the road but owes me money, if he has any about him: therefore, as you are one of my debtors, if you do not pay me instantly, your blood shall satisfy my demand." The captain exchanged several shots with Cady; but his horse being killed under him, he surrendered his watch, a diamond ring, and a purse of twenty guineas. William, having collected all he could, tied the captain neck and heel, nailed the skirts of his coat to a tree, and rode off in search of more booty.

His next encounter was with Viscount Dundee, who commanded the forces of James II. and fell in the battle of Killicrankie. Dundee was mounted upon horseback, attended by two servants. Cady rode up to them at full speed, and enquired if they had not seen a man ride past with more than ordinary haste, " Yes," he was presently answered. Cady replied, " the villain has robbed me of twenty pounds that I was going to pay my landlord, and I am ruined!" The man who had ridden by was a confederate, and had done so by express concert. His lordship was moved with compassion, and ordered the two footmen to pursue the robber. When the servants seemed to have got to a sufficient distance, Cady turned upon his lordship, and robbed him of a gold watch, a gold snuff-box, and fifty guineas. He then shot the Viscount's horse, and rode after the footmen, whom he found about a mile off with the supposed robber as their prisoner. These men were surprised when Cady desired them to let him go, and laughed at them for what they had done. They, however, refusing to part with their prey, a scuffle ensued, and one of the footmen being slain; the other fled, and found that his master had been dismounted and robbed.

Dundee complained of this injury at Court, and a reward of two hundred pounds was offered to any person who should apprehend either Cady or his companion, who were both minutely described. To evade the diligent search which he was certain this proclamation would occasion, he went over to Flanders. As he had received a liberal education, he entered himself of the English seminary of Douay, and, joining the fraternity of Benedictine Friars, soon acquired an extraordinary character for learning and piety. The natural result was, that many penitents resorted to him for confession. The rigid sanctity and ecclesiastical duties of Cady were, however soon found rather troublesome companions, and he resolved to return to England, preferring his rambles upon the highway to the devotions of the convent. But as money was necessary for his voyage, his invention was again set in motion.

To effect his purpose, he feigned himself sick, and, being confined to his bed, was visited by many of those who had formerly employed him as their father-confessor. He particularly fixed his attention upon two young women, who generally came together, and were both very rich and very handsome. He had previously procured a brace of pistols. When the ladies next came to him, and had made their confession, he desired them presently to attend to him. He briefly informed them that he was greatly in want of money, and that if they did not instantly supply his wants, he would deprive them of their lives, holding at the same time a pistol to their breasts. He then proceeded to rifle their pockets, where he found fifty pistoles. In addition to this, he compelled them to make an offering of two diamond rings from their fingers; then binding them both together, he informed the father of the convent that he was going to walk a little in the fields, and would soon return.

H

It is needless to say that he returned no more to his religious habitation, but renewed his former mode of life.

Scarcely was he arrived in England, when he met a hop-merchant, accompanied by his wife, upon Blackheath, and commanded them to stand and deliver. The merchant made a stout resistance, firing two pistols, but without effect; so that he was left to the mercy of the robber, who killed his horse, and, examining their pockets, found twenty-eight pounds upon the merchant, and half-a-crown upon his wife.

Cady then addressed her thus: "Is this your way of travelling? What! carry but half-a-crown in your pocket, when you are to meet a gentleman-collector on the highway? I'll assure you, Madam, I shall be even with you, therefore off with that ring from your finger." She begged him to spare her marriage-ring, as she would not lose it for double the value, having kept and worn it these twenty years. "You whining old woman," quoth William, "marriage is nothing to me;—am I to be more favourable to you than any other woman, I'll warrant? Give me the ring in a moment, without any more cant, or I shall make bold to cut off your finger for dispatch, as I have served several of your sex before." The good woman, seeing all her entreaties vain, hastily pulled the ring off her finger, and thrust it into her mouth. Cady then stamped, raged, and swore, that he would be even with her; and instantly shooting her through the head, went away perfectly unmoved, while the husband, being tied to a tree, was a spectator of this horrid barbarity.

Cady rode instantly to London, but fearing that even that great city could not conceal the author of a crime so unparalleled, he left the metropolis, and went to Scotland. Either his inclinations did not lead him, or he deemed that country too poor to afford him sufficient booty, he therefore soon returned again to England. On his road to the capital, between Ferrybridge and Doncaster, he met with Dr. Morton, a prebendary of Durham, well mounted; but whether meditating upon the amount of his tithes, or the next Sabbath's sermon, is uncertain. Cady instantly rode up to him, and cried, "Deliver or you are a dead man!" the doctor unaccustomed to such language, began to admonish him concerning the atrocity of his conduct, and the danger he was in, both with respect to his body and soul. Cady stared him in the face with all the ferocity that he could muster, and informed him that his remonstrances were in vain, saying that if he did not deliver him what he had, he should speedily send him out of the world. "But then," added Cady; "that is nothing, because all the gentlemen of your cloth are prepared for death. "What, you unreasonable, you unmannerly dog!" continued he, in a rage, unable to discover the doctor's cash: "what do you mean, to meet a man in the midst of his journey, without bringing him any money to pay his charges?" For the doctor had taken care, to hide his money in a hedge, so that Cady, upon examining him, found his pockets completely empty. The ruffian, convinced that a man of his appearance could not travel without money, with dreadful imprecations threatened that if he would not inform him what he had done with it, he should never go home alive. The doctor insisting that he had none, the wretch shot him instantly through the heart.

He next undertook a journey into Norfolk to visit his relations, but meeting a coach near that place, in which were three gentlemen and a lady, he rode up to it and addressed them in his own language. The gentlemen, however, were resolved to stand upon the defensive, and one of them fired a blunderbuss at him, which only grazed his arm, without doing any material injury. This put him into a violent passion, and, after taking a hundred and fifty pounds from the company, he brutally added, that the gentleman who fired at him should not pass unpunished, and instantly shot him through the heart; then, cutting the reins of the horses, he went off in search of new plunder, and declined visiting his relations upon that occasion, lest he should have been detected.

Directing his course to London, he came up with a lady taking a ride for the benefit of the air, attended by a single footman, and fell upon her in a very rude manner, pulling a diamond ring from her finger, a gold watch out of her pocket, and a purse with eighty guineas; insulting her meanwhile with opprobrious language. Though the lady had commanded her footman not to interfere, yet the man could not help complimenting Cady with some well-merited appellations. The ferocious monster, without uttering a word, saluted him with a brace of bullets in the head, and he fell upon the spot. Cady was just about to prosecute his journey, when two gentlemen, perceiving what he had done, rode up to him with pistols in their hands. Cady seeing his danger, fired at them, and shots were exchanged with the greatest rapidity, until Cady's horse was shot under him; and even then he struggled with the greatest violence with the gentlemen, until his strength was exhausted; he was then apprehended, and carried to Newgate under a strong guard. There he remained until the assizes, without showing the least signs of repentance, or tokens of regret. Upon his trial he behaved with the most daring insolence, calling the judges "a huddle of alms-women," and treating the jury in the same manner. The crime for which he was accused was so clearly proved, that he was sentenced to death, and committed to the condemned hole. But this place of darkness and horror had no effect upon his mind. He continued to roar, curse, blaspheme, and get drunk, as he had always done. It is probable that the hope of pardon, by the influence of some friends at court, tended to harden him the more; but the number and enormity of his crimes prevented the extension of royal mercy to such a miscreant. The day of execution being come, and the cart stopping as usual under St. Sepulchre's wall, while the bellman rang his bell, and repeated his exhortations, instead of being moved, he began to swear and rail, because they stopped him to hear an old puppy chatter nonsense. At Tyburn he acted in a similar manner; without either taking any notice of the ordinary, praying by himself, or addressing the people, he rushed into an eternal state to suffer the just punishment of his great and numerous offences. He died in the twenty-fifth year of his age, in the year 1687.

PATRICK O'BRIAN.

PATRICK O'BRIAN was a native of Ireland, and his parents were very indigent. He came over to England, and enlisted in the Coldstream Guards. He was, however, not so dexterous in the use of his arms as he was in the practice of all manner of vice. Patrick was resolved not to want money, if there was any in the country. He first ran into debt at all the public-houses and shops that would trust him; then borrowed from every person, as long as any one could be found to believe him.

When fraud failed him, he had recourse to force. Doctor Clewer, rector of Croydon, was the first whom he attacked. This man had been, in his youth, tried at the Old Bailey, and burned in the hand, for stealing a silver cup. Alluding to this, Patrick said, "That he could not refuse lending a little assistance to one of his old profession." The Doctor assured him, "That he had not any money about him; not even so much as a single farthing."

"Then," said Patrick, "I must have your gown, sir." "If

you can win it," cried the Doctor, " you shall; but let me have the chance of a game at cards; they commenced, Patrick was victorious, and obtained the black gown.

One day, he attacked a famous posturemaster, and commanded him to " Stand and deliver!" the latter instantly jumped over his head, which led Patrick to suppose that it was the devil come to sport with him before his time. By this display of his agility, the harlequin escaped with his money, and had the good fortune never to afford an opportunity to O'Brian to be revenged of him for his fright.

Our adventurer at last commenced highwayman. For this purpose he purchased a horse and other necessaries, and began in due form." He one day met with the celebrated Nell Gwynne in her coach, and addressed her, saying :—" Madam, I am a gentleman; I have done a great many signal services to the fair sex, and have, in return, been all my life maintained by them. Now, as I know you to be a charitable woman, I make bold to ask you for a little money, though I never had the honour of serving you in particular. However, if any opportunity shall ever fall in my way, you may depend upon it I will not be ungrateful." Nell made him a present of ten guineas, and he went off in quest of more plunder.

It was with O'Brian as with every other wicked man; he was solicitous to lead others to the same line of conduct. In particular, he seduced a young man, of the name of Wilt, who was apprehended, and suffered for his first offence. O'Brian was also apprehended, and executed at Gloucester; and when he had hung the usual time, his body was cut down, and given to his friends; but when carried home, he was observed to move, on which a surgeon was immediately sent for, who bled him; and other means being used, he recovered life. This fact was kept a secret, and it was hoped, that it would have had a salutary effect upon his future conduct. His friends were very willing to contribute towards his support, in order that he might live in the most retired manner, and O'Brian engaged to reform his life, and for some time kept his promise; but the impressions of death, and all its tremendous consequences, soon wearing off his mind, he returned to his vicious courses. Abandoning his friends, and purchasing a horse and other necessaries, O'Brian again visited the road.

In about a year after his execution, he met the very gentleman who was his former prosecutor, and attacked him in the same manner as before. The gentleman was surprised to see himself stopped by the very same person who had formerly robbed him, and who was executed for that crime. His consternation was so great, that he could not avoid exhibiting it, and he addressed O'Brian, saying, "How comes this to pass? I thought that you had been hanged a twelvemonth ago?" "So I was, and therefore you ought to imagine that what you now see is only my ghost. However, lest you should be so uncivil as to hang my ghost too, I think it my best way to secure you." Upon this, he discharged a pistol through the gentleman's head, and, alighting from his horse, cut his body in pieces with his hanger.

This barbarity was followed by a greater. O'Brian, accompanied by four others, attacked the house of Launcelot Wilmot, Esq. of Wiltshire, entered, and bound all the servants; then went up to the gentleman's own room, and bound him and his wife. They next proceeded to the daughter's chamber, whom they stabbed to the heart, and having returned, in the same manner butchered the old people, and rifled the house to the value of £2500.

This miscreant continued his depredations two years longer, until one of his accomplices confessed his crimes, and informed upon all who were concerned. Our adventurer was seized at his lodgings at Little Suffolk-street, and conveyed to Salisbury, where he was tried and condemned. He was a second time executed, and, to prevent another resuscitation, was hung in chains, near the place where the crime was perpetrated, on the 30th of April, 1689.

THOMAS RUMBOLD.

RUMBOLD was the son of honest and industrious parents, who lived at Ipswich, in Suffolk. In his youth he was apprenticed to a bricklayer; but evil inclinations gaining an ascendancy over his mind, he quitted his employment before a third part of his time was expired. In order to support himself after having absconded, and conceiving a great desire to see London, he repaired thither, and soon confederated himself with a gang of robbers. In conjunction with these he shared in many daring exploits; but, wishing to try his skill and fortune alone, he left them, and repaired to the road.

He travelled from London with the intention of waylaying the Archbishop of Canterbury. Having got sight of the party between Rochester and Sittingbourne in Kent, he went into a field, and placing a tablecloth on the grass, on which he placed several handfuls of gold and silver, took a box and dice out of his pocket, and com menced a game at hazard by himself. His Grace observing him in this situation, sent a servant to inquire the meaning; who upon coming near Rumbold, heard him swearing and rioting about his losses, but never paid the least attention to his questions. The servant returned, and informed the prelate, who alighted, and seeing none but Rumbold, asked him whom he played with? " Pray, Sir," said Rumbold, " be silent—five hundred pounds lost in a jiffey!" His Grace was about to speak again;—" Ay," continued Rumbold, continuing to play on, " there goes a hundred more!" " Pr'ythee," said the archbishop, " do tell me whom you play with." Rumbold replied, " With ——," naming some one who perhaps never had existence. " And how will you send the money to him?" " By his ambassadors," quoth Rumbold; " and, considering your Grace as one of them extraordinary, I shall beg the favour of you to carry it to him." He accordingly rose, and went up to the carriage, and, placing in the seat about six hundred pounds, rode off. He proceeded on the road he knew the archbishop had to travel, and both, after having refreshed at Sittingbourne, again took the road, Rumbold preceding the bishop by a short distance. He waited at a convenient place, and again seated himself on the grass in the same manner as before, only having very little money on the cloth. The bishop again observed him, and now believing him really to be a mad gamester, walked up to him, and just as his Grace was going to accost him, Rumbold cried out with great seeming joy, " Six hundred pounds!" " What," said the archbishop, " losing again?" " No, by G—!" replied Rumbold, " won six hundred pounds! I'll play this hand out, and then leave off while I'm well." " And of whom have you won them?" said his grace. " Of the same person that I left the six hundred pounds for with you, before dinner." " And how will you get your winnings?" " Of his ambassador, to be sure," said Rumbold; so, presenting his pistol and drawn sword, he rode up to the carriage, and took from the seat his own money, and fourteen hundred pounds besides, with which he got clear off.

With part of this money Rumbold bought himself an eligible situation; but still he could not give up his propensity of appropriating to himself the purses of others. For many miles round London he had the waiters and chambermaids of the inns enlisted into his service; and though, to all appearance, he was in an honest way of gaining a livelihood, yet he continued his nefarious courses to a great extent. He was not, indeed, always successful; but, having once been apprised of two rich travellers being at an inn where one of his assistants was, he left London immediately, and waited on the road which he had been informed the travellers were to take : long, however, he might have waited, for they were too cunning, and pretended to be travelling to the place which they had last left. Determined, however, not to return without doing some business, he loitered about, till the Earl of Oxford, attended by a single footman appeared, and, being known to his lordship, he disguised himself by throwing his long hair over his face, and holding it with his teeth. In this clumsy mask he rode up, demanded his lordship's purse, and threatened to shoot both the servant and him if they made the least resistance. Expostulations were vain, and he proceeded to rifle the earl, in whose coat and waistcoat he found nothing but dice and cards, and was much enraged, till, feeling the other pockets, he discovered a nest of "goldfinches," *(guineas,)* with which he was mightily pleased, and said he would take them home and cage them; recommending his lordship to return to his regiment, and attend to his duty, giving him a shilling as an encouragement.

As Rumbold was riding along the road, he met a country girl with a milk-pail on her head, with whose beauty and symmetry of shape he was greatly taken. Having entered into conversation, Rumbold alighted, and, excusing himself for the freedom, sat beside her while she milked her cows. Pleased with each other's company, they made an assignment the same evening ; our adventurer was to come to her father's house at a late hour, and, pretending to have lost his road, solicit a night's lodging. The plan was accordingly followed out; but they were disappointed in each others society that evening, for some one of the family kept astir all night. Determined, however, not to leave his fair convert, he pretended in the morning to be taken dangerously ill, and the good farmer rode off immediately for medical assistance. All the power of surgery, however, could not discover his ailment. The farmer kindly insisted upon his remaining where he was until he should recover, to which he, with great professions of gratitude, assented. Completely overpowered by such generosity, Rumbold wished to make some apparent return ; and, borrowing a name, told him he was a bachelor of property in a certain county; that he had hitherto remained secure against the attacks of beauty, but that he was now vanquished by the attractions of his daughter, and hoped, if the girl had no objection, that a proposal of marriage would not be unacceptable to the family. The farmer, in his turn, overcome by such a mark of condescension, expressed himself highly gratified by the proposal; and, upon communicating it to the family, all were agreeable, and none more than the girl. The idea of adding gentility to the fortune which the farmer intended for his daughter, quite elated him, and made him extremely anxious to gain the favour of the suitor. Rumbold followed out his plans, and his endearments with the daughter were thus more frequent than he expected. His principal design was to sift the girl as to the quantity of money her father had in the house, and where it lay; but he was chagrined when informed that there were only a few pounds; for that, a few days before they met, her father had made a great purchase, which took all his ready money. Seeing, now, that there was no chance of gleaning the father's harvest, he resolved to leave the family, and accordingly, one evening took his march incognito, leaving the girl a present of twenty pieces of gold, inclosed in a copy of verses.

He proceeded on the road, and met with no person worthy his notice until the following day, when a singular occurrence happened to him. Passing by a small coppice between two hills, a gentleman, as he supposed, darted out upon him, and commanded him to stand and deliver. Rumbold requested him to have patience, and he would surrender all his property; when, putting his hand in his pocket, he drew a pistol, and fired at his opponent without the shot taking effect. "If you are for sport," cried the other, "you shall have it!" and instantly shot him slightly in the thigh: and at the same moment drawing his sword, he cut Rumbold's reins at one blow; thus rendering him unable to manage his horse. Rumbold fired his remaining pistol, and again missed his adversary, but shot his horse dead. Thus dismounted, the gentleman made a thrust at him with his sword, which missing Rumbold, penetrated his horse, and brought them once more upon an equality. After hard fighting on both sides, our adventurer threw his adversary, bound him hand and foot, and proceeded to his more immediate object of rifling. Upon opening his coat he was amazed to discover that he had been fighting with a woman. Raising her up in his arms, he exclaimed, " Pardon me, most courageous Amazon, for thus rudely dealing with you: it was nothing but ignorance that caused this error; for, could my dim-sighted soul have distinguished what you were, the great love and respect I bear your sex would have deterred me from contending with you: but I esteem this ignorance of mine as the greatest happiness, since knowledge, in this case, might have deprived me of the opportunity of knowing there could be so much valour in a woman. For your sake, I shall for ever retain a very high esteem for the worst of females." The Amazon replied, that this was neither a place nor opportunity for eloquent speeches, but that, if he felt no reluctance, she would conduct him to a more appropriate place; to which he readily assented. They entered a dark wood and, following the winding of several obscure passages, arrived at a house upon which, apparently, the sun had not been accustomed to shine. A number of servants appeared, and bustled about their lady, whose disguise was familiar to them; but they were astonished to see her return on foot, attended by a stranger.

Being conducted to an elegant apartment, and having been refreshed by whatever the house afforded, they became very familiar, and Rumbold pressed his companion to relate her history, which, with great frankness, she did in the following words:—

"I cannot, Sir, deny your request, since we seem to have formed a friendship which, I hope, will turn out to our mutual advantage. I am the daughter of a sword-cutler: in my youth my mother would have taught me to handle a needle, but my martial spirit gainsaid all persuasions to that purpose. I never could bear to be among the utensils of the kitchen, but was constantly in my father's shop, and took wonderful delight in handling the warlike instruments he made; to take a sharp and well-mounted sword in my hand, and brandish it, was my chief recreation. Being about twelve years of age, I studied by every means possible, how I might form an acquaintance with a fencing-master. Time brought my desires to an accomplishment; for such a person came into my father's shop to have a blade furnished, and it so happened that there was none to answer him but myself. Having given him the satisfaction he desired, though he did not expect it from me, among other questions I asked him if he was not a professor of that noble science of self-defence, which I was pretty sure of from his postures, looks, and expressions. He answered in the affirmative, and I informed him I was glad of the opportunity, and begged him to conceal my intention, while I requested he would instruct me in the art of fencing. At first, he seemed amazed at my proposal; but, perceiving I was resolved in good earnest, he granted my request, and appointed a time which he could conveniently allot to that purpose. In a short time I became so expert at back-sword and single rapier, that I no longer required his assistance, and my parents never once discovered this transaction.

"I shall wave what exploits I did by the help of my disguise, and only tell you that, when I reached the age of fifteen, an innkeeper married me, and carried me into the country. For two years we lived peaceably and comfortably together; but at length the violent and imperious temper of my husband called my natural humour into action. Once a week we seldom missed a combat, which generally proved very sharp, especially on the head of the poor innkeeper; the gaping wounds of our discontent, were not easily salved, and they in a manner became incurable. I was not much inclined to love him, because he was a man of a mean and dastardly spirit. Being likewise stinted in cash, my life grew altogether comfortless, and I looked on my condition as insupportable, and, as a means of mitigating my troubles, I was compelled to adopt the resolution of borrowing a purse occasionally. I judged this resolution safe enough, if I were not detected in the very act; for who could suspect me to be a robber, wearing abroad man's apparel, but at home a dress more suitable to my sex? Besides, no one could procure better information, or had more frequent opportunities than myself; for, keeping an inn, who could ascertain what booty their guest carried with them better than their landlady?

"As you can vouch, Sir, I knew myself not to be destitute of courage; what, then, could hinder me from entering on such enterprises? Having thus resolved, I soon provided myself with the necessary habiliments for my scheme, carried it into immediate execution, and continued with great success, never having failed till now. Instead of riding to market, or travelling five or six miles about some piece of business (the usual pretences with which I blinded my husband,) I would, when out of sight, take the road to the house in which we now are, where I metamorphosed myself, and proceeded back again in search of prey. Not long since, my husband had one hundred pounds due to him about twenty miles from home, and appointed a certain day for receiving it. Glad I was to hear of this, and instantly resolved to be revenged on him for all the injuries and churlish outrages he had committed against me; I knew very well the way he went, and understood the time he intended to return. I waylaid him, and had not to wait above three hours, when my lord and master made his appearance, whistling with joy at his heavy purse. I soon made him change the tune to a more doleful ditty in lamentation of his bad fortune. I permitted him to pass, but soon overtook him, and keeping close by him for a mile or two, at length I found the coast clear, and, riding up and seizing his bridle, presented a pistol to his breast, and, in a hoarse voice, demanded his purse, else he was a dead man. My cowardly husband, seeing death before him, had nearly saved me the rouble by dying without compulsion; and so terrified did he appear, that he looked more like an apparition than any thing human. 'Sirrah!' said I, 'be expeditious;' but a dead palsy had seized every part of him, so that he appeared incapable of directing his hands to his pockets. I soon recalled his spirits by two or three sharp blows with the flat of my sword, which speedily awakened him, and, with great trembling and submission, he resigned his money. After I had dismounted him, I cut his horse's reins and saddle-girths, beat him most soundly, and dismissed him, saying: 'Now, you rogue, I am even with you; have a care, the next time you strike a woman, (your wife, I mean,) for none but such as dare not fight a man, will lift up his hand against the weaker vessel. Now you see what it is to provoke them. For, if once irritated, they are restless till they accomplish their revenge to their satisfaction: I have a good mind to end your wicked courses with your life, inhuman varlet, but I am loth to be hanged for nothing, I mean for such a worthless fellow as you are. Farewell! this money shall serve me to purchase wine to drink ' confusion to all unmanly and brutal husbands!'"

This extraordinary character was about to proceed with the narration of her exploits, when the servant announced the arrival of two gentlemen. Our heroine left the room, and returning with her friends, apologised to our adventurer for the interruption, but hoped he would not find the company of her acquaintances disagreeable, whom he soon discovered to be likewise females in disguise. The conversation became general, and, upon condition of Rumbold stopping all night with them, the Amazon promised to finish her adventures next day. This accorded with the wishes of Rumbold; and when they retired to rest, he found the same room was destined for them all. His curiosity was, however, overcome by his covetousness; for, rising early next morning, and finding all his companions asleep, he rifled their pockets of a considerable quantity of gold, and decamped with great expedition, thus disappointing the reader in the continuation of a narrative almost incredible from its singularity.

Our adventurer had frequently observed a goldsmith in Lombard Street, counting large bags of gold, and he became very desirous to have a share of the glittering hoard. He made several unsuccessful attempts; but having in his possession many rings, which he had procured in the way of his profession, he dressed himself in the habit of a countryman, attended by a servant, and going to the goldsmith's shop, proposed to sell one of these rings. The goldsmith, perceiving it to be a diamond of considerable value, and from the appearance of Rumbold, supposing he was ignorant of its real worth, after examining it, with some hesitation, estimated its value at ten pounds. To convince the countryman that this was its full value, he showed him a diamond ring very superior in quality, which he would sell him for twenty pounds. Rumbold took the goldsmith's ring to compare with his own, and, fully acquainted with its value, informed him that he had come to sell, but that it was a matter of small importance to him whether he purchased or sold. He accordingly pulled out a purse of gold, and laid down the twenty pounds for the ring. The goldsmith stormed and raged, and cried that he had cheated him, and insisted on having back his ring. Rumbold, however, kept hold of his bargain, and replied, that the other had offered him the ring for twenty pounds; that he had a witness to his bargain; there was his money, and he hoped that he would give him a proper exchange for his gold.

The goldsmith's indignation increasing at the prospect of parting with his ring, he carried the matter before a justice. Being plaintiff he began his tale, by informing the magistrate, " that the countryman had taken a diamond ring from him worth a hundred pounds, and would give him but twenty pounds for it." " Have a care," replied Rumbold, " for if you charge me with taking a ring from you, which is, in other words, stealing, I shall vex you more than I have yet done." He then told the magistrate the whole story, and produced his servant as a witness to the bargain. The goldsmith now became infuriated, exclaiming, that " he believed the country gentleman and his servant were both impostors and cheats!" Rumbold replied, " that he would do well to take care not to make his cause worse; that he was a gentleman of three hundred pounds per annum; and that, being desirous to sell a ring at its just price to the goldsmith, the latter endeavoured to cheat him by estimating it below its value." The magistrate, accordingly, decided in favour of our adventurer, only appointing him to pay the twenty pounds in gold, without any exchange.

The riches of Lombard Street still continuing to attract the attention of Rumbold, he with longing eyes one day traversed that street, attended by a boy whom he had trained in his service. The boy ran into a shop where they were counting a bag of gold, seized a handful, then let it all fall upon the counter, and ran off. The servants pursued, seized the boy, and charged him with having some of the money. Rumbold approached to the assistance of the lad, insisting that the youth had not stolen a farthing of their money, and that the goldsmith should suffer for his audacity. The goldsmith and Rumbold came to high words, and mutual vollies of imprecations were exchanged. The latter then enquired what sum he charged the boy with having stolen? The goldsmith replied, that he did not know, but the bag originally contained a hundred guineas.

Upon this, Rumbold insisted that he would wait until he saw the money counted. He tarried about half an hour, and the money was found complete. The goldsmith made an apology to Rumbold for the mistake; but the latter replied, that, as a gentleman, no one should put such an affront upon him with impunity. After some strong expressions on both sides, Rumbold took his leave, assuring his antagonist that he should hear from him. The goldsmith was arrested the day following, in an action of defamation. The bailiff who arrested him, being bribed by our adventurer, advised him to compromise the matter; urging, that the gentleman he had injured was a person of quality, and if he persisted in the action, it would expose him to severe damages. With some difficulty the matter was settled, by the goldsmith giving Rumbold twenty pounds in damages.

A goldsmith in Foster Lane next supplied the extravagances of Rumbold. He had often disposed of articles for that tradesman, who had full confidence in our hero's fidelity. One day, having observed in his shop a very rich jewel, he acquainted the goldsmith that he could sell it for him. Happy at such information, he delivered it to Rumbold, who carried it to a clever workman to have a false one, exactly similar, prepared; and then embraced an opportunity to leave the counterfeit with the goldsmith's wife, in his absence. Shortly afterwards, he met the husband in the street, who said he never expected to have been so used by him, and threatened to bring the matter under the cognizance of a judge; but Rumbold, fearing the result, retreated to a remote part of the city.

Rumbold was one day reconoitering in the vicinity of Hackney, when his attention was directed towards a house, which he earnestly desired to possess. He approached the house, knocked at the door, and enquired if the landlord was at home. He soon appeared; when Rumbold politely informed him, that, having been highly pleased with the appearance of his house, he was resolved to have one built after the same model, and requested the favour of being permitted to send a tradesman to take its exact dimensions. This favour was readily granted; when our adventurer went to a carpenter, and informed him that he wished him to go along with him to

Hackney to measure a house, in order that he might have one built on a similar construction. They accordingly went, and found the gentleman at home, who kindly entertained Rumbold, while the carpenter took the dimensions of every part of the house.

The carpenter being amply rewarded, was dismissed, and, by the aid of the draft of the house taken by him, Rumbold drew up a lease, with a very great penalty in case of failure to fulfil the agreement. Being provided with witnesses to the deed, he went and demanded possession. The gentleman was surprised, and only smiled at the absurdity of the demand. Rumbold commenced a law-suit for possession of the house, and his witnesses swore to the validity of the deed. The carpenter's evidence was also procured, many other circumstances were mentioned to corroborate the fact, and a verdict was obtained in favour of Rumbold's claim. But the gentleman deemed it proper to pay the penalty rather than lose his house.

Rumbold, disguised in the apparel of a person of quality, one day waited on a scrivener, and acquainted him that he had immediate occasion for a hundred pounds, which he hoped he would be able to raise for him on good security. The scrivener enquired who were the securities, and Rumbold named two respectable cit' zens, whom he knew to be at that time in the country; which satisfying the money-lender, he desired our adventurer to call next day. In the mean time the lender made enquiry after the stability of the securities, and found he had not been imposed upon as to their respectability. Our adventurer again waited upon the scrivener, who having agreed to advance the sum, Rumbold sent for two of his accomplices who personated his securities, and, after a little preliminary caution, signed the bond under the assumed names; and, upon Rumbold's receiving the money, they immediately took their leave. The name which Rumbold assumed on this occasion was of further service to him; for it happened to be that of a gentleman in Surrey, whom he met with, after this adventure, at an inn. Having learned what time the gentleman intended to remain in town, and the name and situation of his estate, he determined to render this chance meeting of service to him. He, accordingly, again waited on the scrivener, and informed him he had occasion for another hundred, but did not wish to trouble any of his friends to become security for such a trifle; for that, as he possessed a good estate, it might be advanced upon his own bond; and that if the scrivener could spare a servant to ride the length of Surrey, he would then learn the extent of his estate, and be enabled to remove any scruple whatever. A servant was accordingly sent, and directed to go and make enquiry after the property of the stranger whom Rumbold had met at the inn. Returning in a few days, Rumbold found the scrivener very condescending, and prodigal of congratulations upon the possession of so pleasant and valuable a property, and said he would not have scrupled though the loan had been for a thousand. Rumbold, finding him thus inclined, doubled the sum, and, after giving his own bond for two hundred pounds, left the scrivener to seek redress as he best could.

Rumbold thus supported himself by exercising his ingenuity at the expence of others, and by this means amassed a considerable sum of money. He was not so much addicted to these bad habits but that he felt an inclination to retire from scenes so fraught with danger and infamy. For this purpose he placed his money in the hands of a private banker, with a design of living frugally and comfortably upon the interest. This banker unfortunately failed, and made off with all Rumbold's property; so that he was once more reduced to the necessity of having recourse to his old employment.

The first exploit recorded of Rumbold after his re-appearance in public, is the following:—He stopped at a tavern, where he called for a flagon of beer, which was handed him in a silver cup, as was customary at that time. Being in a private room and alone, he called for the landlord to partake of his noggin, and they continued together for some time, until the landlord had occasion to leave him. Soon after, he went to the bar, and paid for his beer, while the waiter at the same time went for the cup; missing which, he called Rumbold back, and asked him for it. "Cup!" said Rumbold, "I left it in the room." A careful search was made, but to no effect; the cup could not be found, and the landlord openly accused Rumbold of the theft. He willingly permitted his person to be searched, which proved equally unsuccessful; but the landlord still persisted in maintaining that Rumbold must have it, or at all events, that he was chargeable with the loss, and would have the matter investigated by a justice, before whom he immediately went. The landlord stated the case, while Rumbold complained loudly of the injury done him by the suspicion; and from his never endeavouring to run off when he was called back, and submitting so readily to be searched, the justice dismissed him, and fined the landlord for his rashness.

During their visit to the justice, some of Rumbold's associates entered the same inn, where, according to arrangement, they found the cup fixed under the table with soft wax, and made off with it without the least suspicion.

The last recorded adventure of Rumbold was one which is now very common in the metropolis. Having observed a countryman pretty flush of money, he and his accomplices followed him; but, from Hodge's attention to his pocket, they failed in several attempts to pick it. Our practitioners, however, taking a convenient opportunity and place, one of them went before and dropped a letter, while another kept close by the countryman, and, upon seeing it, cried out " See, what is here?" But, although the countryman stooped to take it up, our adventurer was too nimble for him; and having it in his hand, observed, " There is somewhat else here besides a letter."—" I cry halves," said the countryman.—" Well," said Rumbold, " you stooped, indeed, as well as I; but I have it. However, I will be fair with you; let us see what it is, and whether it is worth dividing :" and thereupon broke open the letter, in which was enclosed a chain or necklace of gold. " Good fortune," said Rumbold, " if this be real gold."—" How shall we know that?" replied the countryman ; " let us see what the letter says," which ran as follows :—

" Brother John,

" I have here sent you back this necklace of gold you have sent me, not from any dislike I have to it, but my wife is covetous, and would have a bigger. This comes not to above seven pounds, and she would have one of ten pounds ; therefore, pray get it changed for one of that price, and send it by the bearer to your loving brother,

JACOB THORNTON.

" Nay, then we have good luck," observed the cheat. " But I hope," said he to the countryman, " you will not expect a full share, for, you know, I found it; and, besides, if one should divide it, I know not how to break it in pieces without injuring it; therefore, I had rather have my share in money."—" Well," said the countryman, I will give you your share in money, provided we divide equally."—" That you shall," said Rumbold, and, therefore, I must have three pounds ten shillings, the price in all being, as you see, seven pounds."—" Ay," said the countryman, thinking to be cunning with our adventurer, " it may be worth seven pounds in money, fashion and all; we must, however, not value that, but only the gold; therefore I think three pounds in money are better than half the chain, and so much I'll give, if you'll let me have it."—" Well, I'm contented," said Rumbold : " but then you shall give me a pint of wine, over and above." To this the other agreed, and to a tavern they went, where the bargain was ratified. There Rumbold and the countryman quickly disposed of two bottles of wine. In the mean time, one of Rumbold's companions entered the inn, inquiring for a certain person who was not there. Rumbold informed the stranger (as he pretended to be) that he would be there presently, as he had seen him in the street, and requested him to come in and wait for him. Upon this the stranger sat down to wait the arrival of his friend. In a little time Rumbold proposed to remove into a larger apartment, where they commenced playing at cards, to amuse themselves until the gentleman who was expected should arrive.

Himself and his associate began their amusement, the countryman being a stranger to the game. After he had continued a spectator of the good fortune of our adventurer, who in general vanquished the stranger, the countryman was at last prevailed upon to run halves with the fortunate gamester. For a while the same good fortune smiled upon them, and the stranger, in a rage at his great losses, refused to proceed. But after a few bottles more were emptied, the long-expected gentleman never appearing, they renewed their amusement; and fortune deserting Rumbold and the countryman who seconded him, in a short time the latter found himself without a shilling.

The landlord was then called to assist in drinking the money gaining, and, being informed how they had cheated the countryman, was resolved to exert his ingenuity at their expence. Meanwhile, several associates of Rumbold, who had been respectively employed in similar adventures, entered the room, joined in their conversation, and participated in their wine. The landlord was at last requested to bring supper, which being done immediately, they commenced with great avidity, and having soon dispatched a shoulder of mutton and two capons; the bottle circulated briskly, until they all, under the influence of the rosy god, fell asleep with the dishes before them.

The landlord embraced this favourable moment of silence to collect all the bones and remnants of the whole day's provisions, and divided them upon the plates which were upon the table. In a short time, one of them losing his balance, embraced the floor, and, by the noise of the fall, awoke the rest of the drowsy company, who all renewed their attacks upon the victuals. "How came these bones here?" cried one of them; "I do not remember that I ate any such victuals."—"Nor I," said another; upon which the landlord was called in and interrogated. "Why, surely, gentlemen, you have forgot yourselves," said he; "you have slept sound and fair indeed! I believe you will forget the collar of brawn you had too, that cost me six shillings out of my pocket." "How, brawn!" said one.—"Ay, brawn," answered the landlord; "you had it, and shall pay for it: you'll remember nothing presently. This is a fine drunken bout, indeed!"—"So it is," said one of the company; "surely, we have been in a dream: but it signifies nothing, my landlord, you must and shall be paid. Give us another dozen bottles, and bring us the bill, that we may pay the reckoning we have run up." This order was obeyed, and a bill presented, amounting to seven pounds, and every man was called upon to pay his share. The countryman shrunk back, wishing to escape; but one of them pulled him forward, saying, "Come, let us tell noses, and every man pay alike." The countryman desired to be excused, and said his money was all exhausted; they, therefore, agreed that he should be exempted,

In the morning, the countryman, in order to procure money to carry him home, resolved to sell the chain in his possession: he accordingly went to a goldsmith, but, to his additional mortification, was informed that, instead of gold, it was only brass gilded over. He acquainted the goldsmith with the whole matter, who went along with him to a justice to obtain a warrant for the apprehension of Rumbold and his associates; but before their arrival, the worthy knights of the pistol had prudently decamped with their spoils.

Rumbold after this adventure had several narrow escapes; but, continuing his nefarious courses, he was at length detected, tried, condemned, and executed at Tyburn in the year 1689.

THOMAS SIMPSON,

CALLED

"OLD MOB."

THOMAS SIMPSON, or, as he was usually called, "Old Mob," was born at Ramsay in Hampshire, and continued to reside there as his only home until he had five children and some grandchildren. As we are unable to find any record of his education, which appears to have been greatly neglected, we shall relate his adventures upon the road in order of time.

One day, near Exeter, he met with Sir Bartholomew Shower, whom he immediately required to deliver his money. Sir Bartholomew obeyed. Old Mob, however, examining his prey, told him that this was not sufficient to answer his present pressing necessities: "therefore, sir," said he, "as you are my banker in general, you must instantly draw a bill upon some one in Exeter for a hundred and fifty pounds, and remain in the next field as security for the payment, until I have received it." The good knight wished to be excused, professing that he knew no one in Exeter who would pay such a sum on demand. But excuses were vain: Old Mob held a pistol to his breast until he complied, and drew upon a rich goldsmith.

Having received the note, he made the knight dismount, cut the bridle and girths of the horse, and turned him off, while he bound Sir Bartholomew hand and foot, and left him under a hedge. The goldsmith knew the handwriting, and paid the money. Old Mob, having received the sum, returned to the knight, saying, " Sir, I am come with a habeas corpus to remove you out of your present captivity;" which he did, leaving him to walk home, a distance of three miles.

One day Old Mob quarrelled with a woman in the neighbourhood, and, in a rage, questioned her virtue. Her husband resented the affront; and commenced an action in a spiritual court against Old Mob, which cost him a considerable sum. Those who have enjoyed the experience well know that spiritual courts are not less litigious and expensive than civil courts.

Not long after, however, Mob met with the proctor who had been the agent in the cause, and had extracted from his purse a considerable sum. He instantly knew him; but, being well disguised, Mob was not recognised by the other. He demanded his purse: the lawyer began to be eloquent in framing excuses; but Mob reiterated his threatenings, and the purse appeared, laden with fifteen guineas. As the proctor was about to draw them from thence, Mob insisted upon having the fine silk purse also. The proctor told him that it was given him by a particular friend, and that he promised to keep it all his life; upon which Old Mob replied, " Suppose that you had a process against me, and were to come to me for your fees; if I had no money, or anything of value but what was given to me by a friend, would you take it for payment, if I told you that I had promised to keep it as long as I lived." —" No, sir."—" Stay there; I love that people should do as they would be done unto. What business had you to promise a thing you were not sure of performing? Am I to be accountable for your vows?" The poor lawyer seeing that if he insisted upon dividing the purse and the gold, his own body and soul might be separated, presented them to Old Mob.

John Gadbury had also the misfortune to fall in with Old Mob. Though this man was an astrologer, yet his knowledge of the stars could not prevent his own misfortune. Poor John trembled when his money was demanded, and turned as pale as death, pretending that he had none. Old Mob, after bantering him, and telling him he could never want money, as he had the twelve constellations always rented to stationers, informed him that his pistol would have his money, in spite of all the stars in the firmament. Dreading that the effect of the pistol would be more violent and sudden than any of the disastrous stars, he surrendered a bag containing about nine pounds in gold and silver.

The next adventure of Old Mob was an attack on the stage-coach from Bath, in which only one lady was passenger. After he had stopped the coachman, he approached the coach, and demanded the lady's money, she replied that she was a poor widow who had just lost her husband, and hoped that he would have compassion upon her. "And is the losing of your husband any argument why I should lose my booty? Your tears, madam, cannot move me; for I remember the old proverb—'The end of a husband is a widow's tears, and the end of those tears another husband.'"

The disconsolate widow made strong encomiums upon the virtues of her departed husband, with strong asseverations that none should ever succeed him in her affections. Old Mob not believing one half she said, and, unwilling to be detained from another adventure, became positive with her; upon which she pulled out a purse with forty guineas, and presented it to him.

Scarcely had he departed from this widow, when he met with the famous Lincoln's-inn-fields mountebank, Cornelius a Tilburgh, going to a stage at Wells. Mob demanded his money in a very rough tone. The poor quack pretended that he himself was a son of necessity. Mob told him he had more wit than to believe a mountebank, whose occupation was lying; "You get your money as easy as I get mine, and it is only fulfilling the proverb, 'lightly come, lightly go;' besides doctor, the next market-day will refund all; and you may excite compassion by informing them that you were robbed of your all in coming to exercise your benevolence towards them."

The doctor could scarce refrain from laughing at the smart strictures of Mob upon his profession; but unwilling to part with the bird he had in hand, he began to read him a lecture on morality, and to remonstrate upon the iniquity of his conduct, reminding him, that the money he thus took, might be the ruin of whole families, and constrain many to employ improper means to regain what they had lost in this manner; "therefore," said he, "you are answerable for their sin." "What," replied Old Mob, "this is the devil reproving sin, with a witness! Can I ruin more people than you, dear Mr. Theophrastus Bombasustus! you are scrupulously conscientious indeed, to tell me of ruining people! I only take their money, you their lives! You with impunity, I at the risk of my own! You have made more blind than the small-pox, more deaf than the cataracts of the Nile, and destroyed more than the pestilence? Unless, doctor, you have a specific against the influence of powder and lead, it is in vain to trifle with me; deliver your money." The quack still delaying, Old Mob seized a portmanteau from his horse, and putting it on his own, took his leave. Arriving at a convenient place to examine the contents, he found fifty-two pounds in money, and a large golden medal, besides all the doctor's instruments and implements of quackery: for the last, however, Mob could find few buyers.

At another time, Old Mob met with the Duchess of Portsmouth, between Newmarket and London. He stopped the coach and demanded her money. Accustomed to command a monarch, she could not conceive how a mean-looking fellow should talk in this style. Upon this, she briskly demanded if he knew who she was? "Yes, madam, I know you to be the greatest harlot in the kingdom, and maintained at the public expense! I know that all the courtiers depend upon your smiles, and that even the king is your slave! But what of all that? a gentleman collector upon the road is a greater man, and more absolute than his majesty is at court. You may now say, madam, that a single highwayman has exercised his authority where Charles II. of England has often begged a favour."

Her grace continued to gaze at him with a lofty air, and told him that he was a very insolent fellow; that she would give him nothing; and that he should certainly suffer for his insolence; adding, "touch me if you dare!" "Madam," answered Mob, "that haughty French spirit will do you no good here: I am an English freebooter, and I insist upon it, as my native right, to seize all foreign commodities. Your money is indeed English, but it is forfeited, as being the fruit of English folly. All you have is confiscated, as being bestowed upon one so worthless. I am king here, madam!

I have use ᴏr money as well as he! The public pay for his follies, and so they must for mine!" Mob immediately attacked her, but she cried for quarter, and delivered him two hundred pounds, a very rich necklace which her late paramour had given her, a gold watch, and two diamond rings.

Abingdon market was in general well stored with corn, and Old Mob being one day there, fell into conversation with a forestaller of grain. Being in possession of a considerable sum of money, he contrived a plan to have a share of the profits acquired by that extensive dealer. He pretended to have come from London to purchase corn; and desiring a sample, seemed satisfied with the quality, and demanded the price. Old Mob instantly made a purchase, paid the money, and sent the corn to a place where he sold it for his own money. Careful to ascertain the time when the corn-dealer was to leave town, and the road he was to take, he was scarcely two miles from the place when Mob approached him, put a pistol to his breast, demanded the money which he had lent him, and whatever more he had about him, as interest for the loan. The countryman was not a little surprised to hear such language from his late companion, and asked him if it was just to take away both goods and money. "Justice!" exclaimed Old Mob, "how have you the impudence to talk of justice, who rob the poor of their food, and rejoice at the misery of your fellow creatures, because you acquire your wealth upon the ruins of your nation? Can any man in the world be more unjust than an engrosser of corn, who buys up the produce of the country, and pretends a scarcity in times of plenty, only to increase his own substance, and leaves behind him abundance of ill-gotten wealth? Such vermin as you are unfit to live upon the earth! Talk no more of justice to me; deliver up your money, or I shall do the world so much justice as to send you out of it!" The countryman hereupon found it necessary to deliver up the large sum of money which he had about him; and Old Mob rode home highly gratified with his exploit.

Sir John Jefferies was the next to supply the wants of our adventurer, who first disabled two servants, and then advancing to the coach, demanded his lordship's money. Jefferies, by his cruelties exhibited in the western assizes, had rendered himself sufficiently infamous, and supposing that his name would carry terror, he informed Old Mob of the quality of the person whom he had accosted in so rude a manner. "I am happy," said he, "in having an opportunity of being revenged on you, for lately putting me in fear of my life. I might," added he, "deliver you over to trial for putting me in dread of death; but shall compound the matter with the money you have in your coach.

The judge began to expostulate with him upon the danger to which he exposed both soul and body by such crimes, reminding him, that if he believed there was a Providence which governed the world, he might expect to meet with justice as the reward of his iniquities. "When justice has overtaken us both," said Old Mob, "I hope to stand as good a chance as your lordship, who have written your name in indelible characters of blood, and deprived many thousands of their lives for no other reason than their appearance in defence of their just rights and liberties. It is enough for you to preach morality upon the bench, when no person can venture to contradict you; but your lessons can have no effect upon me. I know you well enough to perceive that they are only lavished upon me to save your ill-gotten wealth." Then thundering forth a volley of oaths, and presenting a pistol to his breast, he threatened the judge with instant death, unless he surrendered his cash. Perceiving that his authority was of no consequence to him upon the road, Jefferies delivered his money, amounting to fifty-six guineas.

The only person with whom Old Mob ever acted in concert, was the Golden Farmer. Two of their adventures may be selected. Having rendered themselves conspicuous upon the highway, and, by their frequent depredations, exposed themselves to the danger of detection, they resolved to repose themselves in the capital, and to employ their ingenuity, as they had now no occasion to exercise their strength. Their first object was to learn the manners and habits of the citizens, in order to impose upon them in their own way. Those who are acquainted with London, know that all is hurry and bustle; and that if a man dresses well, and for a while makes regular payments, he may obtain credit to a great amount. Even so it was at the period in which our adventurers flourished. They accordingly commenced ostensibly as merchants. They took a large handsome house, hired several servants, and commenced business upon a large scale. The Golden Farmer selected that of a chandler, he being in some measure acquainted with that line of business. Old Mob took up his residence near the Tower, and commenced Dutch trader; for having been in that country when a boy, he had learned a little of the language, and knew the commodities that were usually exported from that quarter. These two pas ed for near relations, of the name of Bryan, and said that they were north-country men.

With singular activity they inquired after goods in their respective circles, purchased all that came in their way, either paying ready money, or drawing notes upon each other for one or two days, which were always regularly honoured. They disposed of their goods at the lowest prices, and thus kept a constant tide of ready money; and their customers being perfectly satisfied, their characters were completely established.

Perceiving their plan ripe for execution, they ordered an immense quantity of goods upon a certain day, drew upon each other for the payment, immediately sold the goods at reduced prices to their usual purchasers, under the pretence that they had a large sum of money to make up, and the next day left town with the sum of 1630*l.* the produce of three months' business. The reader may easily conceive what were the feelings and chagrin of the different merchants, when on the day of payment, it was discovered, that the two extensive dealers and punctual payers had both disappeared.

For some time Old Mob and the Golden Farmer had recourse to their former employment upon the highway, until new dangers constrained them to think of another dexterous adventure by which to recruit their stores. There were two wealthy jewellers, brothers, the one living in London, and the other in Bristol. Old Mob and the Golden Farmer were minutely acquainted with the history of both brothers. These deceitful rogues knew that the jewellers were weak and sickly, which would obtain easy credit to a report of their death. Under this conviction they formed their plan, and wrote the following letter to each brother, only varying the name and place, according to circumstances:

" DEAR BROTHER, *March* 26, 1686.

" This comes to bring you the sorrowful news, that you have lost the best of brothers, and I the kindest of husbands, at a time when we were in hopes of his growing better as the spring advanced, and continuing with us at least one summer longer. He died this morning about eleven o'clock, after he had kept his bed only three days.

" I send so hastily to you, that you may be here before we prepare for the funeral, which was the desire of my dear husband, who informed me that he had made you joint-executor with me. The will is in my hands, and I shall defer opening it until you arrive here. I am too full of grief to add any more; the messenger, who is a very honest man, and a neighbour of mine, will inform you of such particulars as are needful. From your sorrowful sister.

" M. SEALS."

"P. S.—I employed a friend to write for me, which I desire you to excuse, for I was not able to do it myself, nor, indeed, to dictate any more."

These letters being sealed and directed, the one of our adventurers set off for London, and the other for Bristol, regulating matters so as to be at their journey's end at the same time. Being arrived, they delivered their credentials, were cordially received, and hospitably entertained. Many tears were shed upon the opening of letters containing such information, while secret joy arose in each mind, upon the anticipated accession of wealth that would accrue from the death of a brother. These two brothers perhaps indulged common affection for each other, but self-interest rises superior to every other species of affection.

The evening at the respective places was spent in relating various incidents of the family history, together with the narration of what the departed brother said in his last moments. Next morning each of the villains was dispatched to inform the sisters-in-law, that, as soon as mourning was got ready, they would hasten to perform their last sorrowful duties. Old Mob went to Bristol, the Golden Farmer to London. The first, in the evening secured jewels to the value of two hundred pounds. The second having taken his aim better, brought away jewels and other goods to a much greater amount.

In the morning, both set out from their respective places, and met at a spot previously determined. Meanwhile, the brothers were both hastening to set out upon their journey. In the family hurry of both, the shops were neglected, so that the robbers were not discovered. The brothers happened to take up their lodgings at the same inn at Newbury. He from London came in first, and went to bed before the other arrived. The Bristol brother, along with a companion who accompanied him, passed through the chamber of his relative, and slept in an adjoining room. It happened that their conversation disturbed the repose of the London brother, who recognised the voice of the dead relative whom he was going to inter. In a short time, the latter was under the necessity of passing through the room of his brother, who, by the moonlight, was more fully convinced that he had not been deceived in the voice. Upon this he cried out; the other brother was equally astonished, and ran back to his room overpowered with fear. They continued both of them sweating and trembling with dread until day-break, when dressing themselves in their morning apparel, they mutually shunned each other, until they attracted the notice of the people o the house. They were at last with difficulty brought together, and detected the imposition, but remained ignorant of the cause. After spending two days at the inn, they returned home, and the plot was discovered.

Old Mob was at last apprehended in Tothill Street, Westminster, presented with thirty-six indictments, of which thirty-two were proved, and was executed at Tyburn on the 30th of May, 1690.

JOHN BIRD

WAS born of industrious and honest parents, and received an education suitable to their circumstances. He was bound an apprentice to a baker, served three years, then ran away from his master, went to London, and enlisted in the Foot Guards. While in the army, he served at the memorable siege of Maestricht, under the command of the Duke of Monmouth, the general of the English forces in the Low Countries.

His natural avarice and restless disposition excited him to desert his colours, and, flying to Amsterdam, he began his career by stealing a piece of silk, but being detected in the act, was carried before a magistrate. The evidence against him being unquestionable, he was committed to the Rasp-house, and doomed to hard labour, such as rasping log-wood, and other drudgeries, during the space of twelve months. Unaccustomed to hard labour, Jack fainted under the punishment, but to no purpose, as his taskmaster imputed it to indolence. To cure this distemper, he chained him to the bottom of a cistern by one foot, and several cocks at once beginning to pour in their streams upon him, he was obliged to pump for his life. The cistern was much higher than he, so that if the water had not been quickly discharged, he would have been drowned, without either relief or pity. This discipline being limited to the space of one hour, Jack vanquished the various floods which threatened to overwhelm him, and was accordingly relieved. The experience, however, of that hour rendered his labour sweet during the remainder of the year.

Upon the expiration of that period, he took leave of a country where he had been so speedily detected and so severely punished, and returned to England to prosecute his adventures upon the highway. Disdaining the mean employment of a footpad, he stole a horse, provided himself with six good pistols and a broad sword, and, in the dress of a gentleman, commenced his campaign. In three or four robberies fortune was auspicious, and seemed to offer a plentiful harvest to gratify his avarice, and to nourish his extravagance; but like many before him, he soon experienced her fluctuating disposition. On the road between Gravesend and Chatham, Bird met with one Joseph Pinnis, a Pilot at Dover, who had been to London receiving 10*l*. or 12*l*. for conducting a Dutch ship up the river. He had lost both his hands in an engagement, so that when Bird accosted him in the common language of his profession, the old tar replied, " You see, sir, that I have never a hand, so that I am not able to take my money out of my pocket myself. Be so kind, therefore, as to take the trouble of searching me." Jack complied with his reasonable demand, and began to examine the contents of the pilot's purse. Meanwhile the furious tar suddenly clasped his arms about Jack, and, spurring his own horse, drew our adventurer off his, then falling directly upon him, he kept him down, beating him most unmercifully with his shod stumps. During the scuffle, some passengers approached, and, enquiring the cause, Pinnis related the particulars, and requested them to supply his place, and give the ruffian a little more of the same oil to his bones, adding, that he was almost out of breath with what he had done already. The passengers immediately apprehended him, and carried him before a magistrate, who committed him to Maidstone gaol, where he continued until the assizes, and then was tried and condemned.

He, however, had the good fortune to obtain a pardon, and afterwards his liberty. The affront of being so completely buffeted by a man without hands, made such an impression upon Bird's mind, that he resolved to abandon an employment which had been so dangerous and so disgraceful to him. But the want of an occupation by which to supply his necessities, again compelled him to the highway.

The first that he encountered was a Welsh drover. The fellow, being equal in strength and courage to the pilot, began to lay about him with a large quarter-staff. Jack, perceiving the boldness of the Welshman, fled out of the reach of his staff, and said, "I have been taken in once by a villain of a tar without hands, and for that trick, I shall not venture my carcase within the reach of one that has hands, for fear of something worse." Meanwhile, he pulled out a pistol, and shot him through the head. In examining his purse, he found only eighteen pence. Jack, with laconic indifference observed, "This is a price worth killing a man for at any time, and rode off without the least remorse."

At another time, Bird met with Poor Robin, the almanack maker; and, as he exacted contributions from the poor when the rich were not at hand, the astrologer was commanded to halt and surrender. As this was the first time that Robin had heard such language, and he had received no intelligence of the arrival of Bird from the stars, he stood and stared as if he had been planet-struck. Finding that Bird was in earnest, Robin pleaded his poverty. "That," said Jack, " is a common, thread-bare excuse, and will not save your bacon." "But," said the star-gazer, "my name is poor Robin; I am the author of those almanacks that come out yearly in my name, and I have canonized a great many gentlemen of your profession · look in my calendar for their names, and let this be my protection." But all in vain; Bird ransacked his pockets, and from thence extracted the large sum of fifteen shillings, took a new hat from his head, and requested him, since he had now given him cause, to canonize him likewise, which Robin engaged to do as soon as he had suffered martyrdom at Tyburn.

Emboldened by success, Jack procured a good horse, and resolved to perform something worthy of the honour that awaited him; and fortune soon presented a favourable opportunity. The Earl of Dorset and his chaplain were riding along in a coach, attended by two servants. Bird advanced; "Stand and deliver!" was his laconic address. His lordship informed him that he was very little anxious about the small sum he had upon him; "But then," said he, "I hope that you will fight for it." Jack then pulled out a brace of pistols, and let fly a volley of imprecations. "Don't put yourself into any passion, my friend," said the Earl, "but lay down your pistols, and I will beat you fairly for all the money I have, against nothing." "That's an honourable challenge, my Lord," exclaimed Jack, "provided that none of your servants be near us." His Lordship then commanded them to keep at a distance. The chaplain, however, could not endure the thought of the Earl fighting while he was an idle spectator, and requested the honour of espousing his master's cause. Matters were arranged: the divine in a minute went to blows with Jack; but the latter, who once had the misfortune to be deprived of his liberty, and exposed to the danger of his neck, by an old tar without hands, was now determined to retrieve his lost honour; and in less than a quarter of an hour, he beat the chaplain in such a manner, that he had only breath remaining to utter the words, "I'll fight no more." Emboldened by victory, Jack said to his Lordship, "that now, if he pleased he would take a turn with him." "By no means," cried the Earl, "for if you beat my chaplain, you will beat me, he and I having tried our manhood before." Then giving our hero a reward of twenty guineas, he rode off with his vanquished chaplain, well pleased that he had not put his own bones in jeopardy.

Continuing his wicked courses, Bird one day, in company with a woman, with whom he lived, knocked down and robbed a man between Drury-lane and the Strand. Bird escaped, but the woman was seized, and committed to Newgate. He visited her in prison, in the hope of accommodating matters with the prosecutor, but was seized upon suspicion of being an accomplice, and tried for the crime. Upon his trial he confessed the fact; the woman was liberated, and he suffered the just punishment of his deeds on the 12th of March, 1690, being at that time forty-two years of age.

THOMAS COX.

THOMAS Cox was the youngest son of a gentleman of Blandford in Dorset, at which place he was born. His father left him a comfortable patrimony, which he soon consumed in riotous living. Upon the decay of his fortune, he came up to London, where he fell in with a gang of highwaymen, and easily complied with their measures, in order to support himself in his dissolute course of life. He was three times tried for his life, before the last fatal trial, and had, after all these imputations, a prospect once more of making himself a gentleman, so indulgent was Providence to him. A young lady fell in love with him at Worcester, he being a very handsome man; and she went so far as to communicate her passion, and almost make him a direct offer of herself and 1500*l.* Cox married her; but, instead of settling himself in the world, and improving her fortune, he spent it all in less than two years, broke the poor young lady's heart by his ill usage, and then took to his old courses again.

The robberies he committed after this were almost innumerable: we shall briefly mention a few, without dwelling on particulars that are not material. One day he met with Killigrew, who had been jester to King Charles II., and ordered him to deliver. "Are you in earnest, friend?" said the buffoon. Tom replied, "Yes, by G—d am I! for though you live by jesting, I can't." Killigrew found he spoke truth; for, well as he loved jesting, he could not conceive that to be a jest which cost him twenty-five guineas; for so much Tom took from him.

Another time he robbed Mr. Hitchcock, an attorney of New Inn, of three hundred and fifty guineas, on the road between Midhurst and Tetworth, in the county of Sussex, giving him in return a lesson on the corruption of his practice, and throwing him a single guinea to bear his charges. Mr. Hitchcock was a little surprised at the highwayman's generosity, but more at his morality, imagining the world must needs be near its end when the devil undertook to reform it.

Tom Cox was as great a libertine in his sentiments as he was in his practice; for he professed a belief that the *summum bonum* of a man consisted in sensual pleasures, as Epicurus is said to have thought formerly, whose disciple he called himself. It is a common thing to call persons Epicureans who fall into these notions: and we do not know whether, in a work of this nature, it may be worth while to prove that the word is falsely applied, since the idea is all that we are to regard. Let Epicurean signify what it will, they are no followers of Epicurus who are not lovers of virtue, and who do not place their supreme happiness in the most exalted pleasures of the mind, as that great philosopher certainly did.

Our offender was at last apprehended for a robbery on the highway, committed near Chard, in Somersetshire; but he had not been long confined in Illchester goal before he found an opportunity of escaping. He broke out of his ward into the keeper's apartment, who, as good luck would have it, had been drunk over-night, and was now in a profound sleep. It was a moonlight night, and Cox could see a silver tankard on the table in the room, which he secured, and then with quickness let himself out into the street, by the help of the keys, leaving the doors all unlocked as he passed. The tankard he had stolen was worth 10*l*.; besides which, he got into a stable hard by, and took a good horse, with proper furniture to carry him off.

It is reported of Cox, that he more than once robbed persons of his own trade, and that he sometimes robbed in company. One time in particular, he had accomplices, and had formed a project for robbing a nobleman, well attended, who was travelling the kingdom. Tom associated himself with this nobleman on the road, and talked to him, as they passed along, of the adventures he had met with in such an agreeable manner, as ingratiated him very much in his companion's esteem. They had not ridden many miles together, before two of Tom's companions came up, and bade them stand, but immediately fled upon Tom's pulling out a pistol, and making a seeming bluster. The nobleman attributed his delivery to the generosity and bravery of his new companion, putting still more confidence in him, and desiring his company as long as possible. They were to stay a whole day at the next great town, in order to take a ride round the country, and see what was to be seen, according to the custom which this noble friend of Tom's had practised all the way. In the morning, the saddle horses were got ready, and our two fellow travellers set out for the tour of the day, the person of quality refusing to take a footman with him, as usual, that he might the more freely converse with his new acquaintance.

We shall not trouble our reader with what they saw on the way, and how much they were pleased, because that is little to our story. About noon they came to a convenient place, when Cox suddenly threw off the mask, and commanded his companion to deliver his money. " Why, ay," said the nobleman, " such a thing might be done here, for it's a devilish lonesome country : but I can fear no danger while you are with me,—you, whose courage I have so lately experienced." " Such a thing might be done ?" replied Cox : " Why, in the name of Satan, I hope you don't think I have kept your company all this time to play with you at last? If you do, sir, let me tell you, you are mistaken." Upon which, he pulled out a pistol, and presented it to his breast, swearing and cursing like a madman, till he had given sufficient proof that he was in earnest. Filled with astonishment and confusion, our nobleman delivered a diamond ring, a gold watch, and near a hundred guineas in money, staring all the while in Tom's face with much gravity. To prevent a sudden pursuit, Tom then dismounted his companion, bound him hand and foot, and killed his horse, according to the custom of experienced highwaymen, taking his leave with a sneer, and " Good bye, fellow-traveller, till I meet you again. '

After this, he committed two other robberies that were known. One of them was on a grazier, who had been at Smithfield, and received about 300*l.* for cattle, a great part of which was in silver, and consequently, was sufficiently bulky. When he had got the money, he fell to caning the poor sufferer in an unmerciful manner, who desired to know the reason of such usage after he had taken all. " Sirrah," said Tom, " 'tis for loading my horse at this rate; that you may remember another time to get your money changed into gold before you come out of town,—for who the plague must be your porter!" We may reasonably suppose the grazier chose rather to pay for the return of his money for the future, than carry so much about him.

Tom's last robbery was on a farmer, from whom he took about 20l. It was not above a week after the fact, before the farmer had occasion to proceed to London about business, and saw Tom coming out of his lodgings in Essex-street, in the Strand, when, upon crying out " Stop thief!" he was immediately apprehended in St. Clement's Church-yard, and committed by a neighbouring magistrate to Newgate, where he lived till the sessions in an extravagant manner, being very full of money. Receiving sentence of death on the farmer's deposition at Justice Hall, on Wednesday the 3rd of June, 1691, he was hanged at Tyburn, in the twenty-sixth year of his age. He was so resolute to the last, that when Mr. Smith, the Ordinary, asked him a few moments before he was turn-off, whether he would join with his fellow-sufferers in prayer? " D—n you—no!" said he, and kicked both ordinary and executioner out of the cart.

COLONEL JACK.

The account of the life of Colonel Jack, written by himself, naturally excites reflections upon the blessings of education, and the misery and ruin of thousands of the poorer orders who have been unfortunately deprived of it.

It cannot, we think, but be apparent, in the autobiography of Colonel Jack, that the writer, although circumstances and the want of education we have been lamenting, caused him to become a thief, was naturally disposed, and had a yearning towards virtue. A certain rectitude of principle, strangely at variance with his calling, remained with him constantly, causing him to abhor the worst parts of his trade, and at last to leave it off altogether.

We have chosen to give the ensuing narrative almost without the alteration of a word; the spirit of the story must inevitably evaporate during a process of transfusion.

" Seeing that my life has been such a chequer-work of Nature, and that I am able now to look back upon it from a safer distance than is ordinary to the fate of the clan to which I once belonged, I think my history may find a place in the world, as well as that of some, which I see, are every day read with pleasure, though they have in them nothing so diverting or instructing as I believe mine will appear to be.

"My origin may be as high as any body's, for aught I know; for my mother kept very good company:—but that part belongs to her story more than to mine. All I know of it is by oral tradition, thus:—my nurse told me my mother was a gentlewoman, that my father was a man of quality, and that she (my nurse) had a good piece of money given her to take me off his hands, and deliver him and my mother from the importunities that usually attend the misfortune of having a child to keep that should not be seen or heard of.

"My father, it seems, gave my nurse something more than was agreed for, at my mother's request, upon her solemn promise, that she would use me well, and let me be put to school; and he charged her, that if I lived to come to any bigness, capable to understand the meaning of it, she should always take care to bid me remember that I was a gentleman; and this, he said, was all the education he would desire of her for me; for he did not doubt but that some time or other, the very hint would inspire me with thoughts suitable to my birth; and that I would certainly act like a gentleman, if I believed myself to be so.

"My nurse was as honest to the engagement she had entered into as could be expected from one of her employment, and particularly as honest as her circumstances would give her leave to be; for she bred me up very carefully with her own son, and with another son of shame, like me, whom she had taken upon the same terms.

"My name was John, as she told me; but neither she nor I knew any thing of a sirname that belonged to me; so that I was left to call myself Mr. Anything that I pleased, as fortune and better circumstances should give occasion. It happened that her own son, (for she had a little boy about one year older than I,) was called John too; and about two years after, she took another son of shame, as I called it above, to keep as she did me, and his name was John too. But my nurse, who may be allowed to distinguish her own son a little from the rest, would have him called captain, because, forsooth, he was the eldest.

"I was provoked at having this boy called captain, and cried, and told my nurse I would be called captain, for she told me I was a gentleman, and I would be a captain, that I would. The good woman, to keep the peace, told me, 'Ay, ay, I was a gentle man, and therefore I should be above a captain, for I should be a colonel, and that was a great deal better than a captain.' Well, I was hushed indeed with this for the present, but not thoroughly pleased, till, a little while after, I heard her tell her own boy, that I was a gentleman, and therefore he must call me colonel; at which her boy fell a-crying, and said he would be called colonel too; so then I was satisfied that it was above a captain. So universally is ambition seated in the minds of men, that not a beggar-boy but has his share of it. Before I tell you much more of our story, it would be very proper to give something of our several characters, as I have gathered them up in my memory, as far back as I can recover things either of myself, or my brother Jacks; and they shall be brief and impartial.

"Captain Jack, the eldest of us all by a whole year, was a squat big, strong-made boy, and promised to be stout when grown up to be a man, but not tall. He was an original rogue; for he would do the foulest and most villainous things even by his own inclination; he had no taste or sense of being honest, no not even to his brother rogues, which is what other thieves made a point of honour of,—I mean that of being honest to one another.

"Major Jack was a merry, facetious, pleasant boy, and had something of a gentleman in him. He had a true manly courage, feared nothing, and yet, if he had the advantage, was the most compassionate creature alive, and wanted nothing but honesty to make him an excellent man. He had learnt to write and read very well, as will be found in the process of this story.

"As to myself, I passed among my comrades for a bold resolute boy; but I had a different opinion of myself; and therefore shuned fighting as much as I could. I was wary and dexterous at my trade, and was not so often caught as my fellow-rogues; I mean while I was a boy, and never after I came to be a man, no, not once for twenty-six years, being so old in the trade, and still unhanged.

"I was almost ten years old, the captain eleven, and the major eight, when our good old nurse died; her husband was drowned a little before in the Gloucester frigate, which was cast away going to Scotland with the Duke of York, in the reign of King Charles II. and the honest woman dying very poor, the parish was obliged to bury her. The good woman being dead, we were turned loose to the world,—rambling about all three together, and the people in Rosemary-lane and Ratcliffe knowing us pretty well, we got victuals easy enough; as for lodging, we lay in the summer-time on bulk-heads and at shop-doors; as for bed, we knew nothing that belonged to it for many years after my nurse died; but in winter got into the ash-holes, and annealing-arches in the glass-houses, where we were accompanied by several youngsters like ourselves; some of whom persuaded the captain to go a kidnapping with them, a trade at that time much followed; the gang used to catch children in the evening, stop their mouths, and carry them to such houses, were they had rogues ready to receive them, who put them on board ships bound to Virginia, and when they arrived there, they were sold. This wicked gang were at last taken, and sent to Newgate; and Captain Jack, among the rest, though he was not then much above thirteen years old, and being but a lad, was ordered to be three times whipped at Bridewell, the Recorder telling him it was done in order to keep him from the gallows. We did what we could to comfort him; but he was scourged so severely, that he lay sick for a good while; but as soon as he regained his liberty, he went to his old gang, and kept among them as long as that trade lasted, for it ceased a few years afterwards.

" The major and I, though very young, had sensible impressions made on us for some time by the severe usage of the captain; but it was within the year, that the major, a good conditioned easy body, was wheedled away by a couple of young rogues to take a walk with them. The gentlemen were very well matched, for the oldest of them was not above fourteen; the business was to go to Bartholomew-fair, and the end of going there was to pick pockets.

" The major knew nothing of the trade, and therefore was to do nothing; but they promised him a share with them for all that, as if he had been as expert as themselves; so away they went. The two dexterous rogues managed it so well, that by about eight o'clock at night, they came back to our dusty quarters at the glass-house, and sitting them down in a corner, they began to share their spoil by the light of the glass house fire. The major lugged out the goods, for as fast as they made any purchase, they unloaded themselves, and gave all to him, that if they had been taken, nothing might be found about them. It was a lucky day for them; the devil certainly assisting them to find their prey, that he might draw in a young gamester, and encourage him to the undertaking, who had been made backward before by the misfortune of the captain.

" For such a cargo to be brought home clear in one afternoon, or evening rather, and by only two little rogues so young, was, it must be confessed, extraordinary; and the major was elevated the next day to a strange degree; for he came to me very early, and called me out into a narrow lane, and showed me his little hand almost full of money. I was surprised at the sight, when he put it up again, and bringing his hand out, " Here," said he, " you shall have some of it," and gave me a sixpence and a shilling's worth of the small silver pieces. This was very welcome to me, who never had a shilling of money together in all my life, that I could call my own. I was very earnest to know how he came by this wealth; he quickly told me the story; and that he had for his share seven shillings and sixpence in money, a silver-thimble, and a silk handkerchief.

" We went to Rag-Fair, and bought each of us a pair of shoes and stockings, and afterwards went to a boiling cook's in Rosemary-lane, where we treated ourselves nobly; for we had boiled beef, pudding, a penny-loaf, and a pint of strong beer, which cost us sevenpence in all. That night the major triumphed in our new enjoyment, and slept in the usual place, with an undisturbed repose. The next day the major and his comrades went abroad again, and were still successful, nor did any disaster attend them for many months; and by frequent imitation and direction, Major Jack became as dexterous a pickpocket as any of them, and went through a long variety of fortune, too long to enter upon now, because I am hastening to my own story, which at present is the main thing I have to set down.

"Overcome by the persuasions of the major, I entered myself into his society, and went down to Billingsgate with one of them, which was crowded with masters of coal-ships, fishmongers, and oyster-women. It was the first of these people my comrade had his eye upon: so he gave me my orders, which were thus: ' Go you,' said he, ' into all the ale-houses as we go along, and observe where any people are telling money, and when you find any, come and tell me.' So he stood at the door and I went into the houses. As the collier-masters generally sell their coals at the Gate, as they call it, so they generally receive their money in those ale-houses, and it was not long before I brought him word of several. Upon this, he went in and made his observations, but found nothing to his purpose. At length, I brought word that there was a man in such a house, who had received a great deal of money of somebody, or, I believed, of several people; and that it lay all upon the table in heaps, and he was very busy writing down the sums, and putting it up in several bags. ' Is he?' said he; ' I'll warrant him, I will have some of it;' and in he went, walked up and down the house, which had several open tables and boxes in it, and listened to hear if he could learn what the man's name was, and he heard somebody call him Cullum, or some such name; then he watched his opportunity, and stepped up to him, and told him a long story, 'That there were two gentlemen at the Gun-tavern sent him to enquire for him, and to tell him, they desired to speak with him.'

"The collier-master had got his money before him just as I had told him, and had two or three small payments of money, which he had put up in little black dirty bags, and laid by themselves; as it was hardly broad day, the major found means, in delivering his message, to lay his hand upon one of those bags, and carry it off perfectly undiscovered. When he had got it, he came out to me, who stood at the door, and pulling me by the sleeve, 'Run, Jack,' said he, 'for our lives;' and away he scoured, and I after him, never resting, or scarce looking about me, till we got quite into Moorfields. But not thinking ourselves safe there, we ran on till we got into the fields, and finding a by-place, we sat down, and he pulled out the bag. 'Thou art a lucky boy, Jack,' said he, 'thou deservest a good share of this job, truly; for 'tis all along of thy lucky news.' So he poured it all out into my hat.

"How he managed to take such a bag from any man who was awake and in his senses, I cannot tell. There were about seventeen or eighteen pounds in the bag, and he parted the money, giving me one-third, with which I was very well contented. As we were now so rich, he would not let me lie any longer about the glass-house, or go naked and ragged as I had done; but obliged me to buy two shirts, a waistcoat, and a great coat; for a great coat was more proper for our business than any other. So I clothed myself, as he directed, and we lodged together in a little garret.

"Soon after this, we walked out again, and then tried our fortune in the places by the Exchange a second time. Here we began to act separately, and I undertook to walk by myself; and the first thing I did accurately, was a trick I played that argued some skill for a new beginner; for I had never seen any business of that kind done before. I saw two gentlemen mighty eager in talk, and one pulled out a pocket-book two or three times, and then slipped it into his coat-pocket again, and then out it came again, and papers were taken out, and others put in, and then in it went again; and so several times, the man being still warmly engaged with another man, and two or three others standing hard by them the last time he put his pocket-book into his pocket with his hand, when the book lay endway, resting upon some other book, or something else in his pocket, so that it did not go quite down, but one corner of it was seen above his pocket. Having seen the book thus pass and repass, I brushed smoothly, but closely, by the man, and took it clean away, and went directly into Moorfields, where my fellow-rogue was to meet me. It was not long before he came: I had no occasion to tell him my success; for he had heard of the action among the crowd. We searched the book, and found several goldsmith's and other notes; but the best of the booty was in one of the folds of the cover of the book; there was a paper full of loose diamonds. The man, as we understood afterwards, was a Jew, and dealt in those glittering commodities.

" We agreed that Will (which was my comrade's name) should return to the 'Change to hear what news was stirring, and there he heard of a reward of one hundred pounds for returning the things. The next day he went to the gentleman, and told him he had got some scent of his book, and the person who took it, and who, he believed, would restore it for the sake of the reward, provided he was assured that he should not be punished for the fact. After many preliminaries, it was concluded, that Will should bring the book, and the things lost in it, and receive the reward, which on the third day he did, and faithfully paid me my share of it.

" Not long after this, it fell out, we were strolling about in Smithfield on a Friday; there happened to be an old country gentleman in the market, selling some very large bullocks; it seems they came out of Sussex, for we heard him say, there were no such bullocks in the whole county of Sussex. His worship, for so they called him, had received the money for these bullocks at a tavern, the sign of which I have forgotten now, and having some of it in a bag, and the bag in his hand, he was taken with a sudden fit of coughing, and stood to cough, resting his hand with the bag of money in it upon a bulk-head of a shop, just by the cloister-gate in Smithfield; that is to say, within three or four doors of it: we were both just behind him, when Will said to me, ' Stand ready.' Upon this he made an artificial stumble, and fell with his head just against the old gentleman in the very moment when he was coughing ready to be strangled and quite spent for want of breath.

" The violence of the blow beat the old gentleman quite down the bag of money did not immediately fly out of his hand, but I ran to get hold of it, and giving it a quick snatch, pulled it clean away, and ran like the wind down the cloister with it, till I got to our old rendezvous. Will in the mean time fell down with the old gentleman, but soon got up. The old knight (for such it seems he was) was frighted with the fall, and his breath was so stopped with his cough, that he could not recover himself to speak until same time, during which nimble Will was got up again, and walked off; nor could he call out 'stop thief,' or tell anybody he had lost any thing for a good while; but coughing vehemently till he was almost black in the face, he at last brought it out, 'The rogues have got away my bag of money.'

"All the while the people understood nothing of the matter; and as for the rogues, indeed, they had time enough to get clear away, and in about an hour Will came to the rendezvous; there we sat down on the grass, and turned out the money, which proved to be eight guineas, and five pounds eight shillings in silver. This we shared upon the spot, and went to work the same day for more; but whether it was that, being flushed with our success, we were not so vigilant, or that no other opportunity offered, I know not, but we got nothing more that night.

"The next adventure was in the dusk of the evening, in a court which goes out of Gracechurch-street into Lombard-street, where the Quakers' meeting-house is. There was a young fellow, who, as we learned afterwards, was a woollen-draper's apprentice in Gracechurch-street; it seems, he had been receiving a sum of money, which was very considerable, and he came to a goldsmith's in Lombard-street with it, paid in the most of it there, insomuch that it grew dark, and the goldsmith began to shut up his shop, and to light his candles. We watched him in there, and stood on the other side of the way, to see what he did. When he had paid in all the money he intended, he stayed a little longer to take notes for what he had paid. At last he came out of the shop with still a pretty large bag under his arm, and walked over into the court, which was then very dark. In the middle of the court is a boarded entry, and at the end of it a threshold: and as soon as he had set his foot over the threshold, he was to turn on his left hand into Gracechurch-street.

"Keep up,' said Will to me; 'be nimble:' and as soon as he had said so, he flew at the young man, and gave him such a violent thrust that it pushed him forward with too great a force for him to stand, and as he strove to recover the threshold, Will took hold of his feet, and he fell forward. I stood ready, and presently fell out the bag of money, which I heard fall, for it flew out of his hand. I went forward with the money, and Will, finding I had it, ran backward, and, as I made along Fenchurch-street, overtook me, and we scoured home together. The poor young man was hurt a little with the fall, and reported to his master, as we heard afterwards, that he was knocked down. His master was glad the rest of the money was paid in to the bankers, and made no great noise at the loss, only cautioned his apprentice to avoid such dark places for the future.

" This booty amounted to 14*l*. 18*s*. apiece, and added extremely to my store, which began to grow too big for my management; but still I was at a loss with whom to trust it.

" A little after this, Will brought me into the company of two more young fellows: we met at the lower part of Gray's-inn-lane, about an hour before sunset, and went out into the fields towards a place called the Pindar of Wakefield, where are abundance of brick-kilns. Here it was agreed to spread from the field path to the road-way, all the way towards Pancras church, to observe any chance game, which, as they called it, they might shoot flying. Upon the path, within the bank on the side of the road going towards Kentish Town, two of our gang, Will and one of the others, met a single gentleman walking apace towards the town, it being almost dark. Will cried, ' Mark, ho!' which it seems was the word at which we were all to stand still at a distance, come in if he wanted help, and give a signal if anything appeared that was dangerous.

" Will stepped up to the gentleman, stopped him, and put the question, that is, ' Sir, your money !' The gentleman, seeing he was alone, struck at him with his cane; but Will, a nimble, strong fellow, flew upon him, and with struggling got him down ; then he begged for his life, Will having told him, with an oath, that he would cut his throat in a moment. While this was doing, a hackney-coach came along the road, and the fourth man who was that way cried, ' Mark, ho!' which was to intimate that it was a prize, not a surprise; and, accordingly, the next man went up to assist him, where they stopped the coach, which had a doctor of physic and a surgeon in it, who had been to visit some very rich patient, and I suppose had considerable fees, for here they got two gold purses, one with eleven or twelve guineas, the other six, with some pocket money, two watches, one diamond ring, and the surgeon's plaster-box, which was nearly full of silver instruments.

" While they were at this work, Will kept the man down, who was under him ; and though he promised not to kill him, unless he offered to make a noise, yet he would not let him stir till he heard the noise of the coach going on again, by which he knew the job was over on that side. Then he carried him a little out of the way, tied his hands behind him, and bade him lie still and make no noise and he would come back in half an hour, and untie him upon his word; but if he cried out, he would come back and kill him. The poor man promised to lie still, and make no noise, and did so, and had not above 11s. 6d. in his pocket, which Will took, and came back to the rest. But while they were together, I was on the other side of the Pindar of Wakefield, and cried out, 'Mark, ho!' too.

"What I saw was a couple of poor women—one a kind of a nurse, and the other a maid-servant, going for Kentish Town. As Will knew I was but young at the work, he came flying to me, and seeing how easy a bargain it was, he said, 'Go, Colonel, fall to work!' I went up to them, and, speaking to the elderly woman, 'Nurse,' said I, 'don't be in such haste—I want to speak with you;' at which they both stopped, and looked a little frightened. 'Don't be alarmed, sweetheart,' said I to the maid; 'a little of that money in the bottom of your pocket will make all easy, and I'll do you no harm.' By this time Will came up to us, for they had not seen him before; then they began to scream out. 'Hold!' said I, 'make no noise, unless you have a mind to force us to murder you whether we will or no: give me your money presently, and make no words, and we shan't hurt you.' Upon this the poor maid pulled out five shillings and sixpence, and the old woman a guinea and a shilling, crying heartily for her money, and said it was all she had in the world. Well, we took it for all that, though it made my heart bleed to see what agony the poor woman was in at parting with it, and I asked her where she lived? she said her name was Smith, and she lived at Kentish Town. I said nothing to her, but bade them go on about their business, and I gave Will the money. In a few minutes we were all together again. One of the rogues said, 'Come, this is well enough for one road; it's time to be gone.' So we jogged away, crossing the field, out of the path, towards Tottenham-court. 'But, hold,' said Will, ' I must go and untie the man, d—n him.' One of them said, ' Let him lie.' 'No,' said Will, ' I will not be worse than my word : I will untie him.' So he went to the place; but the man was gone: either he had untied himself, or somebody had passed by, and he had called for help, and so was untied, for he could not find him, nor make him hear, though he ventured to call twice for him aloud.

"This made us hasten away the faster, and getting into Tottenham-court road, they thought it was a little too near, so they made into the town at St. Giles's, and crossing to Piccadilly, went to Hyde Park gate ; here they ventured to rob another coach, that is to say, one of the two other rogues and Will did it between the Park-gate and Knightsbridge. There was in it only a gentleman and a woman whom he had picked up, it seems, at the Spring-garden a little farther: they took the gentleman's money, and his watch, and his silver hilted sword; but when they came to the woman, she cursed them for robbing the gentleman of his money, and leaving none for her: as for herself she had not one sixpenny-piece about her though she was, indeed, well enough dressed too. Having made this adventure, we parted, and went each man to his lodging.

"Two days after this, Will came to my lodging, for I had now got a room by myself, and appointed me to meet him the next evening at such a place. I went, but to my great satisfaction missed him, but met with the gang at another place, who had committed a notorious robbery near Hounslow; where they wounded a gentleman's gardener, so that, I think, he died, and robbed the house of a very considerable sum of money and plate. This, however, was not so clean carried, but the neighbours were alarmed, the rogues pursued, and being at London with the booty, one of them was taken; but Will, being a dexterous fellow, made his escape with the money and plate. He knew nothing that one of his comrades was taken, and that they were all so closely pursued that every one was obliged to shift for himself. He happened to come in the evening, as good luck then directed him, just after search had been made for him by the constables; his companion who was taken, having upon promise of favour, and to save himself from the gallows, discovered his confederates, and Will amongst the rest, as the principal party in the whole undertaking. He got notice of it, and left all his booty at my lodging, hiding it in an old coat that lay under my bed, leaving word he had been there, and had left the coat that he borrowed of me under my bed. I knew not what to make of it, but went up-stairs, and finding the parcel, was surprised to see wrapped up in it, above a hundred pounds in plate and money, and heard nothing of brother Will, as he called himself, for three or four days, when we sold the plate after the rate of two shillings per ounce, to a pawnbroker near Cloth-Fair.

"About two days afterwards, going upon the stroll, whom should I meet but my former brother, Captain Jack! when he saw me, he came close to me in his blunt way, and said, 'Have you heard the news?' I asked him, 'what news?' He told me, 'My old comrade and teacher was taken, and that morning carried to Newgate; that he was charged with a robbery and murder, committed somewhere beyond Brentford; and that the worst was, he was impeached.' I thanked him for his information, and for that time parted; but was the very next morning surprised, when, going across Rag-Fair, I heard one call 'Jack.' I looked behind me, and immediately saw three men, and after them a constable, coming towards me with great speed. I was in a great surprise, and started to run; but one of them clapped in upon me, got hold of me, and in a moment the rest surrounded me, and told me they were to apprehend a known thief, who went by the name of one of the 'Three Jacks of Rag-Fair;' for that he was charged upon oath with having been a party in a notorious robbery, burglary, and murder, committed in such a place and on such a day.

"Not to trouble the reader with an account of the discourse that passed between the justice, before whom I was carried, and myself, I shall in brief inform him, that my brother Captain Jack, who had the forwardness to put it to me whether I was among them or no, when in truth he was there himself, had the only reason to fly, at the same time that he advised me to shift for myself; so that I was discharged, and in about three weeks after, my master and tutor in wickedness, poor Will, was executed for the fact.

"I had nothing to do now but to find out the captain, of whom, though not without some trouble, I at last got news, and told him the whole story. He presently discovered, by his surprise, that he was guilty, and after a few words more told me, 'It was all true, that he was in the robbery, and had the greatest part of the booty in keeping; but what to do with it, or himself, he did not know, but thought of flying into Scotland,' asking me if I would go with him?' I consented, and he showed me twenty-two pounds he had in money. I honestly produced all the money I had left, which was upwards of sixteen pounds. We set out from London on foot, and travelled the first day to Ware; for we had learned so much of the road that our way lay through that town; from Ware we travelled to Cambridge, though that was not our direct road. The occasion was this: in our way through Puckeridge, we baited at an inn, and while we were there, a countryman came and fastened his horse at the gate, while he went into to drink. We sat in the gateway, and having called for a mug of beer, we drank it up. We had been talking to the ostler about the way to Scotland, who told us to ask the road to Royston: 'But,' said he, 'there is a turning just here a little farther, you must not go that way, for that goes to Cambridge.'

"We had paid for our beer, and sat at the door only to rest us, when on a sudden a gentleman's coach drove up, and three or four horsemen rode into the yard, and the ostler was obliged to go in with them. Said he to the captain, 'Young man, pray take hold of the horse,' meaning the countryman's horse I mentioned above, ' and take him out of the way that the coach may come up.' He did so, and beckoned to me to follow him. We walked together to the turning; said he to me, " Do you step before, and turn up the lane; I'll overtake you; so I went on up the lane, and in a few minutes he got upon the horse, and was soon at my heels, bidding me get up and take a lift.

" I made no difficulty of doing so, and away we went at a good round rate, having a strong horse under us. We suspected the countryman would follow us to Royston, because of our directions from the ostler; so that we went towards Cambridge, and went easier after the first hour's riding; and coming through a town or two, we alighted by turns, and did not then ride double, but by the way picked a couple of good shirts off a hedge; and that evening got safe to Cambridge, where the next day I bought a horse for myself. Thus equipped, we jogged on through several places, till we got to Stamford in Lincolnshire, where it was impossible to restrain my captain from playing his pranks, even at church; where he went, and placed himself so near an old lady, that he got her gold watch from her side unperceived; and the same night we went away by moonlight, after having the satisfaction to hear the watch cried, and ten guineas offered for it again. He would have been glad of the ten guineas instead of the watch, but durst not venture to carry it home. We went through several other places, such as Grantham, Newark, and Nottingham, where we played our tricks; but at last we got safe to Edinburgh, without any accident but one, which was in crossing a ford, where the captain was really in danger of drowning, his horse being driven down by the stream, and falling under him; but the rider had a proverb on his side, and got out of the water.

" At Edinburgh we remained about a month, when, on a sudden, my captain was gone, horse and all, and I knew nothing what was become of him, nor did I ever see or hear of him for eighteen months after; nor did he so much as leave the least notice for me, either where he was gone, or whether he would return to Edinburgh again or no. I took his leaving me very grievously, not knowing what to do with myself, being a stranger in the place, and on the other hand, my money abated apace too. I had, for the most part of this time, my horse upon my hands to keep; and, as horses yield but a sorry price in Scotland, I found no opportunity to sell him to any advantage, however, at last, I was forced to dispose of him.

"Being thus eased of my horse, and having nothing at all to do, I began to consider within myself what would become of me, and what I could turn my hand to. I had not much diminished my stock of money; for though I was all the way so wary that I would not join with my captain in his desperate attempts, yet I made no scruple to live at his expense. In the next place, I was not so anxious about my money running low, because I had made a reserve, by leaving upwards of 90*l.* in a friend's hands at London; but still, I was willing to get into some employment for a livelihood. I was sick of the wandering life I had led, and resolved to be a thief no more, but stuck close to writing and reading for about six months, till I got into the service of an officer of the Customs, who employed me for a time; but, as he set me to do little but pass and repass between Leith and Edinburgh, leaving me to live at my own expense till my wages should be due, I ran out the little money I had left in clothes and subsistence, and shortly before the year's end, when I was to have 12*l.* English money, my master was turned out of his place, and, what was worse, having been charged with some misapplications, was obliged to take shelter in England; so we that were his servants—for there were three of us—were left to shift for ourselves. This was a hard case for me, in a strange place, and I was reduced by it to the last extremity. I might have gone to England, an English ship being there: the master proffered to take my word for ten shillings, till I got there; but just as I was departing, Captain Jack appeared again.

"I have mentioned how he left me, and that I saw him no more for eighteen months. His ramble and adventures were many; in that time he went to Glasgow, playing some very remarkable pranks there; escaped the gallows almost miraculously; got over to Ireland; wandered about there; escaped from Londonderry over to the Highlands, and, about a month before I was left destitute at Leith by my master, noble Captain Jack came in there, on board the ferry-boat from Fife, being, after all his adventures and successes, advanced to the dignity of a foot soldier in a body of recruits, raised in the north for the regiment of Douglas.

"After my disaster, being reduced almost as low as Jack, I found no better shift before me, at least not for the present, than to enter myself a soldier too; and thus we were ranked together, with each of us a musket upon our shoulders. I was extremely delighted with the life of a soldier; for I took the exercises naturally, so that the sergeant who taught us to handle our arms, seeing me so ready at it, asked me, if I had never carried arms before? I told him, no. At which he swore, though jesting; 'They call you colonel,' said he, 'and I believe you will be a colonel, or you must be some colonel's bastard, or you would never handle your arms as you do, at once or twice showing.' Whatever was my satisfaction in that respect, yet other circumstances did not equally concur to make this life suit me; for, after we had been about six months in this company, we were informed, that we were to march for England, and be shipped off at Newcastle, or Hull, to join the regiment in Flanders. Poor Captain Jack's case was particular; he durst not appear publicly at Newcastle, as he must have done had he marched with the recruits. In the next place, I remembered my money in London, which was almost 100*l.*; and if it had been asked all the soldiers in the regiment, which of them would go to Flanders a private sentinel if they had 100*l.* in their pockets, I believe none of them would have answered in the affirmative.

"These two circumstances concurring, I began to be very uneasy, and very unwilling in my thoughts to go over into Flanders a poor musketeer, to be knocked on the head for 3*s.* 6*d.* a-week. While I was daily musing on the hardship of being sent away as above, Captain Jack came to me one evening, and asked me to take a walk with him into the fields, for he wanted to speak with me. We walked together here, and talked seriously of the matter, and at last concluded to desert that very night; the moon affording a good light, and Jack having got a comrade with him thoroughly acquainted with the way across the Tweed; when on the other side we should be on English ground, and safe enough; from thence we proposed to go to Newcastle, and get some collier ship to take us in, and carry us to London.

"About half an hour past eight in the morning, we reached the Tweed; and here we overtook two more of the same regiment, who had deserted from Haddingdon, where another part of the recruits were quartered. These were Scotsmen, and very poor, having not one penny in their pockets; and when they saw us, whom they knew to be of the same regiment, they took us to be pursuers: upon which they stood upon their defence, having the regiment swords on, as we had also, but none of the mounting or clothing; for we were not to receive the clothes till we came to the regiment in Flanders. It was not long before we made them understand that we were in the same condition with themselves; and so we became one company. Our money had ebbed very low, and we contrived to get into Newcastle in the dusk of the evening; and even then we durst not venture into the public parts of the place, but made down towards the river below the town. Here we knew not what to do with ourselves, but, guided by our fate, we put a good face upon the matter, went into an alehouse, sat down, and called for a pint of beer.

"The woman of the house appeared very frank, and entertained us cheerfully; so we, at last, told her our condition, and asked her if she could not help us to some kind master of a collier, who would give us a passage to London by sea. The subtle devil, who immediately found us proper fish for her hook, gave us the kindest words in the world, and told us she was heartily sorry she had not seen us one day sooner; that there was a collier-master of her particular acquaintance, who went away but with the morning tide; that the ship was fallen down to Shields, but, she believed, was hardly over the bar, and she would send to his house, and see if he was gone on board, (for some masters do not go away till a tide after the ship:) and she was sure, if he was not gone, she could prevail with him to take us all in: but then she was afraid we must go on board immediately, the same night.

"We begged of her to send to his house, for we knew not what to do; for, as we had no money, we had no lodging, and wanted nothing but to be on board. We looked upon this as a mighty favour that she sent to the master's house, and, to our great joy, she brought us word, about an hour after, that he was not gone, and was at a tavern in the town, whither his boy had been to fetch him; and that he had sent word he would call there in his way home. This was all in our favour, and we were extremely pleased with it. In about an hour he came into the room to us. 'Where are these honest gentlemen soldiers,' said he, 'that are in such distress?' We all stood up, and paid our respects to him. 'Well, gentlemen,' said he, 'and is all your money spent?'

"'Indeed it is,' said one of our company, 'and we shall be infinitely obliged to you, sir, if you will give us a passage. We shall be very willing to do any thing we can in the ship, though we are not seamen.'

"'Why,' said he, 'were none of you ever at sea in your lives?'

"'No,' said we, 'not one of us.'

"'You will be able to do me no service, then; for you will all be sick. However, for my good landlady's sake here, I'll do it. But are you all ready to go on board, for I go on board myself this very night.'

"'Yes, sir,' said we again, 'we are ready to go this very minute.'

"'No, no,' said he, very kindly, 'we'll drink together. Come, landlady, make these honest gentlemen a sneaker of punch.'

"We looked at one another, for we knew we had no money; and he perceived it. 'Come, come,' said he, 'don't be concerned at your having no money: my landlady here, and I, never part with dry lips. Come, good wife, make the punch, as I bid you.'

"We thanked him, and said, 'God bless you, noble captain!' a hundred times over, being overjoyed at our good luck. While we were drinking the punch, he told the landlady he would step home, and order the boat to come at high water, and bade her get something for supper, which she did.

"In less than an hour our captain returned, and came up to us, and blamed us that we had not drunk the punch out. 'Come,' said he, 'don't be bashful; when that's out, we can have another. When I am obliging poor men, I love to do it handsomely.'

"We drank on, and drank the punch out; more was brought up, and he pushed it about apace; then came up a leg of mutton. I need not say we fed heartily, being several times told we should pay nothing. After supper, he bade my landlady ask if the boat was come; and she brought word, No, it was not high water by a great deal. Then more punch was called for, and, as was afterwards confessed, something more than ordinary was put into it, so that, by the time the punch was drunk out, we were all intoxicated; and as for me, I fell asleep.

"At last I was roused, and told that the boat was come: so I and my drunken comrades tumbled out, almost one over another, into the boat, and away we went with our captain. Most of us, if not all, fell asleep till after some time, though how much, or how far going, we knew not. The boat stopped, and we were awakened, and told we were at the ship's side, which was true, and with much help, and holding us, for fear we should fall overboard, our captain, as we termed him, called us thus: —'Here: boatswain, take care of these gentlemen; give them good cabins, and let them turn in to sleep, for they are very weary.' And so indeed we were, and drunk too.

"Care was taken of us, according to order, and we were put into very good cabins, where we were sure to go immediately to sleep. In the mean time, the ship, which was indeed just ready to go, and only on notice given had come to anchor for us at Shields, weighed, stood over the bar, and went off to sea; and when we awoke, and began to peep abroad, which was not till near noon the next day, we found ourselves a great way at sea, the land in sight indeed, but at a great distance, and all going merrily on for London, as I thought. We were very well used, and very well satisfied with our condition, for about three days, when we began to inquire, whether we were not almost in the Channel, and how much longer it would be before we should come into the river? 'What river?' said one of the men. 'Why, the Thames,' said my Captain Jack. 'The Thames!' answered the sailor, 'what d'ye mean by that? What! ha'n't you had time enough to be sober yet?' So Captain Jack said no more, but looked very silly, when, awhile after, some other of us asked the same question, and the seamen, who knew nothing of the cheat, began to smell a rat, and turning to the other Englishman who came with us, 'Pray,' said he, 'where do you fancy you are going, that you ask so often about it?' 'Why to London,' said he; 'where should we be going? We agreed with the captain to carry us to London.'

"'Not with the captain,' said he; 'I dare say, poor men, you are all cheated; and I thought so when I saw you come aboard with that kidnapping rogue Gilliman; you are all betrayed, for the ship is bound to Virginia.' As soon as we heard this news, we were raving men, drew our swords, and swore revenge; but we were soon overpowered, and carried before the captain, who told us, ne was sorry for what had happened, but that he had no hand in it, and it was out of his power to help us; and he let us know very plainly what our condition was, namely, that we were put on board his ship as servants to Maryland, to be delivered to a person there; but that, however, if we would be quiet and orderly in his ship, he would use us well in the passage; but if we were unruly, we must be handcuffed, and be kept between decks; for it was his business to take care no disturbance happened in the ship.

"'No hand in it! D—n him,' said my Captain Jack aloud, 'do you think he is not a confederate in this villainy? would any honest man receive innocent people on board his ship, and not enquire of their circumstances, but carry them away, and not speak to them? I tell you he is a villain. Why does he not complete his villainy, and murder us, and then he'll be free from our revenge!'

"All this discourse availed nothing, we were forced to be quiet, and had a very good voyage, no storms all the way; but just before we arrived, one of the Scotchmen asked the captain of the ship, whether he would sell us. 'Yes,' said he. 'Why then, sir,' said the Scotchman, 'the devil will have you at the hinder end of the bargain.' 'Say you so?' said the captain, smiling: 'well, well, let the devil and I alone to agree about that; do you be quiet, and behave civilly, as you should do.'

"When we came ashore, which was on the banks of a river they call Potomack, Jack said, " I have something to say to you, captain; that is, I have promised to cut your throat, and, depend upon it, I will be as good as my word." Our captain or kidnapper, call him as you will, made no answer, but delivered us to the merchant to whom we were consigned, who again disposed of us as he thought fit; and in a few days we were separated.

" As for my Captain Jack, to make short of the story, that desperate rogue had the good luck to have an easy good master, whom he abused very much; for he took an opportunity to run away with a boat, with which his master entrusted him and another to carry provisions to a plantation down the river. This boat and provisions they ran away with, and sailed north to the bottom of the bay, as they call it, and there quitting the boat, they wandered through the woods, till they got into Pennsylvania, from whence they made shift to get a passage to New England, and from thence home; where, falling in among his old companions, and to his old trade, he was at length taken and hanged about a month before I came to London, which was near twenty years afterwards.

" My part was harder at the beginning, though better at the latter end; I was sold to a rich planter whose name was Smith. During this scene of life I had time to reflect on my past hours; and though I had no great capacity of making a clear judgment, and very few reflections from conscience, yet it made some impression upon me. I behaved myself so well, that my master took notice of me, and made me one of his overseers; and was so kind as to send my note of my friend's hand for the 93*l.* before-mentioned, to his correspondent, who received and returned me the money. My good master, a little time after, said to me, ' Colonel, don't flatter me, I love plain dealing: liberty is precious to every body, I give you yours, and will take care you shall be well used by the country, and will get you a good plantation.'

" I insisted I would not quit his service for the best plantation in Maryland; that he had been so good to me, and I believed I was so useful to him, that I could not think of it; and at last I added, I hoped he could not believe but that I had as much gratitude as a negro.

" He smiled, and said he would not be served upon these terms; that he did not forget what he had promised, nor what I had done in his plantation: and that he was resolved in the first place to give me my liberty; so he pulled out a piece of paper, and threw it to me: 'There,' said he, ' is a certificate of your coming on shore, and being sold to me for five years, of which you have lived three with me, and now you are your own master.'

"I bowed, and told him, that I was sure if I was my own master, I would be his servant as long as he would accept of my services. He told me he would accept of my services on these two conditions; first, that he would give me 30*l.* per annum and my board, for my managing the plantation I was then employed in. And secondly, that at the same time he would procure me a new plantation to begin with upon my own account; 'for Jack,' said he, smiling, ' though you are but a young man, 'tis time you were doing something for yourself.'

"Not long after, he purchased in my name about 300 acres of land, near his own plantation, as he said, that I might the better take care of his. My master, for such I must still call him, generously gave it me; 'but Colonel,' said he, ' giving you this plantation is nothing at all, if I do not assist you to support it, and to carry it on, and therefore I will give you credit for whatever is needful; such as tools, provisions, and some servants to begin; materials for out-houses, and hogs, cows, horses for stock, and the like; and I'll take it out of your returns from abroad, as you can pay it.'

"Thus got to be a planter, and encouraged by a kind benefactor, that I might not be wholly taken up with my new plantation, he gave me freely, without any consideration, one of his negroes, named Mouchat, whom I always esteemed. Besides this, he sent to me two servants more, a man and a woman; but these two he put to my account as above. Mouchat and these two fell immediately to work for me; they began with about two acres of land, which had but little timber on it at first, and most of that was cut down by the two carpenters who built my house. It was a great advantage to me, that I had so bountiful a master who helped me out in every case; for in this very first year, I received a terrible blow; having sent a large quantity of tobacco to a merchant in London, by my master's direction, which arrived safe there, the merchant was ordered to make the return in a sorted cargo of goods for me, such as would have made a man of me all at once, but, to my inexpressible terror and surprise, the ship was lost, and that just at the entrance into the Cape, that is to say, the mouth of the bay; some of the goods were recovered, but spoiled. In short, nothing but the nails, tools, and iron-work were good for any thing; and though the value of them was very considerable in proportion to the rest; yet my loss was irreparably great, and indeed the greatness of the loss consisted in its being irreparable.

"I was perfectly astonished at the first news of the loss, knowing that I was in debt to my patron or master so much, that it must be several years before I should recover it; and as he brought me the bad news himself, he perceived my disorder; that is to say, he saw I was in the utmost confusion, and a kind of amazement; and so indeed I was, because I was so much in debt. But he spoke cheerfully to me, 'Come,' said he, 'do not be so discouraged; you may make up this loss.' 'No, sir,' said I, 'that never can be, for it is my all, and I shall never be out of debt.' 'Well,' he answered, ' you have no creditor, however, but me; and, now, remember I once told you, I would make a man of you, and I will not disappoint you.' For this further proof of his friendship I thanked him with more ceremony and respect than ever, because I thought myself more under the hatches than I was before: but he was as good as his word, for he did not baulk me in the least of anything I wanted; and as I had more iron-work saved out of the ship in proportion than I required, I supplied him with some part of it, and took up some linen and clothes and other necessaries from him in exchange. And now I began to increase visibly; I had a large quantity of land cured, that is, freed from timber, and a very good crop of tobacco in view, and I got three servants more, and one negro; so that I had five white servants and two negroes; and with this my affairs went very well on; the first year, indeed, I took my wages or salary of 30l. a-year, because I wanted it very much; but the second and third year I resolved not to take it, but to leave it in my benefactor's hands, to clear off the debt I had contracted.

" At the same time my thoughts dictated to me, that though this was the foundation of my new life, yet it was not the superstructure, and that I might still be born for greater things than these; that it is honesty and virtue alone that made men rich and great, and gave them fame, as well as figure in the world, and that therefore I was to lay my foundation in these, and expect what might follow in time. To help these thoughts, as I had learned to read and write when I was in Scotland, so I began now to love books, and particularly had an opportunity of reading some very considerable ones, some of which I bought at a planter's house, who was lately dead and his goods sold, and others I borrowed. I considered my present state of life to be my mere youth, though I was now above 30 years old, because in my youth I had learned nothing; and if my daily business, which was now great, would have permitted, I would have been content to have gone to school. However, fate, which had something else in store for me, threw an opportunity into my hand, namely, a clever fellow that came over a transported felon from Bristol and fell into my hands for a servant. He had led a *loose* life, he acknowledged, and being driven to extremities, took to the highway, for which, had he been taken, he would have been hanged; but falling into some low-prized rogueries afterwards, for want of opportunity for worse, he was caught, condemned, and transported, and, as he said, was glad he came off so.

"He was an excellent scholar, and I perceiving it, asked him one time if he could give a method how I might learn the Latin tongue; he said, smiling, yes, he could teach it me in three months, if I would let him have books, or even without books if he had time. I told him a book would become his hand better than a hoe, and if he could promise to make me but understand Latin enough to read it and understand other languages by it, I would ease him of the labour which I was now obliged to put him to; especially if I was assured that he was fit to receive that favour of a kind master. In short, I made him to me, what my kind benefactor made me to him: and from him I gained a fund of knowledge infinitely more valuable than the rate of a slave, which was what I paid for it;—but of this hereafter.

"In this posture I went on for twelve years, and was very successful in my plantation, and had gotten by means of my master's favour, whom now I called my friend, a correspondent in London, with whom I traded; shipped over my tobacco to him, and received European goods in return, such as I wanted to carry on my plantation, and sufficient to sell to others also. In this interval, my good friend and benefactor died; and I was left very disconsolate on account of my loss, for it was indeed a great loss to me; he had been a father to me, and I was like a forsaken stranger without him. Though I knew the country, and the trade too, well enough, and had for some time chiefly carried on his whole business for him; yet I seemed greatly at a loss now my counsellor and chief supporter was gone, and I had no confidant to communicate myself to, on all occasions, as formerly; but there was no remedy. I was, however, in a better condition to stand alone than ever; I had a very large plantation, and had near seventy negroes, and other servants.

"I now looked upon myself as one buried alive in a remote part of the world, where I could see nothing at all, and hear but little of what was seen, and that little not till at least half a year after it was done, and sometimes a year or more; and in a word, the old reproach often came in my way, namely, that this was not yet the life of a gentleman. However, I now began to frame my thoughts for a voyage to England, resolving then to act as I should see cause, but with a secret resolution to see more of the world if possible, and realise those things to my mind, which I had hitherto only entertained remote ideas of by the help of books.

"It was three years after this before I could get things in order fit for my leaving the country: in this time I delivered my tutor from his bondage, and would have given him his liberty, but I found that I could not empower him to go for England till his time was expired according to the certificate of his transportation, which was registered; so I made him one of my overseers, and thereby raised him gradually to a prospect of living in the same manner, and by the like steps, that my good benefactor raised me, only that I did not assist him to enter upon planting for himself as I was assisted, neither was I upon the spot to do it; but this man by his diligence and honest application delivered himself, even unassisted any farther than by making him an overseer, which was only a present ease and deliverance from the hard labour and fare which he endured as a servant. However, in this trust he behaved so faithfully, and so diligently, that it recommended him in the country, and, when I came back, I found him in circumstances very different from what I left him in, besides his being my principal manager for near twenty years, as you shall hear in its place.

"I was now making provision for my going to England, after having settled my plantation in such hands as were fully to my satisfaction. My first work was, to furnish myself with such a stock of goods and money as might be sufficient for my occasions abroad, and, particularly, might allow to make large returns to Maryland for the use and supply of all my plantations; but when I came to look nearer into the voyage, it occurred to me that it would not be prudent to put my cargo all on board the same ship that I went in; so I shipped, at several times, five hundred hogsheads of tobacco, in several ships, for England, giving notice to my correspondent in London, that I would embark about such a time to come over myself, and ordering him to insure for a considerable sum proportioned to the value of my cargo.

"About two months after this I left the place, and embarked for England in a stout ship carrying 24 guns, and about 600 hogsheads of tobacco; and we left the capes of Virginia on the first of August ———. We had a very sour and rough voyage for the first fortnight, though it was in a season so generally noted for good weather. We met with a storm, and our ship was greatly damaged, and some leaks were sprung, but not so bad but by the diligence of the seamen they were stopped; after which we had tolerable weather and a good sea, till we came into the soundings, for so they call the mouth of the British Channel. In the grey of the morning, a French privateer, of 26 guns, appeared, and crowded after us with all the sail she could make. Our captain exchanged a broadside or two with her, which was terrible work to me; for I had never seen such before; the Frenchman's guns having raked us, and killed and wounded six of our men. In short, after a fight long enough to show us that if we would not be taken, we must resolve to sink by her side, for there was no room to expect deliverance, and a fight long enough to save the master's credit, we were taken, and the ship carried away for St. Malo's. I had however, besides my being taken, the mortification to be detained on board the cruiser, and to see the ship I was in, manned by Frenchmen, set sail from us. I afterwards heard that she was re-taken by an English man of-war, and carried into Portsmouth

"The Rover cruised abroad again, in the mouth of the Channel, for some time, and took a ship richly laden, bound homeward from Jamaica. This was a noble prize for the rogues, and they hastened away with her to St. Malo's; and from thence I went to Bourdeaux, where the captain asked me if I would be delivered up a state prisoner, get myself exchanged, or pay three hundred crowns. I desired time to write to my correspondent, in England, who sent me a letter of credit, and in about six weeks I was exchanged for a merchant prisoner in Plymouth. I got passage from hence to Dunkirk, on board a French vessel; and having a certificate of an exchanged prisoner from the intendant of Bourdeaux, I had a passport given me to go into the Spanish Netherlands, and so whither I pleased. I went to Ghent, afterwards to Newport, where I took the packet-boat, and came over to England, landing at Deal instead of Dover, the weather forcing us into the Downs. When I came to London, I was very well received by my friend to whom I had consigned my effects; for all my goods came safe to hand, and the overseers I had left behind had shipped, at several times, four hundred hogsheads of tobacco, to my correspondent, in my absence. So that I had above 1000*l.* in my factor's hands, and two hundred hogsheads besides, left in hand, unsold.

" I had nothing to do now, but entirely to conceal myself from all that had any knowledge of me before; and this was the easiest thing in the world to do, for I was grown out of every body's knowledge, and most of those I had known, were grown out of mine.

" My Captain who went with me, or rather who carried me away, I found by enquiring at the proper place, had been rambling about the world, come to London, fallen into his old trade, which he could not forbear, and growing an eminent highwayman, had made his exit at the gallows after a life of fourteen years most exquisite and successful rogueries; the particulars of which would make, as I observed, an admirable history. My other brother Jack, whom I called Major, followed the like wicked trade; but was a man of more gallantry and gen^· ·, and having committed innumerable depredations upon m⌂⌂⌂⌂, had yet always so much dexterity as to bring himself off, till at length he was laid fast in Newgate, and loaded with irons, and would certainly have gone the same way as the Captain, but he was so dexterous a rogue, that no gaol, no fetters would hold him; and he and two more found means to knock off their irons, worked their way through the wall of the prison, and let themselves down on the outside, in the night. So escaping, they found means to get into France, where he followed the same trade, and that with so much success, that the Major grew famous by the name of Anthony, and had the honour with three of his comrades, (whom he had taught the English way of robbing generously, as they called it, without murdering, or wounding, or ill-using those they robbed,) to be broken upon the wheel, at the Grève in Paris.

" All these things I found means to be fully informed of, and to have a long account of the particulars of their conduct from some of their comrades, who had the good fortune to escape, and whom I got the knowledge of without letting them so much as guess at who I was, or upon what account I inquired.

" I was now at the height of my good fortune, and got the name of a great merchant. I lived single, and in lodgings, and kept a French servant, being very desirous of improving myself in that language, and received five or six hundred hogsheads a year from my own plantation, and spent my time in that and supplying my people with necessaries at Maryland, as they wanted them.

" In this private condition I continued about two years more, when the devil, owing me a spleen ever since I refused being a thief, paid me home with interest, by laying a snare in my way which had almost ruined me.

" There dwelt a lady in the house opposite to the house I lodged in, who made an extraordinary figure, and was a most beautiful person, she was well bred, sang admirably fine, and sometimes I could hear distinctly, the houses being over against one another in a narrow court, this lady put herself so often in my way, that I could not in good manners forbear taking notice of her, and giving the ceremony of my hat when I saw her at her window, or at the door, or when I passed her in the court; so that we became almost acquainted at a distance. Sometimes she also visited at the house in which I lodged, and it was generally contrived that I should be introduced when she came. And thus, by degrees, we became more intimately acquainted, and often conversed together in the family, but always in public, at least for a great while. . I was a mere boy in the affair of love, and knew as little of what belonged to a woman, as any man in Europe of my age; the thoughts of a wife, much less of a mistress, had never so much as taken the least hold of my head, and I had been till now, as perfectly unacquainted with the sex, and as unconcerned about them, as I was when I was ten years old, and lay in a heap of ashes at the glass-house.

" She attacked me without ceasing, with the finesse of her conduct, and with arts which were impossible to be ineffectual. She was ever, as it were, in my view, often in my company, and yet kept herself so on the reserve, so surrounded continually with obstructions, that for several months after she could perceive I sought an opportunity to speak to her, she rendered it impossible, nor could I ever break in upon her, she kept her guard so well.

" This rigid behaviour was the greatest mystery that could be, considering at the same time, that she never declined my seeing her, or conversing with me in public; but she held it on. She took care never to sit next me, that I might slip no paper into her hand, or speak softly to her, she kept somebody or other always between, that I could never come up to her. And thus, as if she was resolved really to have nothing to do with me, she held me at bay several months. In short, we came nearer and nearer every time we met, and at last gave the world the slip, and were privately married, to avoid ceremony, and the public inconvenience of a wedding.

" No sooner were we married, but she threw off the mask of her gravity and good conduct, and carried it to such an excess, that I could not but be dissatisfied at the expense of it. In about a twelvemonth she was brought to bed of a fine boy, and her lying-in cost me as near as I can now remember, 136$l.$ which she told me she thought was a trifle. Such jarring continually between us produced a separation; and she demanded 300$l.$ per annum for her maintenance. This, however, made me look more closely into her conduct, and, by means of two trusty agents, I was enabled to detect her infidelity, and to sue her before the Ecclesiastical Court, from which I obtained a divorce.

" Things being at this pass, I resolved to go over to France, where

I fell into company with some Irish officers of the regiment of Dillon, where I bought a company, and so went into the army directly. Our regiment, after I had been some time in it, was commanded into Italy; and one of the most considerable actions I was in, was the famous attack upon Cremona, in the Milanese, where the Germans being treacherously let into the town by night, through a kind of common sewer, surprised the town, and took the Duke de Villeroy prisoner, beating the French troops into the citadel, but were in the middle of their victory so boldly attacked by two Irish regiments, that, after a most desperate fight, and not being able to break through us to let in their friends, they were obliged to quit the town, to the eternal honour of those Irish regiments. Having been in several campaigns, I was permitted to sell my company, and got the Chevalier's brevet for a colonel, in case of raising troops for him in Great Britain. I accordingly embarked on board the French fleet for the Firth of Edinburgh; but they overshot their landing-place; and this delay gave time to the English fleet, under Sir George Byng, to come to an anchor just as we did.

"Upon this surprise the French admiral set sail, and crowding away to the north, got the start of the English fleet, and escaped, with the loss of one ship only, to Dunkirk; and glad I was to set my foot on shore again, for all the while we were thus flying for our lives I was under the greatest terror imaginable, and nothing but halters and gibbets ran in my head, concluding that, if I had been taken, I should certainly have been hanged.

"I took post horses for Flanders, and at last got safe once more to London, from which place I embarked for Virginia, and had a tolerable voyage thither, only that we met with a pirate ship, which plundered us of every thing they could come at which was for their turn; but, to give the rogues their due, though they were the most abandoned wretches that ever were seen, they did not use us ill; and, as to my loss, it was not considerable.

"I found all my affairs in very good order at Virginia, my plantation prodigiously increased; and my manager, who first inspired me with travelling thoughts, and made me master of any knowledge worth naming, received me with a transport of joy, after a ramble of four and twenty years. I was exceedingly satisfied with his management, for he had improved a very large plantation of his own at the same time; however, I had the mortification to see two or three of the Preston gentlemen there, who being prisoners of war, were spared from the public execution, and sent over to that slavery, which, to gentlemen, must be worse than death.

"During my stay here, I married a maid I brought over from England, who behaved herself for some time, extraordinary well, but at last played the fool, and died; and I not liking to stay long in a place where I was so much talked of, sent to one of my correspondents for a copy of the general free pardon then granted, and wherein it was manifest I was fully included.

"After I had settled my affairs, and left the same faithful steward, I again embarked for England, and, after a trading voyage, (for we touched at several places in our way,) I arrived safe, determining to spend the remainder of my life in my native country; for here I enjoy the moments which I had never before known how to employ, and endeavour to atone, as far as possible, for the vices of an ill-spent life.

"Perhaps when I wrote these things down, I did not foresee that the writings of our own stories would be so much the fashion in England or so agreeable to others to read, as I find custom, and the humour of the times, have caused them to be. If any one that reads my story pleases to make the same just reflections which I ought to have made, he will reap the benefit of my misfortunes, perhaps, more than I have done myself. It is evident, by the long series of changes and turns which have appeared in the narrow compass of one private mean person's life, that the history of men's lives may be in many ways made useful and instructive to those who read them, if moral and religious improvement and reflections are made by those who write them."

CAPTAIN ZACHARY HOWARD.

HOWARD was a gentleman born and bred; he came to an estate in Gloucestershire, of fourteen hundred pounds per annum, just about the breaking out of the civil war in 1641; his father dying that year. A sincere love of loyalty inspiring him to fight for his king, he mortgaged his estate for twenty thousand pounds, with which he raised a troop of horse for the service of Charles the First, who gave him the command of them. He remained thus in the army till the republican party became conquerors; when he (with many other cavaliers) was obliged to retire into exile. He, however, returned to England, with King Charles the Second, on whom he attended at Worcester fight, where he performed wonders, and was even applauded by his Majesty. But, as it is well known, the Parliamentarians triumphed.

Howard remained in England; but having lost his estate, and being out of all employment, he could devise no other way of supporting himself, than by robbing on the highway: a very precarious method indeed; but what many great gentlemen in those days were either obliged to adopt, or to want sustenance.

It is said of Howard, that when he resolved on this course of life, he swore, like others of his contemporaries, that he would be revenged, as far as lay in his power, of all persons who were against the interests of his royal master. Accordingly, he attacked all whom he met, and knew to be of that party.

The first of whom he thus assaulted was the Earl of Essex, who had been general in chief of the Parliament's forces. His lordship was riding over Bagshot Heath, with five or six in retinue; nevertheless, Zachary made boldly up to the coach-door, commanded the driver to stand, and my lord to deliver; adding,—that if he did not comply with his demand without ceremony, neither he nor any of his servants, should be spared. It is unaccountable, how a general always used to success, and having so many attendants, should be terrified at the menaces of a single highwayman. But so it was; and his honour gave him twelve hundred pounds, which he had in the coach, and which had been squeezed out of forfeited estates, church lands, and sequestrations; being unwilling to venture his life for such a trifle, at a time when the party had such a plentiful harvest to reap. Zachary was so well contented with this booty, that he let this nobleman pass on, with desiring him to get such another sum ready against the next convenient meeting.

Another time he overtook, on Newmarket Heath, the Earl of Pomfret, so famous for his ludicrous speeches in the House of Commons, attended by only one footman. Zachary held his lordship in discourse for about half a mile; when, coming to a convenient place, he pulled out a pistol, and, with a volley of oaths, ordered him to surrender that minute. "You seem," says the Earl, "by your swearing, to be a ranting cavalier: have you taken a lease of your life, sir, that you dare venture it thus against two men?" Howard answered, "I would venture it against two more, with your idol Cromwell, at their head." "Oh," says Pomfret, "he is a precious man, and has fought the Lord's battles with success!"—Zachary replied, by calling Oliver and all his crew, a company of dastardly cowards; putting his lordship in mind, also, that talking bred delays, and that delays were dangerous! "Therefore," says he, "out with your purse this moment, or I shall out with your soul—if you have any."

The earl, however, still delaying, Howard dismounted him, by shooting his horse, and then took from him a purse full of broad pieces of gold, and a rich diamond ring; then, making him mount behind his man, he tied them back to back, and in that condition left them.

Fairfax, who was also general of the Parliament army after Essex, being with some forces in Northumberlandshire, happened to take up his own quarters at Newcastle-upon-Tyne, at a time that Howard was at the same town. It came to the captain's ear, that Fairfax was about sending a man to his lady with some plate, which had been presented to him by the mayor and aldermen of that corporation; so that when the day came that the fellow set out with the prize, our highwayman also took leave of Newcastle, and rode after the roundhead servant. He overtook him on the road, and fell into deep discourse with him, about the present times, which Howard seemed as well pleased with as the other; who took him really for an honest fellow, as he seemed, and offered still to bear him company. They baited, dined, supped, and lay together, and so continued in this friendly manner till the messenger came within a day's journey of the seat where his lady resided. Next morning being the last day they were to be together, Howard thought it high time to execute his design, which he did with a great deal of difficulty. Being come to a proper place, Zachary pulled out his commission, and commanded the fellow to deliver the portmanteau, in which was the plate, to the value of two hundred and fifty pounds. The other being as resolute to preserve, as Howard was to take it from him, refused to comply; whereupon a sharp combat ensued, in which the Captain had his horse shot under him, after a discharge of two or three pistols on either side. The encounter still lasted: for our highwayman continued to fire on foot, till he shot his adversary through the head, which occasioned him to fall, and breathe his last in a moment.

When Howard saw the man dead, he thought it his best way to get off the ground as fast as possible; so nimbly mounting the horse which carried the treasure, he rode about five miles from the place where the fact was committed, and then deposited the portmanteau in a hollow tree, and tranquilly went to dinner at the next town. From thence he made the best of his way to Farringdon in Berkshire, where Madam Fairfax was, and whither the fellow he had killed was destined. He reached there that evening, and delivered the following letter to the lady, which he found in the pockets of the deceased:—

"Newcastle-upon-Tyne, Aug. 1650.

My dear,
    Hoping that you and my daughter Elizabeth are in good health, this comes to acquaint you that my presence is so agreeable to the inhabitants of this place, that their mayor and aldermen have presented me with a large quantity of plate, which I have sent to you by my man Thomas, a new servant; whom I would have you treat very kindly, he being recommended to me by several gentlemen, as a very honest, worthy man. The Lord be praised, I am very well, and earnestly long for the happiness of enjoying your company, which I hope to do within this month or five weeks at farthest. In the mean time, I subscribe myself,
    Your loving husband, till death,
        FAIRFAX."

The lady, learning by the contents, that a parcel of plate had been sent by the bearer, enquired of him where it was. Her supposed man readily told her that he was in danger of being robbed on such a heath, by suspicious persons; and therefore, lest he should meet with the same men again, or others like them, he had lodged his charge in the hands of a substantial inn-keeper, at such a town; from whence he could fetch it in two days. This affectation of carelessness pleased his new mistress very much, and confirmed the character which her husband had given him; so that she treated him tenderly, and desired he would go to bed betimes, that he might rest after the fatigue of travelling.

The whole family at this time consisted only of the lady, her daughter, two maids, and two men servants. No sooner were all these gone to repose, than Howard arose, dressed himself, and with sword and pistol in hand, went into the servants' apartments, whom he threatened with instant death if they made the least noise. He tied all four with the bed cords, and then gagged them. He next went to Mrs. Fairfax's chamber, and served her and her daughter as he had done the servants. Having committed these vile acts, and taken political revenge, he proceeded to make a strict scrutiny into the trunks, boxes, and chests of drawers; in all which he found two thousand broad pieces of gold, and some silver; when he rode off for his portmanteau in the tree, which he also found, and carried off.

Shortly after this, a proclamation was issued out by the Commonwealth, promising five hundred pounds to any one who should apprehend the offender; whereupon, to avoid being taken, Zachary fled into Ireland, where he pursued his former courses; till being grown as notorious there, as in England, he thought it advisable to return. He landed at Highlake; and came to the city of Chester, at a time that Oliver Cromwell lay there with a party of horse, and even put up at the same inn; where he passed for a gentleman going to travel into foreign countries for improvement.

He, moreover, counterfeited himself a Round-head, and frequently spoke against the royal family, highly applauding the murder of King Charles the First. By this means, he got familiar with Cromwell, who was so pleased with his conversation, that he would seldom dine or sup without this daring adventurer.

About a fortnight after this acquaintance between them had commenced, Howard went, one morning early, to pay old *Noll* (a nickname, bestowed at that period, on the Protector,) a visit in his bed-chamber, which happened to be on the same floor with his own. He found easy admittance; when Cromwell desired that he would join in prayers with him. Zachary most cheerfully consented; but no sooner was Cromwell on his marrow-bones, than he knocked him still lower with the butt-end of a pistol, presenting it afterwards to his breast, and swearing that, if he did but attempt to make the least noise, he would shoot him through the heart. though he were sure to be hanged for it the next minute on the landlord's signpost.

These terrifying words so panic-struck the republican, that he permitted his assaulter to do what he pleased; who, in good truth, gagged and bound him hand and foot; after which, he rifled two trunks, from whence he took about eleven hundred jacobusses; and then, to satisfy his burning revenge, took a well filled pan of water that stood in the room, and placed it topsy-turvy on the protector's head, saying—" As, no doubt, thou aspirest to be king, thus do I crown thee, tyrant as thou art!"

Having finished, he went hastily down stairs, and mounted his horse, which he had before ordered to be ready, under pretence of some urgent business a few miles out of town.

By this means Howard got clear off, before Oliver could make any body hear by his knocking.

At last, several of the family went up stairs, and were guided by the noise to the poor general, whom they found in the miserable pickle before described, and unable to stir. Some of them, at the first sight thought he had put on his head piece; till the water which ran down his face and shoulders, convinced them to the contrary, and induced them speedily to unbind him.

As soon as he was loose he fell on his knees, and gave thanks for so signal a deliverance from the fury of a wicked cavalier; for such he believed Howard.

Our Captain enjoyed his liberty but a very little time after this exploit; for venturing, one day, to attack half a-dozen republican officers together, as they were riding over Blackheath, he was overpowered; and, though he vigorously defended himself, so as to kill one, and wound two more, he was at last taken by the remaining three. These were soon assisted by several passengers, who joined in taking this bold robber before a magistrate; and he was forthwith committed to Maidstone gaol. Thither Oliver went to see and insult him; but to all which Howard replied with his usual bravery and wit, to the utter confusion of *Noll*.

On his trial at the ensuing assizes, evidences enough appeared to convict him, although he had possessed twenty lives. Not only the officers who took him, but even Cromwell, and General Fairfax's wife and daughter gave in their depositions, besides a vast number of others whom he had robbed. So that he was sentenced, for two murders, and numberless robberies, to be hung till he was dead.

At the place of execution, apparelled in white, he confessed himself guilty of everything laid to his charge; but declared he was sorry for nothing but the murders he had committed. Yet, even these, he said, appeared to him the less criminal, when he considered the persons on whom they were acted. He professed further, that if he was pardoned, and at liberty again, he would never leave off robbing the Round-heads, so long as there were any of them left in England.

What was the most remarkable at Howard's death, was, his smiling contemptuously on Oliver, who came into the country on purpose to see the last of him; saying, that, if he, Oliver, had met his reward, he had been in the same circumstances several years ago.

Howard made his final exit in 1651-2; being no more than thirty-two years of age.

NATHANIEL HAWES.

WE have this criminal's own authority for saying that he was the son of a rich grazier in Norfolk, who dying in his infancy, the child suffered the loss of a paternal inheritance, through the villainy of those who were entrusted as guardians. They, however, at proper age, apprenticed Nathaniel to an upholsterer, with whom he faithfully served the first four years: but at the end of that period, finding a relish in the pleasures of libertinism, he greatly increased his connexions with the vicious and the profligate of either sex: and this unfortunate arrangement it was that drove him to the fatal necessity of raising supplies beyond the limits of honour and honesty.

His master naturally became the first sufferer; nor was he discovered for a considerable time; till the largeness of his demands induced him to dip so very deeply, that an explanation was at length the unavoidable consequence. The shame and confusion which attended this serious eclaircissement was quickly obliterated in the haunts of licentiousness, whither he continued to repair, in spite of his master's admonitions, and in defiance of his positive orders to the contrary; for Nat, when all other opportunities were shut up, frequently arose, as soon as he conjectured that the family were asleep; and, unlocking the street door, repaired to his boon companions, with whom he usually continued till within an hour before the ascending sun silenced their nocturnal revels.

When vices of this kind obtain ascendancy over a young person, in the progressive stages from sixteen to three or four and twenty the consequences, without some fortunate intervention, are almost always of a melancholy nature. Persuasion, and particularly example, are the bane of rash and unguarded youth; who, after stifling the first pangs which obtrude at the loss of character and reputation, are incapable of seeing the turpitude of their transactions; transactions on which they had meditated with horror while the mind was unvitiated.

We have already said enough of Hawes to prepare our readers for the next event to be recorded in the sketch. Having now less access to his master's property, he perpetrated a street robbery: but was detected, and committed to prison, where he lay several months, previous to the Assizes; when he was found guilty: but, in compassion to his youth, the Judge humanely granted him a pardon.

It does not appear whether his master, or his guardians, exerted their efforts, at this critical period, to bring about a change of principle: but, for the sake of humanity, let us suppose that neither the one nor the other were, in this respect, deficient. Certain however it is, that Nathaniel most grossly abused the lenity which he had received from the Court, by almost instantly returning to his old companions and to his old vices —Drinking, gaming, and the society of abandoned women, forming the whole routine of their happiness; if that can be called happiness which produces pain, vexation, disappointment, and disease; to say nothing of those imminent dangers which attend the raising of supplies.

Young Hawes was naturally vivacious, sprightly, and daring; qualities which endeared him to the females, and rendered him useful to the other sex; with whom he now undertook several excursions on the road, for the purpose of supplying demands, whose magnitude would have perplexed less diligent *financiers*. Nathaniel's courage was often put severely to the test; and we must do him the justice to say, that, in this respect, he greatly excelled the stoutest of his coadjutors; who, unable to imitate, bestowed on him the most preposterous commendation. By such means he was easily prevailed upon to undertake any thing which they proposed, however badly devised, or dangerously planned: and the unfortunate youth, at length, became so ridiculously elate, that he but too often grossly abused and injured those whom he had so cruelly pilfered. 'This might probably arise,' says one of his predecessors, 'from his whimsical notions!' Led on by these whimsicalities, which doubtless comprehended an idea of invulnerability, Nathaniel Hawes hesitated not to attack singly a carriage filled with gentlemen, whether armed or not; to stop, at the same instant, two or three travellers on horseback; or to rummage the waggons in a successive line, as they passed the Oxford road towards London: and, though now and then apprehended, the county prisons were by no means strong enough to secure him till the day of trial. In proportion, however, as he transferred the theatre of spoliation nearer the metropolis, his dangers seem to have multiplied: for, being committed to New Prison, on suspicion of robbing a gentleman on the Hampstead road, he found that solemn receptacle constructed on different principles than those gaols which he had formerly eluded. Like an experienced General, he continued to reconnoitre, as long as hope or possibility remained: but, by a kind of sympathy, contracting an acquaintance with a female shop-lifter confined in the same place, that lady communicated to Nathaniel and another, a feasible project for procuring the invaluable blessings of liberty; and having, before commitment, hid under her stays a variety of necessary implements, they one night proceeded from theory to practice; when at two in the morning, those determined enemies of coercion bid adieu to the solitary environs of Clerkenwell.

Hawes, being in consequence reduced to a cutting state of poverty, committed a variety of depredations to supply the exigencies of the moment; and, by degrees, arriving again at the dignity of highwayman, he repaired to Finchley Common, and robbed one Richard Hall of four shillings and his horse. He was, however, shortly afterwards apprehended for this fact, and securely lodged in Newgate; where he affected the pomposity of a great man reduced by the vicissitudes of Madam Fortune; declaring he would conduct himself more nobly than any gentleman who had died at Tyburn within the last seven years! But this kind of incoherent expressions rather excited pity than admiration: it was vanity run mad with vengeance!

Nathaniel, when arraigned at the Old Bailey—in conformity to his heroic declarations,—refused to plead, because a good suit of clothes had been taken from him, by which means he could not cut a respectable figure in the Court. And though the Judge reproved him in a pathetic speech, and laid down the consequences of his refusal, our hero insultingly answered 'That, instead of justice, he was likely to receive injustice; but therefore doubted not that they would, some time or other undergo a heavier sentence than could be inflicted on him:—that, for his part, he looked on death with disdain; being determined to leave the world as courageously as he had lived in it!'

Nathan highly congratulated himself on this heroic effort; privately confessing to some Newgate friends, that he had complained of the loss of his clothes in order to seize on a pretence for shewing how excellently he merited the character of an intrepid hero, that Gentlemen of the Road, in succeeding ages, might pay the just tribute due to his memory. Under this very laudable impression, he actually sustained on his breast a weight of two hundred and fifty pounds upwards of seven minutes, all that time admiring what had been related of the indifference of a certain French lacquey, who danced a minuet just before he expired on the wheel! a circumstance which excited universal astonishment in France, and stimulated the Duc de Rochfoucault, though very ridiculously, to make a comparison between that criminal and the Roman Patriot Cato!

Hawes, when seven minutes had expired, fearing that a longer perseverance would rob him of that popularity which he expected to derive at the gallows, consented to plead; when the weight was accordingly removed : but the inward bruises which resulted, gave him such excessive pain, that Nathan, in some sort, laid that

greatness aside which he purposed to be observed. He nevertheless, heard his sentence pronounced with firmness; confessed,
afterwards, some of the numerous villanies committed by him;
particularly two or three in which innocent persons were implicated:
attended the Chapel devotions, contrary to general expectation;
and made exit at Tyburn in September 1721, when scarcely twenty
years of age!—Let us drop the tear of pity on his fate; and
leave the reader of feeling to make his own comments on the depravity of human nature, and the high degree of weakness and
vitiation which it is possible for the mind of mortals to obtain!

TOM ROWLAND AND FRANK OSBORN.

THE first of these notorious malefactors was born at Ware, in
Hertfordshire, and, by his parents, was put an apprentice to a
bricklayer; but after he had served his time, being of a slothful
and idle disposition, he kept such company as soon brought him to
follow evil courses; and to support his extravagancy in a most
riotous way of living, he stole a horse out of the Duke of Beau-
fort's stables, at his seat at Badminton, in Gloucestershire; and
then going on the highway, he committed several most notorious
robberies for above 18 years; but he always robbed in woman's
apparel, which disguise was the means of his reigning so long in
his villainy. Whenever he was pursued, he then rid astride; but
at last being apprehended in this unlawful habit, for robbing a
person on Hounslow-heath, of a quantity of bone-lace, to the
value of 1,200*l.* sterling, he was condemned for this fact, and found
guilty also upon another indictment preferred against him for robbing another person, near Barnet, of eighty-four pounds nine shillings. He was executed at Tyburn, on Friday, the 24th of October,
1699, aged 40 years.

At the same place, were hanged Mercy Harvey, for murdering
her bastard male child, by cutting it into very small pieces:
Anne Henderson, a Scotch woman, for stealing a silver tankard;
Bryant Cane, for felony and burglary, in breaking open the house
of Mr. Baker, at Mary-le-bone, and robbing it, and gagging him
and all the servants in his family; John Dowbridge, a butcher, for
stealing a mare; Jane Eaton, aged nineteen, and Catherine Jones,
for breaking the house of one John Prescot, and stealing from

thence goods of great value. The following persons, viz.—Peter Vallard, a Frenchman, Thomas Rogers, and Thomas Castle, *alias* Cassey, were drawn on a sledge to Tyburn, were the two first were hanged and quartered for clipping and coining; but the other criminal, the night before his execution, so far obtained their majesty's clemency, as to be but only hanged.

Frank Osborn was born of very good friends at Colchester, in Essex, who putting him apprentice to a goldsmith in Lombard-street, in London, he very truly and honestly served out his apprenticeship, and then set up his trade himself in Cannon-street, in the City, where he followed it for seven years; but he had not been his own master above two years, when getting into very loose company, who all bred him to drunkenness and gaming, he ran very much behind hand, and contracted several debts; which coming thick upon him, to make his creditors easy he went on the highway; and meeting once with the Earl of Albemarle in his coach and six horses, between Harwich and Manningtree, in the county of Essex, with four footmen and two gentlemen on horseback to attend him, besides the coachman and postillion, he attempted, with only one person more, to rob his lordship. So, whilst his comrade stopped the coach-horses, he rode up to his lordship, and demanded his money. The attendants seeing the insolence of these bold robbers, who being but two, they thought it would seem a great piece of cowardice if they did not engage them; whereupon one of the gentlemen firing first, all the rest began, even the very coachman and postillion too, who had pistols in their pockets. Now the shot flying about the highwaymen's ears very thick, whilst the earl also discharged a blunderbuss out of his coach, but without doing any execution, they also fired as fast as they could, but with better aim and better success: for in discharging of about eight pistols, they shot both the horses of the two gentlemen dead, wounded two of the footmen very desperately, and the postillion, with the forehorse on which he rode. Then riding up to the earl again, they grossly abused him with ill language, and threatened to shoot him through the head unless he presently delivered what he had, he gave them a purse, in which was 130 guineas, a gold watch, a diamond ring, a pair of diamond buckles, and a gold snuff-box. But whilst they were rifling a trunk that was tied on the coach-box, six or seven officers of the army rode up towards them, when Frank Osborn and his comrade made the best of their way off; but when those gentlemen came up with the Earl of Albemarle, and were informed of the robbery, they made such close pursuit after the robbers that they were forced to ride into Manningtree river, in which one of them was drowned, and also his horse; but Frank swam safe over into the county of Suffolk, and went straight to London without any discovery.

Another time Frank Osborn meeting with the late Duke of Newcastle, when his grace was but Earl of Clare, on the road to Nottingham, riding up to his coach, and most courteously pulling off his hat, quoth he, " My lord, having heard from several creditable persons, what a charitable peer your honour is, in distributing your generous alms among decayed gentlemen; and it being my misfortune, through many losses and crosses in the world, to be reduced to a state poorer than even Job was in his greatest calamity, I humbly make bold to implore your lordship's benevolence, for which I shall be ever grateful the longest day I have to live." Now, this nobleman being not to be tongue-padded out of his money, he in a very angry mood said to Frank, "Prithee, fellow, don't stand talking to me of charitable alms and benevolence, for I know not what you mean by those canting words; therefore, go about your business, for, indeed, I have nothing at all for myself scarce, and much less for beggars." Quoth Frank again, " I am not, Sir, such a mean sort of a beggar as your lordship perhaps may take me to be; for what people will not give me by fair means, I always take away by foul ones." So pulling out a pistol, and presenting it to his lordship's breast, he farther said, " unless your lordship presently deliver your money, expect nothing but present death, for I will certainly shoot you through the body upon the very least refusal." So taking four hundred pounds out of his coach and wishing his lordship a good journey, he rode away with his booty.

He reigned about five years in this villainous practice, without the least mistrust among his neighbours, who took him for a very honest man, because he carried himself with the greatest circumspection imaginable; but at last he and three other highwaymen, setting upon a nobleman on Hounslow-heath, who had a great retinue with him, they made such an obstinate and resolute resistance against them, that they took Frank Osborn; but his other accomplices made their escape, whom he would never discover to the very last gasp. Being committed to Newgate, and condemned for this attempt, whilst he lay under sentence of death, he shewed not much penitence for the wicked courses he had took, but would often say, that he was very sorry that he had disgraced so good and ingenious a profession as his was; and on Friday the 12th of September, 1690, he was executed at Tyburn, aged 29 years. Also on the same day were executed with him William Goff, a trooper, who served the late King James and King William, for robbing on the highway; Thomas Yarrold, a husbandman, born at Ampthill-town, in Bedfordshire, for stealing a gelding; John Daynter, a shoe-maker, for breaking into the house of Mr. Yates, and stealing thence a silver tankard, a dozen of silver spoons, and twenty-one pounds in money; and James Smith, for robbing a gentleman on the highway of twenty-eight guineas and two gold rings. When he was tied up in order to receive the sentence of death, he exceedingly misbehaved himself in court, by calling the Judges, the Lord-Mayor, and Recorder, most opprobious names, and swearing propnane oaths, in which wicked obstinancy he continued till he was hanged.

JAMES WHITNEY.

In general, the biographers of rogues and vagabonds give their heroes a title to wit and ingenuity very far beyond the abilities of the scoundrels they record; to this, in a great measure, is owing the difficulty of finding out, and appreciating as they merit, genuine anecdotes of the characters delineated. If any man becomes distinguished by crime, a hundred stories are immediately put in circulation, attributing matters to his invention, to which he was not only incompetent, but absolutely a stranger to the very circumstances related.

One of this description appears to have been James Whitney, who, in addition to his own depredations, has the credit of many he never probably committed. He was born at Stevenage, in Hertfordshire, and, when fit for servitude, was apprenticed to a butcher, with whom he continued until the expiration of his time; but no sooner did he become his own master, than he gave way to a very irregular course of life.

Going with another butcher to Romford, in Essex, in order to buy calves, they met with one they had a particular fancy to; but the owner demanded what they thought an extravagant price for it, so that they could not strike a bargain; however, as the man kept a public-house, our companions agreed to go in and drink with him. They were much vexed at not being able to purchase the calf, when

Page 168.

Whitney suddenly proposed the stealing of it, to which the other consenting, they sat drinking till night.

In the evening, a fellow came into the town with a great she-bear, which he carried about for a show, and put up at the house where the two butchers were drinking in an inner room; the landlord was some time before he could contrive where to lodge the bear, but at last he resolved to move the calf into another out-house, and tie madam Bruin up in his place, which was done accordingly, without the knowledge of Whitney and his friend, who continued drinking till they were told it was time to go to bed. Upon this warning they paid their reckoning, and went out, staying in the fields near the town till they imagined the time favoured their design. The night was very dark, and they came to the stall without making any noise or disturbance; Whitney was to go in and fetch out the calf, while the other watched without; when he entered he felt about, till he got hold of the bear, which lying after the sluggish manner peculiar to those creatures, he began to tickle it to make it rise; at last, being awaked, the beast being muzzled, rose up on her hind legs, not knowing but it was her master going to show her; Whitney still continued feeling about, wondering at the length of the calf's hair, and that he should stand in such a posture, till the bear cau ht hold of him and hugged him fast between her fore-feet.

In this posture he remained, unable to remove, and afraid to cry out, till the other butcher, wondering at his long stay, put his head in at the door, and said, with a low voice, " What the plague, will you be all night stealing a calf!" " A calf!" quoth Whitney, " I believe it is the devil that I am going to steal, for he hugs me as closely as he does the witch in the statue." " Let it be the devil," says t'other; " bring him out, however, that we may see what he is like, which is something I should be very glad to know." Whitney was too much surprised to be pleased with the jesting of his companion, so that he replied with some choler, " Come and fetch him yourself, for may I be d——d if I half like him." Hereupon the other entered, and, after a little examination, found how they were bit. By his assistance Whitney got loose, and they both swore they would never attempt to steal calves any more.

Whitney, after this, took the George Inn, at Cheshunt, in Hertfordshire, where, for a time, he entertained all sorts of bad company; but this speculation not answering, in a little time he was compelled to shut up his house, and retreat to London, where he began to practice every sort of fraud and villainy. It was some time before he took to the highway, following only the common tricks practised by the sharpers of the town, in which he was the more successful, as he always went dressed like a gentleman.

One morning, as Whitney stood on Ludgate-hill, at a mercer's door, waiting for a friend whom he expected to come by, two ladies of the town came along; these ladies took our gentleman for the master of the shop, and supposing he would be an easy dupe, asked him if he had any fine silks of the newest fashion; Whitney readily replied, " that he had none by him at present he could recommend; but, in a day or two's time, he should have choice, several weavers being to bring him in pieces, made from the last fashions brought up, and begged to know where he might have the honour to wait on them with samples," to which one of the ladies replied, " that being newly come to town, they did not remember the name of the street; but it was not far off, and if he pleased to go with them, they would show him their habitation." Whitney politely consented, and, to make the affair appear with a better face, he stepped into the shop, as if he went to give orders to the shopman, to whom he only put a few trifling questions, and came out again unsuspected. Having accompanied the ladies home, he very civilly offered to take his leave of them. " Nay, Sir," says one of them, " but you shall walk in and take a glass of wine with us, since you have been so good as to give yourself all this trouble." Whitney thanked them, and, with abundance of complaisance, accepted the invitation.

Hitherto both parties were deceived; Whitney really took them for gentlewomen of fortune, and came home with them only to learn something that might forward him to make a prey of them; and they as confidently believed him to be the mercer, who owned the shop at which they picked him up. Their designs were to get his money out of his pocket, and, if they could, a suit or two of silk into the bargain. What confirmed them in this opinion was, the notice he took of several gentlemen as he passed along the street, by pulling off his hat to them, and their returning the compliment.—Whitney did it for this very purpose, and it is natural and common for men of fashion to return the salutation of those who notice them.

The ladies introduced the supposed mercer into an apartment splendidly furnished, where the table was instantly spread with a fine cold collation. This being over, the servant and one of the ladies withdrew, leaving the other alone with our adventurer, who soon discovered the drift of her ladyship; but, willing to keep on the mask, after many amorous professions, promised her as much silk as would make her a complete dress.

Whitney was so well pleased with his adventure and reception at this place, that he was resolved, if possible, to have a little more enjoyment, and to that end went to a mercer, and told him, that such a lady had sent him, to desire that he would send one of his men with two or three pieces of the richest silk he had, for her to choose a gown and petticoat. The mercer knowing the person of quality he named, she having been his customer before, and without mistrusting any thing, sent a youth, who was but newly come apprentice, telling him the prices in Whitney's hearing. Our adventurer led the lad through as many bye-streets as he could, in order to carry him out of his knowledge, till observing a house in Suffolk-street, which had a thoroughfare into Hedge-lane, he desired the young man to stay at the door, while he carried in the silks to shew them to the lady, who lodged there; the youth very readily agreed, and Whitney went into the house, and asked the people for somebody whom they did not know; and, upon their telling him no such person lived in that neighbourhood, he desired leave to go through, which was granted, and he got clear off with his prize, which he immediately carried to his two ladies, and divided between them. After which, he revelled with them in all manner of excess for several days, and then withdrew himself.

He was resolved, however, that nobody but himself should enjoy the fruit of his industry, and since he could not have the profit of his cheat, he thought proper to restore the mercer his goods again. He therefore wrote a letter as to where the women lived, and the shop-keeper, getting a warrant and constable, went and found the silks in their possession; all the excuse they could make, as to receiving them from the real owner, availed nothing; they were hurried before a magistrate, who committed them to Tothill-fields Bridewell, where their backs were covered with stripes of the cat-and-nine-tails, instead of the eleemosynary silks, which they made so sure of.

Whitney had now become a confirmed highwayman, and meeting a gentleman on Bagshot-heath, he commanded him to stand and deliver, to which the other replied, " Sir, 'tis well you spoke first; for I was just going to say the same thing to you." " Why, are you a gentleman thief then?" quoth Whitney. " Yes," said the stranger, " but I have had very bad success to-day." Whitney upon this wished him better luck, and took his leave, really supposing him to be what he pretended. At night it was the fortune of Whitney and this person to put up at the same inn, when our gentleman told some other travellers by what stratagem he had escaped being robbed on the road. Whitney had so altered his habit and speech, that the gentleman did not know him again; so that he heard all the story without being taken any notice of. Among other things, he heard him tell one of the company softly, that he had saved an hundred pounds by his contrivance. The person to whom he had whispered this, was going the same way the next morning, and said, he had also a considerable sum about him, and, if he pleased, should be glad to travel with him for security.

When morning came, the travellers set out, and Whitney about a quarter of an hour after them; all the discourse of the gentlemen was about cheating the highwayman, if they should meet any. When Whitney, at a convenient place, had got before them and bid them stand, the gentleman whom he met before not knowing him, he having disguised himself after another manner, briskly cried out, " We were going to say the same to you, Sir." " Were you so?" quoth Whitney, " and are you of my profession then?" " Yes," said they both, " If you are," replied Whitney, " I suppose you remember the old proverb, two of a trade can never agree, so that you must not expect any favour on that score. But to be plain, gentlemen, the trick will do no longer; I know you very well, and must have your hundred pounds, Sir; and your considerable sum, Sir," turning to the other, " let it be what it will, or I shall make bold to send a brace of bullets through each of your heads. You, Mr. Highwayman, should have kept your secret a little longer, and not have boasted so soon of having outwitted a thief; there is now nothing for you to do, but deliver or die!"

These terrible words put them both into a sad consternation: they were loth to lose their money, but more loth to lose their lives: so of two evils they chose the least, the tell-tale coxcomb disbursing his hundred pounds, and the other a somewhat larger sum, professing that they would be careful for the future not to count without their host.

Another time, Whitney met with one Mr. Hull, an old usurer, in the Strand, as he was riding across Hounslow-heath. He could hardly have chosen a wretch more in love with money; and, consequently, who would have been more unwilling to have parted with it. When the dreadful words were spoken, he trembled like a paralytic, and fell to expostulating the case in the most moving expressions he was master of, professing that he was a very poor man, had a large family of children, and should be utterly ruined, if he was so hard-hearted as to take his money from him. He added, moreover, the illegality of such an action, and how very dangerous it was to engage in such evil courses. Whitney, who knew him, cried out in a great passion: " Sirrah, do you pretend to preach morality to an honester man than yourself; you who make a prey of all mankind, and grind to death with eight and ten per cent. This once. however, Sir, I shall oblige you to lend me what you have without bond, consequently without interest; so make no more words."

Old Hull, hereupon, pulled out about eighteen guineas, which he gave with a great deal of grumbling; telling him withal, that he should see him one time or another ride up Holborn-hill backwards. Whitney was going about his business till he heard these words, when he returned, and pulled the old gentleman off his horse, putting him on again with his face towards the horse's tail, and tying his legs; " Now," says he, " you old rogue, let me see what a figure a man makes when he rides backwards, and let me have the pleasure, at least of beholding you first in that posture." So giving the horse three or four good cuts with his whip, he set him a running so fast, that he never stopt till he came to Hounslow town, where the people loosed our gentleman, after they had made themselves a little merry with the sight.

Whitney always affected to appear generous and noble; meeting one day with a gentleman on Newmarket-heath, whose name was Long, and having robbed him of a hundred pounds in silver, which was in his portmanteau, tied up in a great bag, the gentleman told him, that he had a great way to go, and, as he was unknown upon the road, should meet with many difficulties, if he did not restore as much as would bear his expences. Whitney opened the mouth of the bag, and holding it to Mr. Long, " Here," says he, " take what you have occasion for." Mr. Long put in his hand, and took out as much as he could hold: to which Whitney made no opposition, but only said with a smile, " I thought you would have had more conscience, Sir."

Coming once to Doncaster, he put up at the Red Lion Inn, and made a great figure, having a pretty round sum in his possession. While he resided here, he was informed that the landlord of the house was reputed rich, but withal so covetous, that he would do nothing to help a poor relation or neighbour in distress. On this Whitney set his wits to work, and gave out that he had a good estate, and travelled about the country merely for his pleasure, and so artfully insinuated himself into the good opinion of his host, that he ran most plentifully into his debt, both for his own accommodation, and the keep of his horse.

It happened that while he remained here, there was an annual fair held; upon the fair-day, in the morning, a small box, carefully sealed, and very weighty, came directed to him. He opened it, took out a letter, which he read, and locked it up, and gave it to his landlady, desiring her to keep it in her custody for the present, because it would be safer than in his own hands, and ordered the landlord, at the same time, to write out his bill, that he might pay him the next morning; as soon as he had done this, he went out, as though to see the fair. In the afternoon he came home again, in a great hurry, and desired his horse might be dressed and saddled, he having a mind to show him in the fair, and, if he could, to exchange him for one he had seen, and which he thought was the finest that ever he fixed his eyes on. " I will have him," says he, "if possible, whether the owner will buy mine or not, although he cost me forty guineas;" he then asked for his landlady to help him to his box, but she was gone to the fair; whereupon he fell a swearing like a madman, that he supposed she had locked up what he gave her, and taken the keys with her; "If she has," quoth he, " I had rather have given ten guineas, for I have no money at all, but what is in your possession." Enquiry was made, and it was found to be as he said, which put him into a still greater passion, though it was what he wished for, and even expected, the whole having been invented for the sake of this single scene.

The landlord quickly had notice of our gentleman's anger, and the occasion of it; upon which he comes to him, and begs of him to be easy, offering to lend him the sum he wanted, till his wife came home. Whitney seemed to resent it highly, that he must be obliged to borrow money when he had so much of his own; however, as there was no other way, he condescended, with abundance of reluctance, to accept the proposal; adding, that he desired an account of all he was indebted as soon as possible, as it was not his custom to run hand over head.

Having received forty guineas, the sum he pretended to want, he mounted his horse, and rode towards the fair, but instead of dealing there for another horse, he spurred his own through the crowd, as fast as he could conveniently, and made the best of his way towards London. At night the people of the inn sat up very late for his coming home, nor did they suspect any thing the first, or even the second night, but at the end of two or three days the landlord was a little uneasy; and, after he had waited a week to no purpose, it came into his head to break open the box, in order to examine it. With this view he went to the magistrate of the place, procured his warrant, and, in presence of a constable and other witnesses, broke open the casket, and was ready to hang himself when he found the contents to be nothing but sand and stones.

This was, however, the last of Whitney's adventures, for not long after his arrival in town he was apprehended in White Friars, upon the information of Mother Cozens, who kept a notorious house in Milford-lane, over against St. Clement's Church. The magistrate, who took the information, committed him to Newgate, where he remained till the next sessions at the Old Bailey. Being brought to trial, and found guilty, the Recorder passed sentence of death on him, and exhorted him to a sincere repentance, as it was impossible for him to hope for a reprieve, after such a course of villainies: and, on Wednesday, the 19th of December, 1694, he was carried to the place of execution, which was at Porter's Block, near Smithfield, where he addressed the people in the following words:—

" I have been a very great offender, both against God and my Country, by transgressing all laws, human and divine. I believe there is not one here present, but has often heard my name, before my confinement, and have seen a large catalogue of my crimes, which has been made public since;—why should I then pretend to vindicate a life stained with so many enormous deeds?—The sentence passed on me is just, and I can see the footsteps of a providence, which I had before profanely laughed at, in my apprehension and conviction. I hope the sense which I have of these things has enabled me to make my peace with heaven, the only thing that is now of any concern to me. Join in your prayers with me, my dear countrymen, that God would not forsake me in my last moments." Having spoke thus, and afterwards spent a few moments in private devotion, he was turned off, being about thirty-four years of age.

A portrait of this celebrated highwayman, seated in prison, engraved at the time, is now become extremely rare and valuable. It has been copied in Caulfield's Memoirs of Remarkable Persons, Vol. I. page 57. From the portrait, he appears to have been a remarkably gentlemanly good looking young man.

THE WALTHAM BLACKS.

In the years 1722 and 1723, a singular set of beings, under the denomination of Waltham Blacks, annoyed the peace of society.

the laws, then, being inadequate to the punishment of these offenders. It originated from a partiality which some of the lower orders entertained for venison; an article which, as this banditti could not purchase, they resolved to obtain by force.

At length, these convivial societies so far increased, that the members scoured the country in armed troops, having their faces blackend by way of honorary distinction and also to terrify such game-keepers, and others, who would not civilly administer to their demands, whether for venison, wine, money, or any necessary that was calculated to increase the hilarity of their stated meetings.

Threatening letters were also dispatched to several individuals, who had shewed a reluctance to contribute towards the joys of the table. This grievance at length grew so intolerable, that the Legislature was constrained to frame an act particularly directed to the remedy of these abuses; and rendering the crime capital, which these gentry committed, without benefit of Clergy.

Several, and among them some apparently unfortunate persons, were in consequence apprehended; and among whom, the following suffered death.—Richard Parvin, master of a public-house at Portsmouth, who owned that he was on the King's Forest at the time stated in the indictment, but declared that his business there had no reference to deer-stealing; which, he said, he could have proved by witnesses, if his family had not been reduced to poverty, by the seizure and confiscation of all his goods and effects, when first taken into custody; in consequence of which he could not defray the expences of bringing persons from Berkshire.

He strenuously insisted on his innocence, even under the gallows; and eagerly directed his eyes in expectation of a reprieve, till the pressure of the rope extinguished his hopes and his life together. Edward Elliot, a youth about seventeen, and son of a tailor who resided near Guildford, was the next who suffered He said, in defence, that about a year preceding that time, thirty or forty men met and carried him away, in the county of Surrey, by force; one of them saying, he was enlisted into the service of the King of the Blacks, and that therefore he must disguise his face conformable to their custom; and obey orders of whatever kind, whether to rob and destroy fish-ponds, burn woods, or shoot deer. If he failed, or proved treacherous, they promised to convert him into a four-footed animal by their magic art.

During his continuance with this banditti, the boy said that he had witnessed several instances of their witchcraft; once, a particular, two men who had offended against the laws and manners, were covered up to their chins in earth, when a whole posse set on them like so many dogs, barking and bellowing in their ears in the most horrible strains: when, on promising not to offend the Black Nation again, they were at last liberated, having previously received some very salutary cautions.

Edward Elliot being out with a small deer-stealing party, at Farnham Holt, had wandered from his companions in pursuit of a fawn, when he was surprised, taken, and bound by the keepers, who then left him to pursue the others.

A smart action shortly commenced; in which a servant belonging to Lady Howe was shot, one of the plunderers wounded in the thigh, and two others taken. This miserable youth, who left a good place for so abandoned a course of life, died full of penitence and contrition.

Robert Kingsmill, taken in the fray just mentioned, was but twenty-six years of age; and was seduced from his parents' house the preceding night only by an acquaintance, after the family, and even himself, had retired to bed. An unlucky adventure, which terminated in his death.

Henry Marshall, about thirty-six years of age, was the person who shot the keeper; as related in the sketch of Edward Elliot. This fellow seemed to glory in his villainy; made light of his murderous conduct; and demanded to know, if he had not a right to stand on his own and companion's defence?

John and Edward Pink, carters in Portsmouth, were always accounted extremely honest, till they imbibed a predilection for venison. These brothers, like many of the rest, could not be persuaded that they had committed any wickedness in the eyes of God: deer being wild animals, they could not see by what equitable right the rich could claim an exclusive property in them!

James Ansell, the seventh and last of these unhappy wretches, was a villain by profession; and, in all likelihood, would have found his road to the gallows, if the Black Association had never been instituted. All of them, except this more hardened villain, were so much terrified at the prospect of death, and so greatly exhausted by sickness, that they were scarcely able to stand up, or speak, at the place of execution: some of the spectators even affirmed, that the life was departed ere Mr. Ketch proceeded to his melancholy office. It is highly probable, however, that these misguided, inconsiderate men were only—as a French poet says—

" Dead in fancy, from a *serious* fear."

The following letter, written by a Country Gentleman to his friend in London, at the time, and, as it were, on the spot, is the best elucidation of this singular event that can possibly be given to our Readers :—

'Amongst the odd accidents which you know have happened to me in the course of a very unsettled life, I don't know any which has been more extraordinary, or surprising, than one I met with in going down to my own house, when I left you last in town. You cannot but have heard of the Waltham Blacks, as they are called, a set of whimsical merry fellows, that are so mad to run the greatest hazards for the sake of a haunch of venison, and passing a jolly evening together. For my part, though the stories told of these people have reached my ears, yet I confess I took most of them for fables; and thought that, if there was truth in any of them, it was much exaggerated: but experience, (the mistress of fools) has taught me the contrary, by the adventure I am going to relate; which, though it ended well enough at last, I confess at first put me a good deal out of humour.

'To begin, then:—My horse got, some way, a stone in his foot, and therewith went so lame just as I entered the forest, that I really thought his shoulder slipped: finding it however, impossible to get him along, I was even glad to take up with a little blind ale-house, which I perceived had a yard and stable behind it. The man of the house received me very civilly, but when he perceived my horse was so lame, as scarcely to be able to stir a step, I observed he grew uneasy. I asked him whether I could lodge there that night; for I was resolved not to spoil a horse which cost me twenty guineas, by riding him in such a condition. The man made no answer; we went into the house together; when I proposed the same question to the wife. She dealt more roughly and freely with me; saying, that truly I neither could nor should stay there, and was for hurrying her husband to get my horse out; however, on putting a crown into her hand, and promising her another for my lodging, she began to consider a little; and, at last, told me that there was indeed a little bed above stairs, on which she would order a clean pair of sheets to be put; for she was persuaded I was more of a gentleman than to take any notice of what was passing there. This made me more uneasy than I was before. I concluded now that I had got into a den of highwaymen, and expected nothing less than to be robbed, and have my throat cut into the bargain; however, finding there was no remedy, I even sat myself down, and endeavoured to be as easy as I could. By this time ; oad become very dark; and I heard three or four horsemen alight and lead their horses into the yard.

'As tne men returned, and were coming into the room where I sat, I overheard my landlord exclaiming, ' Indeed, brother, you need not be uneasy; I am positive the gentleman's a man of honour!' To which I heard another voice reply, ' what good could our deaths do a stranger? Faith I don't apprehend half the danger that you do. I dare say the gentleman would be glad of our company, and we should be pleased with his. Come, hang fear! I'll lead the way.'

'So said, so done: in they came, five of them, all disguised so effectually, that I declare, unless it were in the same disguise, I should not be able to distinguish any one of them. Down they sat; and he, who I supposed was constituted their captain *pro hac vice*, accosted me with great civility, asking if I would honour them with my company to supper? I acknowledged I did not yet guess the profession of my new acquaintances; but supposing my landlord would be cautious of suffering either a robbery or a murder in his own house, I knew now how, but, by degrees, my mind grew perfectly easy.

'About ten o'clock, I heard a very great noise of horses, and soon after of men's feet trampling in a room over my head; then my landlord came down, and informed us, supper was just ready to go upon the table.

'Upon this, we were all desired to walk up; and he, whom I be fore called the Captain, presented me, with a humorous kind of ceremony, to a man more disguised than the rest, who sat at the upper end of the table; telling me, at the same time, he hoped I would not refuse to pay my respects to PRINCE OROONOKO, King of the Blacks! It then immediately struck into my head, who those worthy persons were, into whose company I had thus accidentally fallen. I called myself a thousand blockheads in my mind for not finding it out before; but the hurry of things, or to speak truth, the fear I was in, prevented my judging even from the most evident signs.

'As soon as this awkward ceremony had been ended, supper was brought in, which consisted of eighteen dishes of venison in every shape; roasted, boiled with broth, hashed collups, pasties, umble pies, and a large haunch in the middle, larded. The table we sat at was very large, and the company in all twenty-one persons: at each of our elbows there was set a bottle of claret; and the man and woman of the house sat down at the lower end. Two or three of the fellows had got natural voices, and so the evening was spent as merrily as the rakes past theirs at the King's Arms, or the City apprentices with their master's maids at Sadler's Wells.

"About two, the company seemed inclinable to break up, having first assured me that they should take my company as a favour any Thursday evening, if I came that way. I confess I did not sleep all night with reflecting on what had passed; and could not resolve with myself whether these humorous gentlemen in masquerade were to be ranked under the denomination of knights-errant, or plain robbers. This I must tell you, by the bye, that, with respect both to honesty and hardship, their life resembles much that of hussars, since drinking is all their delight, and plundering their employment.

"Before I conclude my epistle, it is fit I should inform you, that they did me the honour (with a design perhaps to have received me into their order) of acquainting me with those rules by which their society was governed. In the first place, the Black Prince assured me, 'that the government was perfectly monarchical; and that, when upon expeditions, he had an absolute command; but in the time of peace, (continued he) and at the table, government being no longer necessary, I condescend to eat and drink familiarly with my subjects as friends.

"We admit no man into our society, till he has been twice drunk among us, that we may be precisely acquainted with his temper, in compliance with the old proverb; 'Women, children, and drunken folks, speak truth!' but if the person who sues to be admitted, declares solemnly he was never drunk in his life, and it appears plainly to the society, in such case this rule is dispensed with, and the person before admission is only bound to converse with us a month.

"As soon as we have determined to admit him, he is then to equip himself with a good mare or gelding, a brace of pistols, and a gun of the size of this, to be on the saddle-bow; then he is sworn upon the horns over the chimney; and having a new name conferred by the society, is thereby entered upon the roll, and from that day forward, considered as a lawful member. I shall only remark one thing more, which is, the phrase we make use of in speaking of one another; viz. 'He is a very honest fellow, and one of us;' for you must know it is the first article in our creed, that there's no sin in deer-stealing.'

"In the morning, having given my landlady the crown piece, I found her temper so much altered for the better, that, in my conscience, I believe she was not in the humour to have refused me any thing, no, not even the last favour: and so walking down the yard, and finding my horse in pretty tolerable order, I speeded directly home, as much in amazement at the new people I had discovered, as the Duke of Alva's huntsmen when they found an undiscovered people in Spain, by following their master's hawk over the mountains."

It may, perhaps, be necessary to remark, that the evil was not wholly eradicated by the executions already related. Several young men, who were not in the least seduced by necessity, supported, for some few months afterwards at the expense of their lives, the character of this Black Society or Nation: more than one keeper was killed in various conflicts which took place; and several families were involved in ruin, by circumstances intimately connected with these very unhappy transactions.

TIMOTHY BUCKELEY.

Tim was reared to the useful occupation of a shoemaker, but leaving his master, he came to London, and soon found out companions suited to his disposition. He and his associates frequented an alehouse at Wapping; and one day being run short of cash, Tim asked the landlord for ten shillings, which he refused. Tim was so exasperated, that, along with some of his associates, he broke into his house, and bound him, his wife, and maid. Whilst Tim was about this operation, the landlord conjured him to be favourable. "No, no, you whose prodigality makes you lord it over the people here like a boatswain over a ship's crew, must not expect any favour from my hands; but I shall go to another part of the town, where I shall be more civilly used, and spend a little of your money there." Accordingly, Tim and his companions robbed the house of forty pounds, three silver tankards, a silver watch, and three gold rings.

Upon another day Tim was airing at Hyde-park-corner, and met with Dr. Catesby, the famous mountebank. At the words "Stand and deliver!" the doctor went into a long harangue about the honesty of his calling, and of the great difficulty with which he made a living. Tim laughed heartily, saying, "Quacks pretend to honesty! here is not such a pack of cheating knaves in the nation. Their impudence is intolerable for deceiving honest simple people, and pretending that more men were not slain at the battle of the Boyne, than they have recovered from death, or beckoned their souls back when they have been many leagues from their bodies; therefore, deliver! or this pistol shall put a stop to your further ramblings and deception." The doctor preferring his life to his gold, presented Tim with six guineas, and a watch, to show him how to keep time while spending the money.

Tim was once apprehended by a baker, in the character of a constable, and sent to Flanders as a soldier. He deserted, and returning to London, one day met the baker's wife. He presented a pistol, and demanded her money; she exclaimed, "Is this justice or conscience, sir!" "Don't tell me of justice, for I hate her as much as your husband can, because her scales are even! And as for conscience, I have as little of that as any baker in England, who cheats other people's bellies to fill his own!—Nay, a baker is a worse rogue than a tailor; for, whereas the latter commonly pinches his cabbage from the rich, the former, by making his bread too light, robs all without distinction, but chiefly the poor, for which he deserves hanging more than I, or any of my honest fraternity." Then, taking from her eleven shillings and two gold rings, he sent her home to relate her adventure to her husband.

Tim next stealing a good horse, commenced business upon the highway, and meeting with a pawnbroker by whom he lost some articles, he commanded him to stand and deliver. The pawnbroker entreated for favour, saying "that it was a very hard thing that honest people could not go about their lawful business without being robbed." "You talk of honesty, who live by fraud and oppression!—your shop, like the gates of hell is always open, in which you sit at the receipt of custom, and having got the spoils of the needy, you hang them up in rank and file, like so many trophies of victory. To your shop all sorts of garments resort, as on a pilgrimage. Thou art the treasurer of the Thieves' Exchequer, for which purpose you keep a private warehouse from whence you ship them off wholesale, or retail, according to pleasure. Nay, the poor and the oppressed have often to pay their own cloth, before they can receive them back by your exorbitant exactions. Come, come, blood-sucker, open your purse-strings, or this pistol shall send you where you are sure to go sooner or later." The poor pawnbroker ransomed his life at the expense of twenty-eight guineas, a gold watch, a silver box, and two gold rings.

Upon another occasion, Tim fortunately met with a stock-jobber (who had prosecuted him for felony,) and robbed him of forty-eight guineas. He requested something to carry him home. Tim refused, saying, "I have no charity for you stock-jobbers, who rise and fall like the ebbing and flowing of the tide, and whose paths are as unfathomable as the ocean. The grasshopper in the Royal Exchange is an emblem of your character. What give you something to carry you home out of the paltry sum of forty-eight guineas! I won't give you a farthing." He then bade him farewell until next meeting.

Though unexpected and unwished, it was not long before the stock-jobber reconnoitered Tim, and caused him to be apprehended and committed to Newgate. He was tried, and received sentence of death; but obtaining a reprieve, and afterwards a pardon, he was determined to be revenged of the man who would not give him rest to pursue his honest employment; he therefore set fire to a country-house belonging to him. To his no small chagrin, however, it was quenched before much harm was done.

Tim then went to Leicestershire, broke into a house, seized eighty pounds, purchased a horse, and renewed his former mode of life. Thus mounted he attacked a coach in which were three gentlemen, and two footmen attending. Tim's horse being shot under him, he killed one of the gentlemen and a footman, but being overpowered, was committed to Nottingham gaol, and suffered the due reward of murder and robbery, at the age of Twenty-nine, and in the year 1701.

THOMAS JONES.

Tom was a native of Newcastle-upon-Tyne, his father was a clothier, whose business he followed until he was two-and-twenty years of age. In that period, however, the prominent dispositions of his mind were displayed by extravagance, and running into debt. In order, therefore, to retrieve his circumstances, he went upon the highway.

Out of gratitude for his father's kindness, he commenced by robbing him of eighty pounds and a good horse. Unaccustomed to such work, he rode, under the impression that he was pursued, and in danger of being taken, no less than forty miles. Arriving in Staffordshire, he attacked and robbed the stage coach of a con-

siderable booty. During the scuffle, several shots were fired
the passengers, but no injury was done.

A monkey belonging to one of the passengers, being tied behind
the coach was so frightened with the firing, that he broke his chain
and ran for his life. At night, as a countryman was coming over
a gate, pug leaped out of the hedge upon his back, and clung very
fast. The poor man, who had never seen such an animal, imagined
that he was no less a person than the devil; and when he came
home, thundered at the door. His wife looked out at the window,
and asked him what he had got. " The devil!" cried he, and
entreated that she would go to the parson, and beg his assistance.
" Nay," quoth she, " you shall not bring the devil in here. If
you belong to him, I don't; so be content to go without my company." Poor Hob was obliged to wait at his door, until one of
his neighbours, wiser than the rest, came, and with a few apples
and pears, dispossessed him of the devil, and got him for his pains.
He accordingly carried him to the owner, and received a suitable
reward.

Tom's next adventure was with a Quaker, who formerly kept a
button shop, but, being reduced in his circumstances, he was going
down to the country, to avoid an arrest. In this situation he was
more afraid of a bailiff than a robber. Therefore, when Tom took
hold of him by the coat, broadbrim very gravely said, " At whose
suit dost thou detain me?"—" I detain thee on thy own suit, and
my demand is for all thy substance." The Quaker having discovered his mistake, added, " Truly, friend, I don't know thee,
nor can I indeed imagine that ever thee and I had any dealings
together."—" You shall find then," said Jones, " that we shall
deal together now." He then presented his pistol. " Pray, neighbour, use no violence, for if thou carriest me to gaol, I am
undone. I have fourteen guineas about me, and if that will satisfy
thee, thou art welcome to take them. Here they are, and give
me leave to assure thee, that I have frequently stopped the mouth
of a bailiff with a much less sum, and made him affirm to my
creditors that he could not find me." Jones received the money,
and replied, " Friend, I am not such a rogue as thou takest me to
be: I am no bailiff, but an honest generous highwayman."—" I
shall not trouble myself," cried the Quaker, " about the distinction
of names: if a man takes my money from me by force, it concerns
me but little what he calls himself, or what his pretences may be
for so doing."

At another time Tom met with Lord and Lady Wharton, and

Page 185.

though they had three men attending, demanded their charity in his usual style. His lordship said, " Do you know me, sir, that you dare be so bold to stop me upon the road ?"—" Not I; I neither know nor care who you are. I am apt to imagine that you are some great man, because you speak so big; but, be as great as you will, sir, I must have you to know, that there is no man upon the road so great as myself; therefore, pray be quick in answering my demands for delays may prove dangerous." Tom then received two hundred pounds, three diamond rings, and two gold watches.

Upon another day, Tom received intelligence that a gentleman was upon the road with a hundred pounds. He waited upon the top of the hill to welcome his approach. A steward of the gentleman discovered him, and suspecting his character, desired that the money might be given to him, and he would ride off with it, as the robber would not suspect him. This was done; Tom came forward, stopped the coach, and the gentleman gave him ten pounds. He was greatly enraged, and mentioned the sum that he knew the gentleman carried along with him. In an instant, however, suspecting the stratagem, he rode after the steward with all possible speed; but the latter observing him in pursuit, increased his pace and reached an inn before Tom could overtake him.

After many similar adventures, Tom was apprehended for robbing a farmer's wife. He was so habituated to vice, that nothing but the gallows could arrest his course, and in the forty-second year of his age, he met with that fate, on the 25th April, 1702.

ARTHUR CHAMBERS.

ARTHUR CHAMBERS was of low extraction, and destitute of every amiable quality. From his very infancy he was addicted to pilfering; and the low circumstances of his parents being unable to support his extravagances, he had recourse to dishonest practices. It is even reported, that before he was dressed in boy's clothes, he committed several acts of theft.

The first thing which he attempted, was to learn, from an experienced master, all those cant words and phrases current among pickpockets, by which they distinguished one another. Chambers was soon an adept in this new language; and being well dressed he was introduced to the better sort of company, and took occasion, when such opportunities offered, to rob his companions.

In a short time he was confined in Bridewell, to answer with hard labour for some small offence. Having obtained his liberty, he left the town, where he again began to be suspected, and went to Cornwall. His social turn gained him a reception in genteel companies, and he became a memorable character in the place. Before he left London, he provided himself with a large quantity of base crowns and half-crowns, which he uttered wherever he went. After many had been deceived, strict search was made, and Chambers detected. For this offence he was committed to gaol, where he remained a year and a half.

As he could no longer abide in Cornwall, he returned to London. Upon his arrival he went to an alehouse, and called for a pot of beer and a slice of bread and cheese. Having refreshed himself, he entered into conversation with some persons in a neighbouring box. The conversation turned upon the superior advantages of a country life, but was insensibly directed to that of robbery. Chambers, improving the hint, regretted that no better provision was made for suppressing such villainies; for added he, death is too scarce a punishment for a man even if he robbed the whole world. "But why do I talk thus?" he continued; "if great offenders are suffered, well may the poor and necessitous say, we must live, and where is the harm of taking a few guineas from those who can spare them, or who, perhaps, have robbed others of them? For my own part, I look upon a dexterous pickpocket as a very useful person, as he draws his resources from the purses of those who would spend their money in gaming, or worse. Look ye, gentlemen, I can pick a pocket as well as any man in Britain, and yet, though I say it, I am as honest as the best Englishman breathing. Observe that country gentleman passing by the window there, I will engage to rob him of his watch, though it is scarcely five o'clock.'

A wager of ten shillings was instantly taken, and Chambers hastened after the gentleman. He accosted him at the extremity of Long Lane, and pulling off his hat, asked him if he could inform him the nearest way to Knave's acre. The stranger replied, that he himself wished to know the way to Moorfields, which Chambers pointed out; and while the other kept his eyes fixed upon the places to which he directed him, he embraced an opportunity to rob him of his watch, and hastening back to the alehouse, threw down his plunder, and claimed the wager.

He next exerted his ingenuity upon a plain countryman, newly come to town. This rustic had got into the company of sharpers, and stood gazing at a gaming-table. Our adventurer stepping up, tapped him on the shoulder, and enquired what part of the country he came from, and if he was desirous to find a place as a gentleman's servant. Robin answered, that it was his very errand to town, to find such a place. Chambers then said, that he could fit him to a hair. " I believe I can afford you myself four pounds a-year standing wages, and six shillings a week board wages, and all cast clothes, which are none of the worst." This was sufficient to make Robin almost leap out of his skin, for never before had such an offer been made to him. Having arranged every thing to his wish, Robin entered upon his new service. He received Chambers' cloak, threw it over his arm, and followed his master. Chambers ordered a coach, and Robin being placed behind, they drove off to an inn. Dinner being ordered, Robin sat down with his master, and made a hearty meal, the former in the mean while instructing him in all the tricks of the town, and inculcating the necessity of his always being upon his guard. He informed him also, that the servants of the inn would be requesting him to join in play at cards, and that he was in danger of being imposed upon therefore, if he had any money upon him, it would be proper to give it to him, and he would receive it back when necessary Robin, accordingly, pulled out his purse, and delivered all that he had, with which Chambers paid his dinner, and went off, leaving Robin to shift for himself, and to lament the loss of his money and his new master.

The next adventure of Chambers was directed against the innkeeper of the Greyhound, St. Alban's. His wife was rather handsome, and exceedingly facetious; and Chambers being often there, was on terms of the greatest familiarity with the household. Directing his steps thither, and pretending to have been attacked by three men near the inn, he went in with his clothes all besmeared. The travellers who were in the inn condoled with him on his misfortune, and gave him a change of clothes until his own should be cleaned. To make amends to himself for this sad disaster, he invited six of his fellow-travellers, with the landlord and his wife, to supper. The glass circulated pretty freely, and the wife entertained them with several appropriate songs. Chambers was careful that her glass never remained long empty. In a short time he saw with pleasure that all his companions, with the solitary exception of the landlord, were sunk in the arms of sleep, and he proposed that they should be conveyed to bed; whereupon two or three stout fellows came to perform that office. Chambers was so obliging as to lend his assistance, but took care that their money and wate. should pay for his trouble.

Left alone with the landlord, he proposed that they should have an additional bottle. Another succeeded before the landlord was in a condition to be conveyed to rest. In aiding the servants with the corpulent innkeeper, he discovered the geography of his bedroom, and finding that the door was directly opposite to his own, he retired, not to rest, but to plot and perfect his villainy.

When he was convinced that the wine would work its full effect upon the deluded pair, he revisited the bedchamber, waited some time, and extracted what property he could most conveniently carry away; by the dawn of day dressed himself in the best suit of clothes which his bottle companions could afford, called for the horse of the person whose clothes he now wore, left two guineas with the waiter to pay his bill, gave half-a-crown to the ostler, and rode off for London.

His first enterprise after his arrival was attacking an Italian merchant upon the Exchange. He took him aside, eagerly enquired what goods he had to dispose of, and, entering into conversation, one of Chambers's accomplices approaching joined the conversation. Meanwhile, our adventurer found means to extract from his pocket a large purse of gold and his gold watch, which he delivered to his accomplice. Not satisfied with his first success, and observing a silk handkerchief, suspended from his pocket, he walked behind him to seize it, but was detected in the act, and kept fast hold of by the merchant, who cried out lustily, "Thief! thief!" In this dilemma, Chambers's accomplice ran to the crier, and requested him to give public proclamation, that if any body had lost a purse of gold, upon giving proper information it would be restored. With the expectation of finding his money again, the merchant let go his hold; and, in the crowd, Chambers and his friends retired with their booty.

But Chambers was now resolved to perform an action worthy of his talents. He hired the first-floor of a house, and agreed with the landlord for 14s. a week. Having, in the first instance, been mistaken for a man of fortune, both from his appearance and style of living, a mutual confidence was gradually established. When his plot was matured, he one day entered, with a very pensive and sorrowful look, the apartment of his landlord, who anxiously inquired the cause of his great uneasiness; when Chambers, with tears in his eyes, informed him, that he had just returned from Hampstead, where he had witnessed the death of a beloved brother who had left him his sole heir, with an express injunction to convey his dear remains to Westminster Abbey. He therefore entreated the favour of being allowed to bring his brother's remains at a certain hour to his house, that from thence they might be conveyed to the place of their destination, which very reasonable request was readily granted by his unsuspecting landlord.

Chambers went off the next morning, leaving word, that the corpse would be there at six o'clock in the evening. At the appointed hour, the hearse, with six horses, arrived at the door. An elegant coffin, with six gilded handles, was carried up-stairs, and placed upon the dining-room table, and the horses were conveyed by the men to a stable in the neighbourhood. They informed the landlord, that Chambers was detained on business, and would probably sleep that night in the Strand.

That artful rogue was, however, confined in the coffin, in which hair holes had been made, the screw-nails left unfixed, his clothes all on, with a winding-sheet wrapped over them, and his face blanched with flour. All the family were now gone to bed, except the maid-servant. Chambers arose from his confinement, went down stairs to the kitchen wrapped in his winding-sheet, sat down, and stared the maid in the face, who, overwhelmed with fear, cried out, "A ghost! a ghost?" and ran up-stairs to her master's room, who chid her unreasonable fears, and requested her to return to bed and compose herself. She, however, obstinately refused, and remained in the room.

In a short time, however, in stalked the stately ghost, took his seat, and conferred a complete sweat and a mortal fright upon all three who were present. Retiring from his station when he deemed it convenient, he continued, by the moving of the doors, and the noise raised through the house, to conceal his design: in the mean time, he went down stairs, opened the doors to his accomplices, who assisted him in carrying off the plate, and every thing which could be removed, not even sparing the kitchen utensils. The maid was the first to venture from her room in the morning, and to inform her master and mistress of what had happened, who, more than the night before, chid her credulity in believing that a ghost could rob a house, or carry away any article out of it. In a little time, however, the landlord was induced to rise from his bed, and to move down stairs, and found, to his astonishment and chagrin, that the whole of his plate, and almost the whole of his moveables, were gone, for which he had only received in return an empty coffin.

A great many other stories of the like nature are told of Chambers; and it is well known, that for the few years he was permitted, by singular good fortune, to go at large, he committed as many artful and daring actions as were ever accomplished by one man.

At length, however one Jack Hall, a chimney-sweeper, being apprehended, to save his own life, made himself an evidence against Chambers, who, being cast upon that information, was, with two other notorious offenders, executed at Tyburn, in 1703, in the twenty-eighth year of his age.

JOHN OVET.

JACK OVET was born at Nottingham, and, after serving an apprenticeship to a shoemaker, for some time, gained his bread by that industrious and useful employment: but his licentious disposition inclining him to profligate and abandoned company, he soon took to the highway.

After having purchased a horse, pistols, and every necessary utensil proper to his projected profession, he rode towards London, and on the way robbed a gentleman of 20*l*. That gentleman, however, not destitute of courage, and unwilling to part with his money, told Ovet, that if he had not taken him unawares, he would not so soon have plundered him of his property. The son of Crispin was not destitute of the essential qualifications of his new profession; he, therefore, replied, that he had already ventured his life for his 20*l*.; "But," continued he, " here's your money again, and whoever is the better man, let him win it and wear it." The proposal being agreed to, and both employing their swords, the gentleman fell, and Ovet had the money.

But having now stained his hands with blood, it was not long before he killed another man in a quarrel. He, however, escaped from justice, and continued his depredations. One day, being greatly in want of money, and meeting one Rogers with some pack-horses, he turned one of them off the way, opened the pack, and extracted about two hundred and eighty guineas, with three dozen of silver knives, forks, and spoons. Then, tying the horse to a tree, he made off with the spoil.

Another time, Jack Ovet, drinking at the Star Inn, in the Strand, overheard a soap-boiler contriving with a carrier how he should send 100*l.* to a friend in the country. At length, it was concluded upon to put the money into a barrel of soap; which project was mightily approved of by the carrier, who answered, " If any rogues should rob my waggon, (which they never did but once,) the devil must be in them if they look for any money in the soap-barrel. Accordingly, the money and soap were brought to the inn, and next morning, the carrier going out of town, Jack Ovet overtook him in the afternoon, and commanding him to stop, or otherwise he would shoot him and his horses too, he was obliged to obey the word of command. Then, cried the honest highwayman, " I must make bold to borrow a little money out of your waggon: therefore, if you have any, direct me to it, that I may not lose any time, which you know is always precious." The carrier told him, he had nothing but cumbersome goods in his waggon, that he knew of; however, if he would not believe him, he might search every box and bundle there, if he pleased.

Ovet soon got into the waggon, and threw all the boxes and bundles about, till, at last, he came to the soap-barrel, which feeling somewhat heavy, said he to the carrier, " What do you do with this nasty commodity in your waggon? I'll fling it away" So throwing it on the ground, the hoops burst, out flew the head, and the soap spreading abroad, the bag appeared: then jumping out of the waggon, and taking it up, said he again, " Is not he that sells this soap a cheating rascal, to put a bag of lead into it, to make the barrel weigh heavy? If I knew where he lived, I'd go and tell him my mind. However, that he may not succeed in his roguery, I'll take it and sell it at the next house I come to, for it will wet one's whistle to the tune of two or three shillings."

He was going to ride away, when the carrier cried after him, " Hold, hold, sir! that is not lead in the bag; it is a hundred pounds, for which (if you take it away) I must be accountable."

' No, no!" replied Jack Ovet, " this cannot be money; but if it is, tell the owner that I will be answerable for it if he will come to me." " Where, sir," said the carrier, " may one find you?" " Why, truly," replied Jack, " that is a question soon asked, but not so easily to be answered; the best direction I can give is, it is likely that you may find me in a gaol before night, and then perhaps, you may have again what I have taken from you, and forty pounds to boot "

Another time Jack Ovet, meeting with the Worcester stage-coach on the road, in which were several young ladies, he robbed them all; but one of them being a very handsome person, he was struck with admiration, and when he took her money from her, said, " Madam, cast not your eyes down, neither cover your face with those modest blushes; your charms have softened my temper, and I am no longer the man I was; what I have taken from you (through mere necessity at present) is only borrowed; for as no object on earth ever had such an effect on me as you, assure yourself, that, if you please to tell me where I may direct to you, I will, upon honour, make good your loss to the very utmost." The young lady told him where he might send to her; and then parting, it was not above a week after that Jack sent a letter to her who had gained such an absolute conquest over his soul that his mind ran now as much upon love as robbery.

Unfortunately, however, the sentimental attachment of our too susceptible highwayman was doomed to suffer a defeat; and still more unfortunately, he was quite as unsuccessful in his profession, for, committing a robbery in Leicestershire, where his comrade was killed in the attempt, he was closely pursued by the county, apprehended, and sent to gaol; and at the next Leicester assizes condemned. Whilst under sentence of death, he seemed to feel no remorse at all for his wickedness, nor in the least to repent o the blood of two persons, which he had shed. So being brought to the gallows, on Wednesday the fifth of May, 1708, he was justly hanged in the thirty-second year of his age.

CAPTAIN EVANS.

THE title of captain did not belong to our hero. He was a native of South Wales, and his father, who was an innkeeper gave him a good education, and bound him apprentice to an attorney. This business did not suit the natural bent of the Captain's temper, and having an opportunity of occasional conversation with the gentlemen of the road, he fell in love with their honourable profession.

It was not long before he became the most dexterous robber in those parts, and soon acquired considerable wealth. One day Evans was being conducted to Shrewsbury gaol under a strong guard, with his legs tied below his horse. One of his guards had

Page 190.

a fine fowling-piece, loaded, and Evans espying a pheasant perched upon a tree, with a deep sigh informed his comrades how dexterous he used to be in shooting at such a mark; and requested that he might be favoured with the piece, that he might show his skill in bringing down the bird. The simple fellow complied with his request; but no sooner was the captain in possession of the gun, than he turned upon his guards, and swore a volley of oaths that he would fire upon them if they moved a step farther. He then retreated to a convenient distance, and commanded one of them who was best mounted to come towards him, to alight from his horse, deliver up his pistols, and untie his legs. This being done, he mounted the fine gelding, leaving his small pony in his stead, and took leave of his guides.

Arriving in London, he, after some time, became clerk to Sir Edmund Andrews, governor of Guernsey, and continued in that station for three or four years. But the return of an annual salary was too dilatory for the patience of Evans; he, therefore, left that employment, and repairing to London assumed the character of a merchant or ship captain; and having dressed his younger brother in livery, employed him as his servant.

In this assumed character he committed several notorious robberies in the vicinity of London. But his most daring robbery was an attack upon Mr. Harvey of Essex in the day time. That gentleman was riding home from St. Paul's cathedral in his coach, when Evans commanded him to surrender, and took from him a diamond ring and a considerable sum of money.

Upon another occasion the captain encountered a writing-master and his wife, and imperiously demanded their money, which they obstinately refused. To punish their obstinacy he rifled them of what money they had; then upon pain of death commanded them to strip themselves, and tying them together, bound them to a tree, and left them in that situation.

In one of his rambles, accompanied by his brother accomplices, he attacked a member of Parliament on Bagshot Heath, riding in a coach and six with three other gentlemen; there were also four on horseback, well armed, besides three footmen, a coachman and postilion. Suspecting Evans and his companions to be robbers, they prepared to receive them, and several shots were exchanged with no other injury than shooting the horse upon which William, the captain's brother, rode. To save farther blood, Evans and the gentleman drew their swords, and engaged in single combat. Evans soon disarmed the squire, but gallantly returned his sword contenting himself with a good horse for his brother, and what money they chose to give him as a free donation. For this generous behaviour, that gentleman afterwards endeavoured to save Evans's life.

One day, the captain meeting Nugent, a bricklayer, whose bulk resembled that of a giant, our hero was at first alarmed; but approaching nearer, commanded him to stand and deliver, and thereupon searching his pockets, robbed him of a watch, and seventeen or eighteen shillings of money, which having converted to his own use, he went to seek a richer booty.

The following was one of the most remarkable of the adventures of Evans and his brother; upon the road to Portsmouth, they met a band of constables, conducting about thirty poor fellows whom they had impressed. Evans asked the reason why they were led like captives and tied together. The officers informed them that these men were for the king's service, and that they had ten shillings for each man. He highly commended them for doing their duty, and rode forward. At a convenient place, he and his brother attacked them with such fury, that they rescued the prisoners and stripped the officers of every shilling. Nor did this suffice, for they bound them neck and heels, and left them in an adjacent field.

At another time, the captain met with one Cornish, an informer upon Finchley Common. He saluted him in his usual phrase, "Stand and deliver, or you are a dead man!" Poor Cornish trembled like an aspen leaf, and begged that he would save his life, informing him, at the same time, that if he robbed him he was undone. "What a plague!" said Evans, "are you a Spaniard, that you carry all your money about you?" "No, sir," replied Cornish, "I am a poor honest man, as all my neighbours in St. Sepulchre's parish know, belonging to the Chamberlain." "Then what inn do you live at?" said Evans. "Perhaps you may do me a piece of service, by informing me of wealthy passengers lodging at your house, and if so, I shall generously reward you." "Sir," replied Cornish, "I belong to no chamberlain of inns, but to the Chamberlain of London, to whom I give information of persons setting up in the city who are not freemen; of apprentices not taking out their freedom when their time is expired; and other such matters as come under the cognizance of that officer." "What, you belong to the Chamberlain of London, then? I thought all this time that you had belonged to some inn, and so might have given me intelligence in my way of business; but as I find the contrary, I have no more time to lose with you; deliver, or you are a dead man!" Then searching the pockets of the informer, in which he only found fivepence, he was enraged that he had lost so much time for nothing. He vented, however, his chagrin and rage, by giving him a severe caning, and went in search of better prey.

Having received intelligence that the Chester coach was coming to London with passengers, Evans sent his brother Will to quarter at Barnet the previous night, and to be at Baldock Lane by a certain hour next morning. It happened that a cheesemonger, a Scotchman, was travelling to Edinburgh, and putting up at the same place, slept with Will all night, and, in the morning, under the pretence of business, Will went part of the road with his bedfellow. But when they came to Baldock Lane, the Scotchman was alarmed by a pistol discharged over Will's head, which was a signal agreed upon between the brothers. They then commanded the Scotchman to stand at a distance, while the two desperate brothers robbed the coach. Scarcely, however, was this done when the captain robbed the Scotchman of seven guineas and two watches. The younger brother however, interceeded in his behalf, and the best watch was delivered back, and three guineas to bear his expences upon the road. But it happened, that these two notorious robbers being apprehended, this man appeared in evidence against them, and they were condemned and executed in the year 1708; the one being twenty-nine, and the other twenty-three years of age.

THOMAS DORBEL.

This robber was bred a glover; but before he had served one half of his time, ran off from his master, and coming to London, soon became acquainted with men of dispositions similar to his own. About the age of seventeen, Tom ventured to appear upon the highway, but was outwitted in his first attempt.

Meeting a Welshman, he demanded Taffy's money, or he would take his life. The Welshman said, " Hur has no money of hur own, but has threescore pounds of hur master's money; but, Cot's blood! hur must not give hur master's money,—what would hur master then say for hur doing so?" Tom replied, " You must not put me off with your cant; for money I want, and money I will have, let it be whose it will, or expect to be shot through the head."

The Welshman then delivered the money, saying, " What hur gives you is none of hur own; and that hur master may not think hur has spent hur money, hur requests you to be so kind as to shoot some holes through hur coat-lappets, that hur master may see hur was robbed." So suspending his coat upon a tree, Tom fired his pistol through it, Taffy exclaiming, " Cots splatter a-nails! this is a pretty pounce; pray give hur another pounce for hur money!" Tom fired another shot through his coat. " By St. Davy, this is a better pounce than the other! pray give hur one pounce more!" —" I have never another pounce left," cried Tom. " Why then," replied the Welshman, " hur has one pounce left for hur, and if hur will not give hur hur money again, hur will pounce hur through hur body." Dorbel very reluctantly but quietly returned the money, and was thankful that he was allowed to depart.

But this narrow escape did not deter Dorbel, and he continued his villainies for the space of five years. It happened, however, that a gentleman's son was taken for robbing on the highway, and as he had been formerly pardoned, he now despaired of obtaining mercy a second time. Tom undertook, for the sum of five hundred pounds, to bring him off. The one half was paid in hand, and the other half was to be paid immediately the deliverance was effected. When the young gentleman came upon his trial, he was found guilty; but just as the judge was about to pass sentence, Tom cried out, " Oh! what a sad thing it is to shed innocent blood! Oh! what a sad thing it is to shed innocent blood!" And continuing to reiterate the expression, he was apprehended, and the judge interrogating him what he meant by such an expression, he said, " May it please your Lordship, it is a very hard thing for a man to die wrongfully; but one may see how hard-mouthed some people are, by the witnesses swearing that this gentleman now at the bar, robbed them on the highway at such a time, when indeed, my Lord, I was the person that committed that robbery."

Accordingly, Tom was taken into custody, and the young gentleman liberated. He was brought to trial at the following assizes; and being asked, whether he was guilty or not? he pleaded, not guilty! " Not guilty!" replied the judge, " why, did not you at the last assizes, when I was here, own yourself guilty of such a robbery!" " I don't know," said Tom, " how far I was guilty then, but upon my word, I am not guilty now; therefore, if any person can accuse me of committing such a robbery, I desire they may prove the same." No witness appearing, he was acquitted.

Tom living at such an extravagant rate in the prison, had scarcely any part of the five hundred pounds remaining when he obtained his liberty; therefore, endeavouring to recruit his funds, by robbing the Duke of Norfolk near Salisbury, his horse was shot, and he himself taken, and condemned at the next assizes. While under sentence, he found a lawyer who engaged, for the sum of fifty guineas, to obtain his pardon. He accordingly rode to London, was successful, and just arrived in time with the pardon, when Dorbel was about to be thrown off,—having rode so hard that his horse immediately dropted down dead. Such, however, was Tom's ingratitude, that he refused to pay the lawyer, alleging, that any obligation given by a man under sentence of death was not valid.

Dorbel was so much alarmed upon his narrow escape from a violent death, that he resolved to abandon the collecting trade, and obtained a situation in several families as a footman. He also served six or seven years with a lady in Ormond Street, who had a brother a merchant in Bristol, whose only daughter, a girl sixteen years of age, prevailed upon her father to allow her to come to London to perfect her education. Dorbel being a person in whom her aunt thought she could place unlimited confidence, was sent to convey the young lady to London. In the last stage he was left alone with her, when the miscreant first shockingly abused her, then robbed her of her gold watch, diamond ring, jewels to the amount of a hundred pounds, and cutting a hole in the back of the coach, escaped, leaving the young lady in a swoon. It was with difficulty she recovered, to inform her relations how she had been treated. Her mother hastened to town to see her, and after speaking a few words to her, the poor girl breathed her last. The disconsolate father soon after lost his senses.

Dorbel was pursued in different directions, and apprehended just after he hed robbed a gentleman of three pounds five shillings. He was tried, and condemned to be executed and hung in chains which well merited sentence was put in force against this hardened villain, on the 23rd of March, 1708.

DICK ADAMS

THE parents of this worthless fellow lived in Gloucestershire, and gave him an education suited to his station. Leaving the country, and coming to London, the abode of the most distinguished virtue as well as the most consummate villainy, he was introduced into the service of a great Duchess at St. James's, and stayed there for two years. He was at last dismissed for improper conduct; but while he remained there, he had obtained a general key which opened the lodgings in St. James's. Accordingly, he went to a mercer, and desired him to send, with all speed, a parcel of the best brocades, satins, and silks, for his Duchess, that she might select some for an approaching drawing-room. Having often gone, upon a similar errand, the mercer instantly complied. His servant,, and a porter to carry the parcels, accompanied Dick, and when arrived at the gate of some of the lodgings, he said, "Let's see the pieces at once, for my Duchess is just now at leisure to look at them. So receiving the parcel, he conveyed it down a back-stair, and went clear off. After waiting with great impatience for two or three hours, the porter and man returned home, much lighter than when they came out.

About a month after, one evening when Dick had been taking his glass pretty freely, he unfortunately came by the mercer's shop, while the mercer was standing at the door; the latter recollected and instantly seized him, saying, "Oh Sir, have I caught you! you are a fine spark indeed! to cheat me out of two hundred pounds worth of goods! but before I part with you, I shall make you pay dearly for them!" Adams was not a little surprised at being so unexpectedly taken; but instantly seeing the Bishop of London coming up in his carriage, he said to the mercer, "I must acknowledge that I have committed a crime to which I was forced by extreme necessity; but I see my uncle, the Bishop of London, coming this way in his coach; therefore, I hope that you will be so civil as not to raise any hubbub of a mob about me, by which I should be exposed and utterly undone: I'll go speak to his Lordship about the matter, if you please to step with me; and I'll engage he shall make you satisfaction for the damage I have done you."

The mercer, eager to receive his money, and deeming this proposal a better method than sending him to gaol, consented. Adams went boldly up, and desiring the coachman to stop, requested a few words of his Lordship. Seeing him in the dress of a gentleman, he was pleased to listen to him, upon which Adams said, "Begging your lordship's pardon for my presumption, I make bold to acquaint your Reverence that the gentleman standing behind me is an eminent mercer, keeping house hard by, and is a very upright, Godly man; but being a great reader of books of divinity, especially polemical pieces, he has met therein with some intricate cases, which very much trouble him, and his conscience cannot be at rest until his doubts and scruples are cleared about them; I humbly beg, therefore, that your Lordship would vouchsafe him the honour of giving him some ease before he runs utterly to despair."

The Bishop, always ready to assist any person troubled with scruples of conscience, requested Adams to bring his friend the following day: "but," said Adams, deferentially, "it will be more satisfactory to the poor man, if your Lordship will speak to him yourself." Upon which the Bishop bowing to the mercer, the latter approached the coach, when the Bishop said, " The gentleman has informed me of all the matter about you, and if you please to give yourself the trouble of coming to my house at Fulham, I will satisfy you in every point." The mercer made many grateful bows, and taking Adams to a tavern, gave him a good entertainment.

The next morning Adams waited upon the mercer, who was making out his bill to present to the Bishop, and pretending that his coming in haste to attend him to the Bishop's house had made him forget to bring money with him, entreated that he would grant him the loan of a guinea, and put it down in the bill. They then went off to wait upon the Bishop at the time appointed. After being regaled in the parlour with a bottle of wine, the mercer was introduced to the Bishop, who addressed him, saying, "I understand that you have been greatly troubled of late; I hope that you are better now, sir?" The mercer answered, "My trouble is much abated, since your Lordship has been pleased to order me to wait upon you." So pulling out his pocket-book, he presented his lordship with a bill containing several articles, including a guinea of borrowed money, amounting in all to two hundred and three pounds nineteen shillings and ten pence.

His Lordship, staring upon the bill, and examining its contents, said, " What is the meaning of all this? The gentleman last night might very well say your conscience could not be at rest, and I wonder why it should, when you bring a bill to me of which I know nothing." "Your Lordship," said the mercer, bowing and scraping, " was pleased last night to say, that you would satisfy me to-day." " Yes," replied the prelate, " and so I would with respect to what that gentleman told me; who said that you, being much troubled about some points of religion, desired to be resolved therein, and, in order thereto, I appointed you to come to-day." " Truly, your Lordship's nephew told me otherwise; for he said you would pay me this bill of parcels, which, upon my word, he had of me, and in a very clandestine manner too, if I were to tell your Lordship all the truth; but out of respect to your honour, I will not disgrace your nephew." "My nephew! he is none of my nephew! I never, to my knowledge, saw the gentleman in my life before!"

Dick not long after went into the Life-Guards, but as his pay would not support his extravagance, he sometimes collected upon the highway. Along with some of his companions upon the road, they robbed a gentleman of a gold watch and a purse of a hundred and eight pounds. Not content with his booty, Adams went after the gentleman, saying, " Sir, you have got a very fine coat on ; I must make bold to exchange with you." As the gentleman rode along, he thought he heard something making a noise in his pocket, and examining it, to his great joy he found his watch and all his money, which Adams in his hurry had forgot to remove out of the pocket of his own coat when he exchanged with the gentleman. But when Adams and his associates came to an inn, and sat down to examine their booty, to their unspeakable chagrin they found that all was gone.

Adams and his companions went out that very same day to repair their loss, and attacked the stage-coach, in which were several women, with whom, irritated by their recent misfortune, they were very rough and urgent. While Dick was searching the pockets of one of the women, she said, " Have you no pity or compassion on our sex ? Certainly, you have neither christianity, conscience, nor religion, in you!" " Right, we have not much christianity nor conscience in us: but, for my part, you shall presently find a little religion in me." So falling next upon her jewels and ear-rings, " Indeed, Madam," exclaimed Adams, "supposing you to be an Egyptian, I must beg the favour of you, being a Jew, to borrow your jewels and ear-rings, according as my forefathers were commanded by Moses ;" and having robbed the ladies to the amount of two hundred pounds in money and goods, allowed them to proceed.

After a course of depredations, Dick, in robbing a man between London and Brentford, was so closely pursued by the person who was robbed, and a neighbour whom he fortunately met upon the road, that in a little time afterwards he was apprehended, carried before a magistrate, committed to Newgate, tried, condemned, and executed, in March, 1713. Though rude and profligate before, he was penitent and devout after receiving his sentence.

Page 201.

WILLIAM GETTINGS,
CALLED
"THE HEREFORD BOY."

THE father of this man was a grazier in Herefordshire; and he lived with him until he was sixteen years old, and then came up to London. Sometimes in the capacity of a footman, and sometimes in that of a butler, he spent five years in a very irreproachable manner. Unfortunately, however, he became acquainted with evil company, was soon corrupted in principles, and became a rogue in practice.

He began his course under the name of William Smith, and traded in the smaller matter of pilfering. In the dress of a porter he one evening went into the house of a doctor of medicine, took down a rich bed, and packed it up. In carrying it off he fell down stairs, and had almost broken his neck. The noise alarming the old doctor and his son, they came running to see what was the matter; whereupon Gettings, puffing and blowing as if he was quite out of breath, perceiving them nearer than they should be, said to the doctor, "Is not your name Young?"—"Yes," replied the doctor, "and what then?"—"Why, then, sir," said Gettings, "There's one Mr. Hugh Hen and Penhenribus has ordered me to bring these goods hither (which have almost broken my back,) and carry them away to a new lodging, which he has taken somewhere hereabouts."—"Mr. Hugh Hen and Penhenribus?" replied the doctor again; "pray, who's he? for, to the best of my knowledge, I don't know such a gentleman."—"I can't tell," said Gettings, "but, indeed, the gentleman knows you, and ordered me to leave the goods here."—"I don't care," said the doctor, "how well he knows! I tell you I'll not take the people's goods, unless they were here themselves; therefore, I say, carry them away!"—'Nay, pray sir," said Gettings, "let me leave the goods here, for I am quite weary already in bringing them hither."—"I tell you," replied the doctor, "there shall none be left here; therefore take them away, or I'll throw them into the street!"—"Well, well," said Gettings, "I'll take the goods away then; but I'm sure the gentleman will be very angry, because he ordered me to leave them here."—"I don't care," replied the doctor, "for his anger, nor your's either! I tell you, I'll take no charge of other people's goods, unless they are here themselves to put them into my custody!"—" Very well, sir," said Gettings, " since I must carry them away, I beg the favour of you and the gentleman there to lift them on my back."—" Ay, ay, with all my heart," replied the doctor. " Come son, and lend a hand to lift them on the fellow's back."

Scarcely was William gone, when the doctor's wife coming home from the market, and going into the room, saw the bed taken down, and came running in a great passion to her husband, exclaiming, " Why, truly, this is a most strange business, that I can never stir out of doors, but you must be making some whimsical alteration or other in the house!"—" What's the matter," replied the doctor, " with the woman? 'Are you beside yourself?'"—" No, said the wife, " but truly you are, in thus altering things as you do, almost every moment!"—" Certainly, my dear," replied the doctor, " you must have been spending your market-penny, or else you would not talk at this rate, as you do, of alterations, when not the smallest have been made since you have gone out."—" I am not blind, I think," retorted the wife, " for I am sure the bed is taken out of the two-pair-of-stairs back-room; and pray, husband, where do you design to put it now?" The doctor and his son then went upstairs, and not only found that the bed was stolen, but that they had assisted the thief to carry it off.

Our hero next resolved to try his fortune upon the highway, and meeting with a sharper on the road, commanded him to "stand and deliver?" He robbed him of two-pence halfpenny, when the sharper remarked, that " the world was come indeed to a very sad pass, when one rogue must prey upon another."

He next robbed a man of twelve shillings and a pair of silver buckles. From hence he proceeded to rifle a stage-coach, and took away some money and a silver watch. Not long after, he robbed Mr. Dashwood and his lady of a gold watch and money.

These, however, were only smaller exhibitions of his dexterity. One evening, well mounted, he passed through Richmond, and perceiving a gentleman walking in his gardens, enquired of the gardener, if he might be permitted to view the gardens, of which he had heard so much.

The gardener, well acquainted with the harmless vanity and benevolence of his master, granted his request. Giving his horse to the gardener, Gettings walked forward, and in a very respectful manner, accosted the gentleman. who received him very courteously; when, setting down together in an arbour, Gettings said, "Your worship has got a fine diamond ring upon your finger."—"Yes," replied the owner, "it ought to be a very fine one, for it cost me a very fine price."—"Why, then," said Gettings, "it is the fitter to bestow on a friend; therefore, if your worship pleases, I must make bold to take it and wear it for your sake." The gentleman stared at his impudence, but Gettings, presenting a pistol, made a short process of the matter. Having taken the ring, the villian added, "I am sure you do not go without a good watch too." Making free with that also, and some guineas, he bound the gentleman, and went off with his booty, after requesting him to be patient, and he would send some person to set him at liberty. When he came to the gate, he gave the gardener a shilling, informing him that Sir James wanted to speak to him. The botanical retainer accordingly went and untied his master, who with a grim smile returned him thanks for sending a man into his own garden to rob him.

Upon another day, Gettings undertook a long journey, for the express purpose of robbing the house of a friend; and being well acquainted with all parts of the house, was successful, and brought off money, plate, and goods, to a considerable amount. He at last, in an unlucky moment, robbed a Mr. Harrison of four guineas, some silver, and a watch; and being detected, was tried, condemned, and executed, on the 25th September, 1713, in the twenty-second year of his age.

EDWARD BONNET.

Edward Bonnet was born of respectable parents in the isle of Ely, in Cambridgeshire, received an education superior to many of his companions, and when he was only ten years old, gave the following proof of his promising genius. He was sent to the parson with the present of a sparerib of pork, wrapped up in a cloth, in a basket. Ned knocked with some degree of importance at the door, which a servant answered, enquiring his business. "I want to speak with your master." The master came, "Well, my lad, what is your business?" "Why, only my father has sent you this," said young Ned; and gave him the basket, without moving his hat. "O fie! fie; child, have you no manners? you should pull hat, and say,—Sir, my father gives his service to you, and desires you to accept this small token. Come, go you out again with the basket, and knock at the door, and I'll let you in, and see how prettily you can perform it." The parson waited within until his impatience to receive and examine the contents of the basket, incited him to open the door. But Ned was at a considerable distance, walking off with the present. " So ho! so ho! sirrah! where are you going?" " Home, sir," replied Ned, in an equally loud voice. " Hey, but you must come back and do as I bade you first." "Thank you for that, sir, I know better than that; and if you teach me manners, I'll teach you wit." The father smiled at the story, and retained his spare-rib.

At the age of fifteen Bonnet was sent apprentice to a grocer, served his time with credit, was afterwards married to a young woman in the neighbourhood, and continued in business, for some time, until he had acquired about six hundred pounds. Unfortunately, however, he was reduced to poverty by an accidental fire. Unable to answer the pressing demands of his creditors, he left the place, and came up to London. Here he soon became acquainted with a band of highwaymen, and began with them to seek from the highway what had been lost by fire.

Nor did he long continue in the inferior walks of his new profession, but providing himself with a horse which he taught to leap over ditch, hedge, or toll-bar, and to know all the roads in the country, whether by day or by night, he quickly became the terror of Cambridgeshire.

Upon this horse, he one day met a Cantabrigian, who was possessed of more money than good sense, morality, or wit, in a calash with a dashing courtesan. Ned commanded the student to "stand and deliver." Unwilling to show his cowardice before his companion, he refused. Without any respect to the venerable University to which he belonged, Ned by violence took from him about six pounds, and presenting a pair of pistols, constrained the hopeful pair to strip themselves, then bound them together, and giving the horse a lashing, the animal went off at full trot with them to the inn to which he belonged. But no sooner did these Adamites enter the town, than men, women, and children, came hallooing, shouting, and collecting the whole town to behold such an uncommon spectacle. The student was expelled for disgracing the University, and the courtesan was sent to the house of correction.

Humourous Ned next met with a tailor and his son, who had arrested him for five pounds. He commanded him to surrender and received thirty-five in place of his five. "I wonder," said the innocent son, "what these fellows think of themselves? surely they must go to the place below for committing these notorious actions." "God forbid," replied the tailor, "for to have the conversation of such rogues there, would be worse than all the rest."

Ned's next adventure was with an anabaptist preacher, whom he commanded to deliver up his purse and scrip. The latter began by reasonings, ejaculations, and texts, to avert the impending evil. Ned instantly put himself in a great passion, and replied, " Pray, sir, keep your breath to cool your porridge, and don't talk of religious matters to me, for I'll have you to know, that, like all other true-bred gentlemen, I believe nothing at all of religion; therefore deliver me your money, and bestow your laborious cant upon your female auditors, who never scold with their maids without cudgelling them with broken pieces of scripture." Whereupon, taking a watch and eight guineas, he tied his legs under his horse, and let him depart.

On another occasion, Bonnet and a few associates met a nobleman and four servants in a narrow pass, one side of which was enclosed by a craggy and shattered rock, and the other by an almost impenetrable wood, rising gradually considerably higher than the road; and accosted them in his usual style. The nobleman pretended that he supposed they were only in jest, and said, "that if they would accompany him to the next inn, he would give them a handsome treat." He was soon informed that they preferred the present to the future. A sharp dispute ensued, but the nobleman and his men were conquered; and the lord was robbed of a purse of gold, a gold watch, a gold snuff-box, and a diamond ring.

Being conducted into the adjacent wood, and bound hand and foot, the robbers left them, saying, "that they would bring them more company presently." Accordingly, they were as good as their word, for in less than two hours they contrived to increase the number to twelve, on which Ned cried, "There are now twelve of you, all good men and true; so bidding you farewell, you may give in your verdict against us as you please, when we are gone, though it will be none of the best; but to give us as little trouble as possible, we shall not now stay to challenge any of you. So, once more, farewell."

Ned Bonnet and his comrades now going to the place of rendezvous, to make merry with what they had got, which was at a by sort of an inn standing somewhat out of the high road between Stamford and Grantham, it happened at night to rain very hard, so that one Mr. Randal, a pewterer, living near Marygold-Alley, in the Strand, before it was burnt down, was obliged to put in there for shelter. Calling for a pot of ale, on which was the innkeeper's name, which was also Randal, the pewterer asked him, being his name-sake, to sit and bear him company.

They had not been long chatting, before Ned and one of his comrades came down stairs and placed themselves at the same table; and understanding the name of the stranger, one of the rogues, fixing his eyes more intently than ordinary upon him, in a fit of seeming joy leaped over the table, and embracing the pewterer exclaimed, "Dear Mr. Randal! who would have thought to have seen you here! it is ten years, I think, since I had the happiness to be acquainted with you."

Whilst the pewterer was recollecting whether he could call this spark to mind or not, for it came not into his memory that he had ever seen him in his life, the highwayman again cried out, "Alas! Mr. Randal, I see now I am much altered, since you have forgotten me." Here, being arrived at a *ne plus ultra*, up started Ned, and with as great apparent joy said to his companion, "Is this Harry, the honest gentleman in London, whom you so often used to praise for his great civility and liberality to all people? Surely then we are very happy in meeting thus accidentally with him."

By this discourse they would almost have persuaded Mr. Randal that they perfectly knew him; but being sensible of the contrary, he very seriously assured them, that he could not remember that he ever had seen any of them in his life. "No!" said they, struck with seeming astonishment; "it is strange we should be altered so much within these few years."

But to evade further ill-timed questions, the rogues insisted upon Mr. Randal's supping with them, which invitation he was by no means permitted to decline.

By the time they had supped, in came four more of Ned's comrades, who were invited also to sit down, and more provisions were called for, which were quickly brought, and as rapidly devoured.

When the fury of consuming half a dozen good fowls and other victuals was over, besides several flasks of wine, there was not less than three pounds odd money to pay. At this they stared on each other, and held a profound silence, whilst Mr. Randal was fumbling in his pocket. When they saw that he only brought forth a mouse from the mountain of money the thieves hoped to find piled in his pocket, which was only as much as his share, he that pretended to know him started up, and protested he should be excused for old acquaintance sake; but the pewterer, not willing to be beholden, as indeed they never intended he should, to such companions, lest for this civility they should expect greater obligations from him, pressed them to accept his dividend of the reckoning, saying, if they thought it equitable he would pay more.

At last one of them, tipping the wink, said, "Come come, what needs all this ado? let the gentleman, if he so pleases, present us with this small treat, and do you give him a larger at his taking his farewell in the morning." Mr. Randal not liking this proposal, it was started that he and Ned should throw dice to end the controversy; and fearing he had got into bad company, to avoid mischief, Randal acquiesced to throw a main who should pay the whole shot, which was so managed that the lot fell upon Randal. By this means Randal, having the voice of the whole board against him, was deputed to pay the whole reckoning; though the dissembling villains vowed and protested they had rather it had fallen to any of them, that they might have had the honour of treating him.

Mr. Randal concealed his discontent at these shirking tricks as well as he could; and they perceiving he would not engage in gaming, but counterfeited drowsiness, and desired to be a-bed, the company broke up, and he was shown to his lodging, which he barricaded as well as he could, by putting old chairs, stools, and tables against the door. Going to bed and putting the candle out, he fell asleep; but was soon awaked by a strange walking up and down the room, and an outcry of murder and thieves.

At this surprising noise he leaped out of bed, and ran to the door, to see whether it was fast or not: and finding nothing removed, (for the highwaymen came into his chamber by a trap-door which was behind the hangings,) he wondered how the noise should be there in his apartment, unless it was enchanted; but as he was about to remove the barricade to run and raise the house, he was surrounded by a crew, who, tying and gagging him, took away all his clothes, and left him to shift for himself as well as he could.

One day, having the misfortune to have his horse shot under him, Bonnet embraced the first opportunity to take a good gelding from the grounds of the man who kept the Red Lion inn. Being again equipped like a gentleman, he rode into Cambridgeshire, and met with a gentleman, who informed him that he had well nigh been robbed, and requested him to ride along with him for protection. As a highwayman is never out of his way, he complied, and, at a convenient place, levied a contribution, as protector of the gentleman, by emptying his pockets of eighty guineas. He however, had the generosity to give him half-a-crown to carry him to the next town.

After having, according to computation, committed three hundred robberies, another thief, being apprehended, in order to save his own life, informed against Bonnet, who was apprehended, not upon the highway, but in his own lodgings, and sent to Newgate, and at the next assizes carried down to Cambridge, sentenced, and executed before the castle, on the 28th March, 1713, to the great joy of the county, which had suffered severely by his depredations.

RICHARD KEELE.

THIS man was born at Ramsey, in Hampshire, and was bound an apprentice to a barber in Winchester. In that station he acquitted himself so well, that he received his master's daughter in marriage; but, after remaining with her about seven or eight years, he went to reside with another woman, who had an annuity of 50*l*.

To gratify his vicious inclinations, his time was chiefly spent in the company of the most abandoned men and women; and it was not long before he excelled them in every species of wickedness.

Not long after he went to reside with the annuitant, he set up an alehouse, but was soon arrested on an action at the instance of a soldier in the foot-guards, for keeping company with his wife, whom he aided in her robberies, until she was condemned. When arrested, no person would bail him out; and he had not been long confined before no less than forty robberies were laid to his charge ; but no prosecution being instituted against him, he was admitted to bail. Being a prisoner on the first action, he removed himself by a writ of *habeas corpus* to the Fleet-prison, but was, not long after, removed to Newgate, upon an accusation of blasphemy. He was tried before Justice Parker, who sentenced him to stand twice in the pillory, once at Charing-cross, and once without Temple-bar, and to suffer imprisonment during a year.

His time being expired, he became a bailiff's follower; but, th being a poor trade, he again began to make free with other men's property. A coat and two periwigs became his prize, for which he was unluckily committed to Newgate. He was found guilty, burned in the hand, and ordered to hard labour in Bridewell for twelve months.

Accordingly, along with William Lowther and Charles Houghton, he was carried to Bridewell, but when Captain Bureman was going to put them in irons they rebelled. Houghton was shot dead, Lowther wounded, and Keele had one of his eyes shot out. But having killed Edward Perry, one of the turnkeys, they were committed again to Newgate, Keele was maintained in prison by Isabel Thomas, for whom an arrest was formerly issued against him by her husband. She was a notorious thief, had been married to many husbands, and was burnt several times in the hand; but was at last tried, condemned, and executed for theft.

In addition to the villainies of Keele, before he was committed on this occasion, he was one time in want of money, having paid twenty or thirty pounds to an adversary, and meeting an *honest* man called Bond and Judgment, from his lending money on bond and when it became due pushing very hard for payment, he commanded him to "Stand and deliver!" Bond and Judgment answered, "Do you know me, sir?"—"Ay," replied Dick, "you villain! I know you to be a mercenary rogue, who would send your mother and father to gaol for the fillip of a farthing: therefore it is but a just judgment befallen you, to take all you have from you." So clapping a pistol to his breast, poor Bond and Judgment was under the necessity of stopping the force of the bullet by threescore guineas. This so lessened his stock, that when he was, not long after, lodged in Newgate, he found a difficulty in raising as much money as would suffice to remove his carcase to the King's Bench prison.

At another time, Keele being well mounted, and accoutred with sword and pistol, met an officer, lately a tradesman, on Hounslow-heath. Keele gave him the word of command, " Stand and deliver!" He was indeed at a stand, but supposing that the colour of his coat would inspire Dick with fear, said, " Don't you see what livery I wear?"—"See whose livery you wear!" replied Dick. " You are *a* footman?"—" No," said the other, " I am an officer in the army, therefore at your peril be it, if you presume to stop me when I am upon lawful occasions."—" Nay," said Dick, " if you go about lawful occasions, I am about unlawful; therefore, deliver what you have, or we must try who is the better man."—" I don't bear a commission to fight with highwaymen," cried the quandum shopkeeper; " I only wear her Majesty's cloth to fight for my queen and country."—" Why then," replied Dick, " neither this cloth, nor any other, must be protection against my arrest; therefore, as the pistol is my tip-staff, I demand your money upon pain of death." But finding no money, he stripped off his coat, waistcoat, and small-clothes, and ordered him to get another suit, and place it to the account of the regiment.

Dick was at last brought to his trial, and the evidence being decisive against him, he and William Lowther were both sentenced to death. In consequence of the influence of a sister who lived with a gentleman of rank, he was confident that he should obtain a pardon, but was miserably disappointed.

It may be proper to remark, that it was his usual custom to boast in all manner of wickedness, and to say, that should he ever come under sentence of death, he would never behave himself similar to the generality of those in that condition; that he should neither confess his crimes, shed a tear, nor show the least contrition or uneasiness. But when he came to be in that situation, he was neither without his dread, nor the expression of his awful forebodings. He suffered for his offences on the 23rd of December, 1713.

WILL OGDEN AND TOM REYNOLDS.

THE first of these was a waterman, and born in Southwark. The second was a dung-bargeman, and born in Barnaby-street. Entering into company, they robbed shops and ships, during the space of two years with considerable success: they then ascended to the second degree of robbery, and broke several houses in Southwark. Associating themselves with another, they broke into a watchmaker's shop, and extracted twenty-six watches; but the stranger becoming evidence, our two trusty friends were lodged in Newgate, tried and condemned, but received a pardon, in consequence of which they were again let loose upon the community. Ogden one evening met a parson walking home under the light of the moon, and approached him in the character of a seaman in great poverty and distress. His dismal narrative excited the compassion of the parson, who gave him a sixpence. The parson had not proceeded far when Ogden met him again, and renewed his request. " You are the most impudent beggar that ever I met with," cried the reverend gentleman. Ogden told him that he was in very great want, and that the sixpence he had received would not supply his necessities. He then gave him half-a-crown. Ogden said, "These are very sad times, for there's horrid robbing abroad, therefore, if you have any more money about you, you may as well let me have it as another, who perhaps may abuse you, and binding you hand and foot, make you lie in the cold all night; but if you'll give me your money, I'll take care of you, and conduct you very safely home."

The parson made a virtue of necessity, and gave him all his money, which was about 40s. Ogden then said, " I see you have a watch, sir; you may as well let me have that too." The parson complied, and as they were plodding along, two or three fellows came out upon them, to whom Ogden cried " the moon shines bright," when they let them proceed. They had only gone a short way, when the same scene was repeated, but at last the parson was brought safely to his own door. He requested his guide to go in, assuring him that he should receive no injury; but the latter declined his offer. The good parson then brought a bottle of wine, and drinking to Ogden, gave him the bottle and the glass to help himself, upon which he ran off with both.

Upon another day, meeting Beau Medlicote, he was commanded to " stand and deliver." The beau pretended to make some resistance with his sword, but pistols being produced, he was constrained to yield. There were only two half-crowns found in his pocket, and one of them was bad. Upon this he received a complete caning for presuming to carry counterfeit money.

Some time after this, Ogden and Reynolds, in company with one Bradshaw, the grandson of Serjeant Bradshaw, who condemned King Charles I. to death, were watching in a wood for some booty. A poor servant girl was returning home from her service, with a box upon her head: Bradshaw was deemed a sufficient match for her; accordingly, he alone rushed out of the wood, and seized her box in which were her clothes and 15s. being all her wages for three months' services. When he had broken up her box and was rifling it, there happening to be a hammer in it, she suddenly seized the hammer, and gave him a blow upon the temple, which was followed by another equally well directed, with the claw of the hammer, into his windpipe, on which the villain immediately expired.

In a short time a gentleman came up, to whom she related the whole adventure; he went up to the deceased, and found in his pockets 80 guineas, and a whistle. Perceiving its use, he immediately whistled, when Ogden and Reynolds in a moment rushed from the wood; but discovering that it was a wrong person who gave the signal, they with equal speed ran back. The gentleman carried the girl before a magistrate, became bail for her appearance, and being tried, she was acquitted.

At another time, these two men met a tallyman, well known for his commerce of two kinds with the hawkers in St. Giles's. They employed the common phrase, "stand and deliver!" In a piteous tone the victim entreated them to spare a poor man who was at great pains to acquire his daily bread. In a violent passion Ogden exclaimed, "Thou spawn of hell! have pity on thee! No, sirrah! I know you too well, and I would almost as soon be kind to a bailiff or an informing constable. A tallyman and a rogue are terms of similar import. Every Friday you set up a tenter in the Marshalsea Court, upon which you rack and stretch poor prisoners, like English broad-cloth, beyond the staple of the wool, till the threads crack, which causes them with the least wet to shrink, and presently wear threadbare. I say that you and all your calling are worse rogues than ever were hanged at Tyburn." After this eloquent harangue, he took whatever he found upon him, stripped him naked, bound him hand and foot, and left him under a hedge to ruminate on his former villainies.

These two rogues continued their depredations until justice at length overtook them, and at Kingston-upon-Thames they were sentenced. They were unsuccessful in attempting to break out of the Stock-house; and such was the indifference of Ogden, that when he was going to the place of execution, he threw a handful of money among the crowd, saying, "Gentlemen, here is poor Will's farewell."

They were executed on the 2d of April, 1714.

JOHN PRICE.

THE depravity of human nature was exemplified in its full extent in the character of John Price. The indigence and profligacy of his parents were such, that he received no education, and he was sent into the world to shift for himself, at the age of seven. Before this period, he was a proficient both in cursing and lying. It is rather a singular fact, that his habitual lying was once a means of saving his life.

About the age of eighteen he was serving a gentleman in the

country, who turned him off for his notorious falsehoods. In going to London he robbed a woman of eighteen shillings, was apprehended in the act, and convicted; but his late master, who was sheriff, took pity upon his situation, and saved his life. Informed of this, the judges at the next assizes blamed the gentleman's conduct for allowing a man to escape who had pleaded guilty. The sheriff acknowledged that such a man had been condemned at the last assizes; but then, he knew the fellow to be such an unaccountable liar, that there was no believing one word he said; so he pleading guilty to what was laid to his charge, was in his opinion a sufficient reason for his being believed innocent of the fact, and he would not hang an innocent man for the world. This reply made the judges smile, and he was dismissed with a severe reprimand, and cautioned not to come before them again.

Upon obtaining his liberty, Price went to London; associated with a band of robbers, and in a short time was apprehended diving into another person's pocket instead of his own, and for that crime committed to Newgate. He was accordingly sentenced to a severe whipping, and sent on board a man-of-war; but after he had received the punishment assigned to stealing from the sailors, he was discharged from the ship.

He hastened again to London, joined another association of thieves, and abandoned himself to all manner of wickedness. One evening his gang divided themselves into three companies. The first met an attorney, near Hampstead, whom they robbed of eight guineas. The unfortunate lawyer had not gone far when he was attacked by the second party, to whom he related his misfortunes, and into what cruel hands he had fallen. "Cruel!" said one of them: "how dare you use these terms? And who made you so bold as to talk to us with your hat on? Pray, sir, be pleased henceforward to learn more manners." They then snatched off his hat and wig; and took a diamond ring from his finger. As he was plodding his way home, uncertain which road was safest, the third division came up to him near Kentish Town, bringing with them a man whom they pretended to have completely stripped, and constrained the lawyer to clothe the naked with his own coat and waistcoat; then told him he might be thankful he got off with his life, which he employed in sowing division amongst society.

In a short time after this, Price and a companion one evening entered a garret, in which there was nothing but lumber, with the intention of robbing the house when all was silent. But in the dark, as Price was laying his hand upon a pistol which he had placed upon the table, it went off and alarmed the whole house. His comrade instantly ran to the window, where they fastened a rope for their escape, and his companion attempting to slide down, the rope soon broke, though he was not so much injured but he got away. Price seeing the extreme danger of being caught, removed the rope to another window, and it conveyed him to a balcony. He was, however, scarcely there, when all the people in the house were alarmed; on which he leaped into a large basket of eggs which a man was carrying upon his head, from Newgate market; so that the fall being broken, he was able to make his escape amid the cry of thieves!

Jack now began to be so well known about town, that he found it necessary to remove to tne country. He was there most industrious in stripping the hedges of the linen that he found upon them. Putting up at an inn, the landlord soon understood from his discourse, that he was a servant who would suit him, and therefore hired him as his tapster. It was this miscreant landlord's custom to murder travellers who put up at his house; but one gentleman being warned by a maid of his danger, provided for his safety.

Among other things the maid informed him that it was usual for the landlord to ring a bell, on which an assassin, pretending to be a servant, entered the chamber, snuffed out the candle, when the other villains rushed in and murdered the stranger. The gentleman caused the maid to place a lantern with a candle in it under a stool, and he laid his arms ready and stood upon his guard. Scarcely had he sat himself down when it happened as the girl had mentioned; but the gentleman, with the assistance of his servant, killed two of the villains and put the rest to flight. He then seized the innkeeper and his wife, carried them before a magistrate, and they were indicted to stand trial at the next assizes. From the maid's deposition it appeared that fourteen strangers had been murdered by them, and that their bodies were concealed in an arched vault in the garden, to which there was a passage from the cellar. Both were executed, and the innkeeper hung in chains.

Jack having once more escaped death, returned to his pilfering trade, was committed to Newgate, and whipped for his crimes. But Jack was now determined to follow the example of the great ones of the earth, and to better his circumstances by marriage. Accordingly, he married one of the name of Betty, who gained her livelihood by running of errands to the prisoners of Newgate.

Nor was Jack, like too many, disappointed in his matrimonial connexion, for he was soon elevated to be hangman to the county of Middlesex. In this station he assumed great importance, and held a levee every day that he did business at Tyburn; but though he sometimes ran in debt, yet he was always very willing to work in order to pay his obligations. But envy reached even him, and he lost his place by means of one who had greater ministerial interest. But Jack could never be destitute while he had hands and fingers to lay hold of whatever was within his reach.

He at last suffered from having assaulted a watchman's wife, whom he met in Bunhill Fields, and used in such a barbarous manner that she died in a few days of her wounds. Two men suddenly came up to him, and, being seized, he was secured in Newgate. After his trial and condemnation, he remained impenitent, and endeavoured, by intoxication, to stifle the forebodings of conscience. He was hanged on the 31st of May, 1718.

JOSEPH BLAKE.

There are some rogues who are far elevated above ordinary culprits. They aspire to eminence in the awful field of criminality. Among this number was Joseph Blake, who, it would appear, was solicitous to acquire distinction, by superior acts of villainy alone.

He was a native of London, and received a decent education from his parents, but it was his misfortune to associate with a wicked companion, who, at an early period, initiated him into the mysteries of iniquity. When he returned from school, he refused to go to any industrious employment, and boldly commenced robber at the age of seventeen. It was his fortune, almost on every occasion, to meet with detection, but still he pursued his course.

Blake entered at last into a famous gang of highwaymen, and one evening they robbed a man of 8s. and a gilt-handled sword. A woman perceived it from a window, and gave the alarm; one of the thieves fired at her, but drawing in her head, she was saved, and the ball grazed the sill. Blake was also with the same gang when they attacked Captain Langley, but that gentleman made such a stout resistance that they could not rob him. Wilkinson, one of the chief of this gang, was apprehended, and in order to save himself, informed against several others. By means of hievidence, no fewer than seventy were discovered; and even Wilkinson was a second time seized, on account of farther guilt being charged against him.

The inclination to discovery being begun, Blake also commenced informer, and by his means no less than about twelve robberies were revealed. On making these discoveries, he obtained his liberty, and when he was discharged at the Old Bailey, a person humorously asked him how long it would be before he was there again? A gentleman replied, "Three years." Blake kept his time.

The moment he was at liberty, he again commenced with Jack Shepherd. One day they met with one Purgitor considerably intoxicated, when Blake knocked him down, and threw him into a ditch, where he must have perished, had it not been for the compassion of Shepherd, who kept his head above water. For this crime two brothers in the Guards were tried, and if they had not been saved by several persons swearing that they were upon duty at the time, they would certainly have suffered; for the fact was sworn against them. The eldest of these brothers died within a week after his liberation, and did not live to see his innocence vindicated by the confession of Blake.

At another time, Blake and Shepherd broke into a house, and carried off goods to a considerable amount. They were both apprehended, tried, and condemned; but the latter escaping from the condemned hole, his life was prolonged for a little time.

Blake behaved in the most audacious manner at his trial; and when he saw that nothing could save him from death, he was resolved to deserve it better. Accordingly, taking the opportunity of Jonathan Wild coming to speak with him, he cut Wild's throat with a penknife. Of this wound Wild languished long, but at last recovered. But if the wound of Blake had proved mortal, it would have prevented a more shameful death. It may, however, be remarked, that whatever Wild might merit from the hands of others, this was ungrateful enough on the part of Blake, because Wild was not only at the expense of curing a wound that the other had received, but gave him 3s. 6d. after his sentence, and promised him a decent coffin.

During the whole time of his confinement in prison, he displayed the most hardened indifference and contempt, and seemed only to regret that he had not been guilty of more numerous and nefarious actions. He was executed in 1724, in the twenty-eighth year of his age.

JACK SHEPHERD.

The father of the celebrated John Shepherd was a carpenter in Spitalfields, of good character, and exceedingly solicitous to train up his children in the path of sobriety and religion. They, however, afforded a melancholy proof that the most virtuous example, and the soundest principles, are frequently unsuccessful in influencing the conduct of children. Two of his sons followed evil courses, and were convicted at the bar of the Old Bailey.

After his father's death, young Shepherd was sent to a school in Bishopsgate-Street, where he received the rudiments of education, and was bound apprentice to a cane chair-maker. His master used him very well, and he lived very comfortably with him; but this master dying, he was sent to another, who treated him so very harshly that he eloped. In a short time, he commenced his depredations, and, in place of his former sober mode of life, his time was spent in drinking all day, and retiring to an infamous abode all night.

The history of this unfortunate man adds another to the many examples already given in this volume, that the company of profligate women has plunged men into scenes of dissipation and vice, to which they would have been entire strangers, had it not been for such associates. He was first enamoured of one Elizabeth Lion, a woman remarkable for her stature and strength. Having separated from her, he associated with one who stimulated him to all manner of pilfering, in order that he might be the better able to feed her extravagances.

One day, informing her that she had received his last half-crown, she instigated him to rob a wealthy pawnbroker. Shepherd left her about one in the morning, and returned with goods to the amount of twenty-two pounds. It was not long before the two who had planned the robbery, exhausted the booty.

The first favourite of Shepherd was committed to St. Giles's round-house, for some pilfering pranks. Jack went to see her, broke open the doors, beat the keeper, and set Bess Lion at liberty. It is scarcely necessary to add, that this action gained him great fame among ladies of her description, and stimulated him to more daring acts of depredation.

About this period Jack supplied his brother with a little money to equip him for the honourable profession he himself followed; and they broke into a linen draper's shop, from whence they extracted goods to the amount of fifty pounds. The younger brother, however, being rather a novice in the art, was too open in the disposal of the goods, by which means he was detected, and his first return for the kindness of his brother was to inform upon him and several of his confederates. Jack Shepherd was accordingly apprehended, and committed to the round-house for farther examination. This place could not long retain so bold a spirit, and marching off, he that very evening committed a robbery, and vowed to be revenged upon Tom for his ungenerous conduct.

Detection proved no reformation. Jack, in company with one Benson, attempting to steal a gentleman's watch, was discovered and committed to New Prison. The first person whom he discerned was his old favourite Bess Lion, who had been sent there upon a similar errand. After exerting all his cunning and stratagem in vain, Bess and he by force escaped, and instantly repaired to her old lodgings. There he remained concealed for some time, but, taking leave of his friend, he again associated with one Grace in raising contributions. These two villains becoming acquainted with one Lamb, an apprentice to Mr. Carter, they enticed him to introduce them into his master's house, from whence they extracted goods to a considerable amount. Shepherd and Grace, however, differed in the division of the spoil, and betrayed each other; when Grace and Lamb were apprehended. The misfortune of poor Lamb, who was so simply inveigled, excited the compassion of some gentlemen, who, by their exertions, succeeded in mitigating his sentence to transportation.

The confederates of Shepherd, in order to obtain a ready market for their goods, employed one Field to sell them, but he being occasionally dilatory, they hired a warehouse, and there deposited what goods they stole. Field, displeased at being turned off from his lucrative employment, importuned them to show him their stores, as he had several orders for goods, and could therefore dispose of them to advantage. He was conducted to the warehouse and shown the goods, and though he had not the courage manfully to rob any person, yet he emptied the warehouse of every rag it contained.

In the course of business, Shepherd robbed a Mr. Kneebone, and was tried at the ensuing sessions. He appeared simple and almost foolish at his trial, alleging, as his principal defence, that Jonathan Wild had disposed of part of the property, and ought therefore to be punished as well as himself. He was however sentenced, and conducted himself, in the whole of his defence, more like an ignorant simple man, than one who was formed to excel in his own, or any other profession.

But necessity is the mother of invention. While in the condemned hole, he prevailed upon one Fowls, who was also under sentence of death, to lift him up to the iron spikes that were over the top of the door which looks into the lodge. By the aid of a strong tall woman, and two others, his head and shoulders were got through, and the whole of his body following, he was by them let down, and without the least suspicion of the keepers, conveyed through the lodge, put into a hackney coach, and out of reach before the least notice of his escape could be given.

But Jack had scarcely breathed the fresh air when he returned to business. He associated with one Page, a butcher, who dressed him in one of his frocks, and both betook themselves to the highway. They went to a watchmaker's shop, in a daring manner broke open one of the glasses, and seized three watches before the boy who kept the shop could detect them. Upon this occasion Shepherd had the audacity to pass under Newgate.

But as Shepherd would not conceal himself nor give over his depredations, he was soon apprehended and again committed to Newgate, was put into the stone-room, loaded with irons, and stapled down to the ground. Being left alone, he with a crooked nail opened the lock, got free of his chains, wrought out two stones in the chimney, entered the red-room, where no person resided, threw down a door, got into the chapel, broke a spike off the door, and by it opened four other doors, got upon the roof, and from thence, by the means of his blanket, went in at a garret window belonging to an adjacent house, and through that house into the street.

The whole of this almost incredible exertion was rendered the more extraordinary in that his irons were on all the time. When at liberty, he went into an adjoining field and knocked them off; and, astonishing to relate, that very evening robbed a pawnbroker's house, where, among other things, he found a handsome suit of black clothes, in which he dressed himself and carried his booty to two of his female companions.

He now went to visit his companions in their scenes of iniquity, and drinking at a brandy shop was discovered by a boy who knew him. The boy had no sooner recognized Jack than he ran to give information, so that he was almost immediately apprehended and reconducted to his old quarters in Newgate, amid a vast crowd, who ran from all parts to see such an extraordinary character; but he was so intoxicated at the time that he was scarcely conscious of his miserable situation. To prevent the possibility of a third escape, they never permitted him to be alone, and made the contributions of those who came to see and converse with such a singular character pay for their additional trouble.

He was now the topic of general conversation, and multitudes, not only of the common ranks of society, but many in the more elevated ranks of life, flocked to see him. In the most ludicrous and jocular manner he related his adventures, exerting all his low wit and buffoonery to amuse those who visited him, and to exact money from them. In this manner were the last days of this unhappy mortal spent, in diverting his mind from serious reflection, and the awful scene before him. Nor was he even destitute of the hope of pardon, from the distinguished persons who visited him, and who seemed to pity his misfortune. But these hopes were vain, and the attentions of these persons proved worse than useless.

He was removed to the bar of the Court of King's Bench, in November, 1724, and an affidavit made that he was the same John Shepherd mentioned in the record of conviction. Judgment was awarded against him, and the day of his execution fixed. But such was his strong desire of life, and his belief that his resources would never fail him, that he prepared a knife to cut the ropes of the cart which should carry him to Tyburn, in hopes of running off among the crowd. This knife was, however, with no small difficulty taken from him by force. As his last refuge to provide against every possible event, he employed a friend, to whom he had given all the money which he had reserved from his visitors, to take his body away with all possible haste,—put it into a warm bed, and draw a little blood, thus to use every possible means to recover life. He finally enjoined, that if all means should prove unsuccessful, his body should be decently interred, and the remainder of the money given to his poor mother.

He was conducted to the place of execution in a cart, strongly handcuffed, when he behaved very gravely, confessed some of the robberies laid to his charge, and exculpated himself from others. His general dexterity, and the various scenes through which he had passed, operated to excite in no common degree, the sympathy of the multitude.

JONATHAN WILD.

THE notorious Jonathan Wild was the son of a carpenter, whose family consisted of three sons and two daughters. Jonathan was the eldest, and having received such an education as his father's circumstances would permit, he served an apprenticeship in Birmingham. He came up to London, and was for some time a gentleman's servant. But not relishing that mode of life, he returned to his business, and wrought very diligently.

Having come back to London, he during some time worked as a journeyman. He, however, living above his income, was arrested for debt. In prison he was scarcely able to exist upon the charity of the prisoners, but was, however, soon made under-keeper to the disorderly persons who were brought in at night.

Jonathan now learned the way of getting money from these people, in return for instructing them how to obtain their liberty. Here was a woman called Mary Miller, who taught him how to acquire money by means to which he was an entire stranger. By her he was made acquainted with all those gangs of profligate persons that infested the town, and the manner in which they prosecuted their schemes. Thus instructed, he became a director among them, and though he never went upon the road, he obtained more money than some who submitted to the danger and the toil of procuring it.

It was no easy matter formerly for thieves to find persons ready to receive and dispose of their goods; but an act being passed, by which those who purchased or received stolen goods, knowing them to be so, were guilty of a capital crime, it became more difficult for them to dispose of their booty. The result was, that the trade was almost reduced to nothing. But the ingenuity of Wild gave a new turn to their commerce.

Upon any person being robbed, Wild obtained intelligence where the goods were deposited, and the persons from whom they had been taken; and upon pretence of restoring them again, received a considerable gratuity. He in a short time had all the villains in the town under his control, and was sure to hang a few of them every season, to maintain his consequence among them, and to inspire terror, not for the law, but for himself. If any title could sufficiently exhibit Jonathan's character, it was that of " Director General of the united forces of highwaymen, house-breakers, footpads, pickpockets, and private thieves."

In process of time, however, he laid aside his caution, took a larger house, and both he and the woman, who was called his wife, dressed more elegantly, and opened a public office for restoring stolen goods. His fame soon circulated, and persons of no small distinction applied to Wild for the recovery of watches they had lost in their night ramblings, or goods which were extracted from their houses.

When any came upon business to the office, a crown was deposited to meet incidental expences. A large book was kept, the loser was examined with great minuteness, as to the time, the place, the manner, and the quantity of goods stolen. The person was dismissed with assurances that every possible search would be made. When he returned, the same would be repeated, and the person informed that they were not yet found, though perhaps they were in the house the first time the person called. Perhaps after a few more calls, Wild would inform the person, " That, provided no questions were asked, and he gave so much money to the porter who brought them, the goods would be returned at such an hour." At the same time Wild would protest, in the most open and frank manner, " That what he did was purely from a principle of doing good; as to a gratuity for the trouble he had taken, he left it entirely to themselves." And when money was presented, he received it with apparent negligence and reluctance.

In this manner he evaded the power of the law. He neither saw the thief, nor received the goods from him. It was not long, however, before he had become so necessary to these gentry, that when he received the goods in his possession, he gave the thief what share of the plunder he pleased, and if he was not satisfied with Wild's offer, he was pretty certain of detection and the gallows.

After Wild had carried on his plan for several years, an act of parliament was passed, chiefly directed against him, declaring it capital to recover stolen goods in this way. Though Wild was prudent and cautious in the extreme, during the first years of his practice, yet in his latter years, he became hardened and careless; therefore, continuing his practices, in defiance of that law, he was apprehended, tried, and condemned. When the usual question was put to him, " What have you to say why judgment of death shall not pass upon you?"—he, in a very feeble voice, said, " My Lord, I hope I may, even in the sad condition in which

I stand, pretend to some little merit, in respect of the services I have done my country, in delivering it of some of the greatest pests with which it was ever troubled. My Lord, I have brought many a bold and daring malefactor to just punishment, even at the hazard of my own life; my body being covered with scars received in these undertakings. I presume, my Lord, to say I have some merit, because at the time these things were done, they were esteemed meritorious by the government; and therefore I beg, my Lord, some compassion may be shown upon the score of these services. I submit myself wholly to his Majesty's mercy, and humbly beg a favourable report of my case." Under sentence of death, his conduct was little calculated to excite pity for his untimely end; and the day before his execution, he drank a large quantity of laudanum, but having emitted it, the poison had not the desired effect. Instead of expressing compassion, the multitude, when he was being conveyed in the cart to Tyburn, threw stones and mud, and exulted in his fall. He was allowed to sit a little in the cart, but the multitude became enraged, calling upon the executioner to dispatch him, or they would tear him to pieces.

Jonathan Wild is immortalized by the inimitable work of Fielding bearing his name; but there is nothing in the mean and dastardly nature of the man that renders him worthy even of being "damned to everlasting fame," by our great Novelist.

RICHARD TURPIN.

There never, perhaps, was a man in the particular profession to which this notorious fellow devoted himself, whose name was more familiar in the mouths of the common people than that of Richard Turpin. But, since it invariably happens that a certain proportion of curiosity respecting the life and actions of a man is sure to beget a corresponding desire to satisfy it, we cannot wonder if the perplexed biographer should sometimes resort to fiction to supply the deficiencies of fact. Hence it has happened that certain exploits have been attributed to Turpin which do not properly belong to him; amongst others, the unparalleled ride from York to London in an unprecedentedly short period, performed, it is averred, on a single horse. We have never been able to find any authentic account of this feat, nor have we, as yet, discovered any conceivable necessity that should compel him to such a rapid journey. Turpin was never tried but once, and that was, indeed, at York, but the reader will perceive that he had no opportunity of escape, nor did he attempt any thing of the kind after his first apprehension.

Richard Turpin was the son of John Turpin, of Hempstead in Essex, and was put apprentice to a butcher in Whitechapel, where he served his time, during which period he was frequently guilty of misdemeanors, and conducted himself in a loose and disorderly manner. As soon as his time was up, he married, and set up in business for himself at Suson in Essex, where having no credit in the market, and no money in his pocket, he was shortly reduced to the necessity of maintaining himself by indirect practices; and, accordingly, very often used to rob the neighbouring gentry of sheep, lambs, and oxen. Upon one occasion, he stole a couple of oxen from a farmer at Plaistow, which he caused to be conveyed to his own house and cut up. Two of the men belonging to the farm, having a suspicion of Turpin, went to his house, and seeing an ox slaughtered, were convinced of his guilt; and having traced the sale of the hides, returned to Suson to apprehend him. Turpin, apprized of their intention, left them in the front-room, jumped out of a window and made his escape.

By this time his character had become notorious, and he never could entertain a thought of returning to Suson, or of following the trade of a butcher in that county. He, accordingly, resolved to commence smuggler, and raising as much money as he could scrape together, he betook him to the hundreds of Essex, where he soon became connected with a gang of smugglers. This his new profession he followed for some time with tolerable success; but fortune taking a turn, he lost all that he had acquired; upon which he began to turn his thoughts to another, but by no means a more honest, way of life. In a word, he connected himself with a gang of deer-stealers, who, finding him a desperate fellow, and fit for their purpose, admitted him among them. This desperate gang, afterwards known and feared under the title of the Essex Gang, not only robbed the forest of deer, but thinned several gentlemen's parks of them, insomuch that they obtained a considerable sum of money. They followed deer-stealing only for some time; but not finding the money come in so quickly as they wished, and being narrowly watched by the park-keepers, they, by Turpin's direction, resolved to go round the country at nights, and when they could find a house that had any thing valuable in it, one was

Page 223.

to knock at the door, which being opened, the rest should rush in and plunder it, not only of plate, but of household goods.

The first person attacked in this manner was a Mr. Strype, an old man who kept a chandler's-shop at Watford; from whom they only took the money he had by him; but Turpin informed his companions that he knew an old woman at Loughton, who, he was certain, had seven or eight hundred pounds in her possession. The plan being declared feasible, away they went, and coming to the door, one of them knocked, and Turpin and the rest of the gang rushed in. The first thing they did was to blindfold the old lady and her maid. Turpin then examined the former touching her money, upon which she declared that she had none, being naturally loth to part with it. Some of the gang were inclined to believe her, but Turpin, with an oath, declared that if she remained obstinate he would set her on the fire. The poor old lady, imagining that this was a mere threat, suffered herself to be lifted on the fire, till the anguish she had endured for a long time, compelled her to disclose, and the gang retired with about 400*l.*

They then consulted together who should be their next victim, and agreed to wait upon a farmer, near Ripple Side. The people within not answering the door so soon as they would fain have had it opened, they broke in, and according to their old custom, tied the old man, the old woman, the servant-maid, and the farmer's son-in-law. They then ransacked the house, and robbed the old farmer of about 700*l.* Turpin, seeing so considerable a booty, cried, "Ay, this would do, if it were always so," their share being about 80*l.* a man.

The success the gang met with, made them resolve to proceed against those who had attempted to detect them. They accordingly agreed to attack the house of Mason, the keeper of Epping Forest. The time was fixed when the house was to be attacked; but Turpin having still a great deal of money in his possession, could not refrain from coming up to London to spend it; and, getting drunk, forgot the appointed time for putting their design into execution; however, the rest, resolving not to be baulked, set out for Mason's after having bound themselves by oath not to leave one whole piece of goods in the house. Accordingly they went, broke open the door, beat poor Mason in a cruel manner, and finally killed him under the dresser. An old man sitting by the fireside, who declared that he knew nothing of them, got off untouched. After ransacking the lower part of the house, and doing much mischief, they proceeded up-stairs, and broke every thing in their way; at last, emptying a punch-bowl, they broke that, when out dropped a hundred and twenty guineas, which they seized upon and made off with.

Turpin, with five others, in January, 1735, came to the door of Mr. Saunders, a wealthy farmer, at Charlton in Kent, and knocking, inquired if the gentleman of the house was at home: he was answered he was, and that being the signal, they rushed in, and going directly to the parlour where Mr. Saunders, his wife, and some friends were amusing themselves at a quiet game of cards, desired them on no account to be alarmed, for that they would not hurt their persons, if they sat still and made no disturbance. A silver snuff-box that lay upon the table, Turpin at once appropriated to himself, and the rest having bound the company, obliged Mr. Saunders to accompany them about the house, and open his closets and boxes, to prevent the necessity of laying violent hands upon them, and perhaps upon himself. They then possessed themselves of upwards of a hundred pounds in money, besides other property, including all the plate in the house. While this was proceeding, the maid-servant, a girl with some presence of mind, ran up-stairs, and barring herself in one of the rooms, called out lustily at the window for assistance; but one of the rogues following her, broke open the door with a poker, and brought her down again. In their search for all things of value in the house, they hit upon some bottles of wine, a bottle of brandy, and some mince-pies, with which they immediately sat down and regaled themselves, inviting the company to partake, indeed compelling them to drink a dram of brandy each, to work off the fright. Mrs. Saunders, however, fainted, and a glass of water with some drops in it was instantly provided, with which they bathed her temples, and were very anxious for her recovery. After staying about two hours in the house, they packed up their plunder, and made off with it, threatening the inmates of the house, that, if they stirred within two hours, they would murder them.

The names of Turpin's principal associates were Fielder, Rose, and Walker; there was another, also, whose name we have not learned. These made an appointment to rob a gentleman's house at Croydon, and for that purpose, agreed to meet at the Half Moon tavern, which they accordingly did, about six o'clock in the evening. Walker, having some knowledge of the house, went at the head of his companions into the yard, and found the coachman dressing his horses; him they bound, and going from thence met Mr. Sheldon the master, whom they seized and compelled to show them the way to the house. As soon as they entered, they tied

Mr. Sheldon's hands behind him with cords, and having served the rest of the family after the same fashion, fell to plundering the house. Eleven guineas, and several pieces of plate, jewels, and other things of value, was the result of this adventure; but before they left the place they returned two guineas, thanked Mr. Sheldon for the very courteous manner with which they had been received, and bade him good night.

Their next design was upon the house of Mr. Lawrence, at Edgeware-bury near Stanmore. About five o'clock they went from the Queen's Head at Stanmore, and proceeded to the destined spot. On their arrival, they left their horses at the outer gate, and climbing over the hatch into the sheep-yard, met with a boy just putting up some sheep. They seized him, and presenting a pistol, told him they would shoot him if he offered to cry out, but if he would inform them truly what servants Mr. Lawrence kept, and who was in the house, they would give him money. The boy, terrified at their threats, told instantly what they desired, and one of them thereupon knocked at the door. When it was opened they all rushed in with pistols in their hands, and seizing Mr. Lawrence, rifled his pockets, out of which they took one guinea, a Portugal piece of thirty-six shillings, about fifteen shillings in silver, and his keys. Dissatisfied with so small a booty, they then drove him up-stairs, and breaking open a closet, plundered it of money, silver cups and spoons, gold rings, and many other things of value. A bottle of elder wine which they found, they divided amongst the servants, lifting it to their mouths, as their hands were pinioned behind them. A maid-servant who was churning in an outhouse, hearing a noise, suspected there were thieves in the house, and put out the candle to secret herself. One of them, however, discovered her, and dragging her from her hiding-place, menaced her with the most horrid threats if she raised an alarm. All of them, indeed, disappointed and enraged at their ill-success, (for they had calculated upon a rich return for their trouble and hazard,) practised, on this occasion, the most savage cruelties. Having stripped the house of every thing of worth, even to the sheets from the beds, they dragged Mr. Lawrence down stairs again, and declared, with the most dreadful oaths, they would cut his throat if he hesitated to confess what money was in the house! and being answered that there was none excepting that which they had taken, they beat him barbarously with the but-ends of their whips, and inflicted a terrific cut upon his head with a pistol. One of them took a chopping-bill, and swore he would cleave his legs off;

another a kettle of water from the fire, and flung on him, which happening, however, to have been recently filled, did no serious injury. In their search, besides the beforementioned particulars, they met with a chest belonging to one of Mr. Lawrence's sons, which they broke open, taking therefrom twenty pounds, and all his linen. Some of these things were afterwards traced to a place called Duck-lane, where two of these fellows were apprehended.

Although in this robbery they got about 26*l.* in money in the whole, yet they made no fair distribution of it amongst themselves. The honour mentioned as existing amongst thieves, was, in this instance, at any rate, something of that character which distinguishes their dealings with others not of their profession; for it appeared upon evidence, that those who were most fortunate in the plunder, on the division of the spoil, could bring their minds to produce no more than three pounds nine shillings and sixpence.

These frequent and daring burglaries induced His Majesty to offer a pardon to any one of the criminals who had been concerned in entering the house of Mr. Lawrence, and committing such atrocities on the evening of the fourth of February; and further, a reward of 50*l.* to every person who should be instrumental in the discovery of any of the offenders.

Notwithstanding which, on the 7th of February, the party again met by appointment, having fixed upon the White Hart in Drurylane, as the best place whereat to concert future depredations. Accordingly, they agreed upon making an attempt to rob Mr. Francis, a large farmer near Mary-le-bone, at whose house they arrived shortly after seven. The details of this outrage are much the same as the previous robberies in which they were engaged. They succeeded in obtaining thirty-seven guineas and ten pounds in silver, a quantity of jewels and linen, and the unfortunate Mr. Francis's wig, all of which they carried off; not forgetting the latter, the value of which, excepting to the owner, we are quite at a loss to conceive.

They also formed a design to rob the house of a country justice, and with that intention met at a public-house near Leigh. Not rightly knowing, however, the way into the justice's domicile, they concealed themselves under some furze bushes; but while they were thus lying in wait, they heard several persons riding along together, who happened to be some of the neighbouring farmers returning from the table of the rustic Rhadamanthus in a state of noisy mirth, induced, doubtless, by the genial fumes of the justice's wines; and by their conversation it was plain that there were others still remaining there, who, dreading neither riotous spouses, nor the midnight bottle, might probably have determined with wine and song to "outwatch the bear;" they therefore deemed it advisable not to attempt it that night, and adjourned accordingly their attack to some more promising period, which so far proved of advantage to them, that it thereby prevented their being taken, as otherwise they unavoidably would have been; for they had been observed by some of the neighbourhood, and being suspected as smugglers, information was given to the custom-house, and a party of dragoons sent out after them, whom they met; when after a strict search, nothing having been found upon them, they were suffered to pass. Thus the justice escaped.

These daring robberies at length roused the country, and one of the King's keepers waited on the Duke of Newcastle, and obtained His Majesty's promise of a reward of one hundred pounds to him who should be fortunate enough to apprehend any of them. This made them lie a little more concealed; but some of the keepers and others receiving intelligence that they were regaling themselves at an ale-house in Westminster, they pursued them there, and bursting open the door, took three, after a stout resistance; two of whom, the third turning evidence against them, were hanged in chains accordingly. Turpin, however, made his escape by leaping from a window.

The gang thus broke up, and Turpin quite left to himself, made a determination never to command another, but to go altogether upon his own bottom; and with this view he set out for Cambridge, as he was not known in that county.

Notwithstanding this resolve, the following strange encounter provided him with his best companion (as he would call him) before he reached his journey's end. King, the highwayman, who had been towards Cambridge on professional business, was returning to town. Turpin seeing him well mounted, and bearing the appearance of a gentleman, thought it was an excellent opportunity to recruit his pockets, and accordingly, with a loud voice, commanded King to stand. King, enjoying the joke, though at the prospect of a bullet through his head if he carried the jest too far, assumed all the conduct of a person so unceremoniously addressed. "Deliver!" shouted Turpin, "or by —— I'll let day-light through you." "What," said King, laughing heartily, "what! dog eat dog! Come, come! brother Turpin, if you don't know me, I know you, and should be glad of your company." After mutual assurances of fidelity to one another, and that nothing should part them till death, they agreed to go together upon some exploit, and met with a small booty that very day; after which they continued together, committing divers robberies for nearly three years, when King was accidentally shot.

King being very well known about the country, as likewise was Turpin, insomuch that no house would entertain them, they formed the idea of dwelling in a cave, and to that end pitched upon a place inclosed with a large thicket, between Loughton Road and King's-Oak-Road; here they made a place large enough to receive them and two horses, and while they lay concealed there, they could see through several holes, purposely made, what passengers went by on either road, and as they thought proper sallied out and robbed them. This they did in such a daring manner, and so frequently, that it was not safe for any person to travel that way, and the very higglers were obliged to go armed. In this cave they drank and lay; Turpin's wife supplied them with food, and frequently remained in the place all night with them.

From the forest, King and Turpin once took a ride to Bungay in Suffolk, where the latter had seen two young market-women receive thirteen or fourteen pounds, and was determined to rob them of it. King attempted to dissuade him from it, saying, they were pretty girls, and he would never be engaged in an attempt to deprive two hard-working women of their little gains. Turpin, however, persisted, and coming up with them relieved them of the burden of their coin, which exploit occasioned a dispute between them.

As they were returning, they robbed a gentleman, who was taking an airing in his chariot, with his two children. King first attacked him, but found him so powerful and determined a person, returning such sound replies in the shape of blows to poor King's civilities, that he was fain to call upon his companion for assistance. Their united strength at last overcame him, and they took from him all the money he had about him, and then demanded his watch, which he declined on any account to part with; but one of the children became frightened, and persuaded its father to let them have it. They then insisted upon taking a mourning ring which they observed he wore, and an objection was raised on his part, even to that proposition. Finding, however, it was useless to oppose them, he at length resigned it, telling them it was not worth eighteen pence, but that he much valued it. Upon which information they returned it to him, saying, they were too much of gentlemen to take anything which another valued so much.

About this time the reward offered for the apprehension of Turpin had induced several poor, but resolute men, to make an attempt to get him into their power. Among the rest a man, groom to a Mr. Thompson, tempted by the placard setting forth the golden return in the event of success, connected himself with a higgler to ward off suspicion, and commenced his search. Turpin one day standing by himself in the neighbourhood of his cave, observed some one who, he supposed, was poaching for hares, and saluted him with, "No hares near this thicket; it's of no use seeking, you'll not find any."—"Perhaps I shall a *Turpin*, though," replied the fellow, and levelled his piece at him. Seeing his danger, Turpin commenced a parley, retreating at the same time by degrees towards his cave, the groom following him with his gun presented. "I surrender," said Turpin, when he reached the mouth of the cavern, and the man dropping the point of his piece, the former seized his carbine, and shot him dead on the spot. Turpin instantly made off to another part of the country, in search of King, and sent his wife a letter to meet him at a certain public-house, at which in a few days, enquiring for her under a feigned name, he found she was awaiting his appearance. The kitchen where she was, happened to be at the back through a public room, where some farmers and others were regailing themselves. On passing through, a butcher, to whom he owed five pounds, recognized him, and taking him aside said, "I know you have money now, Dick; if you'd pay me it would be of great service,"—"My wife has certainly money to some amount," replied Turpin, with a most unmoved countenance; "she is in the next place; I'll get it of her, and pay you presently." When Turpin was gone, the butcher apprized the company who he was, and added, "I'll just get my five pounds of him, and then we'll take him." Turpin, however, was not to be so caught, and instead of going to his wife, leaped out of the next window, took horse, and was off in an instant, much to the discomfiture of the knight of the cleaver and the assembled company, who doubtless had calculated most correctly the proportion of the reward that would be due to each by virtue of the king's signet.

Having discovered King, and one of his associates whose name was Potter, they determined to set out at once for London; and coming over the forest about three hundred yards from the Green Man, Turpin found that his horse, having undergone great fatigue, began to tire. On such an occasion it was no question with Turpin how he should provide himself with another, for, overtaking a gentleman, the owner of several race-horses, he at once appropriated his steed and a handsome whip to his own peculiar use, and recommending his own broken-down jade to the kind consideration of the party, speaking highly of his points, left him to mount the sorry courser, and urge the wretched quadruped forward in the best way he could.

This robbery was committed on a Saturday night, and on the Monday following the gentleman received intelligence, that such a horse as he had lost and described was left at an inn in Whitechapel; he accordingly went there, and found it to be the same. Nobody came for it at the time appointed, but about eleven o'clock at night, King's brother called for the horse, and was seized immediately. The whip he carried in his hand, the gentleman instantly identified as that stolen from him, although the button upon which his name had been engraved was half broken off; the latter letters of his name, however, were plainly distinguishable upon the remaining part. They charged a constable with him, but he becoming frightened, and on the assurance that if he spoke the truth he should be released, confessed, that there was a lusty man, in a white duffel coat, waiting for it in a street adjoining. One Mr. Bayes immediately went out, and finding the man as directed, perceived it was King. Coming round upon him, Mr. Bayes (the then active landlord of the Green Man, to whom the gentleman at the time had related the robbery,) attacked him. King immediately drew a pistol, which he pointed to Mr. Bayes's breast, but it luckily flashed in the pan. A struggle then ensued, for King was a powerful man, and Turpin hearing the skirmish, came up, when King cried out, " Dick, shoot him, or we are taken, by ——!" at which instant Turpin fired his pistol, but it missed Mr. Bayes, and shot King in two places. " Dick, you have killed me, make off," were King's words as he fell, and Turpin, seeing what he had done, clapped spurs to his horse, and made his escape. King lived for a week afterwards, and gave Turpin the character of a coward, telling Mr Bayes that if he pleased to take him, he was to be found at a certain house near Hackney Marsh, and that when he rode away, he had three brace of pistols about him, and a carbine slung. Upon inquiry, it was found that Turpin had actually been at the house which King mentioned, and made use of something like the following expressions to the man. " What shall I do? where shall I go? Dick Bayes, I'll be the death of you; for I have lost the best fellowman I ever had in my life; I shot poor King in endeavouring to kill that dog." The same resolution of revenge he retained to the last, though without the power of effecting it.

After this, he still kept about the forest, till he was harrassed almost to death; for he had lost his place of safety, the cave, which was discovered upon his shooting Mr. Thompson's groom. When they found the cave, there were in it two shirts in a bag, two pair of stockings, part of a bottle of wine, and some ham. Turpin was very nearly taken, while hiding in these woods, by a Mr. Ives, the king's huntsman, who, thinking he was secreted there, took out two dry-footed hounds; but Turpin perceiving them coming, climbed up a tree, and saw them stop beneath it several times, as though they scented him, which so terrified Turpin, that as soon as they were gone, he made a resolution of retiring that instant to Yorkshire.

Soon after this, a person came out of Lincolnshire to Brough, near Market-Cave, in Yorkshire, and stayed for some time at the Ferry-house. He said his name was John Palmer; and he went from thence sometimes to live at North Cave, and sometimes at Welton, continuing in these places about fifteen or sixteen months, except such part of the time as he went to Lincolnshire to see his friends, which he frequently did, and as often brought three or four horses back with him, which he used to sell or exchange in Yorkshire. While he so lived at Brough, Cave, and Welton, he very often went out hunting and shooting with the gentleman in the neighbourhood. As he was returning one day from shooting, he saw one of his landlord's cocks in the street, and raising his gun, shot it dead. A man, his neighbour, witnessing so wanton an act, complained of such conduct, asking him by what authority he shot another man's property. "Wait one moment," said Mr. Palmer, "just stay till I have charged my piece, and I'll shoot you too." The landlord being informed of the loss he had sustained by the death of his favorite bird, and the man who saw the act, being enraged at the threat Palmer had used towards him, they both obtained a warrant against him, and he was brought up at the General Quarter Sessions, where he was examined. Sureties for his good behaviour in future were the penalty alone exacted from him, which, however, refusing to find, he was committed to the House of Correction. His conduct thus excited great suspicion; for it was strange that a man who was in the habit of bringing from his friends in Lincolnshire half-a-dozen horses at a time, and plenty of money, should be so forsaken as not to be able to provide sureties; and still stranger, that on so trivial an occasion as the present, if he could find them at all, he did not produce them. A man's pride under other circumstances might be concerned, or a consciousness of innocence that excluded the possibility, or the benefit of release, under other conditions than free acquittal; but on a charge of this nature, which might have been made up even by the purchase of a fowl, or a simple excuse, his refusal was very suspicious. Enquiries were set on foot in all quarters; and the magistrate, not contented with the accounts he gave of himself of having been a grazier in Lincolnshire, despatched officers to learn how far that statement was consistent with truth. The result was a confirmation of Palmer's account, so far as the fact of his having lived in Lincolnshire, and having been a grazier there; that is, that there he had something to do with sheep, confined principally to the expert practice of stealing them. Mr. Palmer, upon the receipt of this information, was removed from the Beverley house of correction to York castle, and accommodated on the way with the use of hand-cuffs, and a guard of honour. When he arrived at his new abode, two persons from Lincolnshire challenged a mare and a foal which he had sold to a gentleman, and also the horse on which he rode when he came to Beverley, to be stolen from them off the fens in Lincolnshire. We need not add that Mr. Palmer was one and the same person with Dick Turpin, the notorious highwayman.

Turpin at one time, with another fellow, laid a scheme for seizing the Government money, ordered to be paid to the ships at Portsmouth. Both of them were to have attacked the guard in a narrow pass, with sword and pistol in hand ; but Turpin's courage failed him, and the enterprize dropped. Gordon, his accomplice in this design, was afterwards taken on a charge in which he alone was concerned; and while in Newgate he declared that " after that, Turpin would be guilty of any cowardly action, and die like a dog."

Turpin was tried and convicted of stealing the horse and the foal and mare from the fens, and was executed on Saturday, April 7th, 1739. He behaved himself with remarkable assurance, and bowed to the spectators as he passed. It was observed that as he mounted the ladder his right leg trembled, on which he stamped it down with violence, and with daunted unfortitude looked around him. After speaking to the executioner for nearly half an hour, he threw himself off the ladder, and expired in about five minutes.

His corpse was brought back from the gallows and buried in a neat coffin in St. George's churchyard. The grave was dug deep, and the persons he appointed to follow him (mourners we hesitate to call them, for we cannot imagine anybody to mourn upon the death of such an unprecedented ruffian,) those persons whoever they were, however, took all possible care to secure the corpse; notwithstanding which, some men were discovered to be moving off the body, which they had taken up; and the mob having got information where it might be found, went to a garden in which it was deposited, and brought it away in a sort of triumph, and buried it in the same grave having first filled the coffin with slacked lime.

HENRY COOK.

HENRY COOK was one of nineteen or twenty of a family, and his parents were industrious and respected in their station. The father being a leather merchant, young Cook was instructed in the same business, and provided with a suitable stock. He conducted himself with propriety for some years, and being married to a reputable woman, seemed to promise a life of respectability and usefulness. It happened, however, that running in debt, he was forced to abscond, lest he should be arrested. In these unpleasant circumstances, he went from place to place, and being informed that the bailiff threatened he would have him if he stayed above ground, he provided a pair of pistols, and sent that officer word that he was prepared for his approach, and that the moment he came it should be his last. He therefore heard no more of him.

After skulking about for some time, he ventured home to his wife one evening; but finding a stranger there, he resolved to live no longer with her. He emptied his shop of what things he could carry, and went to secrete himself in his sister's house. He next provided himself with a pair of pistols, and commenced highwayman. Though he began on foot, he soon obtained a horse, and with no small success carried on his depredations. After four robberies, from which he only received thirteen pounds, thirteen shillings, his career was nearly terminated. Having robbed a gentleman of his horse, and some days after, riding along, seven or eight men came up to him, and had not rode a mile, when one of them challenged his horse, as the one advertised to have been stolen by a highwayman at such a time and place. "Accordingly," says Cook, "he imperiously demanded of me an account of myself, and how I came by that horse. I told him that I lived in

London, and had purchased the horse of a man at the Bell Inn, at Edmonton, and that if he would go there along with me, he would be satisfied of the truth of what I said." By this stratagem, Cook hoped to have separated him from his companions, given him his friend's horse instead of his own, and taken his cash for giving him so much trouble. But all the party went along with him, so that, when he came near the inn, he was greatly at a loss how to extricate himself from this unpleasant dilemma; but at the gate of the inn he put spurs to his horse, and rode down a lane; their horses however, being fresher, he took toward a wood, when, his horse refusing to leap, four of his troublesome companions were within forty yards of him, when he fired, and demanded them to stand off. They stopped, when he alighted from his horse, and ran into the wood.

Having been thus alarmed, he remained inactive for some days, but venturing out again, he attacked an old man, robbed him of his money and horse; and had not proceeded far, when he met another man with a better horse, which he took, and what money and useful articles he found upon him. The latter gentleman had not proceeded far on his journey, when he met the old man, who claimed his horse, else he would inform upon him as a robber. The other then gave him his horse, and walked home upon foot. After some days' carousing, till his money was spent, Cook went out again; but, to his astonishment, within a little of the place where he had robbed the man of his money and his horse, he was dismounted, seized, carried before a magistrate, and committed to Newgate. His accuser, however, was so favourable as not to swear that he was the man who robbed him, though the animal upon which Cook rode was certainly the prosecutor's horse. This being the first time that he had been apprehended, his father and neighbours appeared in his behalf, got him clear off, and, elated with his acquittal, took him home with them to his wife and family.

Upon his return, he found his affairs in an embarrassed condition, and inquiring of William Taylor, the man who conducted his business, he found there were no good debts outstanding, nor any funds wherewith to renew his operations with apparent success. Thus circumstanced, he resolved to go to London, and purchase a pair of pistols, in order to rob between his own house and the forest until his funds were recruited. Having done so, he soon gained 30*l*. and consulting with Taylor how to lay out the money, he told him how he had gained it, and added, " let us go and make it ten times more, and then think of buying leather." The proposal was accepted, and repairing to London, they purchased what things were necessary. They then commenced with great boldness stopping all coaches and individuals, so that they soon found their present employment a speedier way of making money than selling leather or making shoes. But one day attacking the stage-coach at Colchester, a captain Mawley shot Taylor, and his companion ran off.

This accident rendered it impossible for Cook to return home; he therefore concealed himself for a few days, and again provided himself with a good horse, and went forth with the most desperate resolution of revenging Taylor's death, by taking the life of Captain Mawley, if he could possibly find him. After various daring robberies, he was at last discovered by a woman that knew him, and was taken; and several witnesses appearing against him, he was sentenced to suffer the due reward of his numerous and aggravated crimes.

HENRY SIMMS,

CALLED

" THE YOUNG GENTLEMAN."

WE prefer giving an abstract of the life and adventures of this notorious criminal in his own words, since it will serve to show far better than any moral reflections of our own, that when once the principles become vitiated, whether by early abuse or habitual moral recklessness, the very nature is changed, and the conscience remains in a state of abeyance. There is an easy unconcern, a ' young gentleman' flippancy in the style in which our adventurer has chosen to narrate his exploits, that indicates too plainly the utter want of common or decent feeling in his nature, and leaves us to the unavoidable conclusion that under no possible circumstances, nor in any conceivable condition, could ' Young Gentleman Harry' have become or have been made a respectable member of society. He begins his narrative thus:—

" I am now thirty years of age, born in London, October 19, 1716, of honest industrious parents, in the parish of St. Martin's-in-the-Fields. Having the misfortune to lose both my father and mother when very young, I was left to the care of an indulgent grandmother, who tenderly loved me, had me educated with maternal fondness, and early began to instil into me sentiments of virtue, honour, and honesty, from which I too early swerved. My grandmother having been many years in the service of a nobleman, was an old servant much respected, and on that account not only indulged with having her grandson with her, but was likewise indulged with my being permitted to go to Eton School with two sons of the noble lord. I remained at Eton School some time, and even there began to show an early inclination to vice, without an opportunity of committing it. When I arrived at the age of fourteen, my grandmother put me apprentice to a breeches-maker, but a life of servitude ill suited my constitution. I stayed with him no longer than a month, in which short time I procured to myself several *choice* acquaintances, particularly two (since hanged,) and was easily persuaded to accompany them in many robberies, which we committed in and about Mary-le-bone fields, and the money we got we riotously spent among thieves and bullies, and when that was gone, turned out (as we called it) for more.

" Thus some months passed on in a round of wickedness which not all the counsel in the universe could restrain. My poor grandmother with tears in her eyes entreated me to leave off my wicked courses, and to follow her instructions. But I little regarded her advice, and still pursued my old schemes. There was hardly a place round London famed for wickedness, but I was there. Tottenham Court Fair, when it came, I rejoiced at, for there I lived riotously, and there too I became a proficient in the dexterous art of picking pockets, by which I gained for some time pretty handsomely. But at length that business grew dead, and, as I lived at a large rate, money was wanting. Accordingly, having mustered up a sufficient quantity of cash, I purchased a pair of pistols and a horse, and set out; and on Epping Forest, near Woodford, I stopped two gentlemen in a chaise and pair, from whom I took only a little silver, and proceeded on to Newmarket, where I arrived that night, and early next morning set out again, stopped the Norwich coach, and took from the passengers thirty guineas, a gold watch, and a diamond ring, and then rode away; and about three hours after, near Littlebury, met the Cambridge coach, from the passengers of which I took about five pounds, and came on for London. I now began to frequent a noted gaming-house in Covent Garden, where, for several nights I had a prodigious run of luck, and won a considerable sum of money. I bought myself a silver hilted sword, had several new suits of clothes made, particularly one suit of black velvet, and appeared at all my usual haunts with surprising eclàt. It was at this time that I gained the name of 'Gentleman Harry,' for though I was before only called plain Harry, yet, on this my sudden grand appearance, I was christened 'Gentleman Harry,' which name I retained for ever. But fortune not continuing her favours at the gaming-table, I was once more reduced, and obliged to take up again my old trade. Hitherto, what business I had done was by myself; but being out one day with a companion, we agreed to attack the first person we met with powder and shot. We saw nothing for some days that we either cared or dared to attack, till we came to a place called Eversley Bank, where we met a collector of Shrewsbury; we ordered him to stand and deliver, and took from him near three hundred pounds. For this robbery two men were taken up a short time after, tried at the assizes, capitally convicted, and executed: and I cannot but own, that, notwithstanding my hardened villainy, so often as I remembered it, I felt a good deal of sorrow at being the cause of shedding innocent blood, which I always avoided and abhorred.

"About a month after this I robbed a lady on Blackheath, in her coach. After the robbery, riding down the hill that leads to Lewisham Wash, I was overtaken by six or seven butchers, one of whom seizing the cape of my coat, pulled me off my horse, and the cape giving way, he tore it quite off. I then pulled out my pistols, swearing I would shoot the first man who dared to advance; which none of them caring to do, I retreated into the fields and got off with the loss of my horse, which cost me seventeen pounds. But I was not long without a horse, for, going towards Bromley, I met a gentleman on horseback, to whom I presented my pistols, ordering him to dismount or I would shoot him through the head; which he did, and I took from him eight guineas and seventeen shillings in silver, and, mounting the horse, left him to pursue his journey on foot. I sold the horse the next day at the George, in Farnham, and bought another, which cost me thirteen guineas. From thence I proceeded to Tunbridge, at which place I stayed a day or two, and then came to London, where I found an old companion, a sailor, who agreed to turn out with me. At the bottom of Shooter's Hill we robbed a gentleman of his gold watch, and about seventeen pounds: the watch I afterwards sold for nine pounds at the gaming-table, in Covent Garden, and lost the money when I had done.

"Being by this time pretty well known, I ran great hazards; it was but a very few days after I lost my money as above, I was attacked by several soldiers in Drury Lane, and should have been carried to the Savoy, had I not been rescued by some of my friends from Covent Garden; and in about a week after that, I was taken out of a tavern for the robbery of a gold watch which I had about me, and was again rescued by my companions. Some little time after this, I was attacked by about nine gentlemen thief-takers, in Bridewell Walk, Clerkenwell, but having my pistols about me, I soon dispersed the cowardly rascals, and walked off. Another time, riding on horse-back through Covent Garden, I was pursued by a party of thief-takers, but got clear.

"Being in this manner continually beset on all sides, I was at length, by the perfidy of some ladies with whom I was in company at Goodman's Fields Wells, taken by a party of thief-takers, and conducted to Clerkenwell Bridewell, where several prosecutions were commenced against me, and I was obliged to come to a composition with divers of them, which drained me very low. One gentleman in particular, whom I had robbed of only eleven shillings and a small medal, made me pay him forty-seven guineas. By these means, having got rid of my several prosecutors, I was by order of the Court of Justice, confined in Clerkenwell Bridewell two months for an assault, at the end of which time I was set at liberty, giving sureties for my good behaviour for two years. It was not long after I was discharged, before I was pressed and sent on board His Majesty's ship the Rye, where I continued for about three months, though much against my inclination; being continually forming some scheme for an escape, not one of which schemes took effect till the following was hit upon. Whilst we were at Leith, we had pressed several hands out of some colliers, who, I found by talking to, were as little desirous of staying on board as myself; I therefore proposed to eight of them this scheme: —that when the cutter, which had been on shore pressing, came alongside at night, one of them should fall out of the main-chains into the river, and the rest of us should immediately jump into the boat and take the man up, and row away, which we put in practice with success, only, just as we had got up our man, the boatswain jumped on board and threatened us. My companions were for throwing him over-board, but on his promising to be quiet they were over-ruled, and he was suffered to sit still; and, notwithstanding several guns were fired after us, we rowed safe to shore, and left the boat to the care of the boatswain to carry back if he thought proper. Being safe on shore, we took leave of each other:

they set out for Scarborough, and I for Edinburgh, in which city I stayed about a week, and during that time became acquainted with a Scotch lassie, who not only furnished me with money to purchase my former implements, but lent me seven guineas to bear my expenses to London, which lasted me no farther than Grantham; and between Grantham and Stamford I was obliged to *speak* with the York stage, from the passengers of which I took eight guineas, about seventeen shillings in silver, a silver watch, and three plain gold rings, with which I came to London.

" In a short space of time after this, I committed many robberies by myself, which I did not exactly minute down. My general rendezvous was about Epping Forest, where I robbed the Harwich coach, the Cambridge coach, the Norwich coach, &c., to a pretty large amount, which I spent as fast as I got. About this time, I kept company with another man's wife, who was so fond of me, that I could persuade her either out of cash or any valuables she had, to supply my present necessities: as was the case when I persuaded her out of her gold watch, and some other things, which her husband took me up upon and I was committed to Newgate, tried at the Old Bailey, and acquitted by the court, who very justly saw through the prosecution. After my being discharged on this affair, I unluckily, in a quarrel, ran a crab-stick into a woman's eye in Goodman's-fields, for which I was sent to New Prison. In the mean time, I was informed that the wife was arrested on an action and sent to a sponging-house. Being determined to relieve her, if possible, I contrived in what manner I could make my escape, and, accordingly, by the help of sheets I let myself down out of my window and got off, I immediately went to a friend of mine in Leather-lane, who furnished me with two pistols, with which I went to the sponging-house in Gray's-inn-lane, expecting to find my lady; but when I came there I found she had been removed to Newgate. Being thus disappointed, and having no hopes of getting her out of Newgate, I determined to go to work at my old trade.

" In Broad-street, St. Giles's, about nine at night, I stopped a coach which contained a single gentleman, from whom I took about seventeen shillings, and from thence went to my old haunts in Covent Garden, and after drinking pretty freely, I had a quarrel with a gentleman, who calling the watch to his assistance, I was taken and carried to the Covent Garden round-house. Being very much fuddled, I soon went to sleep: but when I waked next morning, and found myself in a prison, after having escaped from one but the night before, I was almost distracted, and began to contrive an escape, but to no purpose; for after calling for the keeper of the round-house, under pretence of being hungry, I got toast and ale, and therewith a knife, with which I hoped once more to make a breach whereby to escape. But I was doomed to be disappointed; for notwithstanding my cutting down the plaster and laths of the ceiling, the joists were so firm that I could not make an opening. I then grew desperate, broke all the things I could find in the room, cut the sheets to pieces, pulled off some tiles from the roof, and did every offensive act in my power, till at length the constable with a large posse of myrmidons arrived, who carried me before Sir Thomas De Veil, where, after a long examination, I laid my information of the robbery of Mr. Smith in Southwark, which robbery I was actually concerned in, though not with the persons I swore against at Croydon assizes, but with three others. We committed the robbery in December, 1745, getting in at the two-pair-of-stairs window by a *Jacob*, that is, a ladder of ropes, which was fixed to the sign-post first, drawn afterwards into the balcony, and then attached to the two-pair-of-stairs window. We took from Mr. Smith's house, after frightening Mrs. Smith almost to death, two bags of money containing 514*l.* and a 20*l.* bank-note, and carried off in bags goods to the value of 800*l.* The cash we divided equally amongst us at a house in the Mint; the plate we sold; and we carried the goods to a house near the Pindar of Wakefield, near Pancras; but for my share of the goods I never received one penny; they were carried to Ireland by my three accomplices, who promised to remit me my part, but were never so good as their words. After my examination I was removed to the New Gaol, Southwark, to give evidence at the assizes at Croydon.

"After this affair at Croydon, I was removed by habeas to Newgate, on the oath of a barber at Westminster, whom I had robbed, which barber was found out by some of my enemies to prosecute me; and upon his indictment I was tried, found guilty, and sentenced to transportation; and, about two months after, was with several other convicts put on board the Italian Merchant, which carried us to Maryland. On our passage I had formed several plans for an escape, one of which had nearly been successful, and was agreed upon between me and the rest of the transports. We were at a certain time to have secured the Captain and sailors, as well as the fire-arms, and to have run away with the ship, but one of them discovered it to the captain, who put us in irons, and kept a watchful eye on us during the remainder of the voyage. When we arrived at Maryland, I was disposed of to the master of the

Two Sisters, who was in want of sailors, and with whom I went to sea. We had not been out many days before we were taken by a privateer of Bayonne, and carried into Spain. We were all sent on shore, and had papers given to us to go to Portugal. When I arrived at Oporto, I was pressed on board his Majesty's ship the King Fisher, where I remained about four months, in which time we took several prizes. But not liking my station, I left her at Oporto, travelled to Lisbon, and got in the Hanover packet to Falmouth, where I stayed about a month. My companions endeavoured to persuade me to go a privateering with them in the Warner galley; but I refused, and leaving Falmouth travelled to St. Ives, where I found a vessel ready to sail for Bristol, on board of which I went, and arrived at Bristol in two days. I was not long there before I determined to set up my old trade, and procured a pair of pistols, though I still wanted a horse; but having observed several horses in a field near Lawford's-gate, I soon marked out one for myself, and that night got into a stable, from whence I stole a saddle and bridle, and without much difficulty caught my horse, and set out for London.

"When I reached London, I was soon informed the thief-takers were after me. The night I came to town, I put my horse up at the White Swan, in Whitechapel, but went no more near him, fearful, as I had stolen him, he might be advertised. But I was not long without a horse, for one Saturday night, about eight o'clock, coming from St. James's, where I had been regaling with some friends, I perceived a boy in Rider-street walking a horse about, apparently waiting for somebody. I called and persuaded him to step on an arrand into Duke-street while I held the horse, and, as soon as the boy was gone, I mounted and rode away, and crossing the country reached Harrow-on-the-Hill, where I passed the night, and the next day set out towards London in hopes of meeting some of the farmers returning from the hay-markets, after having sold their hay. I had drunk pretty freely at dinner and was somewhat elevated. I had not ridden far before I met three gentlemen, whom I commanded to 'stand and deliver their money,' which they did very quietly. From the first I got about three pounds, from the second I had about five pounds, and from the third thirteen or fourteen shillings.

"The next person I robbed was Mr. Sleep, my prosecutor, and though neither he nor I recognized each other at that time, yet he, it seems, has known me from a child. I took from him his watch and six shillings, and made off.

"After robbing Mr. Sleep, I still kept travelling towards London, in hopes of meeting the farmers; at length, five of them appeared, whom I commanded 'to stop,' and took from them about 5*l*. in silver. I felt in their pockets for watches, but they had none. Next I met three men, whom I ordered 'to stop;' but they, not regarding my orders, refused, and rode full speed, and I along side of them, for at least five or six minutes, presenting my pistol, swearing I would shoot if they did not stop: but they still rode on; and I turned from them, giving them a hearty d—n, not caring to let off my pistol; for I had determined to shoot no man, unless he attempted to take me. But after this, on the same road, I robbed two more men; from one I took about fifteen shillings, from another about seven shillings. Turning from them I let off one of my pistols into the air, and went on for London.

"That night I made a sort of perambulation among the thief-takers, determining to do mischief to some of them, if possible, especially to those who, I heard, had been after me. The first I went to was one W. H. in Chancery-lane. Being on horseback, I knocked at the door, which his wife opened, demanding my business. I told her, 'to speak with her husband.' She replied, 'he was gone to bed,' at the same time desiring to know my name and business. 'I am a gentleman of his acquaintance,' said I; 'he will know me when he sees me.' My blunderbuss, which I then carried, being mounted with brass, and having a brass barrel, by the light of her candle she perceived it, and directly slapped to the door, called to her husband, and told him (mentioning my name) that I was at the door. I could hear him ask for his piece, on which I cried out, 'You rascal, come to the door, and I'll piece you;' and if he had come I should certainly have killed him, but he thought better of it, and I rode away.

"From my friend H. I went to another of the same sort of gentry in Holborn, one I. S. I got off my horse and went into his house threatening destruction; but the moment he saw me enter at one door, he went out at another, and after venting a few oaths, I remounted my horse, and went to the Greyhound inn, in Drury-lane, where I lay that night.

"Next morning I set out for Epping Forest, and dined at the Bird-in-Hand, at Stratford: after dinner, about two o'clock, I set out on the Romford road. I met on the forest a chaise, and from a man therein took about fourteen shillings. This robbery was done within sight of the Spread Eagle, at the door of which several people were drinking on horseback. From thence I rode through

Ilford, then came on the forest again, and stayed till it was almost dark, and rode towards Laytonstone, within half a mile of which I robbed a captain of his gold watch, ten guineas, and some silver. After speaking with the captain, I came off the forest for London. Perceiving a hurly-burly, and a great mob at Snaresbrook turnpike, I rode up to see what was the matter, and on enquiry amongst the mob, found that they had stopped a gentleman whom they mistook for me. As it was dark and they could not distinguish me, I thought it most prudent to ride through the turnpike, and go directly for London, which I did, and putting up my horse at the Saracen's Head, Aldgate, and calling a coach, I went to a tavern, where I lay all night.

In the morning I began to reflect that, it being well known I was in England returned from transportation, and as well known too that I had committed a great many robberies, there were many thief-takers after me, and I was surrounded with danger; and I therefore determined to set out for Chester immediately, and from thence to Dublin, resolving, as I had now a handsome sum, as well as a parcel of diamond rings and watches, to live entirely on my stock, and rob no more, at least while that lasted. I dined that day at St. Alban's, and as I generally drank both at and after my meals pretty freely, I soon grew warm, and after dinner, setting out for Dunstable, I found my resolution to rob no more would not hold, for within a quarter of a mile of Redbourne, I ordered three gentlemen to stand and deliver. Presenting my pistol at the first, he replied, that he would not be robbed, and rode on; the second hit me on the head with his whip, and at the same time the other rode by me. Having a good beast under me, I was quickly up with them, and putting on one of my terrible countenances, with bitter imprecations I vowed that I would instantly shoot the first man dead who refused to deliver: when one of them quietly gave me about nine shillings; from the second I took an old-fashioned watch and seventeen shillings; and from the third, two guineas and about five shillings, and taking my leave immediately, attacked two more gentlemen, who likewise rode for it; but their horses being as good as mine, I ran them into Redbourne, and then gave it up. About an hour after, I stopped a single man on horseback, who telling me he had but eighteen-pence, I bade him keep that; but he seeming to have a very good horse and mine beginning to fail, I made him dismount and change with me. He had a portmanteau on his horse, which he was very industriously going to take off, but I told him he might as well let it remain where it was, which he did, though I had no opportunity to see what was in it; for being now become, perhaps, one of the most industrious of my profession, I could no more let a coach, chaise, or man go by without speaking with them in my way, than I could fly, and perceiving a coach coming along, which proved to be the Warrington stage, I directly made up to it, and got from the passengers therein about three pounds. The ladies seemed terribly frightened, and begged I would take my pistol away, which I did, and after taking their money I went on for Dunstable, and calling at several houses before I got there, I became pretty fatigued, not only with my business, but with liquor too. Being very much fuddled, I was so cunning as to think of putting up at the Bull inn, at Dunstable, the very house where the Warrington coach went to. After dismounting my horse, and calling for a quartern of brandy, I saw some of the passengers in the kitchen, belonging to the coach I had just then robbed, on which, I never stayed for my brandy, but went out of the house, mounted my horse, and rode as fast as I could make him go, till I came to Hockcliffe, and as it rained very hard, I resolved to put up, and accordingly went into the Star inn. After I had been there about an hour, and had drunk very freely, I became intoxicated, and fell asleep by the kitchen fire; but was soon awakened by three troopers and some others with pistols at my head, swearing they would shoot me if I offered to put my hand to my pockets. Being half asleep as well as drunk, they soon disarmed me, and took from me one gold watch, two silver ones, four diamond rings, forty-seven guineas in gold, and four pounds in silver: three of the best diamond rings I had secreted in my neckcloth. I desired them to give me my money again, and to let me go to bed; they gave me about nine pounds in gold and silver back, and then conducted me to a chamber, where I went to bed, after putting my money under my pillow, and fell asleep, guarded by the troopers, who took my money from under my head, which, when I awoke and missed, I charged them with, telling them it was using me exceedingly ill indeed, as they had gotten so much from me already, to take that from me too; whereupon, they returned it to me. Presently, I got up and sat by the fire-side, a good deal chagrined at my unfortunate fate. I resolved in my mind a thousand different methods of escape, but none appeared feasible even to myself. At length, a thought came into my head, of which I was resolved to make a trial. As I knew these troopers, from their behaviour, to be hungry hounds, and having two seals, the one gold and the other silver about me; as I sat over the fire, I determined to throw them in, naturally supposing, from their eagerness after plunder, they would endeavour to get them out, and I might thus, by some means or other, become master of their firearms. It happened as I had imagined; eager for their prey they fell down to rake them from the ashes, when I at the same time snatched a pistol from one of their hands and snapped it at his head: it missed fire, and I was immediately overpowered by the rest of the troopers, the landlord and others coming to their assistance; and I was the next day carried before the justice at Dunstable, where I insisted upon the troopers returning me my money and watches again, before I would answer any questions, and, accordingly, I *undressed* their pockets both of money and watches, asking them if they thought I had nothing else to do than to venture my life to dress the pockets of such fellows as they, who knew not how to wind up a watch; for in endeavouring to wind up one of the watches they had broken it.

" I was eventually committed to Bedford gaol for robbing the Warrington stage-coach, where I remained about four months, till I was removed by habeas corpus to Newgate, and in February last was tried at the Old Bailey for robbing Mr. Francis Sleep of his watch and six shillings, of which I was found guilty, and received sentence of death."

The above is an abstract containing all the most interesting or prominent transactions in the life of Henry Simms, who appears to have laboured in his vocation with a zeal worthy of better calling, and with a wantonness deserving of the gallows to which, at length, he was compelled to ascend. Young Gentleman Harry was executed at Tyburn, in June, 1747; and after hanging till he was dead, his body was cut down by a mob appointed for that purpose, and carried to a surgeon's in Covent Garden.

JAMES MACLAINE.

JAMES MACLAINE, called in his own time by the distinguished title of "The gentleman highwayman," seemed at his birth to be far removed from the common temptations which too frequently lead to an infamous death. Until the decease of his father, which took place when he was about eighteen years of age, a fair prospect of prosperity was presented to him; but, unhappily, being conscious of his birth, which entitled him, by a slight straining of courtesy, to the designation of a gentleman, he imbibed, together with an inordinate vanity, an aversion from business, and an immoderate desire to appear a gay young fellow.

Lauchlin Maclaine, the father of our adventurer, was a Presbyterian divine, and pastor of a congregation of that communion at Monaghan, in the North of Ireland. He designed James, his second son, for a merchant, and bestowed upon him a sound education, but died before he could put his intentions into effect of sending him to Rotterdam, to be placed in the counting-house of a Scotch merchant of his acquaintance.

Young Maclaine, the instant his father's breath was out of his body, proceeded to take possession and to dispose of his father's substance; and treated with perfect contempt the remonstrances of his friends and relations, and the exortations of his aunt, who, finding all her entreaties ineffectual took his only sister into her charge, and left him to pursue what course he pleased.

Thus left to himself, Maclaine forgot altogether the projected Dutch counting-house, and equipping himself in the gayest apparel that part of the country could afford, and purchasing a gelding, set up fine gentleman at once, and in a twelvemonth dissipated almost the whole of his property. During his extravagances, however, his ear had been frequently troubled with the remonstrances of his aunt and his other relations, which he at length found so disagreeable, that he was fain to set out for Dublin without communicating his intention to any one. It was here, it appears, that he first conceived the notion of making his fortune by marriage; and having no disagreeable person, he gratuitously gave himself credit for many more excellencies than, unfortunately, other people could discover in him. The demands for the maintenance of such an appearance as would realize his hopes of a rich marriage, soon swept away the remainder of his property; and he had now full time to reflect on his folly and vanity, and to regret not a little having despised the advice of his relations, who had for some time turned a deaf ear to his entreaties by letter for a supply of money. But upon them, nevertheless, he felt was now his sole dependance. He had long spent his all—he was an entire stranger to a single individual of worth or substance in the place, and his credit and clothes, even to the last shirt, were gone. Selling his sword, therefore, the last piece of splendour that remained to him, he raised as much as would bear his charges on foot, and with a heavy heart set out to return to Monaghan, his native place.

Not a hand was outstretched to welcome the prodigal home again; his aunt refused to see him, all his other relations followed her example, and the companions of his former riots not only refused him relief, but rendered him the sport and ridicule of the town. His sister, however, sometimes contrived to see him by stealth to give him her pocket-money, but that could not long support him. Here, then, he must inevitably have starved, had not a gentleman on his way to England, passing through the town, compassionately offered him the place of a servant who had recently died. Want, and the dread of starving, had by this time entirely banished all unnecessary and superfluous pride, and our young gentleman accepted the offer with joy. But, unhappily, the extreme pressure of want once removed, old thoughts return, old vanities are renewed; and so it was with Mr. Maclaine. His master's commands, though uniformly softened by good-nature and benevolence, appeared to him as so many insults offered to his birth and breeding; it is no wonder, therefore, that in a few months he was discharged from his service. Depending on his sister, who was about to be married to a man of some wealth, he set out once more for Ireland, to endeavour to obtain enough from his relations to fit him out for America or the West Indies; but here again he was doomed to disappointment. His sister's marriage had been broken off—she was unable to do anything for him;—and his other relations, deeming themselves scandalized by his having been a footman, were even less tractable than before, treated him with great indignity, and finally refused all manner of assistance.

Again reduced to starvation, he was obliged to think of service as his only resource. With much difficulty he obtained a situation as butler to a gentleman near Cork, with whom he did not live long, being discharged for some breach of trust. Here he remained for many months out of place, wandering about, without any settled abode or means of subsistence, except occasional remittances from his elder brother, a pastor of the English congregation at the Hague, whose friendly assistance was less relished, because it was accompanied by warm remonstrances on the past, and wholesome advice on the future conduct of his life.

Fortune was at length favourable; his old master, though he refused him a character to another family, generously paid his passage to England, and allowed him, for a limited period after his landing, a shilling a day for subsistence.

Once again on this side of the water, his notions of gentility returned; he scorned being a menial servant; and valuing the *minimum* of his ambition at a pair of colours, he actually had the impudence to attempt to borrow the purchase money on the bond he had obtained from his master. This absurd scheme failing, he threw up his shilling a-day in disgust, and heroically cast himself for support on a celebrated courtesan, a countrywoman of his own, who maintained him for some months in great magnificence, and enabled him to attend the public places with something like splendour.

But having disgusted this lady by his pusillanimous conduct in a rencontre with a certain peer,—who bestowed upon him a severe castigation, and very nearly ran him through the body, though he was much stronger, and as well armed as the nobleman,—he was once more without resources. His grandeur now suffered an eclipse for two or three months, and his last suit had been laid by in lavender, or, in other words, pawned, when he inspired the regard of a lady of quality, the consequence of which was, that for five or six months longer he flourished away as an idle fellow in all the public places.

But Maclaine inwardly was not idle. He was extremely anxious for an independent settlement, and the thought of inveigling some woman of fortune by the charms of his person was still uppermost in his mind. Among other schemes to this end, there was none he built so much upon as a very hopeful and grateful plot he had laid for the daughter of his patroness and benefactress, who had a considerable fortune. But the young lady's waiting-maid, who had either more honesty than abigails in general are furnished with, or had not received the price with which they are usually rewarded, discovered the affair to the old lady, who forthwith dismissed Maclaine from her services, but when, in a few months after, he was much reduced, she privately bestowed upon him fifty pounds in order to fit him out for Jamaica, where he had proposed to go and seek his fortune, and where the lady was willing enough that he should retire, that she might be free from fears on her daughter's account.

But Maclaine was no sooner possessed of this sum than he forgot his Jamaica expedition, and returned to his favourite scheme of fortune-hunting; for he never could rid himself of the idea that one day or other he should succeed in the main object of his existence. He released, therefore, his best clothes from the durance vile in which they had been plunged, and after various treatise with match-makers and chambermaids, relating to ladies of great reputed fortune, all which treaties ended in disappointment, he reluctantly contracted his ambition, and made suit to the daughter of a considerable innkeeper and dealer in horses, with whom he was fortunate enough to succeed, and whom he married with her parents' consent, and five hundred pounds.

Here it would seem that Maclaine had laid aside all thoughts of the fine gentleman, and had really determined to make the most of his wife's fortune by industry and dilligence. He took a house in Welbeck-street, and set up a grocer's and chandler's shop; was very obliging to his customers, punctual in his dealings, and, while his wife lived, was esteemed by his neighbours a careful and industrious man. However, though at times, and while he was in his shop, he appeared to like his business, yet in parties of pleasure, which he made but too often, and on holidays, he affected the dress of a gentleman, and thus created expences which only a gradual encroachment on his capital enabled him to meet; insomuch, that when his wife died, which was about three years after their marriage, he resolved to leave off business, and converted his furniture and goods into the miserable sum of eighty-five pounds, which, perhaps, with frugality, might have supported him in business, but which was at all times too small a sum for Mr. Maclaine.

His mother-in-law consenting to take charge of his only daughter, and once more in a manner a single man, with his eighty-five pounds in his pocket, again did the desire of appearing the gay fine gentleman obtrude itself upon his mind, and his old project of marrying a rich fortune engrossed all his faculties. For this purpose, Mr. Maclaine, who, but a few weeks before was not ashamed to appear in a patched coat, or to carry a halfpenny-worth of coal or sand to his customers, now hired handsome apartments near Soho-square, and resumed his laced clothes, and a hat and feather.

But, however unreasonable to others this sudden transition from the grub to the butterfly might appear, Mr. Maclaine had very good private reasons for his actions. It appears that during his wife's last illness, she had been attended by one Plunket, as a surgeon and apothecary; this Plunket, after the decease of the poor woman, opened his mind to Maclaine, saying, that though the latter had lost a good wife, yet, seeing that she was gone, it was of no use to despond or to repine, particularly as it might eventually turn out the most lucky circumstance in his life. He added at the same time that if Maclaine would agree to share the fortune with him, he could help him to a lady with ten thousand pounds at least in her own right.

This motion was too agreeable to Mr. Maclaine to be rejected. It is hardly necessary to detail with what zeal this affair was followed up, or how often they flattered themselves with the deceitful prospects of success. The young lady having been taken to the wells, Maclaine followed her, passing for a man of fortune, and in every part of his dress and equipage appearing in that character. Plunket acted as his partner, and was a sort of under agent, while Maclaine himself was ogling, dancing, and flirting with the young lady. But an ill-timed quarrel with an apothecary, one evening in the public room, placed a quietus upon his hopes for ever; for the disciple of Galen enlisting a "gallant son of Mars" in his quarrel, the latter had the effrontery to kick our adventurer down stairs, declaring publicly that he knew the rascal a footman a few years ago. This statement, which was believed by every body present, amongst whom was his mistress, whose credulity he had ascertained before, and was therefore not in a situation to doubt, compelled him and his footman Plunket to decamp without the ceremony of leave-taking, and, indeed, without any ceremony at all.

Returning to town from this woeful expedition, and examining the state of their cash, these faithful friends discovered that five guineas were the whole that remained,—a sum too little to support them, or to enter into any new project, or to keep up their assumed grandeur. Maclaine now found himself in a worse plight than he had brought himself to for some years past, without any visible hope of a supply, and yet engaged in a mode of life highly expensive, which it went to his heart either to retrench or relinquish. He now thought seriously of embarking for Jamaica, where he hoped to find employment as an accountant, and flattered himself that his person might be turned to account amongst the rich planter's daughters or widows. But no money was forthcoming for this purpose, nor could he think of any possible scheme whereby it might be raised.

Certainly, never had man less cause to complain of Fortune than Maclaine, and it would seem throughout his life, that she had determined to make his ruin entirely the work of his own hand, and leave him at last utterly without excuse or palliation; for meeting on 'Change with a gentleman, a countryman of his own, to whom he had formerly related his hopes of making a fortune in the manner we have related, he told him his situation at the present moment adding that he was now undone, that he had spent his all in that unhappy project, and had not wherewithal to subsist here, or to carry him from a place in which he felt he was cutting a very ridiculous figure. Hereupon the gentleman spoke in his behalf to some others of his countrymen; and as his conduct heretofore, according to the notions of the age, had been rather imprudent than vicious, they actually raised sixty guineas to fit him out for Jamaica, which they gave him promising him letters of recommendation from some merchants of respectability to their own correspondents. Here, then, was a prospect at once opened to him, of future happiness and prosperity. Let us see how it terminated.

He had agreed for the passage, paid part of the money in advance, and bespoken some necessaries fitted for the climate, when unhappily for the infatuated man, he was prompted to go to a masquerade, to take leave, as he said, for the last time, of the bewitching pleasures of London, and to bid a final farewell to this species of enjoyment, which he should have no hope of partaking in the West Indies. He went with the whole of his money in his pocket. The strange appearance of the place and of the company amused him for a while, but the noise of the gamesters drew his attention to the gaming-table, where the quick transition of large sums from one hand to another awakened his avarice, and lulled his prudence asleep. In short, he ventured, and in half an hour had possessed himself of a hundred guineas, with which he resolved, according to their phrase, " to tie up;" but avarice had now attacked him; and after taking a turn or two round the room, he again returned, and in a few minutes was stripped to the last guinea.

It is needless to describe his agony on this occasion. His money gone, his expedition utterly disconcerted, and his friends lost past redemption! What was now to be done?

In this extremity, his evil genius, now in the ascendant, prompted him to send for Plunket to advise with, and from that moment his ruin commenced. This was the favourable moment for Plunket. Himself a man of no honour, an utter stranger to all ties or principles of religion or honesty, an old sharper, and a daring fellow into the bargain, this was an opportunity, when his friend was agitated almost to madness, to propose, at first by distant hints, and at last in plain English, going on the highway.

Had he approached him in a calm hour, it is more than probable that his proposal had been rejected with horror; but the former strongly represented the necessity of a speedy supply before his friends could discover that his money was gone, which, he said, would expose him to universal scorn and contempt. A strange infatuation, the dread of shame—the shame of appearing a fool, diminished the horror of being a villain, and decided him to recruit his losses by means the most hazardous and wicked.

Having agreed upon a plan of co-partnership, and hired too horses, Plunket furnishing the pistols; for this was not his first entrance upon business of that nature, they set out on the evening after the masquerade, to lie in wait for passengers coming from Smithfield-Market. They met on Hounslow-heath with a grazier, next morning about four o'clock, from whom they took, without opposition, between sixty and seventy pounds.

In this, and other expeditions of the same kind, they wore Venetian masks; but this covering could not stifle conscience in Maclaine, nor animate him into courage. He accompanied Plunket, it is true, and was by at the robbery, but strictly speaking, had no hand in it; for his fears were so great that he had no power to utter a word, or to draw a pistol. The least resistance on the part of the countryman would have given wings to his heels, and have caused him to leave his more daring accomplice in the lurch.

Even when the robbery was over, and the countryman out of sight, Maclaine's fears were intolerable. He followed Plunket for some miles without speaking a word; and when they put up at an inn, nearly ten miles from the place of the robbery, he called for a private room, fearful of every shadow, and terrified at every sound. His agonies of mind were so great, that Plunket was fearful that his folly would raise suspicion in the house, and he would fain have persuaded him to return immediately to London; but he would not stir till it was dusk, and then would not appear at the stables from which they had hired the horses, but left the care of them to Plunket.

He was now, by his share of this ill-acquired booty, very nearly reimbursed his losses at the masquerade, and might have easily undertaken his voyage; but he had lost all peace of mind, and was become entirely void of prudence. So great was his dread of a discovery, though Plunket represented the impossibility of it, that he would not stir out of his room for some days, and even then did not think himself safe, but proposed going down to the country for a week or two. Plunket did not oppose his departure, especially as he was to direct the route, and had gotten some intimation of a prize coming that day from St. Alban's, towards which place they set out. When they had gone a few miles, Plunket imparted to him his design, which Maclaine promised to second with a great deal of reluctance. When they came within sight of the coach, in which was their expected booty, Maclaine would have persuaded

Plunket to desist; but the other, turning his qualms of conscience into ridicule, and dropping some hints of cowardice, Maclaine prepared for the attack, crying, " He needs must whom the devil drives. I am over shoes and must over boots;" but notwithstanding, conducted himself in so distracted a manner as went nigh to lose them their prey. They took, however, from a gentleman and lady in the coach, two gold watches, and about twenty pounds in money, with which they got clear off; but did not think fit to keep that road any longer, but turned off, and before morning put up at an inn at Richmond, where Maclaine was as much in the horrors as in London; had no rest, no peace of mind, and stayed there two or three days, sulky, sullen, and perplexed as to what course he was to pursue. His wish, however, to be in town in time for the ship's departure for Jamaica, determined him to return to London in a fortnight, when he found that the ship had sailed two days before,— a disappointment that added to his former perplexity. Nevertheless, having money in his pocket, he contrived to excuse himself to his friends for his untoward absence, and promised, and seriously designed, to set out on the very next opportunity.

But the expensive company he kept in the interim, and further losses at play, once more stripped him of his money; and his evil genius, Plunket, was ever at his elbow, ready to suggest the former method of supply, with which he now complied much less reluctantly than before. The bounds of honour once overstepped, especially when success and security attend the villainy, the habit of vice grows strong; and the checks of conscience gradually less regarded at length pass without notice. In a word, Maclaine hardened himself by degrees to villainy, left the company of his city acquaintance that they might not tease him about his voyage to Jamaica, and took lodgings in St. James's-street, a place excellently suited to his purpose, for his appearance glanced off all suspicion, and he had a favourable opportunity, when gentlemen came to town, of knowing and watching their motions, and consequently of following and waylaying them on the road.

In the space of six months, he and Plunket, sometimes in company and sometimes separately, committed fifteen or sixteen robberies in Hyde Park, and within twenty miles of London, and obtained some large prizes. But still the money went as it came, for Plunket loved his bottle and intrigue, and Maclaine was doatingly fond of fine clothes, balls, and masquerades, at all which places he made a conspicuous figure. As he still had fortune-hunting in view, he was very assiduous in his attentions to women, and was not altogether unsuccessful; but, we imagine, made sincere return to none but such as had money in their own hands, or could be useful in helping him to an introduction to such as had.

And here it were needless and not productive of much interest to recount several intrigues in which Maclaine was engaged, and it were not a little painful to narrate two instances of wanton seduction on his part, which, were there no other counts in the moral indictment against him, would be sufficient to consign him to eternal infamy.

Mr. Maclaine applied himself also to his old profession of fortune-hunting, and in company with his old and worthy coadjutor Plunket, made several attempts to entrap heiresses, all of which proved abortive. While he was intent upon these schemes, he had no opportunity of making excursions on the road, and to defray his expenses had borrowed from a citizen's wife, with whom he had an intrigue, about twenty pounds, which he promised faithfully to repay before her husband should return from the country. The time of the citizen's arrival being at hand, the good wife became exceedingly anxious about the coin; and as a similar favour might be wanted by him at a future time, Mr. Maclaine made it a point of conscience to keep his word with her, and appointed her to come to him at his lodgings at Chelsea, where he paid her the money. He, however, took care that his friend Plunket should ease her of the trouble of carrying it home, by waylaying her in the five-fields.

Soon after this, a supply of cash being wanted, Plunket and he prepared for an expedition, and took the road to Chester; and in three days committed five robberies between Stony Stratford and Whitchurch, one of which was upon an intimate acquaintance, by whom Maclaine had been handsomely entertained but two days before. However, the booty in the whole five robberies did not amount to thirty pounds in cash, but they had watches, rings, &c. to a much greater amount. On the very evening of their return to town, they obtained information that an officer in the East India company's service had received a large sum of money with which he was about to return to Greenwich. They waylaid and robbed him of a very considerable sum, and it would seem that on this occasion they were under some dread of a discovery; for, in a few days after the commission of it, Maclaine set out for the Hague and Plunket for Ireland.

On the arrival of the former at the Hague, he pretended a friendly visit to his brother, who received him with cordiality and affection, and as honesty is never suspicious, he was easily induced to give credit to the specious tale which his brother related to him. He told him that he had got a considerable fortune with his late wife, and that her father, who died some few months before, had left him a valuable legacy, with which he designed to purchase a company in the army. Upon that, and the interest of his other friends, he said, he hoped to live at ease for the remainder of his life. His worthy brother, rejoicing in his prosperity, introduced him to his acquaintance and friends, amongst whom Mr. Maclaine behaved with great politeness, giving balls and large parties; to pay for which, it is surmised, he had the art to extract the gold watches and purses of his guests without suspicion.

However, upon his arrival in London, to which place he had been induced to return by a letter from Plunket, informing him of another rich matrimonial prize, which was, as usual, beyond his reach, or above his ingenuity to ensnare;—he again appears to have taken up his old thoughts of preparing for Jamaica, as a last resource. But these thoughts did not long possess him; for though by the sale of his horses and furniture he might have fitted himself for the West Indies in a very genteel manner, and had still reputation enough left to have procured sufficient recommendations from home; yet he was prevailed upon to try his fate on the road once more, and was but too successful, making several rich prizes. Amongst the rest he and Plunket robbed Horace Walpole, and on a reward being advertised for the watch which they had taken from him, Plunket had the impudence to go and receive it himself, choosing to run the risk rather than trust a third person with their hazardous secret. But all human prudence is in vain to stop the hand of justice, when once the measure of our iniquity is full; our closet secrets take wind, we know not how; and our own folly acts the part of an informer to awaken offended justice. The crisis of Maclaine's fate was at hand. It was he who proposed his last excursion to Plunket, who was ill at the time, and was very unwilling to turn out; but Maclaine, impelled by some uncommon impulse, urged him so earnestly, that he at length complied. They came up, about two o'clock in the morning, near Turnham Green, with the Salisbury stage-coach, in which five men and a woman were passengers. Though this was Maclaine's expedition, yet Plunket was the acting man, and obliged all the men to come out of the coach one by one, and rifled them; and then, putting his pistol in his pocket, lest he should frighten the lady, without forcing her out of the coach, he took what she offered without further search. Plunket would now have gone off; but Maclaine, full of his 'ate, demanded the cloak-bags out of the boot of the coach; each of them took one before him and rode off, bidding a polite adieu to the passengers, and riding as deliberately as though they had been performing some signal service.

On the same morning they met and robbed Lord Eglington, who was the prize for whom they originally went out. They effected this by a stratagem, as his lordship was armed with a blunderbuss. One of them skreened himself behind the post-boy, so that if his lordship fired, he must shoot his servant, while the other with a pistol cocked demanded his money, and ordered him to throw his blunderbuss on the ground. But it appears, the prize obtained at this hazard was but seven guineas, with which, and the cloak-bags, they returned to Maclaine's lodgings before the family were up, and divided their spoil.

But though the clothes were described in the public papers, yet so infatuated was Maclaine, that he sold his share of the booty to a salesman, who instantly recognized them as belonging to a Mr. Higden, and the latter immediately had Maclaine taken into custody.

On his first examination he denied the fact, but afterwards, that he might leave himself no room to escape, he formed a design of saving his life by impeaching his accomplice Plunket, foolishly imagining that justice would promise life to a villain she had in custody, for impeaching another that was out of her reach. But in the words of Massinger—

"Here is a precedent to teach wicked men,
That when they leave religion and turn atheists,
Their own abilities leave 'em."

For though he was forewarned that a confession, without impeaching a number of accomplices, would not avail him, he still insisted upon taking that step, not from compunction or remorse, but with the base design of saving his own life at the expense of that of his quondam friend.

On his second examination he delivered his confession in writing, and behaved in a most dastardly manner, whimpering and crying like a whipped school-boy. This conduct, degrading as it was, drew sympathetic tears from and opened the purses of his fair audience, whose bounty supported him in great affluence while he remained in the Gatehouse, and whose kind offers of intercession gave him hopes of a free pardon.

On his trial, he thought fit to retract his confession, pretending that he was flurried, and in some measure delirious when he made it, and that he had received the clothes from Plunket in payment of a debt. But this evasion had no weight with the jury, who brought him in guilty without going out of court.

On receiving sentence, guilt, shame, and dread deprived him of the power of speech, and disabled him from reading a paper, pathetically enough composed, in which he prayed for mercy.

In Newgate, ample time was permitted him to make his peace with his offended Maker, and there is every evidence to believe, from the testimony of the Rev. Dr. Allen, who attended him constantly to the last moment of his life, that his remorse and contrition was unaffected, sincere, and strong.

He was carried to Tyburn in a cart, like the rest of the criminals, and not, as was expected, in a coach; he stood the gaze of the multitude (which was on this occasion almost infinite,) without the least concern; and when he was about to be turned off, he said, " O God, forgive my enemies, bless my friends, and receive my soul!" His execution took place on Wednesday, October 3, 1750.

In the very amusing Letters of Horace Walpole to Sir Horace Mann, recently published, we find the following spirited and lively sketch of Maclaine.

" I have been in town for a day or two, and heard no conversation but about M'Lane, a fashionable highwayman, who is just taken, and who robbed me among others; as Lord Eglington, Sir Thomas Robinson of Vienna, Mrs. Talbot, &c. He took an odd booty from the Scotch Earl, a blunderbuss, which lies very formidable upon the justice's table. He was taken by selling a laced waistcoat to a pawnbroker, who happened to carry it to the very man who had just sold the lace. His history is very particular, for he confesses every thing, he is so little of a hero, that he cries and begs, and I believe, if Lord Eglington had been in any luck, might have been robbed of his own blunderbuss. His father was an Irish dean; his brother is a Calvinist minister in great esteem at the Hague. He himself was a grocer, but losing a wife that he loved extremely about two years ago, and by whom he has one little girl, he quitted his business with 200*l*. in his pocket, which he soon spent, and then took to the road with only one companion, Plunket, a journeyman apothecary, my other friend, whom he has impeached, but who is not taken. M'Lane had a lodging in St. James's-street over against White's, and another at Chelsea; Plunket one in Jermyn-street: and their faces are as known about St. James's as any gentleman's who lives in that quarter, and who perhaps goes upon the road too. M'Lane had a quarrel at Putney bowling-green two months ago

with an officer, whom he challenged for disputing his rank; but
the Captain declined, till M'Lane should produce a certificate of
his nobility, which he has just received. If he had escaped a month
longer, he might have heard of Mr. Chute's genealogic expertness,
and come hither to the College of Arms for a certificate. There
was a wardrobe of clothes, three-and-twenty purses, and the celebrated blunderbuss found at his lodging, besides a famous kept
mistress. As I conclude he will suffer, and wish him no ill, I don't
care to have his idea, and am almost single in not having been to
see him. Lord Mountford, at the head of half White's, went the
first day: his aunt was crying over him: as soon as they were withdrawn, she said to him, knowing they were of White's, 'My dear,
what did the Lords say to you? have you ever been concerned with
any of them?' Was not it admirable? what a favourable idea people must have of White's!—and what if White's should not deserve
a much better! But the chief personages who have been to comfort and weep over this fallen hero are Lady Caroline Petersham
and Miss Ashe: I call them Polly and Lucy, and asked them if
he did not sing—'Thus I stand like the Turk with his doxies
around.'"

EUGENE ARAM.

THAT Eugene Aram was a very remarkable and ingenious man,
cannot for a moment be doubted; especially as he has left us part
of a Lexicon, deriving the English language from the Chaldee,
Hebrew, Arabic, and Celtic dialects, which is a very learned and
convincing performance; still we cannot help thinking that his
abilities have been greatly over-rated. His defence was doubtlessly
of consummate ingenuity. In fact, the celebrated Archdeacon
Paley, who was present at his trial, attributes his conviction to
this very ingenuity—asserting that " he had a fair claim to a niche
in the Biographia Britannica," having got himself hanged by his
own cleverness, which he certainly had."

The accounts of the life of this man have become of late so widely
circulated, and the particulars respecting the murder of which he
was the perpetrator so generally known, that any notice of him in
this work would appear almost supererogatory were it not that
a charge of oversight and omission could, without injustice, be

reasonably advanced against it, were we to slight over or leave unmentioned a name so notorious. We shall, therefore, give a summary of his history, commencing with an account of his family and early life, furnished by himself at the request of the two gentlemen who, at his own particular desire, attended him at his condemnation.

"I was born at Ramsgill, a little village in Netherdale, in 1704. My maternal relations had been substantial and reputable in that dale, for a great many generations: my father was of Nottinghamshire, a gardener, of great abilities in Botany, and an excellent draughtsman. He served the Right Rev. the Bishop of London, Dr. Compton, with great approbation; which occasioned his being recommended to Newby, in this county, to Sir Edward Blackett, whom he served in the capacity of gardener, with much credit to himself, and satisfaction to that family, for above thirty years. Upon the decease of that Baronet, he went, and was retained in the service of Sir John Ingilby, of Ripley, Bart. where he died; respected when living, and lamented when dead. My father's ancestors were of great antiquity and consideration in the county, and originally British. Their surname is local, for they were formerly lords of the town of Haram, or Aram, on the southern banks of the Tees, and opposite to Stockburn, in Bishopric; and appear in the records of St. Mary's, at York, among many charitable names, early and considerable benefactors to that abbey. They, many centuries ago, removed from these parts, and were settled under the fee of the lords Mowbray, in Nottinghamshire, at Haram, or Aram Park, in the neighbourhood of Newark upon Trent; where they were possessed of no less than three knight's fees in the reign of Edward the Third. Their lands, I find not whether by purchase or marriage, came into the hands of the present Lord Lexington. While the name existed in the county, some of them were several times high sheriffs for the county; and one was professor of divinity, if I remember right at Oxford, and died at York. The last of the chief of this family, was Thomas Aram, Esq. of Gray's Inn, and one of the commissioners of the Salt Office, under Queen Anne. He married one of the co-heiresses of Sir John Coningsby, of North Mimms, in Hertfordshire. His seat, which was his own estate, was at the Wild, near Shenley, in Hertfordshire, where I saw him, and where he died without issue.

"I was removed very young, along with my mother, to Skelton, near Newby, and thence at five or six years old, my father making a little purchase at Bondgate, near Ripon, his family went thither. There I went to school; where I was made capable of reading the Testament, which was all I was ever taught except a long time after, for about a month in a very advanced age for that, with the Reverend Mr. Alcock, of Burnsal.

" After this, about thirteen or fourteen years of age, I went to my father at Newby, and attended him in the family there, till the death of Sir Edward Blackett. It was here my propensity to literature first appeared, for being always of a solitary disposition, and uncommonly fond of retirement and books, I enjoyed here all the repose and opportunity I could wish. My study at that time was engaged in the mathematics: I know not what my acquisitions were, but I am certain my application was intense and unwearied. I found in my father's library there, which contained a very great number of books in most branches, Kersey's Algebra, Leybourn's Cursus Mathematicus, Ward's Young Mathematician's Guide, Harris's Algebra, &c. and a great many more; but these being the books in which I was ever most conversant, I remember them the better. I was even then equal to the management of quadratic equations, and their geometrical constructions. After we left Newby, I repeated the same studies in Bondgate, and went over all parts I had studied before, I believe not altogether unsuccessfully.

" Being about the age of sixteen, I was sent for to London, being thought upon examination by Mr. Christopher Blackett qualified to serve him as bookkeeper in his counting-house. Here, after a year or two, I took the small-pox and suffered most severely under that distemper. I returned home again, and there with leisure on my hands, and a new addition of authors to those brought me from Newby, I renewed not only my mathematical studies, but began and prosecuted others, of a different turn, with much avidity and diligence. These were poetry, history, and antiquities; the charms of which quite destroyed all the heavier beauties of numbers in lines, whose applications and properties I now pursued no longer, except occasionally in teaching.

" I was, after some time employed in this manner, invited into Netherdale, my native air, where I first engaged in a school, and where, unfortunately enough for me, I married. The misconduct of the wife which that place afforded me, has procured me this prosecution, this prison, this infamy, and this sentence.

" During my marriage here, perceiving the deficiencies of my education, and sensible of the want of the learned languages, and prompted by an irresistible covetousness of knowledge, I commenced a series of studies in that way; and undertook the tediousness of the intricacies, and the labour of grammar; I selected Lilly from the rest, all of which I got, and repeated by heart. The task of repeating it all every day was impossible, while I attended the school; so I divided it into portions; by which method it was pronounced thrice every week, and this I performed for years.

"I next became acquainted with Camden's Greek Grammar, which I also repeated in the same manner, *memoriter*. Thus instructed, I entered upon the Latin classics; whose allurements repaid my assiduities and my labours. I remember to have, at first, overhung five lines for a whole day; and never in all the painful course of my reading, left any one passage, but I did, or thought I did, perfectly comprehend it.

"After I had accurately perused every one of the Latin classics, historians and poets, I went through the Greek Testament; first passing every word as I proceeded; I next ventured upon Hesiod, Homer, Theocritus, Herodotus, Thucydides, and all the Greek tragedians: a tedious labour was this; but my former acquaintance with history lessened it extremely: because it threw a light upon many passages, which without that assistance must have appeared obscure.

"In the midst of these literary pursuits, a man and horse from my good friend William Norton, Esq., came for me from Knaresborough, bearing that gentleman's letter inviting me thither; and accordingly I repaired there in some part of the year 1734, and was, I believe, well accepted and esteemed there. Here, not satisfied with my former acquisitions, I prosecuted the attainment of Hebrew, and with indefatigable diligence. I had Buxtorff's grammar, but that being perplexed, or not explicit enough, at least in my opinion at that time, I collected no less than eight or ten different grammars; and thus one very often supplied the omissions of the others; and was, I found, of extraordinary advantage. Then I purchased the Bible in the original, and read the whole Pentateuch, with an intention to go through the whole of it, which I attempted, but wanted time.

"In April, I think the 18th, 1744, I went again to London; and agreed to teach the Latin and writing, for the Rev. Mr. Painblanc, in Piccadilly, which he, along with a salary, returned, by teaching me French; wherein I observed the pronunciation the most formidable part, at least to me, who had never before known a word of it. By continued application every night and every opportunity, I overcame this, and soon became a tolerable master of French. remained in this situation two years and above.

"Some time after this I went to Hays, in the capacity of writing master, and served a gentlewoman there, since dead; and stayed, after that, with a worthy and reverend gentleman. I continued here between three and four years. To several other places I then succeeded, and all that while used every occasion for improvement. I then transcribed acts of parliament to be registered in chancery; and after went down to the free-school at Lynn.

"From my leaving Knaresborough to this time is a long interval, which I had filled up with the farther study of history and antiquities, heraldry and botany; in the last of which I was very agreeably entertained, there being in that study so extensive a display of nature. I well knew Tournefort, Ray, Miller, Linnæus, &c. I made frequent visits to the botanic garden at Chelsea; and traced pleasure through a thousand fields: at last, few plants, domestic or exotic, were unknown to me. Amidst all this I ventured upon the Chaldee and Arabic; and, with a design to understand them, supplied myself with Erpenius, Chappelow, and others: but I had not time to obtain any great knowledge of the Arabic; the Chaldee I found easy enough, because of its connexion with the Hebrew.

"I then investigated the Celtic, as far as possible, in all its dialects; began collections, and made comparisons between that, the English, the Latin, the Greek, and even the Hebrew. I had made notes, and compared above three thousand of these together, and found such a surprising affinity, even beyond any expectation or conception, that I was determined to proceed through the whole of these languages, and form a comparative lexicon, which I hoped would account for numberless vocables in use with us, the Latins, and Greeks, before concealed and unobserved: this, or something like it, was the design of a clergyman of great erudition in Scotland; but it must prove abortive, for he died before he executed it, and most of my books and papers are now scattered and lost."

Such is the account Eugene Aram has given of himself, until the commission of the fatal act that brought down upon him the execration of the world, and the last vengeance of the law. Of all the crimes man is capable of committing, there is none so offensive to Omnipotence as murder; and the Almighty, therefore, seems to be more intent to expose that heinous and accursed offence to mankind; to warn and to admonish them, to show them that rocks cannot hide, nor distance secure them from the inevitable consequences of the violation of that law which nature dictates and man confirms. The extraordinary means by which this murder was brought to light, is one of many instances of this divine interposition.

Daniel Clark was born at Knaresborough, of reputable parents, where he lived and followed the business of a shoemaker. About the month of January, 1744 or 5, he married, and became possessed of property to the amount of two or three hundred pounds. He was at that time in very good credit at Knaresborough, and it is supposed a scheme was then laid by Eugene Aram, at that time a school-master in the town, and one Houseman, a flax-dresser, to defraud several tradesmen of great quantities of goods and plate, Clark having been chosen as the fittest person to carry their plan into execution; for, as he then lived in very good reputation, and, moreover, was lately married, he was the person of all others best calculated to effect the intended purpose. Accordingly, Clark for some days went about to various tradesmen in the town, and under the pretext that, as he was just married, it was not altogether irrational to suppose that cloth, and table and bed-linen would considerably contribute to his matrimonial comfort, he took up great quantities of linen and woollen-drapery goods; the worthy dealers of Knaresborough rendering up their commodities with the greatest zeal and expedition on so interesting an occasion. After this, he went to several innkeepers and others, desiring to borrow a silver tankard of one, a nicely worked silver pint of another, and the like, alleging that he was to have company that night, and should be glad of the use of them at supper; and in order to give a colour to his story, he procured of the innkeepers (of whom he had borrowed the plate) ale and other liquors to regale his visitors.

Some suspicious circumstances, however, appearing that night, and the following morning, a rumour got wind that Clark had absconded; and upon inquiry, most certainly, he was not to be found. An active search was immediately made for the goods and plate with which he had provided himself when some part of the goods was found at Houseman's house, and another part dug up in Aram's Garden; but as no plate could be found it was concluded somewhat naturally, that with them Clark had decamped. The strictest inquiry was instantly set on foot to discover his retreat; persons were dispatched to all parts; advertisements describing his person, inserted in all the papers; but to no purpose.

Eugene Aram, being suspected to be an accomplice, a process was granted against him by the steward of the honour of Knaresborough to arrest him for a debt due to a Mr. Norton, with a view to detain him till such time as a warrant could be obtained from the justice of the peace to apprehend him upon that charge. To the surprise of all, however, the money was instantly paid, and moreover, at the same time, a considerable mortgage upon his house at Bondgate was also discharged. Soon afterwards, Aram left the town, and was not heard of until the month of June, 1758, when the murder of Clark being traced to him, he was found residing at Lynn.

Upwards of thirteen years after Clark's disappearance, it happened that a labourer employed in digging for stone to supply a lime-kiln, at a place called Thistle-hill, near Knaresborough, striking about half-a-yard and half-a-quarter deep, turned up an arm bone, and the small bone of the leg of a human skeleton. His curiosity being excited, he carefully removed the earth round about the place, and discovered all the bones belonging to a body, presenting an appearance, from their position, as though the body had been doubled at the hips, though the bones were all perfect. This remarkable accident being rumoured in the town, gave rise to a suspicion, that Daniel Clark had been murdered and burried there; for no other person had been missing thereabouts for sixty years and upwards. The coroner was instantly informed, and an inquest summoned.

The wife of Eugene Aram, who had frequently before given hints of her suspicions, was now examined. From her evidence, it appeared that Clark was an intimate acquaintance of Aram's before the 8th of February, 1744-5, and they had had frequent transactions together, and with Houseman also. About two o'clock in the morning of the eighth of February, 1744-5, Aram, Clark, and Houseman, came to Aram's house and went up-stairs, where they remained about an hour. They then went out together, and Clark being the last, she observed that he had a sack or wallet on his back. About four, Aram and Houseman returned, but without their companion. " Where is Clark?" she inquired; but her husband only returned an angry look in reply, and desired her to go to bed, which she refused, and told him, " she feared he had been doing something wrong." Aram then went down stairs with the candle, and she being desirous to know what they were doing, followed them, and from the top of the stairs heard Houseman say, " She's coming; if she does, she'll tell." " What can she tell, poor simple thing?" replied Aram, " she knows nothing. I'll hold the door to prevent her coming." " It's of no use, something must be done," returned Houseman; " if she don't split now, she will some other time." "No, no, foolish," her husband said; "we'll coax her a little till her passion is off, and then."—"What?" said Houseman sullenly, "shoot her," whispered Aram, "shoot her!" Mrs. Aram hearing this discourse, became very much alarmed, but remained quiet. At seven o'clock the same morning they both left the house, and she, immediately their backs were turned, went down stairs, and observed that there had been a fire below, and all the ashes taken out of the grate. She then examined the dunghill, and perceived ashes of a different kind lying upon it, and searching amongst them found several pieces of linen and woollen cloth very nearly burnt, which had the appearance of wearing apparel. When she returned into the house, she found a handkerchief that she had lent to Houseman the night before, and a round spot of blood upon it about the size of a shilling. Houseman came back soon afterwards, and she charged him with having done some dreadful thing to Clark: but he pretended total ignorance, and added, " she was a fool, and knew not what she said." From these circumstances, she fully and conscientiously believed that Daniel Clark had been murdered by Houseman and Eugene Aram, on the 8th of February, 1744-5.

Several other witnesses were examined, all affirming that Houseman and Eugene Aram were the last persons seen with Clark, especially on the night of the 7th of February, being that after which he was missing. Upon hearing these testimonies, Houseman, who was present, was observed to become very restless, discovering all the signs of guilt, such as trembling, turning pale, and faltering in his speech. Few men, guilty of the crime of murder, have the strength of heart and self-command to conceal it: by some circumstance or other, the truth will out; a look, a dream, and not unfrequently, as in this case, their own unfaithful tongue, is the involuntary agent that brings at last the blackened culprit to that punishment which unerringly awaits the man that sheds his brother's blood. Accordingly, upon the skeleton being produced, Houseman, taking up one of the bones, dropped this most unguarded expression; "This is no more Daniel Clark's bone than it is mine." "What remarked the coroner instantly—"what? —how is this? How can you be so sure that that is not Daniel Clark's bone?" "Because I can produce a witness," replied Houseman, in evident confusion—" I can produce a witness who saw Daniel Clark upon the road two days after he was missing at Knaresborough." This witness was instantly summoned, and stated that he had never seen Clark after the 8th of February; a friend however, had told him (and this only had he mentioned at first) that he met some one very like Clark; but, it being a snowy day, and the person having the cape of his great coat up, he could not say with the least degree of certainty who he was. This explanation, so far from proving satisfactory, increased the suspicion against Houseman; and accordingly a warrant was issued against him, and he was apprehended and brought before William Thornton, Esq., who, examining him, elicited a full acknowledgment of the fact of his having been with Clark on the night in question, on account of some money (twenty pounds) that he had lent him, and which he wanted at the time very pressingly. He further stated, that Clark begged him to accept the value in goods, to which proposition he assented, and was necessarily, therefore, several times to and fro between Clark's house and his own, in order to remove the goods from one to the other. When he had finished, he left Clark at Aram's house, with Aram and another man whom he had never seen before. Aram and Clark, immediately afterwards, followed him out of the house of the former, and the stranger was with them. They then went in the direction of the Marketplace, which the light of the moon enabled him to see, and he lost sight of them. He disavowed most solemnly that he came back to Aram's house that morning with Aram and Clark, as was asserted by Mrs. Aram; nor was he with Aram, but with Clark, at the house of the former on that night, whither he only went to seek Clark in order to obtain from him the note.

Being then asked if he would sign this examination, he said he would rather waive it for the present, for he might have something to add, and, therefore desired to have time to consider of it. The magistrate then committed him to York Castle, when, expressing a wish to explain more fully, he was again brought before Mr. Thornton, and in his presence made the following confession:— That Daniel Clark was murdered by Eugene Aram, late of Knaresborough, a schoolmaster, and, as he believed, on Friday the 8th of February, 1744-5; for that Eugene Aram and Daniel Clark were together at Aram's house early that morning, and that he (Houseman) left the house and went up the street a little before, and they called to him, desiring he would go a short way with them; and he accordingly went with them to a place called St. Robert's Cave, near Grimble Bridge, where the two former stopped, and there he saw Aram strike Clark several times over the breast and head, and saw him fall, as if he were dead; upon which he came away and left them; but whether Aram used any weapon or not to kill Clark, he could not tell, nor did he know what he did with the body afterwards, but believed that Aram left it at the mouth of the cave; for that, seeing Aram do this, lest he might share the same fate, he made the best of his way to the bridge-end, where, looking back, he saw Aram coming from the cave-side, (which is in a private rock adjoining the river,) and could discern a bundle in his hand, but did not know what it was: upon this he hastened away to the town, without either joining Aram or seeing him again till the next day, and from that time he had never had discourse with him. He stated, however, afterwards, that Clark's body was buried in St. Robert's Cave, and that he was sure it was there, but desired it might remain till such time as Aram was taken. He added further, that Clark's head lay to the right, in a turn at the entrance of the cave.

Proper persons were instantly appointed to examine St. Robert's Cave, when agreeably to Houseman's confession, the skeleton of a human body (the head lying as he had described,) was soon found. A warrant was instantly issued to apprehend Eugene Aram, who was discovered to be living at Lynn in the capacity of usher at a school. He confessed before the magistrate that he was well acquainted with Clark, and, to the best of his remembrance, about or before the 8th of February, 1744-5, but utterly denied any participation in the frauds which Clark stood charged with at the time of his disappearance. He also declared he knew nothing of the murder, and that the statements made by his wife were without exception false: he, however, declined to sign his examination on the same plea preferred by Houseman, that he might recollect himself better, and lest anything should be omitted which might afterwards occur to him. On being conducted to the castle, he desired to return, and acknowledged that he was at his own house when Houseman and Clark came to him with some plate, of which Clark had defrauded his neighbours. He could not but observe that the former was very diligent in assisting; in fact, it was altogether Houseman's business; and there was no truth whatever in the statement that he came there to sign a note or instrument. All the leather which Clark had possessed himself of, amounting to a considerable value, was concealed under flax at Houseman's house, with the intention of disposing of it little by little, to prevent any suspicion of his being concerned in the robbery. The plate was beaten flat in St. Robert's Cave. At four o'clock in the morning, they, thinking it was too late to enable Clark to leave with safety, agreed that he should stay there till the next night, and he accordingly remained there all the following day. In order, then, the better to effect his escape, they both went down to the cave, Houseman only entering, while he watched without, lest any person should surprise them. On a sudden he heard a noise, and Houseman appeared at the mouth of the cave, and told him that Clark was gone. He had a bag with him, containing plate, which he said he had purchased of Clark, money being much more portable than such cumbersome articles. They then went to Houseman's house, and concealed the property there, he fully believing that Clark had escaped. He never heard anything of Clark subsequently, and was as much surprised to hear there was a suspicion of his being murdered, as that be (Eugene Aram) should be considered to be the murderer. Notwithstanding this surprise, however, his examination having been signed, he was committed with his companion to York Castle, there to await the assizes.

On the 3rd August, 1759, they were both brought to the bar. Houseman was arraigned on the former indictment, acquitted, and admitted evidence against Aram, who was thereupon arraigned. Houseman was then called and deposed to the same effect as that which has already appeared in his own confession. Several witnesses were called who gave evidence as to finding several kinds of goods buried in Aram's garden, Aram's knowledge of the fact of Clark's possessing two hundred pounds, and to show that they both had been seen together on the evening of the 7th February. After which the skull was produced in court; on the left side there was a fracture, from the nature of which it was impossible to have been done but by the stroke of some blunt instrument. The skull was beaten inwards, and could not be replaced but from within. The surgeon gave it as his opinion, that no such breach could proceed from natural decay; that it was not a recent fracture by the spade or axe by which it might have been dug up; but seemed to be of some years' standing.

Eugene Aram's defence, which he read, was marked with an undoubted manifestation of very considerable powers. It was learned and argumentative; and in some passages, glowing and eloquent. He attempted to show, that no rational inference can be drawn that a person is dead who suddenly disappears;—that hermitages such as St. Robert's Cave were the constant repositories of the bones of the recluse; that the proofs of this were well authenticated; and, that therefore the conclusion that the bones found were those of some one killed in battle, or of some ascetic, remained no less reasonably than impatiently expected by him. A verdict of guilty was however returned, and he was condemned to be hanged accordingly.

On the morning after his condemnation, he confessed the justice of his sentence to the two gentlemen who attended him, and acknowledged that he had murdered Clark. He told them, also, that he suspected Clark of having an unlawful commerce with his wife; and that at the time of the murder he felt persuaded he was acting right, but since, he had thought otherwise.

It was generally believed, as he promised to make a more ample confession on the day he was executed of every thing prior to the murder, that the whole would have been disclosed; but he put an end to any further discovery, by an attempt upon his own life. When he was called from his bed to have his chains taken off, he refused, alleging that he was very weak. On moving him, it was found he had inflicted a severe wound upon his arm, from which the blood was flowing copiously. He had concealed a razor in the condemned hold some time before. By proper and prompt appliactions he was brought to himself and though weak from loss of blood conducted to Tyburn in York, where being asked if he had any thing to say, he answered, " No." He was then executed, and his body conveyed to Knaresborough Forest, and hung in chains August 6, 1759, pursuant to his sentence.

That Eugene Aram murdered Clark is beyond all question, since we have his confession; that he committed the murder, actuated by the cause he alleges, is open to great suspicion. The strange solicitude which all men, even the most vicious, manifest, to leave behind a memory mingled with some little good, prompted him, doubtless, to give his crime the ennobling, or at least, mitigatory motive to which he attributes it. Whether the perpetration of a murder can be justified, even urged by the wrong Aram states himself to have suspected, may be left to the consideration of the casuist; but whether the dreadful act can be extenuated by as deliberate and foul an attack on the virtue and character of an innocent and industrious woman, whom he upon all occasions treated with infamous barbarity, is a question we can confidently leave to the judgment and moral sense of every man. That Eugene Aram was leagued with Clark and Houseman in their fraud at Knaresborough, there can be little doubt; that he plundered his unhappy victim after he had murdered him, there can be less; that no sense of domestic injury would urge a man to rob another who had wronged him after he had slain him, needs only to be mentioned to ue admitted; and therefore, believing conscientiously from these facts that the charge against his wife was not maintainable, a double indignation is entailed upon the wretch who could add to the measure of his crime this gratuitous calumny.

Notwithstanding these facts and the inferences that every attentive reader must inevitably draw from them, Eugene Aram has . een deemed a fit hero for a popular novel; and the execration with which he should have been consigned to posterity has been attempted to be converted into a sentimental commiseration for a gentle student who beat out his friend's brains on philosophical principles, and converts his property to his own use purely with a view to the interests of science and the intellectual progression of the world at large.

There is a remarkable similarity in crime and conduct between Aram and Thurtell, though they were so totally dissimilar in other particulars. Both were cold blooded, determined murderers—both selected for their victim an individual with whom they had been concerned in deeds of plunder; though Thurtell had the advantage in being incited to his atrocity by revenge, Weare having cheated him at play. The defence of both was conducted on the same principle, that of endeavouring to overturn the evidence, by citing a variety of instances to prove witnesses might be mistaken; for an uneducated man, Thurtell's defence was as clever as Aram's, and made a great impression on his judge, who complimented him upon it. Thurtell committed his defence to memory, and delivered it as if extemporaneously. Aram committed his to paper, and read it in court. Much has been said of Aram's general gentleness, love of learning, &c., and an attempt has been made to create an interest in his favour from these circumstances. Human nature is full of strange anomalies—we do not conceive this to argue any thing;—Aram murdered Clark for the mere sake of his money—he would have shot his wife if he had had the opportunity; and it appears from a statement in the Literary Gazette, emanating from Dr. L., Master of the Grammar School in Lynn, where Aram was arrested, that on one occasion when the doctor had received a considerable sum of money from the parents of his pupils, he was awakened by a noise at his bed-room door, in the middle of the night, and detected Aram there, dressed and in great confusion. The impression of the doctor was, that Aram, knowing he had the money in his bed-room, intended to rob, and no doubt to murder him, if it had been rendered necessary by discovery or opposition. Thurtell could bring forth as many claims to favourable consideration as Aram. Determined murderer as Thurtell was, nothing could be more frank and good-natured than his general conduct;—and we have heard of many acts of disinterestedness, humanity, and even honour emanating from him. Thurtell was as passionately attached to oratory and the drama as ever Aram could have been to philological researches; and the manly and decent manner with which Thurtell resigned himself to his fate certainly gives him the advantage over the cowardly shrinking, at the eleventh hour, of the linguist.

GEORGE BARRINGTON

Was originally a native and inhabitant of Ireland; and, as it will appear in the sequel that the name of Barrington was assumed, let it suffice to remark that his father's name was Henry Waldron, and that he was a working silversmith; while his mother, whose maiden name was Naish, was a mantua-maker, and occasionally a midwife.

Our adventurer was born about the year 1755, at the village of Maynooth, in the county of Kildare. His parents, who bore a good character for their industry, integrity, and general good behaviour, were however, never able to rise to a state of independence, or security from indigence, owing to their engagement in a law-suit with a more powerful and opulent relative, in order to the recovery of a legacy, to which they conceived they had a legal right. To the narrowness of their circumstances, the neglect of their son's education is imputed; and therefore, they were incapable of improving, or of giving a proper bias to those early indications of natural abilities, and a superiority of talents, which must inevitably have unfolded themselves even in the dawn of young Barrington's existence. He was, notwithstanding these obstacles, instructed in reading and writing at an early age, at their expence; and afterwards, through the bounty of a medical gentleman in the neighbourhood, he was initiated in the principles of common arithmetic, the elements of geography, and the outlines of English grammar.

This ill-fated youth, however, enjoyed but for a short time the benefits he derived from the kindness of his first patron, a dignitary of the church in Ireland; for the violence of his passions

T

which equalled at least the extent of his talents, precipitated him into an action by which he lost his favour for ever, and which, in its consequences, finally proved his ruin. When he had been about half a year at the grammar-school in Dublin, to which he had been sent by his patron, he unluckily got into a dispute with a lad, much older, larger, and stronger than himself; the dispute degenerated into a quarrel, and some blows ensued, in which young Waldron suffered considerably; but in order to be revenged, he stabbed his antagonist with a penknife; and had he not been seasonably prevented, would have in all probability murdered him. The discipline of the house, (flogging) however, was inflicted with proper severity on the perpetrator of so atrocious an offence, which irritated the unrelenting and vindictive temper of the young man to such a degree that he determined at once to run away from school, from his family, and from his friends; thus abandoning the fair prospects that he had before him, and blasting all the hopes that had been fondly, though vainly, formed of the great things that might be effected by his genius when matured by time and improved by study.

His plan of escape was no sooner formed than it was carried into execution; but previously to his departure, he found means to steal ten or twelve guineas from the master of the school, and a gold repeating watch from Mrs. Goldsborough, the master's sister. With this booty, a few shirts, and two or three pair of stockings, he silently but safely effected his retreat from the school-house, in the middle of a still night in the month of May 1771; and pursuing the great northern road all that night, and all the next day, he late in the evening arrived at the town of Drogheda, without interruption, without accident, and in a great measure without halting, without rest, and without food.

The first place of safety at which young Waldron thought proper to halt, was at an obscure inn at Drogheda, where a company of strolling players happened to be at that time, it was the occasion of a new series of acquaintance, which, though formed on precipitation and on the spur of the occasion, was retained from choice and affection for a number of years.

One John Price, the manager of the strolling company, became quickly the confidant and from the confidant the sole counsellor of the young fugitive Waldron, who, influenced by the ardour, the natural and unguarded ingenuousness of a youthful mind, communicated to this new friend, without reserve, all the circumstances of his life and story. By his advice this unhappy youth renounced his paternal name, assumed that of Barrington, entered into the company, and in the course of four days, became so absolutely and formally a strolling son of Thespis, that he performed the part of Jaffier in " Venice Preserved," with some applause, to a crowded audience, in a barn in the suburbs of Drogheda; and this without the assistance of a prompter.

Though the reception he met with on his debut was very flattering to a mind like his, Price, as well as himself, thought it would not be proper for him to appear in public so near the scene of his late depredations in the capital. It was therefore resolved on by them that the whole company should without delay move to the northward, and, if possible, get to the distance of sixty or eighty miles from Dublin before they halted for any length of time. In order to enable so numerous a body to move with all their baggage, it was necessary to raise money; and in doing this, Barrington's assistance being the first thing that offered, was indispensably necessary. He was accordingly applied to, and acquiesced with a good grace, giving Price Mrs. Goldsborough's gold repeater, which was disposed of for the general benefit of the strollers.

As soon as the necessary funds were procured, all these children of Thespis set out for Londonderry, which was the place at which they first designed to play. Travelling but slowly they were a considerable time on their journey; and during the course of it, the penetrating eyes of the experienced actresses discovered that Barrington had made a tender impression on the heart of Miss Egerton, the young lady who played the part of Belvidera when he acted that of Jaffier at Drogheda. This poor girl was the daughter of an opulent tradesman at Coventry. She was young and beautiful, sweet tempered and accomplished, but now friendless; and, though like the rest, inured to misfortune, she was destitute of the experience which is generally acquired during a series of sinister and untoward events. At the age of sixteen, she was seduced by a lieutenant of marines, with whom she fled from her father's house to Dublin, where in less than three months he abandoned her, leaving her a prey to poverty, infamy, and desperation.

Having been thus deceived in the simplicity of innocence by the cunning and falsehood of one of the vilest and most profligate of human beings, she had no other resource from the most extreme want than closing with Price, who proposed to her to join his company; which, situated as she was, she readily agreed to do, and had been with him but a very short time when she saw Barrington, of whom, being of a warm constitution, she became rather sudden ly enamoured. But to the credit of our adventurer, although his affection was as ardent as her own, it was not of that brutal and profligate cast that so frequently disgraces the devious paths of youthful imprudence and indiscretion. On the part of Miss Egeron, the symptoms of her affection for him were so obvious, that, inexperienced as he then was in matters of gallantry and intrigue, he not only perceived her passion but was sensible of her merit, and returned her love with perfect sincerity.

It was not long before Price, urged a second time by want of money, found it expedient to insinuate to the unfortunate Barrington, that a young man of his address and appearance might very easily find means to introduce himself into some of the public places to which the merchants and chapmen of that commercial city generally resorted; and that he there might, without any great difficulty, find opportunities of picking their pockets unnoticed, and of escaping undetected, more especially at that particular time, when, the fair being held, a favourable juncture afforded itself of executing a plan of such a nature with safety and facility. The idea pleased our needy adventurer, and the plan formed on it was carried into execution by him and his trusty confidant John Price. the very next day, with great success; at least such it appeared to them at that time, their acquisitions having amounted, on the close of the evening, to about forty guineas in cash, and about 150*l.* Irish currency, in bank-notes; which, however, they artfully determined not, on any account, to circulate in the part of the kingdom in which they were obtained. This precaution became peculiarly necessary; for several gentlemen having been robbed, the town took the alarm, which was the greater, or at least made the more noise, from the rarity of such events in that part of the kingdom, where the picking of pockets is said to be very little practised or known. But whatever the alarm was, or whatever noise it made, neither Barrington nor his accomplice was suspected. They however resolved to leave Derry as soon as they could with any appearance of propriety depart from thence: so that, having played a few nights as usual, with more applause than profit, they and their associates of the sock and buskin removed from Londonderry to Ballyshannon, in the county of Donegal, and never more returned into that part of the kingdom, where George Barrington may be considered as having commenced the business of a regular and professed pickpocket, in the summer of the year 1771, being at that time little more than sixteen years of age, and having just laid by the profession of a strolling player.

This wretched company having now become thieves as well as vagrants in the eye of the law, and compelled to subsist upon the plunder above mentioned, after travelling about a fortnight, arrived at Ballyshannon. Here Barrington, with the company to which he belonged, spent the autumn and the winter of the year 1771, playing generally on Tuesdays and Saturdays, and picking pockets with John Price every day in the week, whenever opportunity offered; a business which, though attended with danger and certain infamy, he found more lucrative and more entertaining than that of the theatre, where his fame and his proficiency were by no means equal to the expectations he had raised, or to the hopes that had been formed of him on his first appearance at Drogheda.

From Ballyshannon, at length, having left the company of his friend Price, he moved to the southward, with his faithful Miss Egerton, whom he had the misfortune to lose for ever in crossing the river Boyne, in which she was drowned, through the ignorance, or the more culpable negligence of a ferryman.

Barrington, however, virtuous in his attachment to Miss Egerton, was for some time inconsolable for the loss which he had just sustained; but being neither of an age nor of a temper propitious to the continuance of sorrowful sensations, he hastened to Limerick, where he hoped to meet Price, his old accomplice. On his arrival in that city, he learned that the person after whom he had enquired had set out for Cork ten days before, and thither our adventurer followed him, and found him within an hour after he entered the town gates. On their meeting, it was agreed on by them never more to think of the stage; a resolution which was the more easily executed, as the company to which they originally belonged was now broken up and dispersed. It was besides settled between them that Price should pass for Barrington's servant, and Barrington should act the part of a young gentleman of large fortune and of a noble family, who was not yet quite of age, but, until he should attain that period, travelled for his amusement. In pursuance of this hopeful scheme, horses were purchased, and the master and man, now united as knight errant and esquire, and well equipped for every purpose of depredation, accordingly took their determination to act their several parts in the wild field of adventure; and thus, in the summer of 1772, as the race grounds in the south of Ireland presented themselves as the fairest objects, they hastened to these scenes of spoliation, and were successful even beyond their expectation.

Picking pockets being rather new amongst the gentry of Ireland, their want of precaution rendered them a more easy prey to Mr. Barrington and his accomplice, who found means to retire to Cork on the setting in of winter, with a booty of nearly 1000*l.* In this city, they found it convenient to fix their residence, at least till the next spring. And now it was that Barrington first determined within himself to become what has been called a gentleman pickpocket, and to affect both the airs and importance of a man of fashion.

In this desperate career of vice and folly, it was the fate of Price, the preceptor of Barrington, to be first detected in the act of picking the pocket of a gentleman of high rank, for which he was tried, convicted, and in a very short period, sentenced to transportation, for the term of seven years, to America.

Barrington, naturally alarmed at the fate of his iniquitous preceptor, without loss of time converted all his moveable property into cash, and taking horse, made as precipitate a journey to Dublin as he possibly could.

On his arrival there, he lived rather in a private and retired manner, only lurking in the darkest evenings about the playhouses, where he occasionally picked up a few guineas or a watch. But he was soon weary of the sameness, and disgusted with the obscurity of a life of comparative retirement, such as that he led in the Irish capital; so that when the spring and the fine weather that accompanied it returned, he embarked on board the Dorset yacht, which was then on the point of sailing with the Duke of Leinster for Parkgate; and before the expiration of the week, he found himself for the first time of his life on English ground.

With Sir Alexander Schomberg, who commanded the Dorset yacht, there were three other persons embarked, and of some distinction, from whence it appeared that the connexion which our adventurer formed with them had considerable effect afterwards in the course of the long succession of transactions in which he was engaged. A young captain was one of the three who was most conspicuous, and as it will appear, a striking, though an innocent cause of Barrington's success in his projects of depredation.

It did not require so much sagacity and penetration as Barrington at the time certainly possessed, to penetrate into the character of this young gentleman, and to predict the good consequences that might follow an intimacy with a young man of his rank, disposition, and family. Actuated by a sordid sense of the utility of such a connexion to one in his circumstances, the adventurer employed all those base arts of flattery and insinuation, of which he had been long a perfect master, to ingratiate himself with this gentleman; and in this design he succeeded to the utmost extent of his wishes. Barrington formed an artful tale, which he told as his own story, the purport of which was, that his father was a man of a noble family in Ireland, and illustrious in England, to which country he himself now came to study law in one of the inns of court, more, however, to avoid the illnatured severity of a harsh, unrelenting step-mother, which rendered his paternal mansion in a great measure intolerable to him, than from any predilection for the profession to which he intended to apply himself, but the exercise of which the ample fortune that he was heir to would render unnecessary.

The story took as well as could be desired by the inventor of it, and it was settled between him and his new friend that he should, on his arrival in town, enter himself of the Middle Temple, where Mr. H——n had some relations and a numerous acquaintance, to whom he said, he should be happy to introduce a gentleman so eminently distinguished by his talents and his accomplishments, as well as by his fortune and birth, as Mr. Barrington was.

It was also further agreed on between them, that they should travel together to London; and they accordingly the next day took a post-chaise at Parkgate, and continuing their journey by easy stages through Chester, Nantwich, and Coventry, where they stopped two or three days, arrived by the end of the week at the Bath Coffee-house in Piccadilly, which, on the recommendation of the captain, who had been several times before in the metropolis, was fixed upon as their head-quarters for the remaining part of the summer.

But the expensive manner in which he lived with Mr. H——n, and those to whose acquaintance that gentleman introduced him, all of them gay, sprightly young fellows, who had money at command, in less than a month reduced the funds which Barrington had brought with him from Ireland to about twenty guineas, which to him, who had been now for some years accustomed to live like a man of affluent fortune, seemed to afford a very inconsiderable resource: he therefore resolutely determined to procure a supply of money by some means or other. One evening, while he was deliberating with himself on the choice of expedients to recruit his finances, he was interrupted in his meditations on the subject, by the arrival of a party of his friends with the captain, who proposed to accompany them to Ranelagh, where they had agreed to meet some of their acquaintance, and to spend the evening. Their proposal was, without much hesitation, acceded to by Barrington, and they, without further loss of time, ordered coaches to set them down at that celebrated place of amusement.

Walking in the middle of the gay scenes that surrounded him, he chanced to espy the two other companions of his voyage in the Dorset Packet, to whom he only made a slight bow of recognition; and in less than a quarter of an hour afterwards he saw the Duke of Leinster engaged deeply in conversation with two ladies and a Knight of the Bath, who, it afterwards turned out, was Sir William Draper; and near these he placed himself, quitting for a short time the company to which he belonged. While he was stationed there, an opportunity, which he considered a fair one, offered itself of making a good booty, and he availed himself of it; he picked the Duke's pocket of about eighty pounds, Sir William's of five-and-thirty guineas, and one of the ladies of her watch, with all which he got off undiscovered by the parties, and joined the captain and his party as if nothing had happened out of the ordinary and common routine of affairs in such places of public recreation as Ranelagh.

A degree of fatality, rather unfortunate for Barrington, it seems, occurred during the perpetration of the robbery just related; that is to say, he was observed in the very act by one of the persons who came with him in the Dorset yacht from Ireland to Parkgate; and this man, who was also a practitioner in the same trade of infamy, lost no time in communicating what he saw to Barrington himself, and that in a manner not by any means calculated to conceal his triumph on the occasion: in fact, this gentleman's affairs being pressing, he made very little ceremony of informing Mr. Barrington that, unless he was willing to give him a share of the plunder, he should communicate to the parties robbed, without delay, the particulars of what he had seen. The consequence of a proposal of this nature presenting a disagreeable alternative, Mr. Barrington, as it may be imagined, naturally chose the least of two evils, and, under pretence of being attacked with a sudden complaint, immediately retired with his new acquaintance to town, and putting up at the Golden Cross inn, at Charing-cross, the booty acquired at Ranelagh was in some sense divided, the new intruder contenting himself with taking the lady's watch, chain, &c., which were of gold, and a ten pound note, leaving all the rest of the money and bank-papers with Mr. Barrington, who, he probably conceived, had run the greatest risk to obtain them at first.

But in order to cement the connexion which these two were now on the point of forming, Mr James (for by that name this new accomplice called himself) insisted upon Barrington supping with him; and as Mr. James knew the town much better than himself, Barrington thought he would be a real acquisition, particularly in helping him to dispose of the valuables he might acquire. Picking pockets, therefore, was proposed by Mr. Barrington as a joint concern.

The outlines of the future operations of these adventurous colleagues being adjusted, it was further agreed upon to have another interview on the next day at a tavern in the Strand, there to regulate the plan of their future conduct; and affairs being so far arranged, Barrington returned to his lodgings at the Bath Coffeehouse, where, luckily enough, neither Captain H——n nor any of his party were at that time arrived from Ranelagh.

The next morning, at breakfast, he informed his friend the captain, that on his return last night he chanced to meet a very worthy relation of his, Sir Fitzwilliam Barrington, who engaged him that day to dinner; so that it would be out of his power to make one of the party that were to spend the day with the captain at the Thatched-house tavern; but that, however, he would endeavour to contrive matters so as to join them early in the evening, and stay to supper with them, if they were bent upon keeping it up to a late hour.

This apology was received without any suspicion by the gentleman to whom it was made, as it accounted plausibly enough for his fellow traveller's absenting himself, notwithstanding his prior engagement to Mr. H——n.

Afterwards, Barrington being dressed, called a coach and drove to the Crown and Anchor tavern, where he found Mr. James, who had been for some time waiting for him. The cloth being removed, and the servants withdrawn, these worthy gentlemen entered upon business. It was agreed upon, that whatever either acquired, should be equally divided between them; and that in the sale of watches, jewels, or any other articles they might have to dispose of, both should be present. By this provision, no suspicion of fraud could be entertained: and thus Barrington got what he extremely wished, and greatly wanted, an introduction to a receiver of stolen goods. It was farther settled by them, that while the captain remained in town, they should take care not to be seen together, and that Mr. James should resume his long neglected habit of a clergyman. These weighty conditions, and some others of equal magnitude and importance, being ultimately adjusted to the satisfaction of these systematic plunderers, it was determined on that they should meet regularly twice a week, that is, on Tuesdays and Fridays, to settle with each other; but never, if it could possibly be avoided, twice at the same house. Having then adjourned to the next Tuesday, and fixed on the Devil tavern, at Temple-bar, as the place of their next meeting, our adventurers separated for that time, Barrington going, according to his appointment, to the Thatched-house tavern, and reaching it about eight in the evening, where he found his friend the Captain, and a large party of his acquaintance. Though rather far gone in liquor, most of them knew him personally, and considering him in the light in which he was represented to them by Captian H――n, as a young man of condition, they were delighted with his company. He only waited till the bills were called for, and the reckoning discharged, when, there being no farther obstacle to a hasty retreat, he plundered those who were most off their guard; or rather those who, as he supposed, were possessed of the most portable kind of property. Still, as the prey then made consisted more of watches and trinkets than ready cash, he was under the necessity of calling upon Mr. James, his new friend, next morning, who readily introduced him to a man, a receiver of stolen property, and, who paying them what they deemed an adequate consideration, they made the first division with as much apparent satisfaction as if they had been lawful dealers in the commodities of which they had unjustly deprived the right owners.

So strongly did appearance plead for him at this time, that Barrington's depredation was never imputed to him by those who suffered in consequence of it; and though similar offences were at different seasons, for upwards of two years, committed by him without suspicion or detection, he preserved his fame, and even extended his acquaintance. With certain superficial qualifications for shining in company, and yet a stranger to honour or honesty, in the summer of the year 1775, in the course of his depredations, he visited, as his custom was, the most celebrated watering-places; and among the rest he went to Brighton, which at that time, though frequented by genteel company, was far from having arrived at the celebrity which it has since acquired, especially since the conclusion of the peace with France. But notwithstanding the paucity of numbers at this watering-place, he is said to have had the address to ingratiate himself into the notice and favour of the late

Duke of Ancaster, with several other persons of rank and property, who all considered him as a man of genius and ability, and as a gentleman of fortune and noble family.

But, in tracing all Mr. Barrington's very singular connexions, it is necessary to remark, that about the conclusion of this winter he got acquainted with one Lowe, a very singular character, and one who, like his friend James, he occasionally made use of to vend his ill-gotten property.

Mr. Barrington's new junction with Mr. Lowe, having rendered Mr. James rather a dead weight upon his hands, he began to think about breaking with him, which he did not find a difficult matter, as James, having at bottom some remorse of conscience for his neglect of the laws of justice and moral obligation, very easily quitted Mr. Barrington's connexion; and what is more extraordinary, being a Roman Catholic by profession, retired to a monastery upon the Continent, there in all probability to end his days in piety and peace. Barrington, on the other hand, seemed to increase in temerity and desperation; for on his forming a connexion with Lowe, which was but a short time previous to that evening of the month of January which was observed as the anniversary of the queen's birth-day, it was resolved on between them, that, habited as a clergyman, he should repair to court, and there endeavour, not only to pick the pockets of some of the company, but what was a bolder and a much more novel attempt, to cut off the diamond orders of some of the knights of the Garter, Bath, and Thistle, who on such days usually wear the collars of their respective orders over their coats. In this enterprize he succeeded beyond the most sanguine expectations that could have been formed by either his new accomplice Lowe or himself; for he found means to deprive a nobleman of his diamond order, and also contrived to get away from the palace without suspicion. This being an article of too much value to dispose of in England, it is reported that it was sold to a Dutchman, or rather to a Dutch Jew, who came over from Holland once or twice a-year for the sole object of buying jewels that had been stolen; and though a stranger, he is generally reported to have given a much higher price for such articles, than could have been gotten from the eceivers in town.

The celebrated Russian Prince Orloff paid his first visit to England in the winter of 1775. The high degree of estimation in which that nobleman had long been held by the late Empress Catherine, had ultimately heaped upon him not a few of her distinguishing favours. Among other things of this nature, she had expressed her approbation of his merits by presenting him with a gold snuff-box, set with brilliants, generally supposed to have been worth no less a sum than thirty thousand pounds. This distinguishing trophy having caught the eye of Barrington, impelled him to contrive means to get it into his possession, and he thought a fit opportunity presented itself one night at Covent Garden Theatre, where getting near the prince, he had the dexterity to convey it out of his excellency's waistcoat pocket into his own; when, being immediately suspected by the prince, he seized him by the collar; but, in the bustle that took place, Barrington slipped the box into his hand, which that nobleman gladly retained, though Barrington, to the astonishment of all around, was secured and lodged in Tothill-fields Bridewell till the Wednesday following, when his examination took place at the public office in Bow-street.

Sir John Fielding being at that time the magistrate, Barrington represented himself to him as a native of Ireland, of an affluent and respectable family. He said that he had been educated in the medical line, and came to England to improve himself by the extent of his connexions. To this plausible representation he added so many tears, and seemed to rest so much upon his being an unfortunate gentleman, rather than a guilty culprit, that Prince Orloff declining to prosecute him, he was dismissed with an admonition from the magistrate to amend his future conduct; but this, it will appear, had no manner of influence upon his subsequent proceedings. In fact, Barrington having gone too far to recede, every one now taking alarm at his character and conduct, and the public prints naturally holding him up as a cheat and impostor, he was even forsaken by those who, until that discovery of his practices, generally countenanced him, and enjoyed his company as a young gentleman of no common abilities.

Being in the lobby of the Lords one day, when an appeal of an interesting nature was expected to come on, so that Barrington thought to profit by numbers of genteel people that generally attend; unhappily for Barrington's projects, a gentleman recognised his person, and applying to the Deputy Usher of the black rod, Barrington was disgracefully turned out, and of course, totally disappointed of the harvest he had promised himself.

Barrington, having by some means heard that this gentleman was the person who had denounced him to the keeper of the lobby, was so indiscreet as to threaten him with revenge for what he deemed an unmerited injury; but the magistrates thinking otherwise, they granted, upon that gentleman's complaint, a warrant against Barrington to bind him over to keep the peace. His credit having sunk so very low, that not one of all his numerous acquaintance would become a surety for him, he was compelled to go to Tothill-field's Bridewell, where he remained a considerable time under confinement, from his inability to procure the bail that was required. However, having again obtained a release from that disagreeable quarter, he had no alternative but that of his old profession, and therefore, in about three months afterwards, we find him detected in picking the pocket of a low woman, at Drury-Lane Theatre, for which, being indicted and convicted at the Old Bailey, he was sentenced to ballast-heaving, or in other words, to three year's hard labour on the river Thames, on board of the hulks at Woolwich. As soon as it was convenient, in the spring of 1777 Barrington was put on board one of these vessels.

A sudden remove from ease and affluence to a scene of wretched servitude and suffering, and the privation of almost every comfort in life, could not but have a most sensible effect upon a man in his condition. In short, he was not only harrassed and fatigued with labour, to which he had been unaccustomed, but even disgusted with the filthy language of his fellow convicts, whose blasphemous effusions, which they seemed to make use of by way of amusement, must have been a constant source of the most disagreeable sensations in the mind of almost any person not totally lost to the feelings and the decencies of civilized, or even a savage state of existence. At length the mental as well as the corporeal sufferings of Barrington, did not escape the notice of Messrs. Erskine and Duncan Campbell, the superintendents of the convicts; for, in consequence of Barrington's good behaviour, and through the interference of these gentlemen, he was again set at liberty, after sustaining nearly a twelvemonth's severe suffering on board the hulks of Woolwich.

Still, nothing that Barrington had yet undergone was sufficient to produce any cordial repentance in his mind. He again entered into the full practice of his former profession. In less than six months after his liberation from hard labour, he was detected by one Payne, a very zealous constable in the city, in the very act of picking pockets at St. Sepulchre's church during divine service, and being convicted upon undeniable evidence at the ensuing Old Bailey Sessions, he was a second time sentenced to hard labour on board the hulks, and that for five years.

It was upon his trial on this occasion, that Barrington was first noticed in the public prints as an able speaker. He then essayed, with no small degree of artifice, to interest the feelings of the court in his behalf; but the evidences of his guilt being too forcible and repeated, and all his efforts proving abortive, he was once more removed to the hulks, about the middle of the year 1778. Being a second time in this humiliating and disgraceful situation, he found his imaginary consequence so much hurt, that, failing in a variety of plans to effect his escape, his next attempt was to destroy himself. For this purpose, he took an opportunity to be seen stabbing himself with a penknife in the breast; but as the wound, by the immediate application of medical assistance, was slowly healed, he continued to linger in this new state of wretchedness, till happening to be seen by a gentleman who came to visit the hulks, it produced another event in his favour.

The gentleman just alluded to being most sensibly affected by the dejected and squalid appearance of Barrington, made a most successful use of his influence with government to obtain Barrington's release, upon the condition that he should leave the kingdom. To this as Barrington gladly assented, he generously supplied him with a sum of money to defray the expense of his removal to Ireland, where it is understood this unhappy offender always persisted in stating that he had friends and relatives of credit and character. In London he did not think proper to stay longer than was needful to procure necessaries for his journey; he therefore took the Chester coach, and in the course of a week was enabled to reach the Irish capital, where his fame having arrived before, he was looked upon with such an eye of suspicion, that he was very shortly apprehended for picking the pocket of an Irish nobleman of a gold watch and his money at one of the theatres, and was soon after committed to the New Gaol to be tried upon the charge, but was acquitted for want of evidence.

Though he was acquitted on this occasion, he was perfectly convinced that the Irish capital would be too warm to retain him. He quickly determined to leave Ireland, and accordingly removed to the northern parts of that kingdom, through which he took his way to Edinburgh, where he concluded that he might, for some time at least, commit his depredations with greater safety and facility than he could do either in London or Dublin.

But, in the opinion which he had formed of the character of the Scots, he soon learned by experience that he was grossly mistaken; for he was quickly observed in the capital of Scotland, where the police is more vigilant and severe than in most other parts of the British dominions. He therefore thought it prudent to depart from Edinburgh, where his gleanings were comparatively small.

However, being determined to return to London, he took the Chester in his way, and it being fair-time there, he is said to have contrived to get possession of the amount of six hundred pounds in cash and bank notes, with which he got clear off.

Such are the delusions of vice and the fatal sweets of ill-gotten wealth, that, though additional danger attended his public appearance, from the infraction of the terms on which he was liberated from his confinement on board the hulks, (which were those of his leaving the kingdom and never more returning to it,) still he frequented the theatres, the Opera-House, and the Pantheon, with tolerable success. But he was now too notorious to be long secure: he was closely watched and well nigh detected at the latter of these places; at least, such strong suspicions were entertained by the magistrates of his conduct on the occasion, that he was taken into custody, and committed to Newgate.

Here again, for want of evidence, he got clear of the charge brought against him; but, notwithstanding this, he was unexpectedly detained at the instance of Mr. Duncan Campbell, the superintendent of the convicts, for having returned to England, in violation of the condition on which His Majesty was pleased to grant him a remission of the punishment which he was sentenced to undergo on board the hulks; and the consequence of the detainer was, that he was made what is called a *fine* at Newgate, during the unexpired part of the time that he was originally to have served on the Thames. When the period of his captivity in this prison expired, he was, as a matter of course, set at liberty; and as usual, no sooner obtained his liberty, than he returned to his former practices. He, however, was now more cautious; and being connected with some accomplices of his own cast, he was not so easily detected as he might have been with others less experienced.

In a state of alarm and anxiety, he lived a considerable time in the society of the most profligate and abandoned characters of the metropolis, when he was seen to pick the pocket of Mr. Le Mesurier, at Drury-lane playhouse, and was immediately apprehended. Charge of him was given to one Blandy, a constable, who, through negligence or corruption, suffered him to make his escape. The proceedings against him were carried on to an outlawry, and various methods were made use of to detect him, for nearly two years, without effect.

But while the lawyers were outlawing him, and the constables endeavouring to take him, he was travelling in various disguises and characters through the northern counties of this kingdom He visited the great towns in those parts as a quack-doctor, or as a clergyman; sometimes he went with an E. O. table, and sometimes he pretended to be a traveller to a manufacturing house at Birmingham or Manchester; and travelling on horseback, with a decent deportment and grave appearance, the account which he thought proper to give of himself was credited, without any difficulty, by those who questioned him.

But, in spite of all these precautions, it sometimes happened that he was known by gentlemen whom he met, once particularly in Lincolnshire; yet no one offered to molest or intercept him, until he arrived at Newcastle-upon-Tyne, where, on being recognised, he was suspected of picking pockets, and, on enquiry, was discovered to be an outlaw: upon which he was removed by a writ of habeas corpus to London, and imprisoned in Newgate where he arrived miserably and so dejected, that on learning his circumstances, some of his friends made a subscription for him, by which they collected near a hundred guineas for his use, by which he was enabled to employ counsel, and to take legal measures to have the outlawry against him reversed.

This being effected, he was tried for the original offence, that of stealing Mr. Le Mesurier's purse; but, through the absence of the Rev. Mr. Adeane, a material witness for the prosecution, he was acquitted. Being once more enlarged, he again set off for Ireland, in company with a young man of the name of Hubert, well-known in town for his fraud on the Duke of York. With this accomplice he was so infatuated as to endeavour to carry on his depredations in Dublin, where it was never his fortune to remain for any length of time undetected; for, Hubert being taken in the fact of picking a gentleman's pocket, and handing the property to Barrington, he with great difficulty made his escape to England, where he rambled about for some time previously to his arrival in the capital, which he had scarcely entered, when he was taken into custody for picking Mr. Henry Hare Townsend's pocket of a gold watch.

Hubert, his accomplice, was tried at Dublin, and sentenced to transportation for seven years; but he afterwards contrived to make his escape.

On Wednesday morning, September 15th, 1790, Barrington was put to the bar to be arraigned on an indictment charging him with stealing, on the 1st September, 1790, in the parish of Enfield, a gold watch, chain, and seals, the property of Henry Hare Townsend, Esq. Upon this occasion Barrington displayed all the talents which it has been universally admitted he possessed; but in spite of a long speech, which professed, whether sincere or assumed, great contrition for his past offences, and a determination to amend his life for the future, he was convicted, and sentenced by the judge to seven year's transportation.

During the voyage to Port Jackson, Barrington rendered an essential service in quelling a mutiny in the vessel. Upon this occasion the captain evinced his gratitude for the services he had performed, and when they reached the Cape, at the recommendation of the former, he received a hundred dollars reward for his zeal and activity.

On their arrival at Port Jackson, Barrington having been recommended to the governor, was placed in the first instance at Tamgabbe as a subordinate, and was soon advanced to be a principal watchman, in which situation he acquitted himself as a useful and active officer; insomuch that the governor determined to withdraw him from the convicts; and at the same time that he received his instrument of emancipation, he was presented with a grant of thirty acres of land at Paramatta. He was subsequently appointed superintendent of the convicts; and although not permitted to return to England, was invested with all the immunities of a freeman, a settler, and a civil officer, and had the satisfaction to know that his diligence and activity were not only without suspicion, but were fully appreciated.

It was here that Barrington resolved to revise the notes he had taken during the voyage, and of describing more fully the places they had touched at. He has accordingly produced a very useful and instructive work.

In addition to this performance, he compiled a complete history of the country itself, from its first discovery, comprehending an account of its original inhabitants, their customs and manners, accompanied with an historical detail of the proceedings of the colony from its foundation to his own time.

Barrington's good behaviour after his arrival at Sidney, gained him many friends; by whose interest he was appointed constable; and while in that office he wrote a prologue to a play that was brought out at Sidney, the two first lines of which ran as follows:—

> True Patriots we, for, be it understood,
> We left our Country, for our *Country's good.*

This was perfectly understood by the audience, and elicited considerable applause, as the remainder of the prologue was equally witty.

He continued in the situation in which the governor had placed him till his death: and performed the duties of his office with an unwearied assiduity, which at last superinduced a general decay of nature, of which he died in the year 1811.

The life of Barrington presents much food for those who are believers in the pernicious doctrines of Fatality—and has always been brought forward and adduced by them as one proof of the truth of the tenets which they endeavour to promulgate.

That his whole existence was an evidence of the truth of the old saying " that great effects spring from trifling causes" we must allow, but the same may be said of almost every other human being, whether in a high or low state of society.

That there is a secret influence by which the affairs both of men and nations are governed, whether domestic or political, we are willing to allow, but we are fully convinced, that every thing that can tend to benefit a man's estate, must be derivable from himself, must be produced by his own energy of mind, activity of body, and decision of character, in the first instance, or as Shakspeare beautifully expresses it—

" There is a tide in the affairs of men,
Which, taken at the flood, leads on to fortune;
Omitted, all the voyage of their life
Is bound in shallows and in miseries."

Barrington, like too many of his fraternity, lost the golden opportunity in his early life, and his whole existence afterwards was as the waves of the sea—unsubjected to control, unrestrained by licence, and unchecked by religion.

ENGLISH PIRATES.

SIR HENRY MORGAN

Was a native of Wales, and descended from a respectable family. His father was a wealthy farmer; but young Morgan had no inclination to that industrious mode of life. Abandoning his father's house, he hastened to a sea-port town, where several vessels were bound for the Isle of Barbadoes. He went into the service of one of these; and upon his arrival in the island, was sold for a slave. Having obtained his liberty, he proceeded to Jamaica, where finding two pirate vessels ready to go to sea, he went on board one of them, with the intention of becoming pirate. Having performed several successful voyages, he agreed with some of his companions to unite their wealth to purchase a vessel; which being done, he was unanimously chosen captain.

With this vessel he went to cruise upon the coasts of Campeachy, and capturing several vessels, returned in triumph to Jamaica. Upon his arrival, one Mansvelt, an old pirate, was equipping a fleet, with the intention of landing upon the continent and pillaging the country. The success of Morgan induced Mansvelt to choose him for his vice-admiral. With a fleet of fifteen ships and five hundred men, they set sail from Jamaica, and arrived at the Isle of St. Catherine. Here they made a descent, and landed the greater part of their men.

They soon forced the garrison to surrender, and to deliver up all the forts and castles, which they demolished, only reserving one, in which they placed a hundred men, and the slaves they had taken from the Spaniards. Then proceeding to an adjoining small island, and having destroyed both islands with fire and sword, and made what arrangements were necessary at the castle, which they had garrisoned, they set sail in quest of new spoils. They cruised upon the coasts of Costa Rica, and entered the river Calla, with the intention of pillaging all the towns upon the coast.

Informed of their arrival, and of their former depredations, the governor of Panama collected a force to oppose the pirates. They fled at his approach, and hastened to the Island of St. Catherine to visit their companions who were left in the garrison. Le Sieur Simon, the Governor, had put the large island in a posture of defence, and cultivated the small island with such care, that it was able to afford fresh provisions to the whole fleet. The vicinity of these islands to the Spanish dominions, and the ease with which they could be defended, strongly inclined Mansvelt to retain them in perpetual possession.

With this view he returned to Jamaica to send out greater numbers, that they might thus be able to defend themselves in case of an attack from the Spaniards. He signified his intentions to the Governor of Jamaica upon his return home; but, afraid of offending the King of England, and of weakening the strength of his own island, the governor declined complying with his wishes. Baffled in his designs, he went to the Island of Tortuga to solicit reinforcements from the governor; but before he could effect his purpose, death suddenly put an end to his wicked career.

Meanwhile, the governor of the garrison of St. Catherine, receiving no intelligence of his admiral, was extremely anxious concerning the cause of his long absence. The Spanish governor of Costa Rica, apprised of the injury that would accrue to his master by those two islands remaining in the hands of the pirates, equipped a considerable fleet to retake the islands. But, before proceeding to extremities, he wrote to Le Sieur Simon to inform him that, if he willingly surrendered, he should be amply rewarded; but, if he resisted, severely punished. Having no hope of being able to defend the islands against such a superior force, he surrendered them into the hands of their rightful owner. A few days after this, an English vessel arrived from Jamaica with a large supply of men, women, and stores. The Spaniards, seeing the ships from the castle, prevailed upon Le Sieur Simon to go on board to decoy them into the harbour: which he dexterously effecting, they were all made prisoners.

But the active and intrepid mind of Morgan was soon employed in the execution of new plans He at first equipped one ship, with the intention of collecting as many as he possibly could to form a strong fleet to carry on his depredations. Being successful in collecting a fleet of twelve sail, with seven hundred men, he rendezvoused in a certain part of the island of Cuba.

Captain Morgan had only been two months in the south of Cuba, when he called a council of his fleet to concert measures for attacking some part of the Spanish dominions. Several proposals were agitated; but it was finally resolved to attack the town of El Puerto del Principe. When arriving in the bay of that place, a Spaniard, who was on board the pirate fleet, swam on shore during the night, and gave intelligence of their designs to the governor and inhabitants of the town. They hastened to conceal their riches, and to muster their whole force to oppose the invaders. Having collected about eight hundred men, cut down trees and placed them across the road to impede the march of the pirates, and formed several ambuscades, taking besides possession of a pass through which they had occasion to penetrate; the governor, with the remainder of his forces, drew up on an extended plain in the vicinity of the town.

Captain Morgan, finding the passage to the town impenetrable, made a circuit through the woods, escaped several of the ambuscades, and with great difficulty arrived at the plain where the Spaniards were waiting to give him a warm reception. A detachment of horse first attacked him, but Morgan formed his men into a semi-circle, and so valiantly and dexterously assailed the Spaniards, that they fled towards the woods for safety, but before they could reach the covert, the greater part fell under the swords of the invaders. After a skirmish of four hours, Morgan and his men entered the town, but the inhabitants having shut themselves up in their houses, fired upon the enemy. Being severely annoyed by the inhabitants in this position, Captain Morgan threatened them, "that if they did not surrender willingly, they should soon behold their city in flames, and their wives and children torn to pieces before their eyes." Thus intimidated, they submitted to the discretion of the pirates.

The pirates then proceeded to unexampled cruelty; shut up the men, women, and children in the several churches, and plundered the town; then searched and pillaged the whole adjacent country, and began to feast and rejoice, while they left their prisoners to starve. Unsatisfied even with this, they began to torment them, in order to constrain them to reveal where their money or goods were concealed.

Finding no more to pillage, and provisions becoming scarce, the pirates meditated a departure. With this intention, they intimated to the wretched inhabitants, " that if they did not ransom themselves, they should all be transported to Jamaica, and their city laid in ashes." The Spaniards accordingly sent some of their numbers to search the woods and country for the required contributions. In a short time they returned, informing Captain Morgan that they had been unsuccessful, but requested the space of fifteen days in order to obtain the required ransom. To this he consented, but in a short time a negro was taken with letters from the governor of St. Jago, requiring the prisoners to endeavour to gain time from the invaders until he should come to their assistance.

Upon this, Captain Morgan ordered all the spoils to be put on board the ships, and informed the Spaniards that, if they did not on the following day pay the ransom, he would set fire to the city.

The inhabitants replied, that it was utterly impossible for them to raise such a sum in so short a time, since the messengers whom they had sent were not in the neighbourhood. Morgan knew their intention, but deeming it unsafe to remain longer in that place, demanded of them four hundred oxen, or cows, together with sufficient salt to prepare them, with the additional condition, that they should put them on board his ships. Under this stipulation he retired with his men, taking six of the principal inhabitants as hostages for the performance of the contract. With all possible expedition the oxen were slain, salted, and put on board, the hostages were relieved, and Captain Morgan took leave of that place, and directed his course to a certain island, where he intended to divide his booty.

Arrived at that place, he found that he had only fifty thousand pieces of eight in money and in goods. This sum being insufficient to pay his debts in Jamaica, the Captain proposed to his men that they should attempt new exploits before returning home. To secure success he admonished them to confide implicitly to his direction, and he would certainly accomplish the desired object. The Frenchmen, however, disagreeing with the English, departed, and left Captain Morgan and his countrymen, to the amount of four hundred and sixty, to seek their fortune in their own way. This rupture did not intimidate the adventurous Captain, but labouring to inspire his men with the same spirit, he, with a fleet of nine ships, directed his course towards the Continent.

Meanwhile, he concealed his intentions from every person in the fleet, only assuring them that, by following his directions, he would certainly enrich them with immense spoil. Arrived upon the coast of Costa Rica, he informed them that his intention was to attack the town of Puerta Vela by night. He encouraged them to this bold enterprise with the assurance of success, saying, that as he had communicated his design to none, the inhabitants would be taken by surprise. To this some objected, on account of the fewness of their numbers; but the Captain replied, "if our number is small, our hearts are great, and the fewer persons we are, the more union, and the better shares of the spoil." Stimulated with the hope of great riches, unanimously agreed upon the attack.

This place was esteemed the strongest that the King of Spain possessed in the West Indies, except Havannah and Carthagena. There were two castles situated in the entry of the harbour, which were deemed almost impregnable. The garrison consisted of three hundred men, and the town was inhabited by about four hundred families. The place being unhealthy, on account of certain noxious vapours which descend from the mountains, the merchants only resided there when the galleons came and went from Spain.

Captain Morgan being thoroughly acquainted with the whole coast, and all the approaches to the city, arrived in the dusk of the evening at a place about ten leagues west of the town. He proceeded up the river to another harbour called Puerta Pontia, and came to anchor. Leaving the vessels with a few men, the rest got into the boats and canoes, and about midnight they went on shore, and marched to the first watch of the city. An Englishman who had been prisoner in that town, was their guide; and he was commanded, with some others, either to take or slay the sentinel. They seized him before he could give the alarm, bound his hands, and brought him to Captain Morgan, who asked him, "how matters went in the city, and what force they had," with many other questions, threatening him with instant death upon his refusing to declare the truth. He then advanced towards the city, with the sentinel walking before; and when he arrived at the first castle, surrounded it with his men.

In this position, he commanded the sentinel to accost those within the walls, and inform them that, if they did not surrender, they would all be cut to pieces without the least mercy. But regardless of his threatenings, they instantly began to fire, which gave the alarm to the whole city. The pirates, however, took the castle; and having shut up the officers and men in one room, they blew up the castle with all its inhabitants. Pursuing their victory, they attacked the city. The governor not being able to rally, the citizens fled to one of the castles, and from thence fired upon the pirates. The assault continued from the dawn of the morning until noon; and victory remained in great suspense, until a troop of those who had taken the other castle, came to meet their Captain with loud shouts of victory. This inspired the Captain with new resolution to exert every effort to take this castle also. He was the more stimulated to this, as the principal inhabitants, with their riches, and all the plate belonging to the different churches were deposited in that fort.

With this view, he caused ten or twelve ladders to be constructed with all expedition; and having brought a number of the religious men and women from the cloisters, he commanded them to place these upon the walls. The governor of the castle was, however, little influenced by the superstition of his countrymen; he was therefore, deaf to all their cries and entreaties to surrender and save their lives and his own. That brave commander declared, that he would never surrender the castle; and continuing to fire upon the besiegers, many of the holy brothers and sisters were slain before the ladders could be fastened on the wall. This, however, being at length effected, the pirates ascended in vast numbers, carrying in their hands fire-balls and earthern pots full of powder, which they kindled at the top of the walls, and threw among the Spaniards.

Unable any longer to defend the castle, they threw down their arms and surrendered. But the brave governor would not submit, and not only slew many of the invaders, but even some of his own men, because they would not continue to repulse the enemy. Unable to take him prisoner, they were constrained to put him to death, for, notwithstanding the lamentation and entreaties of his wife and daughter, he remained inflexible, declaring " that he would rather die as a valiant soldier, than be hanged as a coward." Having taken the castle, they placed all the wounded by themselves, leaving them to perish of their wounds, and the men and women in separate apartments, with a strong guard upon them, and gave themselves up to all manner of debauchery and riotous excess. They next proceeded to torture the prisoners, to constrain them to inform them where they had deposited their money or their goods.

Meanwhile, intelligence of their disasters, and of the taking of the city, was conveyed to the president of Panama, who immediately endeavoured to raise such a force as might expel the pirates. The unhealthiness of the climate, their own debaucheries, and the sword, having greatly lessened the number of his men, Captain Morgan gave orders to carry on board all their spoils, and to prepare to sail to another port. While these preparations were advancing, Captain Morgan requested the inhabitants to pay one hundred thousand pieces of eight as the ransom of their city, or he would reduce it to ashes.

In this unhappy dilemma, two messengers were despatched to the president of Panama to inform him of their misfortunes, and to solicit his assistance. Having an army collected, he marched towards Puerta Vela; but Morgan stationing a hundred of his men in a narrow pass, through which it was necessary he should come, the Spaniards were instantly put to flight, and the president returned home with the remainder of his forces. Thus abandoned to their cruel fate, the wretched inhabitants collected the sum demanded; and Captain Morgan having victualled his fleet, and taken several of the best guns from the castle, sailed for the island of Cuba to divide his spoils. These he found to amount to two hundred and fifty thousand pieces of eight, with a large quantity of cloth, linen, silks, and other goods. With this immense wealth the pirates sailed for Jamaica, and arriving there, gave loose to their usual riot and excess.

After having lavished the wealth which they had acquired, Morgan gave orders to his fleet to rendezvous at Cow Island. Rendered famous by his recent adventure, many other pirates joined him, and he soon saw himself at the head of a more powerful fleet than he had ever commanded. The French, however, that joined him, distrustful of his fidelity to them, abandoned his flag, and went to pursue their own measures. Leaving that place, Captain Morgan set sail for the island of Savona, with a fleet of fifteen ships, and a full complement of men. He proceeded on his voyage until he arrived at the port of Ocoa. Here he landed some of his men, and sent them into the woods to seek water and fresh provisions. They returned with several beasts which they had slain; but the Spaniards, dissatisfied with their conduct, laid a snare to entrap them in their second attempt to hunt in their territories.

They ordered three or four hundred men from Santo Domingo to hunt in all the adjacent woods, and emptied them of animals. The pirates returning in a few days to the hunting, could find none, which induced them to venture farther into the woods. Watching all their motions, the Spaniards collected a herd of cows, and committed the care of them to two or three men. The pirates slew several of them; but the moment they were about to carry them off, the Spaniards fell upon them with desperate fury, and constrained them to retreat to their ships; but, during their retreat, they frequently fired upon their pursuers, so that they fled in their turn, and were pursued into the woods, and many of them slain. Enraged at this attack upon his men, Captain Morgan next day landed two hundred men, and ranged the woods; but finding no enemy, he set fire to the scattered cottages of the peasants, and so returned to his ships.

Having waited with no small degree of impatience, for some of his ships that had not arrived, he sailed for the Isle of Savona. Arrived at this place, he was still disappointed in not seeing the remainder of his fleet join him; and while with great impatience waiting for them, he sent some of his men to fetch provisions. The Spaniards, however, were now so vigilant, and so well prepared to defend themselves and their property, that they were constrained to return empty-handed.

Despairing of the arrival of his other ships, Captain Morgan made a review of those who were present, and found them to amount to five hundred men, provided with eight ships. With this small number he was unable to pursue his original plan, and, by advice of a Frenchman who had been at the taking of Maracaibo, he resolved to sack that place a second time. After watering at the Island of Ruba, they arrived at the sea of Maracaibo, and, after some hot actions, in taking possession of the forts at the entrance, arrived at the city in small boats and canoes. The inhabitants deserted the city at their approach; and, after having taken what property they could find, and exercising unheard-of cruelties and tortures upon the prisoners they found in the neighbourhood, Captain Morgan resolved to sail for Gibraltar, and run the hazard of a battle. Some of the principal prisoners he took with him, and sent others to Gibraltar, to tell the inhabitants of the barbarous cruelty they had seen exercised towards their townsmen, and to assure them that, unless they surrendered to Morgan, they would share the same fate. Notwithstanding a show of resistance at first, every person in the city, with the exception of an idiot, fled when the pirates approached, taking with them their riches and gunpowder, and destroying the guns of the fortress.

This solitary individual who had remained in the city, notwithstanding it was evident to Morgan and his associates that he was an idiot, they tortured with unparralled cruelty, to force him to discover to them the retreat of the inhabitants, of which he knew nothing, yet he died under their ferocious hands. Detachments were sent to scour the country round in search of the fugitives, whom, when they found, they treated with the most barbarous inhumanity. One of these detachments was headed by Morgan himself, who directed his search against the governor, but the latter retired to a high mountain, and completely foiled Morgan and his army. The heavy rains and want of ammunition had reduced the pirates to great distress; and if the Spaniards had not been so dismayed, they would at this time have found their invaders an easy prey.

Morgan returned to Gibraltar with a great many prisoners, who negociated a ransom to save the city from being burnt. He then proceeded to Maracaibo, where he was informed that a Spanish fleet, consisting of several large vessels, lay at the entrance of the strait to prevent his escape, which struck his men and himself with great consternation. He assumed a fictitious courage, and sent a letter to the admiral, demanding a very high ransom to prevent the town of Maracaibo from being committed to the flames. This, however, met with no gracious reception, and the Spanish admiral would listen to nothing but the surrender of all the prisoners, hostages, and property. In this dilemma, Morgan assembled his men, and asked them whether they would give up what they had acquired with such toil and danger, or fight their way through the enemy? To the latter proposition they unanimously agreed.

Despair sharpened their invention and their courage. They set about immediately to prepare a fire-ship, with which they intended to destroy the Spanish admiral's ship, and considerably strengthened their other vessels. Captain Morgan sailed with his fleet, and attacked the enemy early in the morning; the fire-ship grappled with the largest vessel, and soon destroyed her; the other two fled towards the castle at the entrance, where one of them was sunk by her own crew, and the other surrendered to the pirates. Elated with this signal victory, the pirates immediately landed, hoping to find the castle surrender at their appearance. In this they were, however, disappointed, for they met with a most spirited resistance, and were at last obliged to fly to their ships.

The Spanish admiral escaped on shore, and was greatly dismayed to see so many of his brave countrymen perish in the waves rather than permit themselves to be taken prisoners by the pirates.

Morgan again sailed for Maracaibo, where he repaired the large ship he had taken, on board of which he hoisted his own flag. He again sent to the Spanish admiral demanding a ransom for the city of Maracaibo, to which that brave officer would not listen, but threatened vengeance on the pirates. The inhabitants, however, offered the sum of 20,000 pieces of eight, besides 500 beeves to victual his fleet, if he would spare the town, and free the Spaniards he had made prisoners. To this last clause, however, he would not agree; he feared the Spanish admiral might destroy his fleet with the guns of the castle, in passing through the strait; and for this purpose he wished to retain the prisoners, to hold out a bribe to the admiral. He sent some of them to the castle, to inform the governor that, unless they were permitted to pass the castle unmolested, he would hang every prisoner in his power. The admiral would not listen to the supplications of these unfortunate prisoners, but accused them of cowardice, and returned for answer, that he would oppose the passage of the pirates by every means in his power.

This resolution made Morgan pause for a while, before he decided what was to be done. In the first place, he divided their plunder, which amounted to 250,000 pieces of eight, besides an immense quantity of merchandize and slaves, Morgan harangued his men, and took counsel what steps they were to follow, in order to get clear of the castle. A stratagem was at length agreed upon, in which they succeeded: during the day-time they sent on shore their boats laden with men, as if they intended to attack the castle by land. The canoes were hid from the castle for some time by the trees on the banks, but in a short time returned, with the appearance of only two or three men in them, to deceive the enemy, while they were all lying in the bottom of the boats. The Spaniards expected the forces that had been landed would attack the castle at night; they removed all their heavy guns to the land side, and left that which commanded the sea without any, by which the pirates passed unmolested during the night.

When the Spaniards perceived that Morgan was about to escape, they transported their guns to the other side of the castle, and commenced a dreadful fire upon the pirates; who, however, effected their escape without much loss or damage. Captain Morgan now sent a canoe to the castle, with some of the prisoners, and fired seven great guns as a farewell salute.

In this voyage the pirates were suddenly overtaken by a great tempest; were constrained to cast anchor, and again to put to sea; and were alternately harrassed with the dread of being overwhelmed in the deep, or cast upon shore and murdered by the Spaniards or Indians. Fortunately, however, for Morgan and his crew, the tempest was calmed, and they arrived safe at Jamaica.

Not long after their arrival here, their excesses emptied their coffers, and constrained them to seek for new spoils. Having collected his men at Port Caullion, he held a council to deliberate upon their next adventure. Meanwhile, it was found necessary to send four ships and one boat, with four hundred men, to the continent, to pillage some coast town for provisions, and to search the woods for wild beasts. These vessels were for some days becalmed in the mouth of the river Cow, which informed the Spaniards of their arrival, and gave them time to hide their money and goods, and to prepare for their own defence. Here they seized a ship richly laden, and landed in defiance of all the resistance of the Spaniards, whom they pursued into the woods, and, by torture, constrained many of them to deliver up their money and property. Dissatisfied with all that they had received, they, upon their departure, exacted a ransom of four thousand bushels of maize as a ransom for the town.

The return of these ships, and their great success, was cause of exultation to Morgan and his men. Having equally divided the maize and the flesh, they directed their course towards Cape Tiburoon; the fleet consisting of thirty-seven sail, with two thousand men, besides marines and boys. The captain divided his fleet into two squadrons, and gave the command of the second squadron to a vice-admiral. He then summoned a council of all his captains, and, besides other directions, enjoined them to carry on hostilities with the Spaniards, as the enemies of the English nation.

From Cape Tiburoon, Morgan sailed for St. Catherine's, then in the possession of the Spaniards, landed a thousand men, and advanced to the governor's residence; but he found that the garrison had retired to the adjacent small island, and had fortified themselves in the strongest manner. Upon their approach, they received such a warm reception, that they were under the necessity of lying all night upon the ground, destitute of every kind of provisions; but a flag of truce being hoisted, a capitulation took place, and it was finally agreed to surrender the island to Morgan and his crew. Having become masters of the island, they hastened to satiate their hungry appetites, and to indulge in all manner of riot and excess. After some time, they pillaged the storehouses of powder and other stores, carried on board the principal guns, destroyed the remainder, and directed their attack upon the castle of Chagre.

This castle is situated at the entrance of the river upon a high mountain, and surrounded with wooden palisades. On the land sides it has four bastions, and is wholly inaccessible by sea. Unintimidated by these obstacles, the pirates made an attack, but were repulsed with some loss. In the action one of the pirates was wounded with an arrow, which he instantly pulled out, wrapped it with cotton, and discharged it from his musket. The arrow fell upon a house thatched with palm-leaves, and the cotton being kindled by the powder set the house on fire, which communicated to a large quantity of powder, that blew up and caused a dreadful consternation. While the Spaniards were labouring to extinguish the flames, the pirates set fire to the palisades; and in a short time entered the place. The governor was slain, and the greater part of his men chose rather to leap into the sea, than await the tortures of the inhuman pirates.

Upon the intelligence of this fortunate adventure, Morgan left St. Catherine's, and hastened to that place, where he was received with every demonstration of joy. Having garrisoned the place, and seized all the vessels, he directed his course towards Panama, at the head of twelve hundred men. But, too confident of the smiles of fortune, he took a small stock of provisions with him. In their march they suffered much from famine, but in the space of nine days he beheld Panama.

On the morning of the tenth day, Captain Morgan arranged his men, but, by the advice of one of his guides, did not take the direct road to the city, and therefore escaped some of the ambuscades that were laid for him. The governor of Panama came out to meet with two squadrons, four regiments, and a number of wild bulls driven by the Indians. Upon the approach of the Spaniards, their number and hostile appearance almost intimidated the unequal numbers of the pirates, but, despairing of all mercy from the hands of those whom they had so often offended, they resolved to give them battle. They were first attacked by a party of horse, but routing them, the foot soon followed their example, and victory declared upon the side of the pirates. The greater part were either slain or taken prisoners. A Spanish captain was also taken prisoner, who informed Morgan concerning the strength and position of the town, which inclined him to attack it in another direction.

Morgan and his men were bravely repulsed, and suffered much from the great guns placed at all points; but in defiance of every opposition and danger, the pirates in three hours carried the town. Thus victorious, they slew all who came in their way, and seized upon the property of the place. To prevent his men from intoxication, that the Spaniards might not have an opportunity to fall upon them, Morgan assembled his men, and prohibited them from tasting the wine, assigning as his reason, that the Spaniards had mingled it with poison.

The captain gave secret orders to set fire to the city in different places. His own men being dissatisfied with this measure, he endeavoured to throw the odium upon the Spaniards themselves. After doing incredible harm, the pirates retired from the town and encamped in the fields. They, however, upon finding themselves safe from a second attack, returned to the city, and conveyed away a large quantity of plate and other valuable articles which the fire had not consumed.

While Morgan continued at Panama, he sent out parties in all directions, who so pillaged the country, that he departed from that place loaded with immense plunder, both in money and in goods. About half way to Chagre they were all searched, beginning with the captain himself, to find whether they had concealed any part of the booty. Several of the company, however, boldly accused the captain of concealing some of the more valuable jewels, as it was impossible that no more than 200 pieces of eight should fall to the share of each man from such an immense spoil.

The captain, finding his authority lessened, endeavoured to escape to St. Catherine's with two or three ships, but the arrival of a new governor in Jamaica, put a period to the depredations of Morgan and many of his associates.

CAPTAIN AVERY

Was a native of Devonshire, and at an early period sent to sea; advanced to the station of a mate in a merchantman, he performed several voyages. It happened, previous to the peace of Ryswick, when there existed an alliance between Spain, England, Holland, and other powers, against France, that the French in Martinique carried on a smuggling trade with the Spaniards on the continent of Peru. To prevent their intrusion into the Spanish dominions, a few vessels were commanded to cruise upon that coast, but the French ships were too strong for them; the Spaniards, therefore, came to the resolution of hiring foreigners to act against them. Accordingly, certain merchants of Bristol fitted out two ships of thirty guns, well manned, and provided with every necessary ammunition, and commanded them to sail for Corunna to receive their orders.

Captain Gibson commanded one of these ships, and Avery appears to have been his mate, in the year 1715. He was a fellow of more cunning than courage, and insinuating himself into the confidence of some of the boldest men in the ship, he represented the immense riches which were to be acquired upon the Spanish coast, and proposed to run off with the ship. The proposal was scarcely made when it was agreed upon, and put in execution at ten o'clock the following evening. Captain Gibson was one of those who mightily love their bottle, and spent much of his time on shore; but he remained on board that night, which did not, however, frustrate their design, because he had taken his usual dose, and so went to bed. The men who were not in the confederacy went also to bed, leaving none upon deck but the conspirators. At the time agreed upon, the long-boat of the other ship, came, and Avery hailing her in the usual manner, he was answered by the men in her, " Is your drunken boatswain on board?" which was the watchword agreed between them. Avery replying in the affirmative, the boat came alongside with sixteen stout fellows, who joined in the adventure. They next secured the hatches, then softly weighed anchor, and immediately put to sea without bustle or noise. There were several vessels in the bay, besides a Dutchman of forty guns, the captain of which was offered a considerable reward to go in pursuit of Avery, but he declined. When the captain awoke, he rang his bell, and Avery and another conspirator going into the cabin, found him yet half asleep. He inquired, saying, "What is the matter with the ship? does she drive? what weather is it?" supposing it had been a storm, and that the ship was driven from her anchors. "No, no," answered Avery, " we're at sea, with a fair wind and good weather." "At sea!" said the captain: "how can that be?" "Come," answered Avery, " don't be in a fright, but put on your clothes, and I'll let you into a secret. You must know that I am captain of this ship now, and this is my cabin, therefore you must walk out! I am bound to Madagascar, with a design of making my own fortune, and that of all the brave fellows joined with me."

The captain, having a little recovered his senses, began to understand his meaning. However, his fright was as great as before, which Avery perceiving, desired him to fear nothing; "for," said he, " if you have a mind to make one of us, we will receive you; and if you turn sober, and attend to business, perhaps in time I

Page 308.

may make you one of my lieutenants; if not, here's a boat, and you shall be set on shore." Gibson accepted of the last proposal; and the whole crew being called up to know who was willing to go on shore with the captain, there were only about five or six who chose to accompany him.

Avery proceeded on his voyage to Madagascar, and it does not appear that he captured any vessels upon his way. When arrived at the north-east part of that island, he found two sloops at anchor, which, upon seeing him, slipped their cables, and ran themselves ashore, while the men all landed, and concealed themselves in the woods. These were two sloops which the men had run off with from the East Indies, and seeing Avery's ship, supposed that he had been sent out after them. Suspecting who they were, he sent some of his men on shore to inform them that they were friends, and to propose a union for their common safety. The sloops' men being well armed, had posted themselves in a wood, and placed sentinels to observe whether the ship landed its men to pursue them. The sentinels only observing two or three men coming towards them unarmed, did not oppose them. Upon being informed that they were friends, the sentinels conveyed them to the main body, where they delivered their message. They were at first afraid that it was a stratagem to entrap them, but when the messengers assured them that their captain had also run away with his ship, and that a few of their men along with him would meet them unarmed, to consult matters for their common advantage, confidence was established, and they were mutually well pleased, as it added to their strength.

Having consulted what was most proper to be attempted, they endeavoured to get off the sloops, and hastened to prepare all things, in order to sail for the Arabian coast. Near the river Indus, the man at the mast-head espied a sail, upon which they gave chase; as they came nearer to her, they discovered that she was a tall vessel, and might turn out to be an East Indiaman. She, however, proved a better prize; for when they fired at her she hoisted Mogul colours, and seemed to stand upon her defence. Avery only cnanonaded at a distance, when some of his men began to suspect that he was not the hero they had supposed. The sloops, however, attacked the one on the bow, and another upon the quarter of the ship, and so boarded her. She then struck her colours. She was one of the Great Mogul's own ships, and there were in her several of the greatest persons in his court, among whom, it was said, was one of his daughters going upon a pilgri-

X

mage to Mecca; and they were carrying with them rich offerings to present at the shrine of Mahomet. It is a well known fact, that the people of the east travel with great magnificence, so that these had along with them all their slaves and attendants, with a large quantity of vessels of gold and silver, and immense sums of money to defray their expenses by land; the spoil therefore which they received from that ship was almost incalculable. .

Taking the treasure on board their own ships, and plundering their prize of every thing valuable, they then allowed her to depart. As soon as the Mogul received this intelligence, he threatened to send a mighty army to extirpate the English from all their settlements upon the Indian coast. The East India Company were greatly alarmed, but found means to calm his resentment, by promising to search for the robbers, and deliver them into his hands. The noise which this made over Europe, gave birth to the rumours that were circulated concerning Avery's greatness.

In the mean time, our adventurers made the best of their way back to Madagascar, intending to make that place the deposit for all their treasure, to build a small fort, and to keep always a few men there for its protection. Avery, however, disconcerted this plan, and rendered it altogether unnecessary.

While steering their course, Avery sent a boat to each of the sloops, requesting that the chiefs would come on board his ship to hold a conference. They obeyed, and being assembled, he suggested to them the necessity of securing the property which they had acquired in some safe place on shore, and observed, that the chief difficulty was to get it safe on shore; adding that, if either of the sloops should be attacked alone, they would not be able to make any great resistance, and thus she must either be sunk or taken with all the property on board. That, for his part, his ship was so strong, so well manned, and such swift-sailing vessel, that he did not think it was possible for any other ship to take or overcome her. Accordingly, he proposed that all their treasure should be sealed up in three chests;—that each of the captains should have keys, and that they should not be opened until all were present;— that the chests should be then put on board his ship, and afterwards lodged in some safe place upon land.

This proposal seemed so reasonable, and so much for the common good, that it was without hesitation agreed to, and all the treasure deposited in three chests, and carried to Avery's ship. The weather being favourable, they remained all three in company during that and the next day; meanwhile Avery, tampering with his men, suggested, that they had now on board what was sufficient to make them all happy; "and what," added he, "should hinder us from going to some country where we are not known, and living on shore all the rest of our days in plenty?" They soon understood his hint, and all readily consented to deceive the men of the sloops, and fly with all the booty; this they effected during the darkness of the following night. The reader may easily conjecture what were the feelings and indignation of the other two crews in the morning, when they discovered that Avery had made off with all their property.

Avery and his men hastened towards America, and being strangers in that country, agreed to divide the booty, to change their names, and each separately to take up his residence, and live in affluence and honour. The first land they approached was the Island of Providence, then newly settled. It however occurred to them, that the largeness of their vessel, and the report that one had been run off with from the Groine, might create suspicion; they resolved therefore to dispose of their vessel at Providence. Upon this resolution, Avery, pretending that his vessel had been equipped for privateering, and having been unsuccessful, he had orders from the owners to dispose of her to the best advantage, soon found a merchant. Having thus sold his own ship, he immediately purchased a small sloop.

In this he and his companions embarked, and landed at several places in America, where, none suspecting them, they dispersed and settled in the country. Avery, however, had concealed the greater part of the jewels and other valuable articles, so that his riches were immense. Arriving at Boston, he was almost resolved to settle there, but, as the greater part of his wealth consisted of diamonds, he was apprehensive that he could not dispose of them at that place, without being taken up as a pirate. Upon reflection, therefore, he resolved to sail for Ireland, and in a short time arrived in the northern part of that kingdom, and his men dispersed into several places. Some of them obtained the pardon of King William, and settled in that country.

The wealth of Avery, however, now proved of small service, and occasioned him great uneasiness. He could not offer his diamonds for sale in that country without being suspected. Considering, therefore, what was best to be done, he thought there might be some person at Bristol he could venture to trust. Upon this he resolved, and going into Devonshire, sent to one of his friends to meet him at a town called Bideford. When he had unbosomed himself to him and other pretended friends, they agreed that the safest plan would be to put his effects into the hands of some wealthy merchants, and no enquiry would be made how they came by them. One of these friends told him, he was acquainted with some who were very fit for the purpose, and if he would allow them a handsome commission, they would do the business faithfully. Avery liked the proposal, particularly as he could think of no other way of managing this matter, since he could not appear to act for himself. Accordingly, the merchants paid Avery a visit at Bideford, where, after strong protestations of honour and integrity, he delivered them his effects, consisting of diamonds and some vessels of gold. After giving him a little money for his present subsistence, they departed.

He changed his name, and lived quietly at Bideford, so that no notice was taken of him. In a short time his money was all spent, and he heard nothing from his merchants, though he wrote to them repeatedly; at last they sent him a small supply, but it was not sufficient to pay his debts. In short, the remittances they sent him were so trifling, that he could with difficulty exist. He therefore determined to go privately to Bristol, and have an interview with the merchants himself,—where, instead of money, he met with a mortifying repulse; for, when he desired them to come to an account with him, they silenced him by threatening to disclose his character; the merchants thus proving themselves as good pirates on land as he was at sea.

Whether he was frightened by these menaces, or had seen some other person who recognised him, is not known; however he went immediately to Ireland, and from thence solicited his merchants very strongly for a supply, but to no purpose; so that he was reduced to beggary. In this extremity he was determined to return, and cast himself upon the mercy of these honest Bristol merchants, let the consequence be what it would. He went on board a trading-vessel, and worked his passage over to Plymouth, from whence he travelled on foot to Bideford. He had been there but a few days, when he fell sick and died; not being worth so much as would buy h. n a coffin.

We shall now turn back and give our readers some account of the other two sloops. Deceiving themselves in the supposition that Avery had outsailed them during the night, they held on their course to the place of rendezvous; but, arriving there, to their sad disappointment no ship appeared. It was now necessary for them to consult what was most proper to do in their desperate circumstances. Their provisions were nearly exhausted, and both fish and fowl were to be found on shore, yet they were destitute of salt to cure them. As they could not subsist at sea without salt provisions, they resolved to form an establishment upon land. Accordingly, making tents of the sails, and using the other materials of the sloops for what purposes they could serve, they encamped upon the shore. It was also a fortunate circumstance, that they had plenty of ammunition and small arms. Here they met with some of their countrymen; and as the digression is short, we will inform our readers how they came to inhabit this place.

Captain George Dew, and Thomas Tew, had received a commission from the governor of Bermuda to sail for the river Gambia, in Africa, that with the assistance of the Royal African Company, they might seize the French Factory situated upon that coast. Dew in a violent storm, not only sprang a mast, but lost sight of his companion. Upon this he returned to refit. Instead of proceeding in his voyage, Tew made towards the Cape of Good Hope, doubled that cape, and sailed for the straits of Babel-Mandel. There he met with a large ship richly laden coming from the Indies, and bound for Arabia. Though she had on board three hundred soldiers, besides seamen, yet Tew had the courage to attack her, and soon made her his prize. It is reported, that by this one prize every man shared near three thousand pounds. Informed by the prisoners that five other ships were to pass that way, Tew would have attacked them, but was prevented by the remonstrances of his quartermaster and others. This difference of opinion terminated in a resolution to abandon the sea, and to settle on some convenient spot on shore; and the island of Madagascar was chosen. Tew, however, and a few others, in a short time went for Rhode Island, and obtained a pardon.

The natives of Madagascar are negroes, but differ from those of Guinea in the length of their hair and in the blackness of their complexion. They are divided into small nations, each governed by its own prince, who carry on a continual war upon each other. The prisoners taken in war are either rendered slaves to the conquerors, sold, or slain, according to pleasure. When the pirates first settled among them, their alliance was much courted by these princes, and those whom they joined were always successful in their wars, the natives being ignorant of the use of fire-arms. Such terror did they carry along with them, that the very appearance of a few pirates in an army would have put the opposing force to flight.

By these means they in a little time became very formidable, and the prisoners whom they took in war they employed in cultivating the ground, and the most beautiful of the women they married; nor were they contented with one, but married as many as they could conveniently maintain. The natural result was, that they separated, each choosing a convenient place for himself, where he lived in a princely style, surrounded by his wives, slaves, and dependants. Nor was it long before jarring interests excited them also to draw the sword against each other, and they appeared at the head of their respective forces in the field of battle. In these civil wars their number and strength were greatly lessened.

The servant, exalted to the condition of a master, generally becomes a tyrant. The pirates, unexpectedly elevated to the dignity of petty princes, used their power with the most wanton barbarity. The punishment of the very least offence was to be tied to a tree, and instantly shot through the head. The negroes, at length, exasperated by continued oppression, formed the determination of extirpating them in one night; nor was it a difficult matter to accomplish this, since they were now so much divided both in affection and residence. Fortunately, however, for them, a negro woman, who was partial to them, ran twenty miles in three hours, and warning them of their danger, they were united and in arms to oppose the negroes before the latter had assembled. This narrow escape made them more cautious, and induced them to adopt the following system of policy :—

Convinced that fear was not a sufficient protection, and that the bravest man might be murdered by a coward in his bed, they laboured to foment wars among the negro princes, while they themselves declined to aid either party. It naturally followed, that those who were vanquished fled to them for protection, and increased their strength. Where there was no war, they fomented private discords, and encouraged them to wreak their vengeance against each other; nay, even taught them how to surprise their opponents, and furnished them with fire-arms, with which to dispatch them more effectually and expeditiously. The consequences were, that the murderer was constrained to fly to them for protection, with his wives, children, and kindred. These, from interest, became true friends, as their own safety depended upon the lives of the protectors. By this time the pirates were so formidable, that none of the negro princes durst attack them in open war.

Pursuing this system of policy, in a short time each chief had his party greatly increased, and they divided like so many tribes, in order to find ground to cultivate, and to choose proper places to build places of residence and erect garrisons of defence. The fears that agitated them were always obvious in their general policy, for they vied with each other in constructing places of safety, and using every precaution to prevent the possibility of sudden danger, either from the negroes or from one another.

A description of one of these dwellings will both show the fears that agitated these tyrants, and prove entertaining to the reader. They selected a spot overgrown with wood, near a river, and raised a rampart with a ditch round it, so straight and steep that it was impossible to climb it, more particularly by those who had no scaling-ladders. Over that ditch there was one passage into the wood; the dwelling, which was a hut, was built in that part of the wood which the prince thought most secure, but so covered that it could not be discovered until you came near it. But the greatest ingenuity was displayed in the construction of the passage that led to the hut, which was so narrow, that no more than one person could go abreast, and it was so contrived in so intricate a manner, that it was a perfect labyrinth; the way going round and round, with several small cross-ways, so that a person unacquainted with it, might walk several hours without finding the hut. Along the sides of these paths, certain large thorns, which grew on a tree in that country, were stuck into the ground with their points outwards; and the path itself being serpentine, as before mentioned, if a man should attempt to approach the hut at night, he would certainly have struck upon these thorns.

Thus like tyrants they lived, dreading, and dreaded by all, and in this state they were found by Captain Woods Rodgers, when he went to Madagascar in the Delicia, a ship of forty guns, with the design of purchasing slaves. He touched upon a part of the island at which no ship had been seen for seven or eight years before, where he met with some pirates who had been upon the island above twenty-five years. There were only eleven of the original stock then alive, surrounded with a numerous offspring of children and grandchildren.

They were struck with terror upon the sight of the vessel, supposing that it was a man-of-war sent out to apprehend them; they, therefore, retired to their secret habitations. But when they found some of the ship's crew on shore, without any signs of hostility, and proposing to treat with them for their slaves, they ventured to come out of their dwellings attended like princes. Having been so long upon the island, their cloaks were so much worn, that their majesties were extremely out at elbows. It cannot be said that they were ragged, but they had nothing to cover them but the skins of beasts in their natural state, not even a shoe or stocking; so that they resembled the pictures of Hercules in the lion's skin; and being overgrown with beard, and hair upon their bodies, they appeared the most savage figures that the human imagination could well conceive.

The sale of the slaves in their possession soon provided them with more suitable clothes, and all other necessaries, which they received in exchange. Meanwhile, they became very familiar, went frequently on board, and were very eager in examining the inside of the ship, talking very familiarly with the men, and inviting them on shore. Their design was to surprise the ship during the night. They had a sufficient number of men and boats to effect their purpose, but the captain suspecting them, kept so strong a watch on deck, that they found it in vain to hazard an attempt. When some of the men went on shore, they entered into a plan to seize the ship, but the captain observing their familiarity, prevented any one of his men from speaking to the pirates, and only permitted a confidential person to purchase their slaves. Thus he departed from the island, leaving these pirates to enjoy their savage royalty. One of them had been a waterman upon the Thames, and having committed a murder, he fled to the West Indies. The rest having been all foremast-men, nor was there one among them who could either read or write.

CAPTAIN MARTEL.

WAR is not the harvest season of pirates. Those who are naturally of a rambling turn of mind, then find employment in privateering. Provincial mobs are most frequent in time of peace; and those turbulent spirits which give energy to tumult, prove brave and useful soldiers when disciplined and introduced into the ranks. In the same manner, pirates under the influence of royal clemency, would prove brave and hardy seamen.

The origin and first adventures of the man upon whose history we are now to enter, are involved in obscurity. He was commander of a private sloop of eight guns and eighty men, upon the coast of Jamaica, where he took the Berkeley galley, Captain

Page 314.

CAPTAIN MARTEL.

Sanders, and plundered him of a thousand pounds; and afterwards he took some money and provisions from a sloop called King Solomon. He proceeded after this to the port of Cavena in the island of Cuba, and in his way captured two sloops, which he plundered and then dismissed. Near the port, he met a fine galley of twenty guns, commanded by Captain Wilson, which was attacked under the black flag, and forced to surrender. Some of the men were put on shore, and others detained. Captain Martel then desired Captain Wilson to inform the owners, that his sloop would admirably answer his purpose, by removing one deck: and as for the cargo, which consisted chiefly of logwood and sugar, he would take care it should be carried to a good market.

This ship being equipped, he mounted her with twenty-two guns and a hundred men, leaving twenty-five hands in the sloop, and went to cruise off the Leeward Islands. Here fortune was propitious to the pirates. After taking two small vessels, they gave chase to a stout ship, which, upon the sight of the black flag, suddenly struck. This was the Dolphin of twenty guns, bound for Newfoundland. The men were made prisoners, and the ship was taken along with our pirates. They seized another vessel on her voyage from Jamaica, put her provisions on board their own ship, and so let her depart. Thus she was obliged to return to Jamaica before she could prosecute her voyage. These fortunate pirates, not long after, captured a small ship and a sloop belonging to Barbadoes, and having taken out the provisions, and such of the men as chose to go along with them, allowed them to depart. Their next prize was the Greyhound galley of London, from Guinea to Jamaica, which they speedily emptied of her valuable cargo, and then permitted to prosecute her voyage.

It was necessary to repair to some harbour, to refit, to obtain provisions, and to dispose of their cargo. Santa Cruz was deemed the most proper place for this purpose, which is ten miles long and two broad, lying south-east by Porto Rico, and belonging to the French settlements. Here they hoped to repose for a while in order to prepare themselves for greater adventures. Nor did fortune forsake these daring adventurers, for on their voyage they captured another vessel, and speedily arrived at the place of their destination. They had now a ship of 20 guns, a sloop of eight, and three prizes. This little fleet they stationed in a small harbour or road upon the north-west of the island.

Their first employment on their arrival was to fortify themselves against any attack. They erected a battery of four guns upon the island, and another of two guns upon the north point of the road. They also stationed one of the sloops, with eight guns, at the mouth of the channel, to prevent any vessel from entering. Having thus fortified themselves, they began to unrig their vessels, in order to clean them.

General Hamilton sent a sloop with an express to Captain Hume to acquaint him that two pirate ships infested the coast. The Scarborough of 30 guns and 140 men, commanded by Captain Hume, had then near 40 of his crew sick, and had buried 20, and was therefore in a bad condition for sea; but having received this intelligence, he left his sick men behind, sailed to the other islands for a supply of hands, and went in search of the pirates. After several disappointments, and about to return, despairing to meet with these marauders, he was informed by a boat which had come from Santa Cruz, that two pirate ships, with some others, were in that place. On Captain Hume's arrival there, the pilot refused to enter the harbour. They were welcomed by the pirates saluting them with red-hot balls from the shore. At length, Captain Hume came to anchor alongside the reef, and cannonaded both the vessels and batteries during several hours. The sloop which guarded the channel was at length sunk, and the man-of-war then directed her fire against the large pirate ships. In the following night it calmed, and Captain Hume, fearing that he might fall upon the reef, weighed anchor, and hovered in the neighbourhood for a few days to block them up. One evening the pirates observed the man-of-war set out for sea, and they took the opportunity to warp out in order to evade the enemy. They soon ran aground, and in this situation saw Captain Hume returning to pay them another visit, which threw them into such dreadful consternation, that they quitted the ship, leaving in it twenty negroes, who all perished. Nineteen of the pirates escaped in a long-boat, while the captain and the rest of the crew fled into the woods, and there, in all probability, terminated their existence.

CAPTAIN TEACH,

OTHERWISE CALLED " BLACKBEARD."

EDWARD TEACH was a native of Bristol, and having gone to Jamaica, frequently sailed from that port as one of the crew of a privateer during the French war. In that station he gave frequent proofs of his boldness and personal courage; but he was not entrusted with any command until Captain Benjamin Hornigold gave him the command of a prize which he had taken.

In the spring of 1717, Hornigold and Teach sailed from Providence for the continent of America, and in their way captured a small vessel with 120 barrels of flour, which they put on board their own vessels. They also seized two other vessels; from one they took some gallons of wine, and from the other, plunder to a considerable value. After cleaning upon the coast of Virginia, they made a prize of a large French Guineaman bound to Martinique, and Teach obtaining the command of her, went upon a cruise. Hornigold, with the two vessels, returned to the island of Providence, and surrendered to the king's clemency.

Teach now began to act an independent part. He mounted his vessel with forty guns, and named her " The Queen Anne's Revenge." Cruising near the island of St. Vincent he took a large ship, called the Great Allan, and after having plundered her of what he deemed proper, set her on fire. A few days after, Teach encountered the Scarborough man-of-war, and engaged her for some hours; but perceiving his strength and resolution, she retired, and left Teach to pursue his depredations. His next adventure was with a sloop of ten guns, commanded by Major Bonnet, whose actions we have already related, and these two having united their fortunes, co-operated for some time: but Teach finding him unacquainted with naval affairs, gave the command of Bonnet's ship to Richards, one of his own crew, and entertained Bonnet on board his own vessel. Watering at Turniff, they discovered a sail, and Richards with the Revenge slipped her cable, and ran out to meet her. Upon seeing the black flag hoisted, the vessel struck, and came-to under the stern of Teach the commodore. This was the Adventure from Jamaica. They took the captain and his men on board the great ship, and manned his sloop for their own service.

Weighing from Turniff where they remained during a week, and sailing to the bay, they found there a ship and four sloops. Teach hoisted his flag, and began to fire at them, upon which Teach the captain and his men left their ship and fled to the shore, burned two of these sloops, and let the other three depart.

They afterwards sailed to different places, and having taken two small vessels, anchored off the bar of Charlestown for a few days. Here they captured a ship bound for England, as she was coming out of the harbour. They next seized a vessel coming out of Charlestown, and two pinks coming into the same harbour, together with a brigantine with fourteen negroes. The audacity of these transactions, performed in sight of the town, struck the inhabitants with terror, as they had been lately visited by some other notorious pirates. Meanwhile, there were eight sail in the harbour, none of which durst set to sea for fear of falling into the hands of Teach. The trade of this place was totally interrupted, and the inhabitants were abandoned to despair. Their calamity was greatly augmented from this circumstance, that a long and desperate war with the natives had just terminated, when they began to be infested by these robbers.

Teach having detained all the persons taken in these ships as prisoners, they were soon in great want of medicines, and he had the audacity to demand a chest from the governor. This demand was made in a manner not less daring than insolent. Teach sent Richards, the captain of the Revenge, with Mr. Marks, one of the prisoners, and several others, to present their request. Richards informed the governor, that unless their demand was granted, and he and his companions returned in safety, every prisoner on board the captured ships should instantly be slain, and the vessels consumed to ashes.

During the time that Mr. Marks was negotiating with the governor, Richards and his associates walked the streets at pleasure, while indignation flamed from every eye against them, as the robbers of their property, and the terror of their country. Though the affront thus offered to the Government was great and most audacious, yet, to preserve the lives of so many men, they granted their request, and sent on board a chest valued at three or four hundred pounds.

Teach, as soon as he received the medicines and his fellow pirates, pillaged the ships of gold and provisions, and then dismissed the prisoners with their vessels. From the bar of Charlestown they sailed to North Carolina. Teach now began to reflect how he could best secure the spoil, along with some of the crew who were his favourites. Accordingly, under pretence of cleaning, he ran his vessel on shore and grounded; then ordered the men in Hand's sloop to come to his assistance, which they endeavouring to do, also ran aground, and so they were both lost. Then Teach went into the tender with forty hands, and upon a sandy island, about a league from shore, where there was neither bird nor beast, nor herb for their subsistence, he left seventeen of his crew, who must have inevitably perished, had not Major Bonnet received intelligence of their miserable situation and sent a long-boat for them.

After this barbarous deed, Teach, with the remainder of his crew, went and surrendered to the governor of North Carolina, retaining all the property which had been acquired by his fleet.

This temporary suspension of the depredations of Black Beard, for so he was now called, did not proceed from a conviction of his former errors, or a determination to reform, but to prepare for future and more extensive exploits. As governors are but men, and not unfrequently by no means possessed of the most virtuous principles, the gold of Black Beard rendered him comely in the governor's eyes, and, by his influence, he obtained a legal right to the great ship called "The Queen Anne's Revenge." By order of the governor, a court of vice-admiralty was held at Bath-town, and that vessel was condemned as a lawful prize which he had taken from the Spaniards, though it was a well-known fact that she belonged to English merchants. Before he entered upon his new adventures, he married a young woman of about sixteen years of age, the governor himself attending the ceremony. It was reported that this was only his fourteenth wife, about twelve of whom were yet alive; and though this woman was young and amiable, he behaved towards her in a manner so brutal, that it was shocking to all decency and propriety, even among his abandoned crew of pirates.

In his first voyage, Black Beard directed his course to the Bermudas, and meeting with two or three English vessels, emptied them of their stores and other necessaries, and allowed them to proceed. He also met with two French vessels bound for Martinique, the one light, and the other laden with sugar and cocoa: he put the men on board the latter into the former, and allowed her to depart. He brought the freighted vessel into North Carolina, where the governor and Black Beard shared the prizes. Nor did their audacity and villainy stop here. Teach and some of his abandoned crew waited upon his excellency, and swore that they had seized the French ship at sea, without a soul on board: therefore a court was called, and she was condemned, the honourable governor received sixty hogsheads of sugar for his share, his secretary twenty, and the pirates the remainder. But as guilt always inspires suspicion, Teach was afraid that some one might arrive in the harbour who might detect the roguery: therefore, upon pretence that she was leaky, and might sink, and so stop up the entrance to the harbour where she lay, they obtained the governor's liberty to drag her into the river, where she was set on fire, and when burnt down to the water, her bottom was sunk, that so she might never rise in judgment against the governor and his confederates.

Black Beard now being in the province of Friendship, passed several months in the river, giving and receiving visits from the planters; while he traded with the vessels which came to that river, sometimes in the way of lawful commerce, and sometimes in his own way. When he chose to appear the honest man, he made their purchases on equal barter; but when this did not suit his necessities, or his humour, he would rob at pleasure, and leave them to seek their redress from the governor; and the better to cover his intrigues with his excellency, he would sometimes outbrave him to his face, and administer to him a share of that contempt and insolence which he so liberally bestowed upon the rest of the inhabitants of the province.

But there are limits to human insolence and depravity. The captains of the vessels who frequented that river, and had been so often harassed and plundered by Black Beard, secretly consulted with some of the planters what measures to pursue, in order to banish such an infamous miscreant from their coasts, and to bring him to deserved punishment. Convinced from long experience, that the governor himself, to whom it belonged, would give no redress, they represented the matter to the Governor of Virginia, and entreated that an armed force might be sent from the men-of-war lying there, either to take or to destroy those pirates who infested their coast.

Upon this representation, the Governor of Virginia consulted with the captains of the two men-of-war as to the best measures to be adopted. It was resolved that the governor should hire two small vessels, which could pursue Black Beard into all his inlets and creeks; that they should be manned from the men-of-war, and the command given to Lieutenant Maynard, an experienced and resolute officer. When all was ready for his departure, the governor called an assembly, in which it was resolved to issue a proclamation, offering a great reward to any who, within a year, should take or destroy any pirate.

Upon the 17th of November 1717, Maynard left James's river in quest of Black Beard, and on the evening of the 21st came in sight of the pirate. This expedition was fitted out with all possible expedition and secrecy, no boat being permitted to pass that might convey any intelligence, while care was taken to discover where the pirates were lurking. His excellency the Governor of Bermuda, and his secretary, however, having obtained information of the intended expedition, the latter wrote a letter to Black Beard, intimating, that he had sent him four of his men, who were all he could meet with in or about town, and so bad him be upon his guard. These men were sent from Bath-town to the place where Black Beard lay, about the distance of twenty leagues.

The hardened and infatuated pirate, having been often deceived by false intelligence, was the less attentive to this information, nor was he convinced of its accuracy until he saw the sloops sent to apprehend him. Though he had then only twenty men on board, he prepared to give battle. Lieutenant Maynard arrived with his sloops in the evening, and anchored, as he could not venture, under cloud of night, to go into the place where Black Beard lay. The latter spent the night in drinking with the master of a trading-vessel, with the same indifference as if no danger had been near. Nay, such was the desperate wickedness of this villain, that, it is reported, during the carousals of that night, one of his men asked him, " In case any thing should happen to him during the engagement with the two sloops which were waiting to attack him in the morning, whether his wife knew where he had buried his money?" when he impiously replied, " That nobody but himself and the devil knew where it was, and the longest liver should take all."

In the morning Maynard weighed, and sent his boat to sound, which coming near the pirate, received her fire. Maynard then hoisted royal colours, and made directly towards Black Beard with every sail and oar. In a little time the pirate ran aground, and so also did the king's vessels. Maynard lightened his vessel of the ballast and made towards Black Beard. Upon this he hailed him in his own rude style, " D—n you for villains, who are you, and from whence come you?" The lieutenant answered, " You may see from our colours we are no pirates." Black Beard bade him send his boat on board, that he might see who he was. But Maynard replied, " I cannot spare my boat, but I will come on board of you as soon as I can with my sloop." Upon this Black Beard took a glass of liquor and drank to him, saying, " I'll give no quarter nor take any from you." Maynard replied, " He expected no quarter from him, nor should he give him any."

During this dialogue the pirate's ship floated, and the sloops were rowing with all expedition towards him. As she came near, the pirate fired a broadside, charged with all manner of small shot, which killed or wounded twenty men. Black Beard's ship in a little after fell broadside to the shore; one of the sloops called the

Ranger, also fell astern. But Maynard finding that his own sloop had way, and would soon be on board of Teach, ordered all his men down, while himself and the man at the helm, whom he commanded to lie concealed, where the only persons who remained on deck. He at the same time desired them to take their pistols, cutlasses, and swords, and be ready for action upon his call, and, for greater expedition, two ladders were placed in the hatchway. When the king's sloop boarded, the pirate's case-boxes, filled with powder, small shot, slugs, and pieces of lead and iron, with a quickmatch in the mouth of them, were thrown into Maynard's sloop. Fortunately, however, the men being in the hold, they did small injury on the present occasion, though they are usually very destructive. Black Beard seeing few or no hands upon deck, cried to his men that they were all knocked on the head except three or four; " and therefore," said he, " let us jump on board, and cut to pieces those that are alive."

Upon this, during the smoke occasioned by one of these case-boxes, Black Beard, with fourteen of his men, entered, and were not perceived until the smoke was dispelled. The signal was given to Maynard's men, who rushed up in an instant. Black Beard and the lieutenant exchanged shots, and the pirate was wounded; they then engaged sword in hand, until the sword of the lieutenant broke, but fortunately one of his men at that instant gave Black Beard a terrible wound in the neck and throat. A most desperate and bloody conflict ensued:—Maynard with twelve men, and Black Beard with fourteen. The sea was dyed with blood all around the vessel, and uncommon bravery was displayed on both sides. Though the pirate was wounded by the first shot from Maynard, though he had received twenty cuts, and as many shots, he fought with desperate valour; but at length, while in the act of cocking his pistol, he fell down dead. By this time eight of his men had fallen, and the rest being wounded, cried out for quarter, which was granted, as the ringleader was slain. The other sloop also attacked the men who remained in the pirate vessels, until they also cried out for quarter. And such was the desperation of Black Beard, that, having small hope of escaping, he had placed a negro with a match at the gunpowder-door, to blow up the ship the moment he should have been boarded by the king's men, in order to involve the whole in general ruin. That destructive broadside at the commencement of the action, which at first appeared so unlucky, was, however the means of their preservation from the intended destruction.

Maynard severed the pirate's head from his body, suspended it upon his bowsprit-end, and sailed to Bath-town, to obtain medical aid for his wounded men. In the pirate sloop several letters and papers were found, which Black Beard would certainly have destroyed previous to the engagement, had he not determined to blow her up upon his being taken, which disclosed the whole villainy between the honourable Governor of Bermuda and his honest secretary on the one hand, and the notorious pirate on the other, who had now suffered the just punishment of his crimes.

Scarcely was Maynard returned to Bath-town, when he boldly went and made free with the sixty hogsheads of sugar in the possession of the governor, and the twenty in that of his secretary.

After his men had been healed at Bath-town, the lieutenant proceeded to Virginia, with the head of Black Beard still suspended on his bowsprit-end, as a trophy of his victory, to the great joy of all the inhabitants. The prisoners were tried, condemned, and executed; and thus all the crew of that infernal miscreant Black Beard were destroyed except two. One of these was taken out of a trading-vessel, only a day before the engagement, in which he received no less than seventy wounds, of all which he was cured. The other was Israel Hands, who was master of the Queen Anne's Revenge; he was taken at Bath-town, being wounded in one of Black Beard's savage humours. One night Black Beard, drinking in his cabin with Hands, the pilot, and another man, without any pretence took a small pair of pistols, and cocked them under the table; which being perceived by the man he went on deck, leaving the captain, Hands, and the pilot together. When his pistols were prepared, he extinguished the candle, crossed his arms, and fired at his company. The one pistol did no execution, but the other wounded Hands in the knee. Interrogated concerning the meaning of this, he answered with an imprecation, " That if he did not now and then kill one of them, they would forget who he was." Hands was eventually tried and condemned, but as he was about to be executed, a vessel arrived with a proclamation prolonging the time of His Majesty's pardon, which Hands pleading, he was saved from a violent and shameful death.

In the commonwealth of pirates, he who goes the greatest length of wickedness, is looked upon with a kind of envy amongst them, as a person of a more extraordinary gallantry; he is therefore entitled to be distinguished by some post, and if such a one has out courage, he must certainly be a great man. The hero of whom are writing was thoroughly accomplished in this way, and some of his frolics of wickedness were as extravagant as if he aimed at making his men believe he was a devil incarnate. Being one day at sea, and a little flushed with drink; "Come," said he, "let us make a hell of our own, and try how long we can bear it." Accordingly he, with two or three others, went down into the hold, and closing up all the hatches, filled several pots full of brimstone, and other combustible matter; they then set it on fire, and so continued till they were almost suffocated, when some of the men cried out for air; at length he opened the hatches, not a little pleased that he had held out the longest.

Those of his crew who were taken alive, told a story which may appear a little incredible. That once, upon a cruise, they found out that they had a man on board more than their crew; such a one was seen several days amongst them, sometimes below and sometimes upon deck, yet no man in the ship could give any account who he was, or from whence he came; but that he disappeared a little before they were cast away in their great ship, and, it seems, they verily believed it was the devil.

One would think these things should have induced them to reform their lives; but being so many reprobates together, they encouraged and spirited one another up in their wickedness, to which a continual course of drinking did not a little contribute. In Black Beard's Journal, which was taken, there were several memoranda of the following nature, all written with his own hand.—"Such a day, rum all out;—our company somewhat sober;—a d——d confusion amongst us;—rogues a plotting;—great talk of separation.—So I looked sharp for a prize; such a day took one, with a great deal of liquor on board; so kept the company hot, d——d hot, then all things went well again."

We shall close the narrative of this extraordinary man's life by an account of the cause why he was denominated Black Beard. He derived this name from his long black beard, which, like a frightful meteor, covered his whole face, and terrified all America more than any comet that had ever appeared. He was accustomed to twist it with ribbon in small quantities, and turn them about his ears. In time of action he wore a sling over his shoulders with three brace of pistols. He stuck lighted matches under his hat, which appearing on both sides of his face and eyes, naturally fierce and wild, made him such a figure that the human imagination cannot form a conception of a fury more terrible and alarming; and if he had the appearance and look of a fury, his actions corresponded with the character.

CAPTAIN CHARLES VANE.

Charles Vane was one of those who stole away the silver which the Spaniards had fished up from the wrecks of the galleons in the Gulf of Florida, and was at Providence when governor Rodgers arrived there with two men-of-war.

All the pirates who were then found at this colony of rogues, submitted and received certificates of their pardon, except Captain Vane and his crew; who, as soon as they saw the men-of-war enter, slipped their cable, set fire to a prize they had in the harbour, sailed out with their piratical colours flying, and fired at one of the men-of-war, as they went off from the coast.

Two days after, they met with a sloop belonging to Barbadoes, which they took, and kept the vessel for their own use, putting aboard five and twenty hands, with one Yeats, the commander. In a day or two they fell in with a small interloping trader, with a quantity of Spanish pieces of eight aboard, bound for Providence, which thay also took along with them. With these two sloops, Vane went to a small island and cleaned; where he shared the booty, and spent some time in a riotous manner.

About the latter end of May, 1718, Vane and his crew sailed, and being in want of provisions, they beat up for the windward Islands. In the way they met with a Spanish sloop, bound from Porto Rico to the Havannah, which they burnt, stowed the Spaniards into a boat, and left them to get to the island by the blaze of their vessel. Steering between St. Christopher's and Anguilla, they fell in with a brigantine and a sloop, freighted with such cargo as they wanted; from whom they got provisions for sea-store.

Some time after this, standing to the northward, in the track which the Old England ships take in their voyage to the American colonies, they took several ships and vessels, which they plundered of what they thought fit, and then let them pass.

About the latter end of August, Vane, with his consort Yeats, came off South Carolina, and took a ship belonging to Ipswich, laden with logwood. This was thought convenient enough for their own business, and therefore they ordered their prisoners to work, and throw all the lading overboard; but when they had more than half cleared the ship, the whim changed, and they would not have her: so Coggershall, the captain of the captured vessel, had his ship again, and he was suffered to pursue his voyage home. In this voyage the pirates took several ships and vessels, particularly a sloop from Barbadoes, a small ship from Antigua, a sloop belonging to Curaçou, and a large brigantine from Guinea, with upwards of ninety negroes aboard. The pirates plundered them all and let them go, putting the negroes out of the brigantine aboard Yeats' vessel.

Captain Vane always treated his consort with very little respect, and assumed a superiority over him and his crew, regarding the vessel but as a tender to his own: this gave them disgust; for they thought themselves as good pirates, and as great rogues as the best of them; so they caballed together, and resolved, the first opportunity, to leave the company, and accept of His Majesty's pardon, or set up for themselves; either of which they thought more honourable than to be servants to Vane: the putting aboard so many negroes, where there were so few hands to take care of them, aggravated the matter, though they thought fit to conceal or stifle their resentment at that time.

In a day or two, the pirates lying off at anchor, Yeats in the evening slipped his cable, and put his vessel under sail, standing into the shore; which when Vane saw, he was highly provoked, and got his sloop under sail to chase his consort. Vane's brigantine sailing best, he gained ground of Yeats, and would certainly have come up with them, had he had a little longer run; but just as he got over the bar, when Vane came within gunshot of him, he fired a broadside at his old friend, and so took his leave.

Yeats came into North Eddisto river, about ten leagues to the southward of Charlestown, and sent an express to the governor, to know if he and his comrades might have the benefit of his Majesty's pardon; promising that, if they might, they would surrender themselves to his mercy, with the sloops and negroes. Their request being granted, they all came up, and received certificates; and Captain Thomson, from whom the negroes were taken, had them all restored to him, for the use of his owners.

Vane cruised some time off the bar, in hopes to catch Yeates at his coming out again, but therein he was disappointed; however, he there took two ships from Charlestown, which were bound home to England. It happened just at this time, that two sloops well manned and armed, were equipped to go after a pirate, which the governor of South Carolina was informed lay then in Cape Fear river, cleaning: but Colonel Rhet, who commanded the sloops, meeting with one of the ships that Vane had plundered, going back over the bar for such necessaries as had been taken from her; and she giving the colonel an account of being taken by the pirate Vane, and also, that some of her men, while they were prisoners on board of him, had heard the pirates say they should clean in one of the rivers to the southward, he altered his first design, and instead of standing to the northward, in pursuit of the pirate in Cape Fear river, turned to the southward after Vane, who had ordered such reports to be given out, on purpose to put any force that should come after him upon a wrong scent; for he stood away to the northward, so, that the pursuit proved to be of no effect. Colonel Rhet's speaking with this ship was the most unlucky thing that could have happened, because it turned him out of the road which, in all probability, would have brought him into the company of Vane, as well as of the pirate he went after, and so they might have been both destroyed; whereas, by the colonel's going a different way, he not only lost the opportunity of meeting with one, but if the other had not been infatuated, and lain six weeks together at Cape Fear, he would have missed him likewise; however, the colonel having searched the rivers and inlets, for several days without success, at length sailed in prosecution of his first design, and met with the pirate accordingly, whom he fought and took.

Captain Vane went into an inlet to the northward, where he met with Captain Teach, otherwise Black Beard, whom he saluted (when he found who he was) with his great guns loaded with shot; it being the custom among pirates when they met, to do so, though they are wide of one another: Black Beard answered the salute in the same manner, and mutual civilities passed between them some days, when, about the beginning of October, Vane took leave, and sailed farther to the northward.

On the 23rd of October, off Long Island, he took a small brigantine bound from Jamaica to Salem in New England, besides a little sloop; they rifled the brigantine, and sent her away. From thence they resolved on a cruise between Cape Meise and Cape Nicholas, where they spent some time without seeing or speaking with any vessel, till the latter end of November; they then fell in with a ship, which it was expected would have struck as soon as their black colours were hoisted; but instead of this she discharged a broadside upon the pirate, and hoisted French colours, which showed her to be a French man-of-war. Vane desired to have nothing further to say to her, but trimmed his sails, and stood away from the Frenchman; however, Monsieur having a mind to be better informed who he was, set all his sails and crowded after him. During this chase the pirates were divided in their resolution what to do: Vane, the captain, was for making off as fast as he could, alleging that the man-of-war was too strong for them to cope with; but one John Rackam, their quarter-master, and who was a kind of check upon the captain, rose up in defence of a contrary opinion, saying, " that though she had more guns, and a greater weight of metal, they might board her, and then the best boys would carry the day." Rackam was well seconded, and the majority was for boarding; but Vane urged, that it was too rash and desperate an enterprise, the man-of-war appearing to be twice their force, and that their brigantine might be sunk by her before they could reach to board her. The mate, one Robert Deal, was of Vane's opinion, as were about fifteen more, and all the rest joined with Rackam the quarter-master. At length the captain made use of his power to determine this dispute, which in these cases is absolute and uncontrollable, by their own laws, viz. the captain's absolute right of determining in all questions concerning fighting, chasing, or being chased; in all other matters whatsoever the captain being governed by a majority; so the brigantine having the heels, as they term it, of the Frenchman, she came clear off.

But the next day, the captain's conduct was obliged to stand the test of a vote, and a resolution passed against his honour and dignity, which branded him with the name of coward, deposed him from the command, and turned him out of the company with marks of infamy; and with him went all those who did not vote for boarding the French man-of-war. They had with them a small sloop that had been taken by them some time before, which they gave to Vane and the discarded members; and that they might be in a condition to provide for themselves by their own honest endeavours, they let them have a sufficient quantity of provisions and ammunition.

John Rackam was voted captain of the brigantine in Vane's room, and he proceeded towards the Caribbee Islands; where we must leave him, till we have finished our history of Charles Vane.

The sloop sailed for the bay of Honduras, and Vane and his crew put her in as good a condition as they could by the way, that they might follow their old trade. They cruised two or three days off the north-west part of Jamaica, and took a sloop and two pettiagas, all the men of which entered with them: the sloop they kept, and Robert Deal was appointed captain

On the 16th of December, the two sloops came into the bay,

where they found only one vessel at anchor. She was called the Pearl of Jamaica, and got under sail at the sight of them; but the pirate sloops coming near Rowland, and showing no colours, he gave them a gun or two, whereupon they hoisted the black flag, and fired three guns each at the Pearl. She struck, and the pirates took possession, and carried her away to a small island called Barnacho, where they cleaned. By the way they met with a sloop from Jamaica, as she was going down to the bay, which they also took.

In February, Vane sailed from Barnacho, for a cruise; but, some days after he was out, a violent tornado overtook him, which separated him from his consort, and, after two days' distress, threw his sloop upon a small uninhabited island, near the bay of Honduras, where she was staved to pieces, and most of her men were drowned: Vane himself was saved, but reduced to great straits for want of necessaries, having no opportunity to get any thing from the wreck. He lived here some weeks, and was supported chiefly by fishermen, who frequented the island with small crafts from the main, to catch turtles and other fish.

While Vane was upon this island, a ship put in there from Jamaica for water, the captain of which, one Holford, an old bucanier, happened to be Vane's acquaintance. He thought this a good opportunity to get off, and accordingly applied to his old friend; but Holford absolutely refused him, saying to him, "Charles, I shan't trust you aboard my ship, unless I carry you as a prisoner, for I shall have you caballing with my men, knocking me on the head, and running away with my ship a pirating." Vane made all the protestations of honour in the world to him; but, it seems, Captain Holford was too intimately acquainted with him, to repose any confidence at all in his words or oaths. He told him, "He might easily find a way to get off, if he had a mind to it:—I am going down the bay," said he, "and shall return hither in about a month, and if I find you upon the island when I come back, I'll carry you to Jamaica, and there hang you." "How can I get away?" answered Vane. "Are there not fishermen's dories upon the beach? Can't you take one of them?" replied Holford. "What?" said Vane, "Would you have me steal a dory then?" "Do you make it a matter of conscience," replied Holford, "to steal a dory, when you have been a common robber and pirate, stealing ships and cargoes, and plundering all mankind that fell in your way! stay here if you are so squeamish:" and he left him to consider of the matter.

After Captain Holford's departure, another ship put into the same island, in her way home for water; none of the company knowing Vane, he easily passed for another man, and so was shipped for the voyage. One would be apt to think that Vane was now pretty safe, and likely to escape the fate which his crimes had merited; but here a cross accident happened that ruined all. Holford returning from the bay, was met by this ship, and the captains being very well acquainted with each other, Holford was invited to dine aboard, which he did. As he passed along to the cabin, he chanced to cast his eye down into the hold, and there saw Charles Vane at work: he immediately spoke to the captain, saying, "Do you know whom you have got aboard there?" "Why," said he, "I have shipped a man at such an island, who was cast away in a trading sloop, and he seems to be a brisk hand." "I tell you," replied Captain Holford, "it is Vane, the notorious pirate." "If it be he," cried the other, "I won't keep him" "Why then," said Holford, "I'll send and take him aboard, and surrender him at Jamaica." This being agreed upon, captain Holford, as soon as he returned to his ship, sent his boat with his mate armed, who, coming to Vane, showed him a pistol, and told him he was his prisoner. No man daring to make opposition, he was brought aboard and put into irons; and when Captain Holford arrived at Jamaica, he delivered up his old acquaintance to justice, at which place he was tried, convicted, and executed, as some time before, Vane's consort, Robert Dale, who was brought thither by one of the men-of-war. It is clear from this how little ancient friendship will avail a great villain, when he is deprived of the power that had before supported and rendered him formidable.

CAPTAIN JOHN RACKAM.

This John Rackam, as has been reported in the foregoing pages, was quarter master to Vane's company, till the crew were divided, and Vane turned out of it for refusing to board the French man-of-war, Rackam being voted captain of the division that remained in the brigantine. The 24th of November, 1718, was the first day of his command; his first cruise was among the Carribbee Islands, where he took and plundered several vessels.

We have already taken notice, that when Captain Woods Rodgers wen. to the Island of Providence with the king's pardon to such of the pirates as should surrender, this brigantine, which Rackam now commanded, made its escape through another passage, bidding defiance to the mercy that was offered.

To the windward of Jamaica, a Madeira-man fell into the pirate's way, which they detained two or three days, till they had their market out of her, and then they gave her back to the master, and permitted one Hosea Tidsel, a Tavern-keeper at Jamaica, who had been picked up in one of their prizes, to depart in her, she being bound for that island.

After this cruise, they went into a small island, and cleaned, and spent their Christmas ashore, drinking and carousing as long as they had any liquor left, and then went to sea again for more. They succeeded but too well, though they took no extraordinary prize for above two months, except a ship laden with convicts from Newgate, bound for the plantations, which in a few days was retaken, with all her cargo, by an English man-of-war that was stationed in those seas.

Rackam stood towards the island of Bermuda, and took a ship bound to England from Carolina, and a small pink from New England, both which he brought to the Bahama Islands, where, with the pitch, tar, and stores, they cleaned again, and refitted their own vessel; but staying too long in that neighbourhood, Captain Rodgers, who was Governor of Providence, hearing of these ships being taken, sent out a sloop well manned and armed, which retook both the prizes, though in the mean while the pirate had the good fortune to escape.

From hence they sailed to the back of Cuba, where Rackam kept a little kind of a family; at which place they stayed a considerable time, living ashore with their Delilahs, till their money and provisions were expended, and they concluded it time to look out for more. They repaired their vessel, and were making ready to put to sea, when a guarda de costa came in with a small English sloop, which she had taken as an interloper on the coast. The Spanish guard-ship attacked the pirate, but Rackam being close in behind a little island, she could do but little execution where she lay; the Dons therefore warped into the channel that evening, in order to make sure of her the next morning. Rackam, finding his case desperate, and that there was hardly any possibility of escaping, resolved to attempt the following enterprize. The Spanish prize lying for better security close into the land, between the little island and the Main, our desperado took his crew into the boat with their cutlasses, rounded the little island, and fell aboard their prize silently in the dead of night without being discovered, telling the Spaniards that were aboard her, that if they spoke a word, or made the least noise, they were all dead men; and so they became masters of her. When this was done, he slipped her cable, and drove out to sea. The Spanish man-of-war was so intent upon their expected prize, that they minded nothing else, and as soon as day broke, they made a furious fire upon the empty sloop; but it was not long before they were rightly apprised of the matter, when they cursed themselves sufficiently for a company of fools, to be bit out of a good rich prize, as she proved to oe, and to have nothing but an old crazy hull in the room of her.

Rackam and his crew had no occasion to be displeased at the exchange, as it enabled them to continue some time longer in a way of life that suited their depraved minds. In August 1720, we find him at sea again, scouring the harbours and inlets of the north and west parts of Jamaica, where he took several small craft, which proved no great booty to the rovers; but they had but few men, and therefore were obliged to run at low game till they could increase their company and their strength.

In the beginning of September, they took seven or eight fishing-boats in Harbour Island, stole their nets and other tackle, and then went off to the French part of Hispaniola, where they landed, and took the cattle away, with two or three Frenchmen whom they found near the water-side, hunting wild hogs in the evening. The Frenchmen came on board, whether by consent or compulsion is not certainly known. They afterwards plundered two sloops, and returned to Jamaica, on the north coast of which island, near Porto Maria Bay, they took a schooner, Thomas Spenlow, master; it being then the 19th of October. The next day Rackam seeing a sloop in Dry Harbour Bay stood in and fired a gun; the men all ran ashore and he took the sloop and lading; but when those ashore found that they were pirates, they hailed the sloop, and let them know that they were all willing to come aboard of them.

Rackam's coasting the island in this manner, proved fatal to him; for intelligence of his expedition, came to the governor, by a canoe which he had surprised ashore in Ocho Bay: upon this a sloop was immediately fitted out, and sent round the island in quest of him, commanded by Captain Barnet, and manned with a good number of hands. Rackam, rounding the island, and drawing round the western point, called Point Negril, saw a small vettiaga, which, at sight of the sloop, ran ashore and landed her men, when one of them hailed her. Answer was made that they were Englishmen, and begged the pettiaga's men to come on board and drink a bowl of punch; which they prevailed upon them to do. Accordingly, the company, in an evil hour, came all aboard of the pirate, consisting of nine persons; they were armed with muskets and cutlasses, but what was their real design by so doing we shall not take upon us to say. They had no sooner laid down their arms and taken up their pipes, than Barnet's sloop, which was in pursuit of Rackam's, came in sight.

The pirates, finding she stood directly towards them, feared the event, and weighed their anchor, which they had but lately let go, and stood off. Captain Barnet gave them chase, and, having the advantage of little breezes of wind which blew off the land, came up with her, and brought her into Port Royal, in Jamaica.

About a fortnight after, the prisoners were brought ashore, viz. November 16, 1720, and Captain Rackam and eight of his men condemned and executed. Captain Rackam and two others were hung in chains.

But what was very surprising, was the conviction of the nine men that came aboard the sloop on the same day she was taken. They were tried at an adjournment of the court, on the 24th of January, the magistracy waited all that time, it is supposed, for evidence to prove the piratical intention of going aboard the said sloop; for it seemed there was no act of piracy committed by them, as appeared by the witnesses against them, two Frenchmen taken by Rackam off the island of Hispaniola; who merely deposed that the prisoners came on board the pirate without compulsion.

The court considered the prisoners' case, and the majority of the commissioners being of opinion that they were all guilty of the piracy and felony they were charged with, viz the going over with a piratical and felonious intent to John Rackam, &c. then notorious pirates, and by them known to be so, they all received sentence of death, and were executed on the 17th of February, 1721, at Gallows Point at Port Royal.

CAPTAIN EDWARD ENGLAND.

THIS adventurer was mate of a sloop that sailed from Jamaica, and was taken by Captain Winter, a pirate, just before the settlement of the pirates at Providence island. After the pirates had surrendered to his Majesty's pardon, and Providence island was peopled by the English government, Captain England sailed to Africa. There he took several vessels, particularly the Cadogan, from Bristol, commanded by one Skinner. When the latter struck to the pirate, he was ordered to come on board in his boat. The person upon whom he first cast his eye, proved to be his old boat swain, who stared him in the face, and accosted him in the following manner: "Ah, Captain Skinner, is it you? the only person I wished to see: I am much in your debt, and I shall pay you all in your own coin." The poor man trembled in every joint, and dreaded the event, as he well might. It happened that Skinner and his old boatswain, with some of his men, had quarrelled, so that he thought fit to remove them on board a man-of-war, while he refused to pay them their wages. Not long after, they found means to leave the man-of-war, and went on board a small ship in the West Indies. They were taken by a pirate, and brought to Providence, and from thence sailed as pirates with Captain England. Thus accidentally meeting their old captain, they severely revenged the treatment they had received.

After the rough salutation which has been related, the boatswain called to his comrades, laid hold of Skinner, tied him fast to the windlass, and pelted him with glass bottles until they cut him in a shocking manner, then whipped him about the deck until they were quite fatigued, remaining deaf to all his prayers and entreaties; and at last, in an insulting tone, observed, that as he had been a good master to his men, he should have an easy death, and upon this shot him through the head.

Having taken such things out of the ship as they stood most in need of, she was given to Captain Davis in order to try his fortune with a few hands.

Captain England, some time after, took a ship called the Pearl, for which he exchanged his own sloop, fitted her up for piratical service, and called her the Royal James. In that vessel he was very fortunate, and took several ships of different sizes and different nations. In the spring of 1719, the pirates returned to Africa, and beginning at the river Gambia, sailed down the coast to Cape Corso, and captured several vessels. Some of them they pillaged, and allowed to proceed, some they fitted out for the pirate service, and others they burned.

Leaving our pirate upon this coast, the Revenge and the Flying King, two other pirate vessels, sailed for the West Indies, where they took several prizes, and then cleared and sailed for Brazil. There they captured some Portuguese vessels; but a large Portuguese man-of-war coming up to them, proved an unwelcome guest. The Revenge escaped, but was soon lost upon that coast. The Flying King in despair ran ashore. There were then seventy on board, twelve of whom were slain, and the remainder taken prisoners. The Portuguese hanged thirty-eight of them.

Captain England, whilst cruising upon that coast, took the Peterborough of Bristol, and the Victory. The former they detained, the latter they plundered and dismissed. In the course of his voyage, England met with two ships, but these taking shelter under Cape Corso Castle, he unsuccessfully attempted to set them on fire. He next sailed down to Whydah road, where Captain La Bouche had been before England, and left him no spoil. He now went into the harbour, cleaned his own ship, and fitted up the Peterborough, which he called the Victory. During several weeks the pirates remained in this quarter, indulging in every species of riot and debauchery, until the natives, exasperated with their conduct, came to an open rupture, when several of the negroes were slain, and one of their towns set on fire by the pirates.

Leaving that port, the pirates, when at sea, determined by vote to sail for the East Indies, and arrived at Madagascar. After watering and taking in some provisions they sailed for the coast of Malabar. This place is situated in the Mogul Empire, and is one of its most beautiful and fertile districts. It extends from the coast of Canora to Cape Comorin. The original natives are negroes; but a mingled race of Mahometans, who are generally merchants, have been introduced in modern times. Having sailed almost round the one half of the globe, literally seeking whom they might devour, our pirates arrived in this hitherto untried and prolific field for their operations.

Not long after their settlement at Madagascar, they took a cruise, in which they captured two Indian vessels and a Dutchman. They exchanged the latter for one of their own, and directed their course again to Madagascar. Several of their hands were sent on shore with tents and ammunition, to kill such beasts and venison as the island afforded. They also formed the resolution to go in search of Avery's crew, which they knew had settled upon the island; but as their residence was upon the other side of the island, the loss of time and labour was the only fruit of their search.

They tarried here but a very short time, then steered their course to Juanna, and coming out of that harbour, fell in with two English vessels and an Ostend ship, all Indiamen, which, after a most desperate action, they captured. The particulars of this extraordinary action are related in the following letter from Captain Mackra

"*Bombay, November* 16*th*, 1720.

" We arrived on the 25th of July last, in company with the Greenwich, at Juanna, an island not far from Madagascar. Putting in there to refresh our men, we found fourteen pirates who came in their canoes from the Mayotta, where the pirate ship to which they belonged, viz. the Indian Queen, two hundred and fifty tons, twenty-eight guns, and ninety men, commanded by Captain Oliver de la Bouche, bound from the Guinea coast to the East Indies, had been bulged and lost. They said they left the captain and forty of their men building a new vessel, to proceed on their wicked design. Captain Kirby and I concluded that it might be of great service to the East India Company to destroy such a nest of rogues, and were ready to sail for that purpose on the 17th of August, about eight o'clock in the morning, when we discovered two pirates standing into the bay of Juanna, one of thirty-four, and the other of thirty-six guns. I immediately went on board the Greenwich, where they seemed very diligent in preparation for an engagement, and I left Captain Kirby with mutual promises of standing by each other. I then unmoored, got under sail, and brought two boats a-head to row me close to the Greenwich; but he being open to a valley and a breeze, made the best of his way from me; which an Ostender in our company, of twenty-two guns, seeing, did the same, though the captain had promised heartily to engage with us, and I believe would have been as good as his word, if Captain Kirby had kept his. About half an hour after twelve, I called several times to the Greenwich to bear down to our assistance, and fired a shot at him, but to no purpose; for though we did not doubt but he would join us, because, when he got about a league from us he brought his ship to and looked on, yet both he and the Ostender basely deserted us, and left us engaged with barbarous and inhuman enemies, with their black and bloody flags hanging over us, without the least appearance of ever escaping, but to be cut to pieces. But God in his good providence determined otherwise; for, notwithstanding their superiority, we engaged them both about three hours; during which time the biggest of them received some shot betwixt wind and water, which made her keep off a little to stop her leaks The other endeavoured all she could to board us, by rowing with her oars, being within half a ship's length of us above an hour; but by good fortune we shot all her oars to pieces, which prevented them, and by consequence saved our lives.

" About four o'clock most of the officers and men posted on the quarter-deck being killed and wounded, the largest ship making up to us with diligence, being still within a cable's length of us, often giving us a broadside; there being now no hopes of Captain Kirby's coming to our assistance, we endeavoured to run ashore; and though we drew four feet of water more than the pirate, it pleased God that he stuck fast on a higher ground than happily we fell in with; so was disappointed a second time from boarding us. Here we had a more violent engagement than before: all my officers and most of my men behaved with unexampled courage; and, as we had a considerable advantage by having a broadside to his bow, we did him great damage; so that had Captain Kirby come in then, I believe we should have taken both the vessels, for we had one of them sure; but the other pirate (who was still firing at us), seeing the Greenwich did not offer to assist us, supplied his consort with three boats full of fresh men. About five in the evening the Greenwich stood clear away to sea, leaving us struggling hard for life, in the very jaws of death; which the other pirate that was afloat, seeing, got a warp out, and was hauling under our stern.

" By this time many of my men being killed and wounded, and no hopes left us of escaping being all murdered by enraged barbarous conquerors, I ordered all that could get into the long-boat, under the cover of the smoke of our guns; so that, with what some did in boats, and others swimming, most of us that were able got ashore by seven o'clock. When the pirates came aboard, they cut three of our wounded men to pieces. I with some of my people made what haste we could to King's-town, twenty-five miles from us, where I arrived next day, almost dead with the fatigue and loss of blood, having been sorely wounded in the head by a musket-ball.

" At this town I heard that the pirates had offered ten thousand dollars to the country people to bring me in, which many of them would have accepted, only they knew the king and all his chief people were in my interest. Meantime, I caused a report to be spread that I was dead of my wounds, which much abated their fury. About ten days after, being pretty well recovered, and hoping the malice of our enemies was nigh over, I began to consider the dismal condition we were reduced to: being in a place where we had no hopes of getting a passage home, all of us in a manner naked, not having had time to bring with us either a shirt or a pair of shoes, except what we had on. Having obtained leave to go on board the pirates with a promise of safety, several of the chief of them knew me, and some of them had sailed with me, which I found of great advantage; because, notwithstanding their promise, some of them would have cut me to pieces, and all that would not enter with them, had it not been for their chief captain, Edward England, and some others whom I knew. They talked of burning one of their ships, which we had so entirely disabled as to be no farther useful to them, and to fit the Cassandra in her room; but in the end I managed the affair so well, that they made me a present of the said shattered ship, which was Dutch built, and called the Fancy; her burden was about three hundred tons. I procured also a hundred and twenty nine bales of the company's cloth, though they would not give me a rag of my own clothes.

" They sailed the 3rd of September: and I, with jury-masts, and such old sails as they left me, made a shift to do the like on the 8th, together with forty-three of my ship's crew, including two passengers and twelve soldiers; having no more than five tons of water aboard After a passage of forty-eight days, I arrived here on the 26th of October, almost naked and starved, having been reduced to a pint of water a day, and almost in despair of ever seeing land, by reason of the calms we met with between the coast of Arabia and Malabar.

" We had in all thirteen men killed and twenty-four wounded; and we were told that we destroyed about ninety or a hundred of the pirates. When they left us, they were about three hundred whites, and eighty blacks in both ships. I am persuaded, had our consort the Greenwich done his duty, we had destroyed both of them, and got two hundred thousand pounds for our owners and selves; whereas the loss of the Cassandra may justly be imputed to his deserting us. I have delivered all the bales that were given me into the company's warehouse, for which the governor and council have ordered me a reward. Our governor, Mr. Boon. who is extremely kind and civil to me, had ordered me home in the packet; but Captain Harvey, who had a prior promise, being come in with the fleet, goes in my room. The governor hath promised me a country voyage to help to make up my losses, and would have me stay and accompany him to England next year."

Captain Mackra was certainly in imminent danger, in trusting himself and his men on board the pirate ship, and unquestionably nothing but the desperate circumstances in which he was placed could have justified so hazardous a step. The honour and influence of Captain England, however, protected him and his men from the fury of the crew, who would willingly have wreaked their vengeance upon them.

It is pleasing to discover any instance of generosity or honour among such an abandoned race, who bid defiance and are regardless of all laws both human and divine. Captain England was so steady to Captain Mackra, that he informed him, it would be with no small difficulty and address that he would be able to preserve him and his men from the fury of the crew, who were greatly enraged at the resistance which had been made. He likewise acquainted him, that his influence and authority among them was giving place to that of Captain Taylor, chiefly because the disposition of the latter was more savage and brutal. They therefore consulted between them what was the best method to secure the favour of Taylor, and keep him in good humour. Mackra made the punch to flow in great abundance, and employed every artifice to soothe the mind of that ferocious villain. A singular incident was also very favourable to the unfortunate captain. It happened that a pirate, with a prodigious pair of whiskers, a wooden leg, and stuck round with pistols, came blustering and swearing upon the quarter-deck, inquiring "where was Captain Mackra." He naturally supposed that this barbarous-looking fellow would be his executioner; but, as he approached, he took the captain by the hand, swearing, that he was an honest fellow, and that he had formerly sailed with him, and would stand by him; and let him see the man that would touch him." This terminated the dispute, and Captain Taylor's disposition was so ameliorated with punch, that he consented that the old pirate ship, and so many bales of cloth, should be given to Mackra, and then sank into the arms of intoxication. England now pressed Mackra to hasten away, lest the ruffian, upon his becoming sober, should not only retract his word, but give liberty to his crew to cut him and his men to pieces.

But the gentle temper of Captain England, and his generosity towards the unfortunate Mackra, proved the origin of much calamity to himself. The crew, in general, deeming the kind of usage which Mackra had received, inconsistent with piratical policy, they circulated a report, that he was coming against them with the Company's force. The result of these invidious reports was to deprive England of his command, and to excite these cruel villains to put him on shore with three others, upon the island of Mauritius. If England and his small company had not been destitute o. every necessary, they might have made a comfortable subsistence here, as the island abounds with deer, hogs, and other animals. Dissatisfied, however, with their solitary situation, Captain England and his three men exerted their industry and ingenuity, and formed a small boat, with which they sailed to Madagascar, where they subsisted upon the generosity of some more fortunate piratical companions.

Captain Taylor detained some of the officers and men belonging to Captain Mackra, and having repaired their vessel, sailed for India. The day before they made land, they espied two ships to the eastward, and supposing them to be English, Captain Taylor ordered one of the officers of Mackra's ship to communicate to him the private signals between the Company's ships, swearing that if he did not do so immediately, he would cut him into pound pieces. But the poor man being unable to give the information demanded, was under the necessity of enduring their threats. Arrived at the vessels, they found that they were two Moorish ships, laden with horses. The pirates brought the captains and merchants on board, and tortured them in a barbarous manner, to constrain them to tell where they had hid their treasure. They were, however, disappointed; and the next morning they discovered land, and at the same time a fleet on shore plying to windward. In this situation they were at a considerable loss how to dispose of their prizes. To let them go would lead to their discovery, and thus defeat the design of their voyage; and it was a distressing matter to sink the men and the horses, though many of them were for adopting that measure. They, however, brought them to anchor, threw all the sails overboard, and cut one of the masts half through.

While they lay at anchor, and were employed in taking in water, one of the above-mentioned fleet moved towards them with English colours, and was answered by the pirate with a red ensign: but they did not hail each other. At night they left the Muscat ships, and sailed after the fleet. About four next morning, the pirates were in the midst of the fleet, but seeing their vast superiority, were greatly at loss what method to adopt. The Victory was become leaky, and their hands were so few in number, that it only remained for them to deceive, if possible, the English squadron. They were unsuccessful in gaining any thing out of that fleet, and had only the wretched satisfaction of burning a single galley. They however that day seized a galliot laden with cotton, and made inquiry of the men concerning the fleet. They protested that they had not seen a ship since they left Gogo, and earnestly implored their mercy; but, instead of treating them with lenity, they put them to the rack, in order to extort farther confession. The day following, a fresh easterly wind blew hard, and rent the galliot's sails; upon this the pirates put her company into a boat, with nothing but a try-sail, no provisions, and only four gallons of water, and, though they were out of sight of land, left them to shift for themselves.

It may be proper to inform our readers, that one Angria, an Indian prince, of considerable territory and strength, had proved a troublesome enemy to the Europeans, and particularly to the English. Callaba was his principal fort, situated not many leagues from Bombay, and he possessed an island in sight of the port, from whence he molested the Company's ships. His art in bribing the ministers of the Great Mogul, and the shallowness of the water, that prevented large ships of war from approaching, were the principal causes of his safety.

The Bombay fleet, consisting of four grabs, the London and the Candois, and two other ships, with a galliot, having an additional thousand men on board for this enterprise, sailed to attack a fort belonging to Angria upon the Malabar coast. Though their strength was great, yet they were totally unsuccessful in their enterprise. It was this fleet returning home that our pirates discovered upon the present occasion. Upon the sight of the pirates, the commodore of the fleet intimated to Mr. Brown the general, that as they had no orders to fight, and had gone upon a different purpose, it would be improper for them to engage. Informed of the loss of this favourable opportunity of destroying the robbers, the governor of Bombay was highly enraged, and giving the command of the fleet to Captain Mackra, ordered him to pursue and engage them wherever they should be found.

The pirates having barbarously sent away the galliot with her men, they arrived southward, and between Goa and Carwar they heard several guns, so that they came to anchor, and sent their boat to reconnoitre, which returned next morning with the intelligence of two grabs lying at anchor in the road. They accordingly weighed, ran towards the bay, and in the morning were discovered by the grabs, who had just time to run under India-Diva castle for protection. This was the more vexatious to the pirates, as they were without water: some of them, therefore, were for making a descent upon the island, but that measure not being generally approved, they sailed towards the south, and took a small ship, which had only a Dutchman and two Portuguese on board. They sent one of these ashore to the Captain, to inform him that, if he would give them some water and fresh provisions, he might have his vessel returned. He replied that, if they would give him possession over the bar, he would comply with their request. But, suspecting the integrity of his design, they sailed to Lacca Deva islands, uttering dreadful imprecations against the captain.

Disappointed in finding water in these islands, they sailed to Malinda island, and sent their boats on shore, to discover if there was any water, or if there were any inhabitants. They returned with the information, that there was abundance of water, that the houses were only inhabited by women and children, the men having fled at the appearance of the ships. They accordingly hastened to supply themselves with water, used the defenceless women in a brutal manner, destroyed many of their fruit-trees, and set some of their houses on fire.

While off this island, they lost several of their anchors by the rockiness of the ground; and one day, it blowing more violently than usual, they were forced to take to sea, leaving several people and most of the water casks; but when the gale was over, they returned to take in their men and water. Their provisions being nearly exhausted, they resolved to visit the Dutch at Cochin. After sailing three days, they arrived off Tellechery, and took a small vessel belonging to Governor Adams, and brought the master on board, very much intoxicated, who informed them of the expedition of Captain Mackra. This intelligence raised their utmost indignation. "A villain!" said they, " to whom we have given a ship and presents, to come against us! he ought to be hanged; and since we cannot show our resentment to him, let us hang the dogs his people, who wish him well, and would do the same, if they were clear." "If it be in my power," said the quarter-master, "both masters and officers of ships shall be carried with us for the future, only to plague them. Now, England we may mark him for this."

They proceeded to Calicut, and attempting to cut out a ship, were prevented by some guns placed upon shore. One of Captain Mackra's officers was under deck at this time, and was commanded both by the captain and quarter-master to tend the braces on the booms, in hopes that a shot would take him before they got clear. He was about to have excused himself, but they threatened to shoot him; and when he expostulated, and claimed their promise to put him on shore, he received an unmerciful beating from the quartermaster; Captain Taylor, to whom that duty belonged, being lame of his hands.

The day following they met a Dutch galliot, laden with limestone, bound for Calicut, on board of which they put one Captain Fawkes; and some of the crew interceding for Mackra's officer, Taylor and his party replied, " If we let this dog go, who has overheard our designs and resolutions, he will overset all our well-advised plans, and particularly this supply we are seeking for at the hands of the Dutch."

When they arrived at Cochin, they sent a letter on shore by a fishing-boat, entered the road, and anchored, each ship saluting the fort with eleven guns, and receiving the same number in return. This was the token of their welcome reception, and at night a large boat was sent, deeply laden with liquors and all kinds of provisions, and in it a servant of John Trumpet, one of their friends, to inform them that it would be necessary for them to run farther south, where they would be supplied both with provisions and naval stores.

They had scarcely anchored at the appointed place, when several canoes, with white and black inhabitants, came on board, and continued without interruption to perform all the good offices in their power during their stay in that place. In particular, John Trumpet brought a large boat of arrack, and sixty bales of sugar, as a present from the governor and his daughter; the former receiving in return a table-clock, and the other a gold watch, the spoil of Captain Mackra's vessel. When their provisions were all on board, Trumpet was rewarded with about six or seven thousand pounds, was saluted with three cheers, and eleven guns; and several handsful of silver were thrown into the boat, for the men to gather at pleasure.

There being little wind that night, they remained at anchor, and in the morning were surprised with the return of Trumpet, bringing another boat equally well stored with provisions, with chests of piece-goods and ready-made clothes, and along with him the fiscal of the place. At noon they espied a sail towards the south, and immediately gave chase, but she out-sailed them, and sheltered under the fort of Cochin. Informed that they would not be molested in taking her from under the castle, they sailed towards her, but upon the fort firing two guns, they ran off for fear of more serious altercation, and returning, anchored in their for ·r station. They were too welcome visitants to be permitted to dep..., so long as John Trumpet could contrive to detain them. With this view he informed them, that in a few days a rich vessel, commanded by the Governor of Bombay's brother, was to pass that way.

That government is certainly in a wretched state, which is under the necessity of trading with pirates, in order to enrich itself; nor will such government hesitate by what means an injury can be repaired, or a fortune gained. Neither can language describe the low and base principles of government which could employ such a miscreant as John Trumpet in its service. He was a tool in the hands of the government of Cochin; and, as the dog said in the fable, " What is done by the master's orders, is the master's action;" or, as the same sentiment is, perhaps, better expressed in the legal axiom; " Qui facit per alium facit per se."

While under the direction of Trumpet, some proposed to proceed directly to Madagascar, but others were disposed to wait until they should be provided with a store ship. The majority being of the latter opinion, they steered to the south, and seeing a ship on shore were desirous to get near her, but the wind preventing, they separated, the one sailing northward and the other southward, in hopes of securing her when she should come out, whatever direction she might take. They were now, however, almost entrapped in the snare laid for them. In the morning, to their astonishment and consternation, instead of being called to give chase, five large ships were near, which made a signal for the pirates to bear down. The pirates were in the greatest dread lest it should be Captain Mackra, of whose activity and courage they had formerly sufficient proof. The pirate ships, however, joined and fled with all speed from the fleet. In three hours' chase none of the fleet gained upon them, except one grab. The remainder of the day was calm, and, to their great consolation, this next day the dreaded fleet was entirely out of sight.

Their alarm being over, they resolved to spend the Christmas in feasting and mirth, in order to drown care, and to banish thought. Nor did one day suffice, but they continued their revelling for several days, and made so free with their fresh provisions, that in their next cruise they were put upon short allowance; and it was entirely owing to the sugar and other provisions that were in the leaky ship that they were preserved from absolute starvation.

In this condition they reached the island of Mauritius, refitted the Victory, and left that place with the following inscription written upon one of the walls. " Left this place on the 5th of

April, to go to Madagascar for Limos." This they did lest any visit should be paid to that place during their absence. They, however, did not sail directly for Madagascar, but the island of Mascarius, where they fortunately fell in with a Portuguese of seventy guns, lying at anchor. The greater part of her guns had been thrown overboard, her masts lost, and the whole vessel disabled by a storm; she, therefore, became an easy prey to the pirates. Condè de Ericeira, Viceroy of Goa, who went upon the fruitless expedition against Angria the Indian, and several passengers, were on board. Besides other valuable articles and specie, they found in her diamonds to the amount of four million of dollars. Supposing that the ship was an Englishman, the Viceroy came on board next morning, was made prisoner, and obliged to pay two thousand dollars as a ransom for himself and the other prisoners. After this he was set ashore, with an express engagement to leave a ship to convey him and his companions to another port.

Meanwhile, the pirates received intelligence that a vessel was to the leward of the island, which they pursued and captured. But instead of performing their promise to the Viceroy, which they could easily have done, they sent the Ostender along with some of their men to Madagascar, to inform their friends of their success, with instructions to prepare masts for the prize; and they soon followed, carrying two thousand negroes in the Portuguese vessel.

Madagascar is an island larger than Great Britain, situated upon the eastern coast of Africa, abounding with all sorts of provisions, such as oxen, goats, sheep, poultry, fish, citrons, oranges, tamarinds, dates, cocoa-nuts, bananas, wax, honey, rice, cotton, indigo, and all other fruits common in that quarter of the globe; ebony, of which lances are made, gums of several kinds, and many other valuable productions. Here, in St. Augustine's bay, the ships sometimes stop to take in water, when they make the inner passage to India, and do not intend to stop at Johanna.

When the Portuguese ship arrived here, they received intelligence that the Ostender had taken advantage of an hour when the men were intoxicated, and risen upon them, and carried the ship to Mozambique, from whence the governor ordered her to Goa.

The pirates now divided their plunder, receiving forty-two diamonds per man, or in smaller proportion according to their magnitude. A foolish jocular fellow who had received a large diamond of the value of forty-two, was highly displeased, and so went and broke it in pieces, exclaiming, that he had many more shares than either of them. Some, contented with their treasure, and unwilling to run the risk of losing what they possessed, and perhaps their lives also, resolved to remain with their friends at Madagascar, under the stipulation that the longest livers should enjoy all the booty. The number of adventurers being now lessened, they burned the Victory, cleaned the Cassandra, and the remainder went on board her under the command of Taylor, whom we must leave for a little while, in order to give an account of the squadron which arrived in India in 1721.

When the commodore arrived at the cape, he received a letter that had been written by the Governor Pondicherry to the Governor of Madras, informing him that the pirates were strong in the Indian seas; that they had eleven sail, and fifteen hundred men; but adding, that many of them retired about that time to Brazil and Guinea, while others fortified themselves at Madagascar, Mauritius, Johanna, and Mohilla; and that a crew under the command of Condin, in a ship called the Dragon, had captured a vessel with thirteen lacks of rupees on board, and having divided their plunder, had taken up their residence with their friends at Madagascar.

Upon receiving this intelligence, Commodore Matthews sailed for these islands, as the most probable place of success. He endeavoured ineffectually to prevail on England, at St. Mary's, to communicate to him what information he could give respecting the pirates; but England declined, thinking that this would be almost to surrender at discretion. He then took up the guns of the Jubilee sloop that were on board, and the men-of-war made several cruises in search of the pirates, but to no purpose. The squadron was then sent down to Bombay, was saluted by the port, and after these exploits returned home.

The pirate, Captain Taylor, in the Cassandra, now fitted up the Portuguese man-of-war, and resolved upon another voyage to the Indies; but, informed that four men-of-war had been sent after the pirates in that quarter, he changed his determination, and sailed for Africa. Arrived there, they put in at a place near the river Spirito Sancto, on the coast of Monomotapa. As there was no correspondence by land, nor any trade carried on by sea at this place, they thought that it would afford a safe retreat. To their astonishment, however, when they approached the shore, it being in the dusk of the evening, they were accosted by several

Page 346

shot. They immediately anchored, and in the morning saw that the shot had come from a small fort of six guns, which they attacked and destroyed.

This small fort was erected by the Dutch East India Company a few weeks before, and committed to the care of a hundred and fifty men, the one half of whom had perished by sickness or other causes. Upon their petition, sixteen of these were admitted into the society of the pirates; and the rest would also have been received, had they not been Dutchmen, to whom they had a rooted aversion.

In this place they continued during four months, refitting their vessels, and amusing themselves with all manner of diversions, until the scarcity of their provisions awakened them to industry and exertion. They, however, left several parcels of goods to the starving Dutchmen, which Mynheer joyfully exchanged for provisions with the next vessel that touched at that fort.

Leaving that place, they were divided in opinion what course to steer; some went on board the Portuguese prize, and, sailing for Madagascar, abandoned the pirate life; and others going on board the Cassandra, sailed for the Spanish West Indies. The Mermaid man-of-war, returning from a convoy, got near the pirates, and would have attacked them, but a consultation being held, it was deemed inexpedient, and thus the pirates escaped. A sloop was, however, dispatched to Jamaica with the intelligence, and the Lancaster was sent after them; but they were some days too late, the pirates having, with all their riches, surrendered to the Governor of Portobello.

Calming their consciences, that others would have acted a similar part, without the least remorse, they took up their residence here, to spend the remainder of their days in living upon the spoil of nations. It is difficult to compute the injury done by this crew during five years. Whether to gratify their humour, to prevent intelligence, or from the want of men to navigate, or the brave resistance made, or from wanton folly and barbarity, the moment the resolution was formed, the vessels they captured were frequently sent to the bottom. After their surrender to the Spaniards, several of them left that place, and it is reported that Captain Taylor accepted of a commission in the Spanish service, and commanded the man-of-war that attacked the English logwood cutters in the bay of Honduras.

CAPTAIN DAVIS

WAS born in Monmouthshire, and, from a boy, trained to the sea. His last voyage from England was in the sloop Cadogan from Bristol, in the character of chief mate. This vessel was captured by the pirate England, upon the Guinea coast, whose companions plundered the crew, and murdered the captain, as already related in England's life.

Upon the death of Captain Skinner, Davis pretended that he was urged by England to become a pirate, but that he resolutely refused. He added, that England, pleased with his conduct, had made him captain in room of Skinner, giving him a sealed paper, which he was not to open until he was in a certain latitude, and then expressly to follow the given directions. When he arrived in the appointed place, he collected the whole crew, and solemnly read his sealed instructions, which contained a generous grant of the ship and all her stores to Davis and his crew, requesting them to go to Brazil, and dispose of the cargo to the best advantage, and make an equal division of the money.

Davis then commanded the crew to signify whether they were inclined to follow that mode of life, when, to his astonishment and chagrin, the majority positively refused. Then, in a transport of rage, he desired them to go where they would.

Knowing that part of the cargo was consigned to merchants in Barbadoes, they directed their course to that place. When arrived there, they informed the merchants of the unfortunate death of Skinner, and of the proposal which had been made to them. Davis was accordingly seized, and committed to prison, but he having never been in the pirate service, nothing could be proved to condemn him, and he was discharged without a trial. Convinced that he could never hope for employment in that quarter after his detection, he went to the island of Providence, which he knew to be a rendezvous for pirates. Upon his arrival there, he was grievously disappointed, because the pirates who frequented that place had just accepted his majesty's pardon, and had surrendered.

Captain Rodgers having equipped two sloops for trade, Davis obtained employment in one of these, called the Buck. They were laden with European goods to a considerable value, which they were to sell or exchange with the French and the Spaniards.

They first touched at the island of Martinique, belonging to the French, and Davis, knowing that many of the men were formerly in the pirate service, enticed them to seize the master, and to run off with the sloop. When they had effected their purpose, they hailed the other ship, in which they knew that there were many hands ripe for rebellion, and coming to, the greater part joined Davis. Those who did not choose to adhere to them were allowed to remain in the other sloop, and continue their course, after Davis had pillaged her of what things he pleased.

In full possession of the vessel and stores and goods, a large bowl of punch was made; under its exhilarating influence, it was proposed to choose a commander, and to form their future mode of policy. The election was soon over, and as a large majority of legal votes were in favour of Davis, and no scrutiny demanded, Davis was declared duly elected. He then drew up a code of laws, to which he himself swore, and required the same bond of alliance from all the rest of the crew. He then addressed them in a short and appropriate speech, the substance of which was, a proclamation of war with the whole world.

They next consulted, what part would be the most convenient to clean the vessel, and it was resolved to repair to Coxon's Hole, at the east end of the island of Cuba, where they could remain in perfect security, as the entrance was so narrow that one ship could keep out a hundred.

They, however, had no small difficulty in cleaning their vessel, as there was no carpenter among them. They performed that laborious task in the best manner they could, and then made to the north side of Hispaniola. The first sail they met with was a French ship of twelve guns, which they captured; and while they were plundering her, another appeared in view. Enquiring of the Frenchmen, they learned that she was a ship of twenty-four guns and sixty men. Davis proposed to his crew to attack her, assuring them that she would prove a rich prize. This appeared to the crew such a hazardous enterprise, that they were rather adverse to the measure. But he acquainted them that he had conceived a stratagem that he was confident would succeed; they might, therefore, safely leave the matter to his management. He then commenced chase, and ordered his prize to do the same. Being a better sailer, he soon came up with the enemy, and showed his black colours. With no small surprise at his insolence in coming so near them, they commanded him to strike. He replied, that he was disposed to give them employment until his companion came up, who was able to contend with them; meanwhile assuring them that, if they did not strike to him, it would most certainly fare the worse with them: then giving them a broadside, he received the same in return.

When the other pirate ship drew near, they, according to the directions of Davis, appeared upon deck in white shirts, which making an appearance of numbers, the Frenchmen were intimidated, and struck. Davis ordered the captain with twenty of his men to come on board, and they were all put in irons except the captain. He then despatched four of his men to the other ship, and called aloud to them, desired that his compliments should be given to the captain, with a request to send a sufficient number of hands to go on board their new prize, to see what they had got in her. At the same time, he gave them a written paper with their proper instructions, even to nail up all the small guns, to take out all the arms and powder, and to go every man on board the new prize. When his men went on board her, he ordered the greater part of the prisoners to be removed into the empty vessels, and by this means secured himself from any attempt to recover their ship.

During three days, these three vessels sailed in company, but finding that his late prize was a heavy sailer, he emptied her of every thing that he stood in need of, and then restored her to the captain with all his men. The French captain was so enraged at being thus miserably deceived, that, upon the discovery of the stratagem, he would have thrown himself overboard, had not his men prevented him.

Captain Davis then formed the resolution of parting with the other prize-ship also, and soon afterwards steered northward, and took a Spanish sloop. He next directed his course towards the western islands, and from Cape de Verd islands cast anchor at St. Nicholas, and hoisted English colours. The Portuguese supposed that he was a privateer, and Davis going on shore was hospitably received, and they traded with him for such articles as they found most advantageous. He remained here five weeks, and he and half of his crew visited the principal town of the island. Davis, from his appearing in the dress of a gentleman, was greatly caressed by the Portuguese, and nothing was spared to entertain and render him and his men happy. Having amused themselves during a week, they returned to the ship, and allowed the other half of the crew to visit the capital, and enjoy themselves in a like manner. Upon their return, they cleaned their ship and put to sea, but four of the men were so captivated with the ladies and the luxuries of the place, that they remained in the island, and one of them married and settled there.

Davis now sailed for Bonavista, and perceiving nothing in that harbour steered for the Isle of May. Arrived there, he found several vessels in the harbour, and plundered them of whatever he found necessary. He also received a considerable reinforcement of men, the greater part of whom entered willingly into the piratical service. He likewise made free with one of the ships, equipped her for his own purpose, and called her the King James. Davis next proceeded to St. Jago to take in water. Davis with some others going on shore to seek water, the governor came to inquire who they were, and expressed his suspicion of their being pirates. Upon this, Davis seemed highly affronted, and expressed his displeasure in the most polite but determined manner. He, however, hastened on board, informed his men, and suggested the possibility of surprising the fort during the night. Accordingly, all his men being well-armed, they advanced to the assault; and, from the carelessness of the guards, they were in the garrison before the inhabitants were alarmed. Upon the discovery of their danger, they took shelter in the governor's house, and fortified it against the pirates: but the latter throwing in some granado shells, ruined the furniture, and killed several people.

The alarm was calculated in the morning, and the country assembled to attack them; but unwilling to stand a siege, the pirates dismounted the guns, pillaged the fort, and fled to their ships.

When at sea, they mustered their hands, and found that they were seventy strong. They then consulted among themselves what course they should steer, and were divided in opinion; but by a majority it was carried to sail for Gambia, on the coast of Guinea. Of this opinion was the captain, who having been employed in that trade, was acquainted with the coast; and informed his companions, that there was always a large quantity of money deposited in that castle, and he was confident, if the matter was entrusted to him, he should successfully storm that fort. From their experience of his former prudence and courage, they cheerfully submitted to his direction in the full assurance of success.

Arrived at Gambia, he ordered all his men below, except just so many as were necessary to work the vessel, that those from the fort, seeing so few hands, might have no suspicion that she was any other than a trading-vessel. He then ran under the fort, cast anchor, and having ordered out the boat, manned with six men indifferently dressed, he, with the master and doctor, dressed themselves like gentlemen, in order that the one party might look like foremastmen, and the other like merchants. In rowing ashore, he instructed his men what to say if any questions were put to them by the garrison.

On reaching land, the party was conducted by a file of musqueteers into the fort, and kindly received by the governor, who inquired what they were, and whence they came? They replied, that they were from Liverpool, and bound for the river Senegal, to trade for gum and elephants' teeth; but that they were chased on that coast by two French men-of-war, and narrowly escaped being taken. " We were now disposed," continued Davis, " to make the best of our voyage, and would willingly trade here for slaves." The governor then inquired what were the principal articles of their cargo. They replied, that they were iron and plate, which were necessary articles in that place. The governor then said, that he would give them slaves for all their cargo; and asked if they had any European liquor on board. They answered, that they had a little for their own use, but that he should have a hamper of it. He then treated them with the greatest civility, and desired them all to dine with him. Davis answered, that as he was commander of the vessel, it would be necessary for him to go down to see if she was properly moored, and to give some other directions; but that these gentlemen might stay, and he would return before dinner, and bring the hamper with him.

While in the fort, his eyes were keenly employed to discover the position of the arms, and how the fort might most successfully be surprised. He discovered that there was a sentry standing near a guard-house, in which there were a quantity of arms heaped up in a corner, and that a considerable number of small arms were in the governor's hall. When he went on board, he ordered some hands on board a sloop lying at anchor, lest, hearing any bustle they should come to the aid of the castle; then desiring his men to avoid too much liquor, and to be ready when he should hoist the flag from the walls, to come to his assistance, he proceeded to the castle.

Having taken these precautions and formed these arrangements, he ordered every man who was to accompany him to arm himself with two pair of pistols, which he himself also did, concealed under their clothes. He then directed them to go into the guard-room, and fall into conversation, and immediately upon his firing a pistol out of the governor's window, to shut the men up, and secure the arms in the guard-room.

When Davis arrived, dinner not being ready, the governor proposed that they should pass the time in making a bowl of punch, Davis's boatswain attending him, had an opportunity of visiting all parts of the house, and observing their strength. He whispered his intelligence to his master, who, being surrounded by his own friends, and seeing the governor unattended by any of his retinue, presented a pistol to the breast of the latter, informing him that he was a dead man, unless he should surrender the fort and all its riches. The governor thus taken by surprise, was compelled to submit; for Davis took down all the pistols that hung in the hall, and loaded them. He then fired his pistol out of the window. His men flew like lions, presented their pistols to the soldiers, and while some carried out the arms, the rest secured the military, and shut them all up in the guard-house, placing a guard on the door. Then one of them struck the union flag on the top of the castle, which the men from the vessel perceiving, rushed to the combat, and in an instant were in possession of the castle, without tumult or bloodshed.

Davis then harangued the soldiers, many of whom enlisted with him; and those who declined, he put on board the small ships, and to prevent the necessity of a guard, or the possibility of escape, carried off the sails, rigging, and cables.

That day being spent in feasting and rejoicing, the castle saluting the ship, and the ship the castle, on the day following they proceeded to examine the contents of their prize. They, however, were greatly disappointed in their expectations, a large sum of money having been sent off a few days before. But they found money to the amount of about two thousand pounds in gold, and many valuable articles of different kinds. They carried on board their vessel whatever they deemed useful, gave several articles to the captain and crew of the small vessel, and allowed them to depart, while they dismounted the guns, and demolished the fortifications.

After doing all the mischief that their vicious minds could possibly devise, they weighed anchor; but in the mean time, perceiving a sail bearing towards them with all possible speed, they hastened to prepare for her reception, and made towards her. Upon her near approach they discovered that she was a French pirate of fourteen guns and sixty four men, the one half French and the other half negroes.

The Frenchman was in high expectations of a rich prize, but when he came nearer, he suspected, from the number of her guns and men, that she was a small English man-of-war; he determined, notwithstanding, upon the bold attempt of boarding her, and immediately fired a gun, and hoisted his black colours: Davis immediately returned the compliment. The Frenchman was highly gratified at this discovery; both hoisted out their boats, and congratulated each other. Mutual civilities and good offices past, and the French captain proposed to Davis to sail down the coast with him, in order to look out for a better ship, assuring him that the very first that could be captured should be his, as he was always willing to encourage an industrious brother.

They first touched at Sierra Leone, where they espied a large vessel, and Davis being the swifter sailer, came first up with her. He was not a little surprised that she did not endeavour to make off, and began to suspect her strength. When he came alongside of her, she fired a whole broadside, and hoisted black colours. Davis did the same, and fired a gun to leeward. The satisfaction of these brothers in iniquity was mutual, at having thus acquired so much additional strength and ability to undertake more formidable adventures. Two days were devoted to mirth and song, and upon the third, Davis and Cochlyn, the captain of the new confederate, agreed to go in the French pirate ship to attack the fort. When they approached, the men in the fort, apprehensive of their character and intentions, fired all the guns upon them at once. The ship returned the fire, and afforded employment until the other two ships arrived, when the men in the fort seeing such a number on board, lost courage and abandoned the fort to the mercy of the robbers.

They took possession, remained there seven weeks, and cleaned their vessels. They then called a council of war, to deliberate concerning future undertakings, when it was resolved to sail down the coast in company; and, for the greater regularity and grandeur, Davis was chosen Commodore. That dangerous enemy, strong drink, had well nigh, however, sown the seeds of discord among these affectionate bretheren. But Davis, alike prepared for council or for war, addressed them to the following purport: " Hear ye, you Cochlyn and La Boise, (which was the name of the French captain) I find, by strengthening you, I have put a rod into your hands to whip myself: but I am still able to deal with you both; however, since we met in love, let us part in love; for I find that three of a trade can never agree long together." Upon this, the other two went on board of their respective ships, and steered different courses.

Davis held down the coast, and reaching Cape Appolonia, he captured three vessels, two English and one Scottish, plundered them and allowed them to proceed. In five days after he met with a Dutchman of thirty guns and ninety men. She gave Davis a broadside, and killed nine of his men; a desperate engagement ensued, which continued from one o'clock at noon until nine next morning, when the Dutchman struck.

Davis equipped her for the pirate service, and called her " The Rover." With his two ships he sailed for the bay of Anamaboa, which he entered about noon, and took several vessels which were there waiting to take in negroes, gold, and elephants' teeth. Davis made a present of one of these vessels to the Dutch captain and his crew, and allowed them to go in quest of their fortune. When the fort had intelligence that they were pirates, they fired at them, but without any effect; Davis fired also, and hoisted the black colours, but deemed it prudent to depart.

The next day after he left Anamaboa, the man at the masthead discovered a sail. It may be proper to inform our readers, that, according to the laws of pirates, the man who first discovers a vessel, is entitled to the best pair of pistols in the ship, and such is the honour attached to these, that a pair of them has been known to sell for thirty pounds.

Davis pursued that vessel, which being between him and the shore, laboured hard to run aground. Davis perceiving this, got between her and the land, and fired a broadside at her, when she immediately struck. She proved to be a very rich prize, having on board the Governor of Acra, with all his substance, going to Holland. There was in money to the amount of fifteen thousand pounds, besides a large quantity of merchant goods, and other valuable articles.

Before they reached the Isle of Princes, the St. James sprang a leak, so that the men and the valuable articles were removed into Davis's own ship. When he came in sight of the fort he hoisted English colours. The Portuguese, seeing a large ship sailing towards the shore, sent a sloop to discover her character and destination. Davis informed them, that he was an English man-of-war, sent out in search of some pirates which they had heard were in this quarter. Upon this, he was piloted into the port, and anchored below the guns at the fort. The governor was happy to have Englishmen in his harbour; and to do honour to

Davis, sent down a file of musqueteers to escourt him into the fort, while Davis, the more to cover his design, ordered nine men, according to the custom of the English, to row him on shore.

Davis also took the opportunity of cleaning and preparing all things for renewing his operations. He, however, could not contentedly leave the fort, without receiving some of the riches of the island. He formed a scheme to accomplish his purpose, and communicated the same to his men. His design was to make the governor a present of a few negroes in return for his kindness; then to invite him, with a few of the principal men and friars belonging to the island, to dine on board his ship, and secure them all in irons, until each of them should give a large ransom. They were accordingly invited, and very readily consented to go: and deeming themselves honoured by his attention, all that were invited, would certainly have gone aboard. Fortunately however, for them, a negro, who was privy to the horrid plan of Davis, swam on shore during the night, and gave information of the danger to the governor.

Under present circumstances, the governor thought proper to dissemble his indignation, and to wait the event. The day arrived, and Davis, the better to secure his prey, and to delude his intended guests on board, along with his fellow nobles, (a title which Davis and his principal officers had assumed,) went on shore to bring the governor and the rest on board to dinner: when they were desired to walk up to the fort to take a little refreshment. An ambush was laid for them, and a whole volley being fired at them, every man fell except one, who ran back and gained the boat. Davis was wounded in the bowels, and, in his dying agony, fired his pistols at his pursuers.

CAPTAIN ROBERTS.

BARTHOLOMEW ROBERTS was trained to a seafaring life. Among other voyages which he made during the time that he lawfully procured his maintenance, he sailed for the Guinea coast, in November, 1719, where he was taken by the pirate Davis. He was at first very averse from that mode of life, and would certainly have deserted, had any opportunity occurred. It happened to him, however, as to many upon another element, that preferment calmed conscience, and reconciled him to that which he formerly hated.

Davis having fallen in the manner related, those who had assumed the title of Lords assembled to deliberate concerning the choice of a new commander. There were several candidates, who, by their services, had risen to eminence among their brethren, and each of them thought himself quallified to bear rule. One addressed the assembled Lords, saying, " That the good of the whole, and maintenance of order, demanded a head, but that the proper authority was deposited in the community at large; so that if one should be elected who did not act and govern for the general good, he could be deposed, and another be substituted in his place."

" We are the original," said he, " of this claim, and should a captain be so saucy as to exceed prescription at any time, why, down with him! It will be a caution, after he is dead, to his successors, to what fatal results any undue assumption may lead; however, it is my advice, while we are sober, to pitch upon a man of courage, and one skilled in navigation,—one who, by his prudence and bravery, seems best able to defend this commonwealth, and ward us from the dangers and tempests of an unstable element, and the fatal consequences of anarchy; and such a one I take Roberts to be: a fellow in all respects worthy of your esteem and favour."

This speech was applauded by all but Lord Simpson, who had himself strong expectations of obtaining the highest command. He at last, in a surly tone, said, he did not regard whom they chose as a commander, provided he was not a papist, for he had conceived a mortal hatred to papists, because his father had been a sufferer in Monmouth's rebellion.

Thus, though Roberts had only been a few weeks among them, his election was confirmed by the Lords and Commons. He, with the best face he could, accepted of the dignity, saying, " that since he had dipped his hands in muddy water, and must be a pirate, it was better being a commander than a private man."

The governor being settled, and other officers chosen in the room of those who had fallen with Davis, it was resolved not to leave this place without revenging his death. Accordingly, thirty men, under the command of one Kennedy, a bold and profligate fellow, landed, and under cover of the fire of the ship, ascended the hill upon which the fort stood. They were no sooner discovered by the Portuguese, than they abandoned the fort, and took shelter in the town. The pirates then entered without opposition, set fire to the fort, and tumbled the guns into the sea.

Not satisfied with this injury, some proposed to land and set the town in flames. Roberts, however, reminded them of the great danger to which this would inevitably expose them; that there was a thick wood at the back of the town, where the inhabitants could hide themselves, and that, when their all was at stake, they would make a bolder resistance; and that the burning or destroying of a few houses, would be a small return for their labour, and the loss that they might sustain. This prudent advice had the desired effect, and they contented themselves with lightening the French vessel, and battering down several houses of the town, to show their high displeasure.

Roberts sailed southward, captured a Dutch Guineaman, and, having emptied her of every thing they thought proper, returned her to the commander. Two days after he captured an English ship, and, as the men joined in pirating, emptied and burned the vessel, and then sailed for St. Thomas. Meeting with no prize, he sailed for Anamaboa, and there watered and repaired. Having again put to sea, a vote was taken whether they should sail for the East Indies or for Brazil. The latter place was decided upon, and they arrived there in twenty-eight days.

Upon this coast our rovers cruised for about nine weeks, keeping generally out of sight of land, but without seeing a sail; which discouraged them so, that they determined to leave the station, and steer for the West Indies; and, in order thereto, they stood in to make the land for the taking of their departure, by which means they fell in, unexpectedly, with a fleet of forty-two sail of Portuguese ships, off the Bay of Los Todos Santos, with all their lading in for Lisbon; several of them of good force, who lay there waiting for two men-of-war of seventy guns each for their convoy. However, Roberts thought it should go hard with him but he would make up his market among them, and thereupon, he mixed with the fleet, and kept his men concealed till proper resolutions could be formed; that done, they came close up to one of the deepest, and ordered her to send the master on board quietly, threatening to give them no quarter, if any resistence or signal of distress was made. The Portuguese, being surprised at these threats, and the sudden flourish of cutlasses from the pirates, submitted without a word, and the captain came on board. Roberts saluted him in a friendly manner, telling him that they were gentlemen of fortune, and that their business with him was only to be informed which was the richest ship in that fleet; and if he directed them right, he should be restored to his ship without molestation, otherwise he must expect instant death.

He then pointed to a vessel of forty guns, and a hundred and fifty men; and though her strength was greatly superior to Roberts, yet he made towards her, taking the master of the captured vessel along with him. Coming alongside of her, Roberts ordered the prisoner to ask, "How Seignior Captain did?" and to invite him on board, as he had a matter of importance to impart to him. He was answered, "That he would wait upon him presently." Roberts, however, observing more than ordinary bustle on board, at once concluded they were discovered, and pouring a broadside into her, they immediately boarded, grappled, and took her. She was a very rich prize, laden with sugar, skins, and tobacco, with four thousand moidores of gold, besides other valuable articles.

In possession of so much riches, they now became solicitous to find a safe retreat in which to spend their time in mirth and wantonness. They determined upon a place called the Devil's Islands, upon the river Surinam, where they arrived in safety, and met with a kind reception from the governor and the inhabitants.

In this river they seized a sloop, which informed them that she had sailed in company with a brigantine loaded with provisions. This was welcome intelligence, as their provisions were nearly exhausted. Deeming this too important a business to trust to foreign hands, Roberts, with forty men in the sloop, gave chase to that sail. In the keenness of the moment, and trusting to his usual good fortune, Roberts supposed that he had only to take a short sail, in order to bring in the vessel with her cargo; but to his sad disappointment, he pursued her during eight days, and instead of gaining, was losing way. Under these circumstances, he came to anchor, and sent off the boat to give intelligence of their distress to their companions.

In their extremity of want, they took up part of the floor in the cabin, and patched up a sort of tray with rope-yarns, to paddle on shore to get a little water to preserve their lives. When their patience was almost exhausted, the boat returned, but instead of provisions, brought the unpleasing information, that the lieutenant, one Kennedy, had run off with both the ships.

The misfortune and misery of Roberts were greatly aggravated by reflecting upon his own imprudence and want of foresight, as well as from the baseness of Kennedy and his crew. Impelled by the necessity of his situation, he now began to reflect upon the means he should employ for future support. Under the foolish supposition that any laws, oaths, or regulations, could bind those who had bidden open defiance to all divine and human laws, he proceeded to form a code of regulations, for the maintenance of order and unity in his little commonwealth.

But present necessity compelled to action, and with their small sloop they sailed for the West Indies. They were not long before they captured two sloops, which supplied them with provisions, and a few days after, a brigantine, and then proceeded to Barbadoes. When off that island they met a vessel of ten guns, richly laden from Bristol; after plundering, and detaining her three days, they allowed her to prosecute her voyage. This vessel, however, informed the governor of what had befallen them, who sent a vessel of twenty guns and eighty men in quest of the pirates. That vessel was commanded by one Rogers, who, on the second day of his cruise, discovered Roberts. Ignorant of any vessel being sent after them, they made towards each other, Roberts gave him a gun, but instead of striking, the other returned a broadside, with three huzzas. A severe engagement ensued, and Roberts being hard put to it, lightened his vessel and ran off.

Roberts then sailed for the Island of Dominica, where he watered, and was supplied by the inhabitants with provisions, for which he gave them goods in return. Here he met with fifteen Englishmen left upon the island by a Frenchman, who had made a prize of their vessel; and they, entering into his service, proved a seasonable addition to his strength.

Though he did not think this a proper place for cleaning, yet as it was absolutely necessary that it should be done, he directed his course to the Granada Islands for that purpose. This, however, had well nigh proved fatal to him; for the Governor of Martinique fitted out two sloops to go in quest of the pirates. They, however, sailed to the above-mentioned place, cleaned with unusual dispatch, and just left that place the night before the sloops arrived.

They next sailed for Newfoundland, arriving upon the banks in June, 1720, and entered the harbour of Trepassi, with their black colours flying, drums beating, and trumpets sounding. In that harbour there were no less than twenty-two ships, which the men abandoned upon the sight of the pirates. It is impossible to describe the injury which they did at this place, by burning or sinking the ships, destroying the plantations, and pillaging the houses.

Roberts reserved a Bristol galley from his depredations in the harbour, which he fitted and manned for his own service. Upon the banks he met ten sail of French ships, and destroyed them all, except one of twenty-six guns, which he seized and carried off, and called her the Fortune. Then giving the Bristol galley to the Frenchman, they sailed in quest of new adventures, and soon took several prizes, and out of them increased the number of their own hands. The Samuel, one of these, was a very rich vessel, having some respectable passengers on board, who were roughly used, and threatened with death if they did not deliver up their money and their goods. They stripped the vessel of every article to the amount of eight or nine thousand pounds. They then deliberated whether to sink or burn the Samuel, but in the mean time they discovered a sail, so they left the empty Samuel, and gave the other chase. At midnight they overtook her, and she proved to be the Snow from Bristol; and, because he was an Englishman, they used the master in a cruel and barbarous manner. Two days after, they took the Little York of Virginia, and the Love of Liverpool, both of which they plundered and sent off. In three days they captured three other vessels, removing the goods out of them, sinking one, and sending off the other two.

They next sailed for the West Indies, but provisions growing short, proceeded to St. Christopher's, when being denied provisions by the governor, they fired on the town, and burnt two ships in the roads. They then repaired to the Island of St. Bartholomew, where the governor supplied them with every necessary, and caressed them in the kindest manner. Satiated with indulgence, and having taken in a large stock of every thing necessary, they unanimously voted to hasten to the coast of Guinea. In their way they took a Frenchman, and as she was fitter for thĕ pirate service than their own, they informed the captain, that, as " a fair exchange was no robbery," they would exchange sloops with him; accordingly, having shifted their men, they set sail. However, going by mistake out of the track of the trade winds, they were under the necessity of returning to the West Indies.

They now directed their course to Surinam, but not having sufficient water for the voyage, they were soon reduced to a mouthful of water a day; their numbers daily diminished by thirst and famine, and the few who survived were reduced to the greatest weakness. They at last had not one drop of water or any other liquid, when, to their inexpressible joy, they anchored in seven fathoms of water. This tended to revive exhausted nature, and inspire them with new vigour, though as yet they had received no relief. In the morning they discovered land, but at such a distance that their hopes were greatly damped. The boat was however sent off, and at night returned with plenty of that necessary element. But this remarkable deliverance produced no reformation in the manners of these unfeeling and obdurate men.

Steering their course from that place to Barbadoes, in their way they met with a vessel which supplied them with all necessaries. Not long after, they captured a brigantine, the mate of which joined their association. Having from these two obtained a large supply, they changed their course and watered at Tobago. Informed, however, that there were two vessels sent in pursuit of them, they went to return their compliments to the Governor of Martinique for this kindness.

It was the custom of the Dutch interlopers, when they approached this island to trade with the inhabitants, to hoist their jacks. Roberts knew the signal, and did so likewise. They, supposing that a good market was near, strove who could first reach Roberts. Determined to do them all possible mischief, he destroyed them one by one, as they came into his power. He only reserved one ship to send the men on shore, and burnt the remainder to the number of twenty.

Roberts and his crew were so fortunate as to capture several vessels, and to render their liquor so plentiful, that it was esteemed a crime against providence not to be continually drunk. One man, remarkable for his sobriety, along with two others, found an opportunity to set off, without taking leave of their friends. But a despatch being sent after them, they were brought back, and in a formal manner tried and sentenced, but one of them was saved by the humorous interference of one of the judges, whose speech was truly worthy of a pirate,—while the other two suffered the punishment of death.

When necessity again compelled them, they renewed their cruising; and, dissatisfied with capturing vessels, which only afforded them a temporary supply, directed their course to the Guinea coast to forage for gold. Intoxication rendered them unruly, and the brigantine at last embraced the cover of night to abandon the commodore. Unconcerned at the loss of his companion, Roberts pursued his voyage. He fell in with two French ships, the one of ten guns and sixty-five men, and the other of sixteen guns and seventy-five men. These dastards no sooner beheld the black flag than they surrendered. With these they went into Sierra Leone, constituting one of them a consort, by the name of the Ranger, and the other a store-ship. This port being frequented by the greater part of the traders to that quarter, they remained here six weeks, enjoying themselves in all the splendour and luxury of a piratical life.

After this they renewed their voyage, and having captured a vessel, the greater part of the men united their fortunes with the pirates. After several cruises they went into a convenient harbour at Old Calabar, where they cleaned, refitted, divided their booty, and for a considerable time caroused, to banish care and sober reflection.

According to their usual custom, the time of festivity and mirth was prolonged until the want of means recalled them to reason and exertion. Leaving this port, they cruised from place to place with varied success; but in all their captures, either burning, sinking, or devoting their prizes to their own use, according to the whim of the moment. The Swallow and another man-of-war being sent out expressly to pursue and take Roberts and his fleet, he had frequent and certain intelligence of their destination; but having so often escaped their vigilance, he became rather too secure and fearless. It happened, however, that while he lay off Cape Lopez, the Swallow had information of his being in that place, and made towards him. Upon the appearance of a sail one of Robert's ships was sent to chase and take her. The pilot of the Swallow seeing her coming, manœuvred his vessel so well, that though he fled at her approach, in order to draw her out of the reach of her associates, yet he at the same time allowed her to overtake the man-of-war.

Upon her coming up to the Swallow, the pirate hoisted the black flag, and fired upon her; but how greatly were the crew astonished, when they saw they had to contend with a man-of-war, and seeing that all resistance was vain, they cried out for quarter, which was granted, and they were all made prisoners, having ten men killed and twenty wounded, without the loss or hurt of one of the king's men.

On the 10th in the morning, the man-of-war bore away to round the cape. Robert's crew, discerning their masts over the land, went down into the cabin to acquaint him of it, he being then at breakfast with his new guest, Captain Hill, on a savoury dish of salmagundy and some of his own beer. He took no notice of it, and his men almost as little, some saying she was a Portuguese ship, others a French slave ship, but the major part swore it was the French Ranger returning; and they were merrily debating for some time on the manner of reception, whether they should salute her or not; but as the Swallow approached nearer, things appeared plainer; and though they who showed any apprehension of danger were stigmatized with the name of cowards, yet some of them now undeceived, declared it to Roberts, especially one Armstrong, who had deserted from that ship, and knew her well. These Roberts swore at as cowards, who meant to dishearten the men, asking them, if it were so, whether they were afraid to fight or not? In short, he hardly refrained from blows. What his own apprehensions were, till she hauled up her ports and hoisted her proper colours, is uncertain; but then, being perfectly convinced, he slipped his cable, got under sail, ordered his men to arms without any show of timidity, dropping a first-rate oath, that it was a bite, but at the same time resolved, like a gallant rogue, to get clear or die.

There was one Armstrong, as was just mentioned, a deserter from the Swallow, of whom they enquired concerning the trim and sailing of that ship; he told them she sailed best upon the wind, and therefore, if they designed to leave her, they should go before it.

The danger was imminent, and the time very short, to consult about means to extricate himself; his resolution in this strait was as follows: to pass close to the Swallow with all her sails, and receive her broadside before they returned a shot; if disabled by this, or if they could not depend on sailing, then to run on shore at the point, and every one to shift for himself among the negroes; or failing in these, to board, and blow up together, for he saw that the greatest part of his men were drunk, passively courageous, and unfit for service.

Roberts himself made a gallant figure at the time of his engagement, being dressed in a rich crimson damask waistcoat and breeches, a red feather in his hat, a gold chain round his neck, with diamond cross hanging to it, a sword in his hand, and two pair of pistols hanging at the end of a silk sling flung over his shoulders, according to the custom of the pirates.

He is said to have given his orders with boldness and spirit. Coming, according to what he had purposed, close to the man-of-war, he received her fire, and then hoisted his black flag and returned it, shooting away from her with all the sail she could pack; and had he taken Armstrong's advice to have gone before the wind, he had probably escaped; but keeping his tacks down, either by the wind's shifting, or ill steerage, or both, he was taken aback with his sails, and the Swallow came a second time very nigh to him.

He had now, perhaps, finished the fight very desperately, if death, who took a swift passage in a grape shot, had not interposed, and struck him directly on the throat. He settled himself on the tackles of a gun; which one Stephenson, from the helm, observing, ran to his assistance, and not perceiving him wounded, swore at him, and bade him stand up and fight like a man; but when he found his mistake, and that his captain was certainly dead, he burst into tears, and wished the next shot might be his portion. They presently threw him overboard, with his arms and ornaments on, according to his repeated request in his life-time.

The prisoners were strictly guarded while on board, and being conveyed to Cape Coast castle, they underwent a long and solemn trial. The generality of them remained daring and impenitent for some time, but when they found themselves confined within a castle, and their fate drawing near, they changed their course, and became serious, penitent, and fervent in their devotions. Though the judges found no small difficulty in explaining the law, and different acts of parliament, yet the facts were so numerous and flagrant which were proved against them, that there was no difficulty in bringing in a verdict of guilty.

CAPTAIN KENNEDY.

It was mentioned in the life of Captain Roberts, that, embracing the opportunity of his absence, the crew of the brigantine ran off, and made one Kennedy their captain. This originated from the following cause. Captain Roberts was insulted by one of his crew when drunk, and, in the violence of his passion, killed the insulter upon the spot. Many in the ship were displeased, but particularly one Jones, the comrade of the man who was slain. When this accident happened, Jones was on land for water, and upon his return, being informed of what had been done, he being a bold active fellow, cursed Roberts, saying that he ought to have been so served himself. Roberts being present, attacked Jones with his sword, and wounded him. Irritated beyond measure by the former and present injury, Jones, though wounded, seized the captain, threw him over a gun, and gave him a severe drubbing. The whole ship was in an instant thrown into violent commotion, some taking part with the captain, and some applauding the spirit and bravery of Jones. "If the one had received a dry chastisement, the other had some of his blood shed. Nor was the provocation upon the one side equal to that upon the other. And, with regard to the captain's rank, if he acted inconsistently with his dignity and power, he was not to be exempted from punishment. Such were the sentiments that were agitated among the crew during the tumult. The quarter-master, employing his authority and influence, calmed the tumult, and the majority were of opinion that the majesty of the vessel was insulted in the person of their captain, and that no private member was at liberty to resent any injury received from him in the manner which Jones had done. The majority, therefore, sentenced Jones to receive two lashes from every man in the ship, as soon as his wound should be healed.

The severity of this sentence did not convince Jones of its equity, and a deep-rooted enmity, and a resolution of revenge, ensued. To accomplish his design, Jones, with a few who were of his sentiments, confederated with Captain Anstis of the brigantine, whom they knew also to be disaffected to Roberts, from the haughty manner in which he behaved. Nor was it merely by his domineering conduct that he irritated Anstis; he was likewise accustomed to leave him nothing but the refuse of the plunder when any prize was taken, though his activity and bravery had perhaps gained the booty. In short, the disaffection became so general, that Lieutenant Kennedy headed the party, and eloped with the privateer and the prize, in the absence of Roberts. Kennedy was chosen Captain, and a division of sentiments ensued, whether they should retire from that mode of life, or pursue their depredations. But as there was no pardon then issued for pirates, they were constrained to retain their present character.

The first act of the new government was to grant liberty to the Portuguese prize. The master was, in their language, a very honest fellow, who, upon his being taken, accosted them, saying that they were welcome to his ship and cargo, and expressed his wish that the vessel had been larger, and the lading richer, for their sakes. In addition to these good wishes, he had given them intelligence of the brigantine after which Roberts had now gone, and though she should never become a prize, yet it had given them an opportunity to move away, without being saluted by the well-known voice of Captain Roberts. In return for all these favours, he received, his ship and men, with his vessel half laden; and having expressed his gratitude in the most obliging terms, he departed.

In the Rover, Captain Kennedy sailed to Barbadoes, and near that island met with a very peaceable prize, commanded by captain Knot, a Quaker. There was neither sword, pistol, nor cutlass on board. After taking what he found most necessary, he allowed the placid Quaker to meditate his way home. Meanwhile, eight of the pirates embraced this opportunity to leave the Rover, and were by him carried to Virginia. During their voyage, they made him handsome presents, and also made several gifts to the sailors, and lived in a merry and jovial manner all the way, Knot not daring to interrupt them, lest they should run off with him and his vessel.

When they arrived off the island, four of the pirates went up the bay towards Maryland, and lived among the planters undiscovered. Captain Knot though he could not, according to his principles, fight, could yet deceive and inform. Accordingly, leaving four of the pirates on board, he went to the governor, and informed him of what passengers he had on board. They were instantly seized, and search being made after the other four, they also were found carousing and rambling about the country. Two Portuguese Jews, whom they had captured upon the coast of Brazil, and had brought along with them, were the principal evidences against them. The honest Quaker, at the same time, surrendered to them every thing which belonged to them, and gave them presents in lieu of those they had bestowed upon him and his men.

Not long after, Kennedy, cruising upon the coast of Jamaica, met with a sloop bound from Boston with bread and flour. Upon this occasion, all those who were disposed to disperse the company went on board, and among the rest Captain Kennedy,—of whom, having been educated as a pick-pocket and house-breaker before he entered the pirate service, his companions now began to entertain such a mean conception, that they were about to throw him overboard, saying that he would inform upon them all the moment he arrived in England. By solemn oaths and protestations he, however, assuaged their rage, and they allowed him to accompany them.

It was their misfortune to have only one man on board who knew any thing of navigation, and even he proved to be a novice. Kennedy was chosen captain on account of his courage and bravery, but he was so ignorant that he could neither read nor write. The pilot was desired to steer towards Ireland, but instead of this, he ran to the north coast of Scotland; and having been tossed about for several days, they thrust the ship into a creek, and all went on shore, leaving her a prize to any who chose to take her.

They passed themselves for shipwrecked mariners, refreshed themselves at the first village, and might have passed without detection, had it not been for their unruly and riotous manner of living. Kennedy and another man left them and shipped for Ireland, where they arrived in safety. A few more separated and went to London; but the body of the gang continued together, and drinking, rioting and debauchery, alarmed the country. In some places they treated the whole village, throwing away their money like stones or sand. Continuing their extravagant course, about eighteen of them were apprehended in the vicinity of Edinburgh, and upon suspicion thrown into prison. Two became king's evidence, and the rest were tried, condemned, and executed.

Kennedy having wasted all his money, left Ireland and kept an infamous house in Deptford road. It was also supposed that he occasionally exacted contributions upon the highway. He was exposed to the same misfortune as befalls all those who associate with persons of abandoned lives and dishonourable principles. One of the females in his house informed upon him as a robber; nor was she disposed to do her work partially, but finding a man whom Kennedy had robbed when a pirate, she took him to visit the latter in Bridewell, where he had been thrown for the robbery. He identified Kennedy, who was committed to the Marshalsea prison.

Kennedy, in order to save his life, turned king's evidence; but though he informed upon eight or ten of his companions, only one could be found, who was a sober man and forced into the service, and therefore pardoned. Kennedy was not so fortunate, but, inasmuch as he had been an old and notorious offender, was condemned and executed.

Those who remained in the Rover soon abandoned her upon the coast of the West Indies, and she was found strolling at sea by a sloop near St. Christopher's island. The greater part of the crew met the fate they deserved.

CAPTAIN WORLEY.

In a small open boat, with only eight companions, Worley entered upon service. Provided with six old muskets, and corresponding ammunition, with a few biscuits, one or two dried tongues, and a keg of water they left New York in September, 1718, and sailed towards Delaware river. Though the distance is about fifty miles, they met with no prey, so they went up the river as far as Newcastle. Near this place they captured a shallop with household goods and plate, and having emptied her of every thing valuable, they permitted her to depart. As this was not done upon the high seas, it could not be construed piracy. The shallop conveyed the intilligence to New York, which alarming government, several vessels were fitted out to go in quest of this formidable rover. But he was not yet destined to be taken; for, after several days cruising, the government vessels returned without their prize.

In sailing down the river, Worley met with a sloop bound for Philadelphia, and quitting his own shallop, he and his men went on board the sloop, and increased their strength by the hands which were in her. In a few days they took a sloop homeward bound for Hull, with all manner of provisions, which enabled them to undertake some bolder scheme.

Upon the success of these pirates, the government issued a proclamation for apprehending all pirates who refused to surrender upon a specified day. To follow out the intention of this proclamation, a vessel of twenty guns was fitted out to cruise upon the coast, and to protect the trade. Informed of this, Worley and his men stood out to sea. In their cruise, they captured a sloop and a brigantine; the former they sunk, as she belonged to New York, and might inform upon them; and they permitted the other to prosecute her voyage.

Worley was now in reality become formidable. He had twenty-five men, six guns, plenty of small arms, and a good vessel. Accordingly, he assumed a more systematic plan, hoisted black colours, formed certain regulations, and swore every man to stand to his colours, and receive no quarter.

They now went into an inlet in North Carolina to clean their vessel; and the government receiving intelligence of their being in that place, two sloops, one of eight and another of six guns, manned with seventy men, were sent in search of them. Worley was gone before they arrived, but, tracing his course, they discovered him off the Capes of Virginia. Upon the supposition that they were two vessels intending to enter St. James's river, Worley hastened to get between them and that entrance of the river, in order to secure his prize. The inhabitants of St. James's Town, supposing that all three were pirates, and that they would land to plunder and destroy the country, the governor ordered all the vessels to haul into the shore, unless they thought that they were in a situation to fight the pirates. He beat to arms, collected all the force that could be mustered, erected a temporary battery with the guns of the ships, and put the island in a posture of defence. But to their surprise they soon saw what they imagined to be pirates fighting with each other.

Meanwhile, as Worley was waiting at the entrance of the river, with the black colours flying, to seize the two vessels as they approached, to his sad mortification they hoisted king's colours, and fired a gun. Thus he found, that, instead of entrapping others, he himself was entrapped and hemmed in by a superior force. Agreeably to their engagements to each other, the pirates determined to conquer or die.

The two sloops gave him a broadside, and immediately boarded, the one upon the quarter, the other upon the bow. Worley and his men drew up on deck, and fought it hand to hand, in a most desperate manner. They were true to their oath; not a man called for quarter, and many were slain before they could be overcome; not one survived, except the captain and another man, who were both severely wounded. They were brought on shore in irons, and, lest they should have died of their wounds, were hanged the following day, in the month of February, 1719. Thus, Worley's beginning was bold and desperate, his course short and prosperous, and his end bloody and disgraceful.

CAPTAIN LOWTHER.

GEORGE LOWTHER sailed from the Thames, in the character of second mate, in the Gambia Castle of sixteen guns and thirty men, belonging to the African Company. There were a number of soldiers under the command of John Massey, intended to garrison a fort which was destroyed by Captain Dawson.

The Gambia Castle arrived safe, and landed Massey and his men; but the military power was overruled by the merchants and traders. To them it belonged to victual the garrison, and, being scanty in their allowance, Massey was highly offended, and remonstrated in terms more suitable to his feelings than their interests. He boldly declared, that he had brought these brave men here under the assurance that they were to have plenty of provisions, and to be treated in the most humane manner; therefore, if they were not so treated, he should be under the necessity of consulting for himself.

The governor was then sick, and, for his better accommodation, was taken on board the Gambia Castle. During this period, the captain being offended with George Lowther, his second mate, ordered him to be punished. The men interfered in behalf of Lowther, and the captain was disobeyed. Lowther and Massey having become intimate during the voyage, they now aggravated their grievances to each other, and the result of their consultation was to seize the ship, and sail for England.

When matters were ripe for execution, Lowther sent a letter to Massey, informing him, "that he must repair on board, as it was now time to put their design into execution." Massey then harangued the soldiers in the barracks, saying, "You that have a mind to go to England, now is the time." They in general agreed, and when all things were ready he sent the boat off with this message to the chief mate, "That he should get the guns ready, for that the King of Barro would come on board to dinner." Lowther knew the meaning; confined the chief mate, and prepared to sail. In the afternoon, Massey came on board with the governor's son, having almost emptied the storehouses, and dismounted the guns of the fort.

The captain of the Gambia Castle, having gone on shore to hold a council with the governor and others, was not permitted to come on board. He called to Lowther and his associates, and offered them what terms they chose, to restore the ship;—but all in vain. They put the governor's son on shore, with three others who did not choose to go along with them, and immediately sailed.

Scarcely were they out at sea, when Lowther addressed them to the following effect: "That it was the greatest folly imaginable to think of returning to England; for that what they had already done could not be justified upon any pretence whatever, but would be looked upon by the government as a capital offence, and none of them were in a condition to withstand the attacks of such powerful adversaries as they would meet with at home. For his part, he told them he was determined not to run such a hazard; and therefore, if his proposal was not agreed to, he desired to be set on shore in some place of safety; that they had a good ship under them, a parcel of brave fellows in her; that it was not their business to starve or be made slaves; and therefore, if they were all of his mind, they would seek their fortunes upon the seas, as other adventurers had done before them." The crew was unanimous, knocked down the cabins, prepared black colours, and named the ship "The Delivery." She was mounted with sixteen guns, and had fifty hands on board.

To enforce order, and to provide for the stability of this government, several articles were drawn up, signed, and sworn to; and they soon began their operations, by capturing a vessel belonging to Boston, which, having emptied her stores, they allowed to depart.

Proceeding to Hispaniola, the Delivery met with a French vessel laden with wine and brandy. In the character of a merchant, Captain Massey went on board, viewed the liquors, and offered a price for the greater part of them, which was not accepted. But after a while he whispered in the Frenchman's ear, "that they must have them all without money." The captain understood his meaning, and with no small reluctance agreed to the bargain. They took out of her about seventy pounds, besides thirty casks of brandy, five hogsheads of wine, several pieces of chintzes, and other valuable goods. Lowther returned five pounds to the Frenchman for his civility.

But this commonwealth was soon to experience the effects of discord. Massey had been trained a soldier, and was solicitous to move in his own sphere; he therefore proposed to land with fifty or sixty men, and plunder the French settlements. Lowther represented the rashness, imprudence, and impracticability of such an adventure. Massey remained absolute in his determination. It became necessary to decide the matter by a reference to the community. A great majority were of the opinion of Lowther. But though overruled, Massey was not convinced, so became fractious and quarrelled with Captain Lowther. The men also were divided; some were land pirates, and some sea pirates, and ere long, they were prepared to decide the matter with the sword.

But employment terminated dissension. The man at the masthead cried, "a sail! a sail!" In a few hours, they came up with her, and found that she was bound for England. They supplied themselves with necessaries, and took a few hands out of her. Lowther proposed to sink her and all the passengers on board, but Massey interfered, and prevented this cruel action. Accordingly, she was permitted to depart, and arrived safe in England.

The next day they captured a small sloop, and detained her. Massey still remaining uneasy, and declaring his resolution to leave the Delivery, Lowther proposed that he and all those who were of his sentiments would go on board the sloop which they had just taken, and seek their own fortunes. This was instantly agreed to, and Massey with ten more went on board, and sailed directly for Jamaica. With a bold countenance he went to the governor, and informed him that he had assisted in running off with the vessel; but his object was to save the lives of His Majesty's subjects, and that his express design was to land them in England; that in opposition to this determination, Lowther and the majority were for becoming pirates; and that he had embraced the first opportunity to leave them, and surrender himself, his men, and his vessel to his excellency.

Massey was kindly received, and sent along with Captain Laws to cruise in quest of Lowther, but not finding him, returned to Jamaica, received certificates of his surrender, and came home a passenger to England. When he came to town, he wrote a narrative of the whole matter to the African Company, who returned him for answer, "That he should be fairly hanged." He was accordingly seized, and, upon his own letter, the evidence of the late captain of the ship, who had been left at the fort, the governor's son, and some others, he was condemned to end his course at Tyburn.

Lowther cruising off Hispaniola, captured a small ship from Bristol and a Spanish pirate. He rifled and burned both ships, sending the Spaniards away in their launch, and constraining the Englishmen to turn pirates. In a few days they took another sloop, which they manned and carried along with them, and then harboured at the small island to clean. Here they spent their time more like demons than men, in all manner of debauchery, drunkenness, and rioting.

Having again set to sea, they met with Edward Low, a pirate, in a small vessel with thirteen hands; and, upon the request of Lowther, he united his strength with theirs. Lowther retaining the command, and Low becoming Lieutenant.

Proceeding on their voyage, they met with a vessel of two hundred tons, called the Greyhound, commanded by Benjamin Edwards. Piratical colours were hoisted, and she was commanded to strike. The captain declined,—an engagement ensued, but finding the pirates too strong for him, he surrendered. Instead of treating the captain and his men with generous lenity, they beat them in a merciless manner, drove them on board their own ship, and then set fire to it.

In their course they took several other ships, rifled and dismissed them; but two they fitted up for their own service. With this small fleet: viz. Admiral Lowther in the Happy Delivery; Captain Low in the Rhode Island sloop; and Captain Harris (who was second mate in the Greyhound) in a sloop formerly belonging to Jamaica,—they sailed to Port Mayo in the gulf of Matique, and made preparations to clean their vessels: with this view they made tents of their sails, stored their provisions in tent also, and then commenced their operations. But scarcely were they at work, when a body of the natives came down upon them, drove them to their ships, seized their tents and stores, and set fire to the Delivery, which was stranded on shore. Lowther and his men now went on board the largest sloop, called the Ranger, and left the other at sea. They were soon reduced to great want, and commotion ensued; but when they had got to the West Indies, they took a prize, which supplied their wants, and having sunk her, sailed for America.

They, in a short time, captured a brigantine, and the company being divided in their sentiments, Low and those who were of his views, got on board the prize, and went off, while those who agreed with Lowther remained in the Ranger. On his way to the main land of America, Lowther took several ships with very little resistance, but upon the coast of South Carolina he met with a ship bound for England. An engagement took place, and Lowther was so hard pressed, that he was under the necessity of running aground, and landing his men; but when the captain of the English vessel had taken the boat in order to burn the pirate ship, a bullet from the pirates on shore put an end to his life, which so discouraged his men, that they returned to their vessel.

After their departure, Lowther got off his sloop, though in a very shattered condition, having suffered much in the engagement, and many of his men having been killed or wounded. With no small difficulty he went to an inlet in North Carolina, where he remained during the winter.

In spring he again took to sea, steered to Newfoundland, took several vessels of similar importance, and in his way to the West Indies captured a brigantine, plundered her, took two men into their own ship, and sent her off. Having cruised a considerable time, it was necessary to clean, and for that purpose he went into the isle of Blanco. While they were keenly employed in this work, the Eagle sloop, belonging to the South Sea Company, with thirty-five men, attacked Lowther, and constrained him to cry for quarter. While they were surrendering, Lowther and twelve of the crew escaped out of the cabin-window, and fled to the woods. Five of them were taken, but the rest remained upon the island.

Informed of this meritorious action on the part of the sloop, the Spanish government condemned the ship to the crew of the Eagle, and sent a small sloop to the island with twenty-five men to search the woods for the other pirates. Three others were found, but Captain Lowther with three men and a boy escaped. As the captain was afterwards found dead with a pistol beside him, it is supposed that in desperation he had shot himself.

The Eagle sloop brought the prisoners to St. Christopher's, where they were all tried in March, 1722: three were acquitted, eleven found guilty, and two recommended to mercy.

CAPTAIN SPRIGGS

SAILED with Lowther for some time, and left him in company with Low. He was quarter-master, and consequently had a large share in all the barbarities of that execrable crew. He quarrelled with Low concerning one of the men who had killed another; Spriggs insisting that he should be hanged, and the other that he should not. After this dispute, Spriggs took an opportunity to leave him in the night, along with eighteen men, having seized upon the Delight, a prize of twelve guns.

Scarcely were they beyond the reach of Lowther and his crew, when Spriggs was elected captain, black colours hoisted, and the guns fired as a salute to themselves and their captain. In their way to the West Indies they took a Portuguese bark, laden with rich plunder, and after using the men in a cruel and barbarous manner, they put them into the boat with a small quantity of provisions, and set the ship on fire.

They took another vessel belonging to Barbadoes, which they plundered, used the men also in a most barbarous manner, then put them into the boat, left them to the mercy of the waves, and set fire to the ship. Some of the men signed their articles, and joined their association. The next capture was a ship from Martinique, and though they did not burn the vessel, the men were used in the same cruel manner. Some days after, they took one coming from Jamaica, robbed her of stores, arms, ammunition, and every thing they pleased, and what they did not think useful, they threw overboard. They forced the two mates and several other hands into their service, and then sent her off. They were not more fortunate in gaining prizes, than they were wantonly cruel to the men. A sloop from Rhode Island fell into their hands: they constrained all the men to join them, but the mate, being a grave sober man, resolutely declined. He was then informed that he should be allowed to go with his discharge written upon his back,— this was a lash from every man in the ship, which was rigorously put in execution.

The next day one of the mates taken out of the prize signed their articles, which was deemed a great acquisition, for he was a good artist. They gave three huzzas, fired all the guns, and appointed him master. The day was devoted to feasting and carousing, and, among other healths, that of George II. was drunk. It had been related to them that the old king was dead, and they expected a general pardon upon the accession of the new sovereign. Thus they proclaimed his Royal Highness the Prince of Wales, saying, that " they doubted not but there would be a general pardon in twelve months, which they would embrace, and come in upon; but if they should be excepted from it, they would murder every Englishman that should fall into their hands."

Not long after, they espied a sail, and gave her chase. They supposed that she was a Spaniard, and so gave her a broadside. But a lamentable cry for quarters being heard from every part of the ship, they ceased firing. How mortified, however, were the rogues, when they found that it was the same vessel that they had sent away not worth a penny. Enraged at this disappointment, about fifteen of these cruel wretches attacked the captain with sharp cutlasses, and would certainly have put an end to his life, had not Burridge, his former mate, rushed in among the thickest of them, and begged for his life. In the madness of their rage, they made a bonfire of the ship, and even when they went down to supper, they called down the unfortunate captain, to have some more cruel sport at his expence. In two days they anchored at an uninhabited island, and, with a musket and some ammunition sent on shore the captain and several of his men, who subsisted there for some time, and were then taken off by one Jones.

Spriggs now anchored at a small island and cleaned, and then sailed in search of the Eagle sloop, which had taken Lowther at Blanco, with the determined resolution to put the captain to death as soon as found, for attacking his friend and brother. But a vessel which he pursued under the impression that it was the Eagle sloop, to his surprise proved to be a French man-of-war, on which Spriggs crowded all the sail he could: he would, however, have been taken, had not the main topmast of the Frenchman been broken.

Spriggs then sailed northward, captured a schooner belonging to Boston, took out the men, sunk the vessel, and having taken another sloop, used the men in the most cruel and barbarous manner, hoisting them as high as the main and fore-tops, and letting them fall upon the deck. After serving them in this manner, they whipped them about the deck until they themselves were fatigued, and then allowed all of them to go except two men.

They next captured a vessel from Rhode Island with provisions and some horses. The brutal pirates mounted the horses and rode at full gallop upon the deck, cursing, swearing, and hollooing, until the animals became infuriated, and threw their riders. They then wreaked their vengeance upon the men, cutting and beating them in a barbarous manner, and telling them it was for bringing horses without boots and spurs, for want of which they were not able to ride them. In this manner these unnatural wretches continued their cruelties as long as they could maintain community, to the disgrace of human nature, and to the sad sorrow of all who were so unfortunate as to fall into their hands.

CAPTAIN ROCHE.

THIS man was a native of Ireland, and was trained up to the sea. When arrived at manhood, he was concerned with some others in insuring ships to a great value, and then destroying them. From a fore-mast man he was raised to be a mate in a vessel that traded between Ireland and France. In this situation he acquired a comfortable subsistence, and might have passed his days in respectability and usefulness; but the love of money, which has often proved the origin of ruin, excited him to abandon the path of honesty.

Having formed the design of becoming pirate, he communicated the same to one Neal, a fisherman at Cork, an ignorant and desperate villain. Neal enticed one Peter Cullen and his brother into the confederacy, and also one Francis Wise. They directed their attention to a French vessel lying in the harbour, Peter Tartoue captain, because there were few hands in her, and, though she was not suitable for the pirate service, yet they hoped soon to be able to exchange her for one more convenient for their purpose.

Accordingly, in November, 1721, all things being concerted, they entered passengers on board her, bound for Nantz; and Roche being an experienced sailor, the master often trusted him with the care of the vessel, while he and the mate went to rest. Upon one of these occasions, Roche and his confederates embraced the opportunity to effect their cruel purpose. The mind of Francis Wise began to relent, and he endeavoured to dissuade them from their nefarious design. Roche was however determined, and said, that he and Cullen had suffered great losses at sea, and were resolved to have them repaired; and if there were any fisherman there who would not join in killing the French rogues, and running away with the vessel, he should certainly share their fate; but on the contrary, if they stood true, they should partake of the booty.

Upon this they all agreed. Meanwhile, Roche commanded three of the Frenchmen and a boy to hand the top-sails. The two who first came down were knocked on the head, and thrown overboard; upon seeing this, the other two ran up to the top-mast head. Cullen followed, threw the boy into the water, and driving down the other man, he was immediately despatched. Those who were sleeping below being aroused by the tumult, and the shrieks of expiring men, rushed up; but before they could apprehend their danger, they were bound together, and, imploring mercy, were also thrown overboard. They were now, as Roche himself confessed, all over as wet with the blood that had been spilt, as if they had been dipped in water, or stood in a shower of rain; nor did they regard it with any other feeling.

This horrible massacre being finished, Roche was made captain, Cullen was to assume the character of a merchant, and the name of Peter Roche was inserted in the papers of the ship. In vain they endeavoured to obtain a few hands from a vessel, under the pretence that some of their men had been swept overboard. By a storm they were constrained to put into Dartmouth in England, and set men to work to alter the form of the vessel, so that she should not be known; and in order to obtain money to pay the workmen, they disposed of several barrels of beef which were in the ship.

They next steered their course for Rotterdam, and disposed of the remaining part of the cargo. From this port they freighted for England, by one Annesly, a merchant, who went passenger along with them. But these execrable villains, in a stormy night, threw him overboard. He swam long round the ship, and entreated them to spare his life, and all his goods should be at their disposal, but they remained unmoved by his entreaties and cries.

They were afterwards under the necessity of coming to the coast of France, and received the intelligence that inquiry had been made after them. Roche abandoned the vessel to Cullen, and went on shore. Cullen having obtained some more hands, sailed for Scotland, and then left the vessel, which was afterwards carried into the Thames.

Roche came to London, and while endeavouring to recover some money under a feigned name, was arrested, examined, and proved to be the person who had run off with the French vessel. Attempting to turn king's evidence, Neal and Cullen were discovered; but, from the cruelty of his conduct, Roche was brought to trial, condemned, and executed at Tyburn, in the 30th year of his age. He was an active genteel man, and under a comely person concealed a black and savage disposition. His whole life was a scene of villainy and murder, and he was alike prepared for the commission of every cruelty.

CAPTAIN GOW

Gow sailed from Amsterdam, in July, 1714, on board the George galley for Santa Cruz, where they took in bee's-wax. Scarcely had they sailed from that place, when Gow and several others, who had formed a conspiracy, seized the vessel. One of the conspirators cried, " There is a man overboard." The captain instantly ran to the side of the vessel, when he was seized by two men, who attempted to throw him over; he however so struggled, that he escaped from their hands. One Winter, with a knife, attempted to cut him in the throat, but missing his aim, the captain was yet saved. But Gow, coming forward, shot him through the body, and he was then cast into the sea. The conspirators proceeded to murder all who were not in their horrid plot, which being done, James Williams came upon deck, and striking one of the guns with his cutlas, saluted Gow in the following words: " Captain Gow, you are welcome, welcome to your command." Williams was declared second lieutenant, and the other officers being appointed, the captain addressed them, saying: " If, hereafter, I see any of you whispering together, or if any of you refuse to obey my orders, let every such man depend upon it, that he shall certainly go the same way as those that are just gone before."

Their first prize was the Sarah Snow, of Bristol. After they had rifled the vessel and received one man from it, they allowed her to prosecute her voyage. The Delight, of Poole, was the next vessel that fell into their hands; but they not long after captured two others, from one of which they received a quantity of fish, and from the other bread, beef, and pork. They also forced two men from the latter ship. A French ship, not long after, furnished them with wine, oil, figs, oranges and lemons, to the value of 500*l*. In a short time after, they captured their last prize, and, as she made no resistance, they plundered and dismissed her.

They next sailed for the Orkney Isles to clean, but were apprehended by a gentleman of that country, brought up to London, and tried before a Court of Admiralty, in May, 1725. When the first indictment was read, Gow obstinately refused to plead, for which the Court ordered his thumbs to be tied together with whipcord. The punishment was several times repeated by the executioner and another officer, they drawing the cord every time till it broke. But he still being stubborn, refusing to submit to the court, the sentence was pronounced against him, which the law appoints in such cases; that is, "That he should be taken back to prison, and there pressed to death." The gaoler was then ordered to conduct him back, and see that the sentence was executed the next morning; meanwhile, the trials of the prisoners, his companions, went forward.

But the next morning, when the press was prepared, pursuant to the order of the Court the day before, he was so terrified with the apprehension of dying in that manner, that he sent his humble petition to the Court, praying that he might be admitted to plead. This request being granted, he was brought again to the bar, and arraigned upon the first indictment, to which he pleaded, Not guilty. Then the depositions that had been given against the other prisoners were repeated, upon which he was convicted, and received sentence of death accordingly, which he suffered in company with Captain Weaver and William Ingram.

The stories of these two men are so interwoven with others, that it will be impossible to distinguish many of their particular actions. They were, however, proved to have been concerned, if not the principal actors, in the following piracies: first, The seizing a Dutch ship in August, 1722, and taking from thence a hundred pieces of Holland, value 800*l*.: a thousand pieces of eight, va.ue

250*l*. Secondly, The entering and pillaging the Dolphin of London, William Haddock, out of which they got three hundred pieces of eight, value 75*l*.; forty gallons of rum, and other things, on the twentieth of November in the same year. Thirdly, the stealing out of a ship called the Don Carlos, Lot Neekins master, four hundred ounces of silver, value 100*l*. fifty gallons of rum, value 30*s*. a thousand pieces of eight, a hundred pistoles, and other valuable goods. And fourthly, the taking from a ship called the England, ten pipes of wine, value 250*l*. The two last charges both in the year 1721. Weaver returned home, and came to Mr. Thomas Smith, at Bristol, in a very ragged condition; and pretending that he had been robbed by pirates, Smith, who had been acquainted with him eight or nine years before, provided him with necessaries, and he walked about unmolested for some time. But Captain Joseph Smith, who knew him when a pirate, one day met him, and asked him to go and take a bottle with him; when they were in the tavern he told him he had been a considerable sufferer by his boarding his vessel,—" Therefore," said he, " as I understand that you are in good circumstances, and plenty of cash, I expect that you will make me some restitution; which if you do, I will never hurt a hair of your head, because you were very civil to me when I was in your hands." But as this recompense was never given, Weaver was apprehended and executed.

Ingram was also a very hardened fellow, and one of the most forward in all their exploits.

CAPTAIN JOHN UPTON

WAS born at Deptford, of honest but poor parents, who gave him an education such as their circumstances could afford. He served an apprenticeship to a waterman upon the river. In the character of boatswain, quarter-master, and other inferior offices, he served on board different men-of-war. After the death of his wife, he found sundry demands made upon him, and several actions raised, for which he was in danger of being arrested; he therefore went on board the John and Elizabeth merchantman, bound for Bonavista in Newfoundland.

When he arrived there he was discharged, and served a planter during a year for the sum of 18*l.* He next went a passenger to Boston, and from thence made a voyage to the Bay of Honduras. He then went on board the Perry galley, bound to Barbadoes and Bristol. At Barbadoes the ship was delivered and loaded again, and set forward to England. The Perry galley in her voyage home was taken by a pirate, and Upton was constrained to enter along with them.

The pirate carried the Perry galley to the island of Ruby, and in a short time they captured a Dutch sloop. Upton and some others were put on board that sloop, and embracing an opportunity, escaped, carrying off the sloop. He left the pirate service, and after moving from place to place, was at last pressed on board his Majesty's ship the Nottingham, where he remained until he was accused of piracy, and brought home for trial.

Upon the trial it was proved, that he had entered with the pirates, signed their articles, been active in their exploits, and received a share of their plunder; that he had advised to burn the Perry galley, with her captain and mate in her; and that he had made a cat-o'nine-tails, with which the mate received 200 lashes. He was condemned, and at the age of 50 years suffered as a pirate.

CAPTAIN EDWARD LOW.

This ferocious villain was born in Westminster, and received an education similar to that of the common people in England. He was by nature a pirate; for even when very young he raised contributions among the boys of Westminster, and if they declined compliance, a battle was the result. When he advanced a step farther in life, he began to exert his ingenuity at low games, and cheating all in his power; and those who pretended to maintain their own right, he was ready to call to the field of combat.

He went to sea in company with his brother, and continued with him for three or four years. Going over to America, he wrought in a rigging-house at Boston for some time. He then came home to see his mother in England, returned to Boston, and continued for some years longer at the same business. But being of a quarrelsome temper, he differed with his master, and went on board a sloop bound for the Bay of Honduras.

While there, he had command of a boat employed in bringing logwood to the ship. In that boat there were twelve men well armed, to be prepared for the Spaniards, from whom the wood was taken by force. It happened one day that the boat came to the ship just a little before dinner was ready, and Low desired that they might dine before they returned. The captain, however, ordered them a bottle of rum, and requested them to take another trip, as no time was to be lost. The crew were enraged, particularly Low, who took up a loaded musket and fired at the captain, but missing him, another man was shot, and they then ran off with the boat. The next day they took a small vessel, went on board her, hoisted a black flag, and declared war with the whole world.

In their rovings, Low met with Lowther, who proposed that he should join him, and thus promote their mutual advantage. We have already related their adventures as long as they remained in company. Having captured a brigantine, Low, with forty more, went on board her; and leaving Lowther, they went to seek their own fortune.

Their first adventure was the capture of a vessel belonging to Amboy, out of which they took the provisions, and allowed her to proceed. On the same day they took a sloop, plundered her, and permitted her to depart. The sloop went into Black Island, and sent intelligence to the governor that Low was on the coast. Two small vessels were immediately fitted out, but, before their arrival, Low was beyond their reach. After this narrow escape, Low went into port to procure water and fresh provisions; and then renewed his search of plunder. He next sailed into the harbour of Port Rosemary, where were thirteen ships, but none of them of any great strength. Low hoisted the black flag, assuring them that if they made any resistance they should have no quarter; and manning their boat, the pirates took possession of every one of them, which they plundered and converted to their own use. They then put on board a schooner ten guns and fifty men, named her the Fancy, and Low himself went on board of her, while Charles Harris was constituted captain of the brigantine. They also constrained a few of the men to join them, and sign their articles.

After an unsuccessful pursuit of two sloops from Boston, they steered for the Leeward Islands, but in their way were overtaken by a terrible hurricane. The search for plunder gave place to the most vigorous exertion to save themselves. On board the brigantine, all hands were at work both day and night; they were under the necessity of throwing overboard six of her guns, and all the weighty provisions. In the storm, the two vessels were separated, and it was some time before they again saw each other.

After the storm, Low went into a small island west of the Carribbees, refitted his vessels, and got provisions for them in exchange of goods. As soon as the brigantine was ready for sea, they went on a cruise until the Fancy should be prepared, and during that cruise, met with a vessel which had lost all her masts in the storm, which they plundered of goods to the value of 1000l. and returned to the island. When the Fancy was ready to sail, a council was held what course they should next steer. They followed the advice of the captain, who thought it not safe to cruise any longer to the leeward, lest they should fall in with any of the men-of-war that cruised upon that coast, so they sailed for the Nores.

The good fortune of Low was now singular; in his way thither he captured a French ship of 34 guns, and carried her along with him. Then entering St. Michael's roads, he captured seven sail, threatening with instant death all who dare to oppose him. Thus, by inspiring terror, without firing a single gun, he became master of all that property. Being in want of water and fresh provisions, Low sent to the governor demanding a supply, upon condition of releasing the ships he had taken, otherwise he would commit them to the flames. The request was instantly complied with, and six of the vessels restored. But a French vessel which was among them, they emptied of her guns and all her men, except the cook, who, they said, being a greasy fellow, would fry well; they accordingly bound the unfortunate man to the mast, and set the ship on fire.

The next who fell in their way was Captain Carter, in the Wright galley; who, because he showed some inclination to defend himself, was cut and mangled in a barbarous manner. There were also two Portuguese friars, whom they tied to the foremast, and several times let them down before they were dead, merely to gratify their own ferocious dispositions. Meanwhile, another Portuguese, beholding this cruel scene, expressed some sorrow in his countenance, upon which one of the wretches said he did not like his looks, and so giving him a stroke across the body with his cutlass, he fell upon the spot. Another of the miscreants, aiming a blow at a prisoner, missed his aim, and struck Low upon the under jaw. The surgeon was called, and stitched up the wound; but Low finding fault with the operation, the surgeon gave him a blow which broke all the stitches, and left him to sew them himself. After he had plundered this vessel, some of them were for burning her, as they had done the Frenchman: but instead of that, they cut her cables, rigging and sails to pieces, and sent her adrift to the mercy of the waves.

They next sailed for the island of Madeira, and took up a fishing-boat with two old men and a boy. They detained one of them, and sent the other on shore with a flag of truce, requesting the governor to send them a boat of water, else they would hang the other man at the yard-arm. The water was sent, and the man dismissed.

They next sailed for the Canary Islands, and there took several vessels; and being informed that two small galleys were daily expected, the sloop was manned and sent in quest of them. They however, missing their prey, and being in great want of provision, went into St. Michael's in the character of traders, and being discovered, were apprehended, and the whole crew conducted to the castle, and treated according to their merits.

Meanwhile, Low's ship was overset upon the careen and lost, so that, having only the Fancy schooner remaining, they all, to the number of a hundred, went on board her, and set sail in search of new spoils. They soon met a rich Portuguese vessel, and after some resistance captured her. Low tortured the men to constrain them to inform him where they had hid the treasures. He accordingly discovered that, during the chase, the captain had hung a bag with eleven thousand moidores out of the cabin window, and that, when they were taken, he had cut the rope, and allowed it to fall into the sea. Upon this intelligence, Low raved like a fury, ordered the captain's lips to be cut off and broiled before his eyes, then murdered him and all his crew.

After this bloody action, the miscreants steered northward, and seized several vessels, one of which they burned, and plundering the rest, allowed them to proceed. Having cleaned in one of the islands, they then sailed for the bay of Honduras. They met a Spaniard coming out of the bay, which had captured five Englishmen and a pink, plundered them, and brought away the masters prisoners. Low hoisted Spanish colours, but when he came nearer, hung out the black flag, and the Spaniard was seized without resistance. Upon finding the masters of the English vessels in the hold, and seeing English goods on board, a consultation was held, when it was determined to put all the Spaniards to the sword. This was scarcely resolved upon, when they commenced with every species of weapons to massacre every man, and some flying from their merciless hands into the waves, a canoe was sent in pursuit of those who endeavoured to swim on shore. They next plundered the Spanish vessel, restored the English masters to their respective vessels, and set the Spaniard on fire.

Low's next cruise was between the Leeward Islands and the main land, where, in a continued course of prosperity, he successively captured no less than nineteen ships of different sizes, and generally treated their crews with a barbarity unequalled even among pirates. But it happened that the Greyhound, of twenty guns and one hundred and twenty men, was cruising upon that coast. Informed of the mischief these miscreants had done, the Greyhound went in search of them. Supposing they had discovered a prize, Low and his crew pursued them, and the Greyhound allowing them to run after her till all things were ready to engage, turned upon the two sloops.

One of these sloops was called the Fancy, and commanded by Low, and the other the Ranger, commanded by Harris; and both hoisted their piratical colours, and fired each a gun. When the Greyhound came within musket shot, she hauled up her mainsail, and clapped close upon a wind, to keep the pirates from running to leeward, and then engaged. But when the rogues found whom they had to deal with, they edged away under the man-of-war's stern, and the Greyhound standing after them, they made a running fight for about two hours; but little wind happening, the sloops gained from her, by the help of their oars; upon which the Greyhound left off firing, turned all hands to their own oars, and at three in the afternoon came up with them. The pirates hauled upon a wind to receive the man-of-war, and the fight was immediately renewed, with a brisk fire on both sides, till the Ranger's mainyard was shot down. Under these circumstances, Low abandoned her to the enemy and fled.

The conduct of Low was surprising in this adventure, because his reputed courage and boldness had hitherto so possessed the minds of all people, that he became a terror even to his own men; but his behaviour throughout this whole action showed him to be a base cowardly villain; for had Low's sloop fought half so briskly as Harris's had done (as they were under a solemn oath to do,) the man-of-war, in the opinion of some present, could never have hurt them.

Nothing, however, could lessen the fury, or reform the manners of that obdurate crew. Their narrow escape had no good effect upon them, and with redoubled violence they renewed their depre-

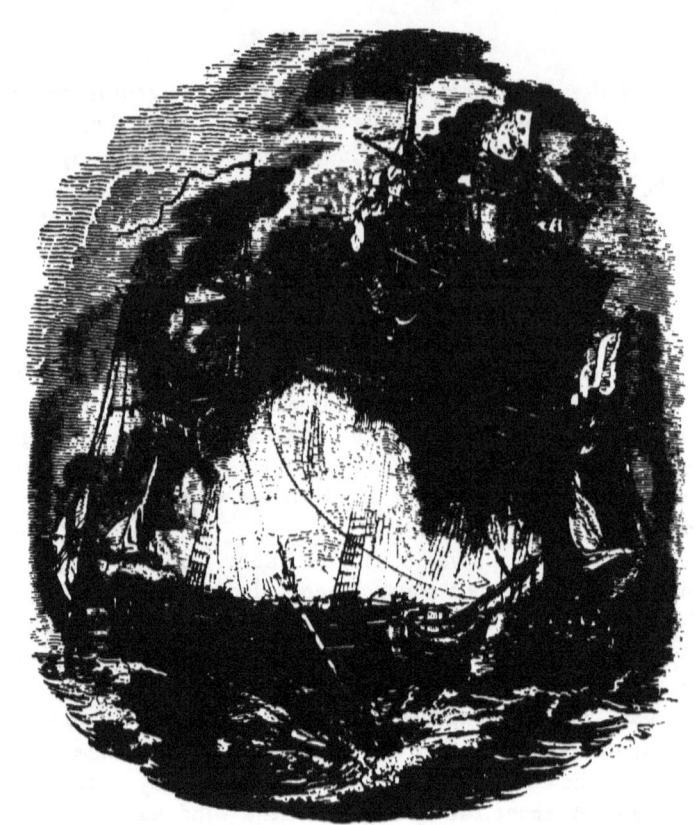

Page 385.

lations and cruelties. The next vessel they captured, was eighty miles from land. They used the master with the most wanton cruelty, then shot him dead, and forced the crew into the boat with a compass, a little water, and a few biscuits, and left them to the mercy of the waves; they, however, beyond all expectation, got safe to shore.

Low proceeded in his villainous career with too fatal success. Unsatisfied with satiating their avarice and walking the common path of wickedness, those inhuman wretches, like to Satan himself, made mischief their sport, cruelty their delight, and the ruin and murder of their fellow men their constant employment. Of all the piratical crews belonging to the English nation, none ever equalled Low in barbarity. Their mirth and their anger had the same effect. They murdered a man from good humour, as well as from anger and passion. Their ferocious disposition seemed only to delight in cries, groans, and lamentations. One day Low having captured Captain Graves, a Virginia man, took a bowl of punch in his hand, and said, "Captain, here's half this to you." The poor gentleman was too much touched with his misfortunes to be in a humour for drinking, he therefore modestly excused himself. Upon this Low cocked and presented a pistol in one hand, and his bowl in the other, saying, "Either take the one or the other."

Low next captured a vessel called the Christmas, mounted her with thirty-four guns, went on board her himself, assumed the title of admiral, and hoisted the black flag. His next prize was a brigantine half manned with Portuguese, and half with English. The former he hanged, and the latter he thrust into their boat and dismissed, while he set fire to the vessel. The success of Low was unequalled, as well as his cruelty; and during a long period he continued to pursue his wicked course with impunity.

PAUL JONES.

ARBIGLAND, in the Stewartry of Kirkenbright, in Scotland, was the birth-place of the celebrated John Paul, where he was born in July, 1747. His father, John Paul, was a gardener, and the first years of his life were passed in the manner usual amongst persons of his station. But we gather from the recollection of persons still alive that he very early evinced a predilection for the sea, and that whilst yet a youth, he was engaged in mercantile speculations of a very extensive character. How the son of a gardener, who had received no other education than that of a parochial school, could launch out thus early into commercial traffic, may at first seem a startling question. A probable solution may perhaps be worked out, by tracing or endeavouring to trace, the cause, hitherto unassigned, of his self-banishment from his own country. In the neighbourhood of his native place, it is supposed that his daring spirit, with his irrepressible love for the sea, recommended him to some persons engaged in a contraband traffic with the western colonies. The extent and precise character of these operations have not transpired, but this association is assigned as the origin of his hatred to this country—other accounts, more definite, and probably more authentic, state that he was bound apprentice to a merchant in the American trade, that his first introduction to America was by that means, and that not till his apprenticeship had expired, did he enter into those connections from which he suffered so much injury; that for some few years subsequent to the termination of his apprenticeship his time was passed chiefly on the sea, and that he visited many parts of Europe and America—that this was the time at which he sustained his losses, in consequence of which, whether from compulsion or disgust, he withdrew into inactive retirement. Be this as it may, the death of his brother in 1773, who left no will, called him to Virginia, to arrange his affairs: about this time, he added Jones to his name.

The spirit which, previously to the assertion of their independence, impelled the Americans to construct a fleet for reprisals on England, found a responsive echo in the breast of Paul Jones; his love of the sea, his appetite for adventure, his smothered ambition for fame, burst out afresh, and supported by a boiling indignation at the conduct of the English, drove him forth from his obscurity. On the 22nd of December, 1775, he was made a lieutenant of the newly-formed American navy. The haste with which this navy was fitted out, the little judgment exercised in the selection of officers, and the great want of naval experience in both officers and men, together with the excitement of the occasion, and their imperfect discipline, were influences, the combined operation of which had very nearly rendered unnecessary any exertions on the part of their enemy. Their first attack on the New Providence, one of the Bahama isles, failed in consequence of the governor having the night before sent away the military stores which they intended to seize; and the fight which they had shortly after with a British man-of-war somewhat resembled the puny efforts of an infant engaged with a full-grown man. Sickness also at this time so lessened their numbers, that scarcely one of the vessels had its compliment of men; and to increase the dilemma, nearly all the seamen had, in obedience to the urgency of the national call, entered the land service, and were at that time acting as soldiers. The discomfiture of their fleet by a single British vessel excited much dissatisfaction, and brought down reproach and obloquy on the heads of the officers. The circumstance of the fight were subjected to judicial examination; the result of which, as respects our hero, was his promotion to the command of the Providence. Paul Jones's superiority in personal courage and energy of mind was evident, and was promptly rewarded: in fact, he seems to have been at that time almost the only officer who entertained enlarged views of the constitution of the navy, or possessed a scientific skill in naval tactics. He always in after-life professed himself to have entered the service for philanthropic motives, and it must be acknowledged that he studied the principles of his profession with the ardour and perseverance of enthusiasm. To raise the American navy to the glorious eminence of acknowledged superiority was certainly to him an ever present object of ambition; but it may be very fairly questioned, if his motives for fighting against his own country were so purely philanthropic as he declared, or as he perhaps believed. His philanthropic indignation at the tyranny and oppression of the colonies by the mother country, has been said to have been not unmixed with rancour and revenge for private injuries, and a malignant spirit of injustice which would wreak revenge on a whole nation for the offences of private individuals. His skill and idomitable courage were, nevertheless, quite equal to the accomplishment of his object; and had he not been thwarted by the narrow-minded jealousy of his brother officers, Dutch, French, and American, the whole British nation would have bitterly rued the unfair dealings of his early connexions. But he very soon found that his desires far exceeded his power of action; for, whether Congress overlooked his claims to promotion, or whether envy and jealousy was already at work, or whether he overrated his merits, or from some other cause, he was not appointed to the command of either of the thirteen frigates built by the Congress in the beginning of 1776, which caused him much mortification. One thing, however, rebounds unquestionably to his credit as a man, and tends in some degree to confirm the assertion that his views were disinterested; in this and all subsequent cases of private mortification and disappointment, he never suffered himself to be checked in his exertions to promote the wellfare of his adopted country. Whilst yet the pain of neglect continued, his thoughts were chiefly directed to the improvement of the American navy, and his letters of this date to the Hon. Mr. Morris contain most valuable advice. He had sense enough to perceive the folly of affecting to scorn " the best regulated navy in the world," and he earnestly recommended that the American navy should be modelled after that of England, but that (the Americans) should " aim at such further improvements as may one day make ours vie with and exceed theirs."

In a short cruise of a few weeks in September and October, of the year 1776, he was very successful, taking sixteen sail, eight of which he destroyed. He then planned an expedition against the Newfoundland fishery, the probable failure of which, in consequence of his men quitting his service for that of privateers, drew from him a powerful letter to Mr. Morris, in which he complains of an insufficiency of the individual emolument to be derived from the service in the navy, and warns him that unless the advantages of the public service be made superior to those of private, the American navy "never can become respectable—never will become formidable; and without a respectable navy, alas, America!" He adverts also, in the same letter, to the mediocre abilities of the naval officers, and shows that efficient officers cannot be secured, but by the establishment of a Board of Admiralty.

Towards the latter end of this year he fell in, whilst cruising, with the Solebay frigate of 23 guns, and the Mitford of 32 guns. Jones's vessel, the Providence, was a sloop with but 12 six-pounders, but he escaped from the Solebay, after a sharp action of several hours, and from the Mitford without any contest at all. At the end of the year, he received a captain's commission and was appointed to the command of a squadron in Rhode Island, destined for an attack on Isle Royal, on his way to which he captured the Mellish, an armed vessel from Liverpool, containing 10,000 suits of uniform intended for the army of General Burgoyne. The value and importance of this prize were much enhanced by the fact that Washington's army was at this time destitute of clothing. By this and other prizes of which he made a considerable number during this voyage, Jones's reputation was much increased. His now elevated rank and formal commission added weight to his opinions, or at least warranted him in advancing them more freely; accordingly, he now devoted himself more particularly to the improvement of every thing connected with the navy. Many of these suggestions have since been acted upon, and his advice followed on a very extensive scale. In the year 1777, " as a reward for the zeal he had shown, and for the signal services which he had performed with little force," Jones was despatched to the American Commissioners in Paris, with an order that they should " invest him with the command of a fine ship."

But the ardour and daring activity of Paul Jones longed for some signal achievement, the very mention of which should fill the Americans with hope and courage, and the English with despair and dismay. He accordingly sent in a communication to the Secret Committee, requesting that he might be sent to Europe *for the purpose of attacking the coasts of England.* The committee wisely deemed that the man who could project such a plan, could carry it in execution; they therefore laid aside the former design and immediately appointed him to the Ranger, leaving him at large to act for himself, where he found the greatest chance of success. This was the mode of operation best suited to Jones's character; so fearless was his daring, and so persevering his courage, that his intrepidity was construed by many into hot-headed rashness, and his "expeditions" into proposals for valorous self-destruction: his prudence, however, and skill were equal to his boldness, and a thorough knowledge of his character would have suggested the possibility, that if left to himself with sufficient means, he would attempt and succeed in projects of daring, from the mere contemplation of which most men would shrink. Such was his proposal for carrying the war to the very shores of the English, of showing them, as he said, "that not all their boasted navy can protect their own coasts, and that the scenes of distress which they have occasioned in America, may soon be brought home to their own door." Jones had been the first who hoisted the standard of American Independence, and now was tne first to hoist the Union flag (thirteen stars, white in a blue field,) and had the honour of the first salute which the American flag ever received from a foreign power: Count D'Orvilliers, who was with the French fleet under his command at Brest when the Ranger arrived there, being the earliest to bestow it. Jones's first object was to make a descent upon Whitehaven,

Having therefore, matured his plans, he sailed from Brest on the 10th of April, 1778. The weather for some days proved unfavourable, but he continued beating about the coast, and to prevent any information of his approach sank all the craft he met. Seeing the Drake, a ship of 20 guns, at anchor in the roads near Carrickfergus, he determined to attack her in the night, but the wind, and some accident to his own vessel, prevented him.

At last, he fixed the 22nd for the descent upon Whitehaven. The term *descent* would be applied to the movement of an army upon a town, and is apt to excite the idea of large numbers and implements of war; but here the reader must exclude from his mind all these accessaries, and merely imagine a handfull of men, attempting the sudden destruction of more than two hundred ships, and a town of sixty thousand inhabitants.

The weather became so calm the night before his intended enterprize, that Jones could not bring the Ranger so near the shore as he wished; at midnight, he therefore left the ship with two boats and thirty-one volunteers. The day dawned before he reached the out pier, but this did not deter him from proceeding. He sent lieutenant Wallingford with the combustibles to the north side of the harbour, and turned his own boat to the southern. Impressed with the vastness of their undertaking, they scaled the walls, Jones at their head. They surprized and secured the sentinels, who were all shut up in the guard-house, and deliberately spiked the cannon of the first fort. This done, Jones, with but one man, spiked all the cannon of the southern fort, distant from the other a quarter of a mile. Having accomplished this, he now, with intense anxiety, looked for the expected blaze on the north side of the harbour. His suspense was the more painful, since the other party had all the combustibles; at last, fearing some accident had occurred, he pulled over to the northern side, and found the whole party in confusion, their light having burnt out the very instant when it became necessary. Nor was Jones's party able to remedy the evil, for their lights also were out: thus by a most untoward accident they were suddenly rendered powerless when they were on the point of accomplishing this most stupendous undertaking. Disappointed, perplexed, wasting time, each moment of which might bring destruction on their heads—what was to be done? Any other than the leader of this party would have been content with cursing fate, and securing a safe return to his ship. Not so Jones—his coolness and presence of mind were at all times equal to the difficulties which might interrupt the progress of his plans.

He dispatched a man to a house to beg a light, with which the
unsuspecting inmate supplied him; the light was obtained, and a
fire soon blazed in the steerage of a ship that was surrounded by
at least a hundred and fifty others, chiefly from two to four hundred
tons burthen. Day had advanced so far, that there was not time
to fire more than one; all his care, therefore, was to prevent that
from being extinguished, to effect which a barrel of tar was hunted
up and thrown upon the fire. The flames now blazed through all
the hatchways, and caught the attention of the inhabitants, who
suddenly appeared in immense numbers. Some attempted to approach, but Jones placed himself between them and the burning
ship, and with a pistol in his hand, commanded them to retire, a
command which, much to the credit of their discretion—that better
part of valour they instantly obeyed. The sun had now risen a
full hour, and it was time to retreat. Jones says in a letter, " After
all my men had embarked, I stood upon the pier for a considerable
time, yet no person advanced; I saw all the eminences around the
town covered with the enraged inhabitants. When we had rowed
to a considerable distance from the shore, the English began to
run in vast numbers to their forts. Their disappointment may be
easily imagined, when they found at least thirty cannon the instruments of their vengeance rendered useless. At length, however,
they began to fire; having, as I apprehend, either brought down
ship guns, or used one or two cannon which lay on the beach at
the foot of the walls, dismantled, and which had not been spiked.
They fired with no direction, and the shot falling short of the boats,
instead of doing any damage, afforded us some diversion, which
my people could not help showing by firing their pistols, &c. in
return of the salute. Had it been possible to have landed a few
hours sooner, my success would have been complete; not a single
ship out of more than two hundred could possibly have escaped,
and all the world would not have been able to have saved the town.
—I was pleased that in this business we neither killed nor wounded
any person; I brought off three prisoners as a sample."

The town, it appears, was indebted for its safety not to the
advance of the day, or to the alarm-fire of the burning vessel,
but to the timely warning of one of Jones's men, whose heart
sank within him at the thought of aiding in so terrible a work of
destruction. The " Cumberland Pacquet extraordinary," for
April 23rd, (the day after the attack,) states that " A little after
three o'clock this morning a man rapped at several doors in Marlborough-street, (adjoining one of the piers) and informed that fire

had been set to one of the ships in the harbour; that matches were laid in several others; that the whole would soon be in a blaze, and the town also destroyed; that he was one belonging to the crew, but had escaped for the purpose of saving, if possible, the town and shipping from destruction."

The news of the descent traversed the country with the speed of the wind: all England was struck with amazement and terror. Every measure of defence was adopted, that fear of instant invasion could suggest. Meetings were held, companies formed by subscriptions; strangers arrested; look-out vessels stationed at every port; forts everywhere repaired, and guns made ready for service. Thus but for the humanity of one of his crew, Paul Jones would have made the English feel in their own homes the dreadful evils of the war they were so eagerly carrying to the shores of another country. Wild and extravagant as the project might seem at first, to the resolute bravery of our hero its execution was easy. That their own coasts were open to attack, that a small part of a single ship's crew would attempt in a couple of open boats the destruction of a town and its whole harbour of shipping, were ideas that had not, and there is but a bare possibility that they could have, entered into the heads of our countrymen. The fact once known, however, they were all activity and watchfulness.

One principal object which Jones had at heart was to effect, by some means, the liberation, or at least to alleviate the sufferings, of the American prisoners: for this purpose, he was anxious to seize the persons, if possible, of some men of importance, and either secure an exchange or check the cruelties inflicted on the Americans. He did not, as might have been anticipated, withdraw precipitately from the neighbourhood of Whitehaven, and thus evade attempts to destroy him, which he must have expected would be the immediate consequence of a knowledge of his daring attack on that town. Trusting to his own resources for his own defence, he, with characteristic judgment, chose rather to avail himself of the interval to attempt a second exploit, scarcely inferior to the other in hardihood, and in one point of view rebounding much more to his honour, inasmuch as it evidenced that in him the rooted hostility of the warrior had not extinguished or diminished the urbanity of the gentleman.

At noon of the very morning on which he had roused the inhabitants of Whitehaven with an alarm almost as dreadful, and quite as little dreamed of, as their being rolled out of their beds by an earthquake, Jones landed with a boat's crew on St. Mary's Isle, on which was the family seat of the Earl of Selkirk, whom he intended to make prisoner, hoping thereby to effect an exchange, or at least, through the Earl's influence, to soften the rigours exercised on the American prisoners. But before he reached the house, he learned that the Earl had lately left St. Mary's for the metropolis. The accomplishment of his purpose being therefore impracticable, he was about to return as gently as he came; to which his boat's crew quickly opposed themselves, declaring that they could not see why they should not follow the example of the English, who in America spared neither life nor property: booty at least they considered their right. These men being the same who had volunteered on the perilous service of the morning, he deemed it prudent to attend to their solicitations; but to shew his disinclination for such excursions of plunder, he retired to the vessel, leaving the men under the command of the lieutenant, with a strict injunction that the most scrupulous politeness should be observed. That "there is honour amongst thieves" has long been acknowledged, when their force is sufficient to render resistance absurd, and they have no fear of interruption; that is, *if they have time*, they can plunder with the most gentlemanly politeness. So it was on this occasion; the delicacy of their captain penetrated the rough breasts of the tars, and under its influence they became sensible of the impropriety of thrusting their uncouth awkwardness into the presence of the Countess of Selkirk. They accordingly, with becoming modesty, refrained from entering the mansion, and deputed the lieutenant to convey to the Countess, with as much delicacy as possible, their moderate request, that she would favour them with the use of the *family plate*. The Countess received the officer with firmness and dignity, the request was not of a nature to be refused, and the lieutenant very shortly conveyed to the longing arms of his men the family plate of the house of Douglas.

The next day, as Paul Jones was meditating an entrance into Carrickfergus, he saw the Drake working out of the harbour, accompanied by some smaller vessels filled with persons who wished to be spectators of the destruction of the terrible Paul Jones and his crew. Jones was eager for the fight, but the tide prevented the Drake from coming within trail, which the Ranger suffered her to do, till late in the afternoon. When near enough, the English hailed, demanding what name, &c. The answer was "The American ship Ranger; we wait for you, and desire that you will come on; the sun is now little more than one hour from setting, it is therefore time to begin." The action was hot, close, and obstinate. The rigging of the Drake was cut to pieces, her masts and yards very much torn, and her hull seriously injured. The captain received a ball in his head, and died just after the boarding of his ship, and his lieutenant survived him but two days. The Drake's crew suffered the more from the number of its crew, but the Ranger's comparatively little. Jones, however, lost his lieutenant.

The consternation produced in the minds of the English by this defeat was indescribable, as it was to them inexplicable. The rapid succession of Jones's exploits: the descent on Whitehaven, the landing at St. Mary's, the capture of the Drake, overwhelmed the public mind with terror, which exhibited itself in the usual form of extravagant reports. Paul Jones was one night seen in all parts of the coast. There was a universal bustle of defensive preparations, companies of volunteers were formed, old forts repaired, and new ones erected.

Jones now released three fishermen whom he had seized, and whose craft he had sunk on the twenty-first, giving them a good boat to go on shore, and money enough to repurchase all they had lost: this generosity left Jones without a guinea in his pocket. As soon as the vessels were fit, he steered for Brest, rejoicing certainly in the extent of his success, but still convinced, that had there been more discipline among the crew, had the officers set an example of proper subordination, he might have accomplished much more. But the American navy was in its infancy, and, whether Paul Jones's courage was too reckless for them, or whether their American spirit of equality could not brook the absolute authority of a sea captain, or whether Jones was too strict a disciplinarian, we know not; but this spirit of insubordination rose to such a height, that Lieutenant Simpson, Jones's first lieutenant, whom he had appointed to the command of the Drake, chose to consider himself equal to Jones, and refused to obey his signals. On the arrival of the ships at Brest, Paul Jones put the refractory lieutenant under arrest for disobedience of orders. Here too he wrote a letter to the Countess of Selkirk, which it is but due to his memory as a man that we should give at full length.

" *Ranger, Brest, 8th May*, 1788.

" Madam,

" It cannot be too much lamented, that in the profession of arms, the officer of fine feelings and real sensibility should be under the necessity of winking at any action of persons under his command, which his heart cannot approve; but the reflection is doubly severe when he finds himself obliged, in appearance, to countenance such acts by his authority.

"This hard case was mine, when on the 23rd of April last I landed on St. Mary's Isle. Knowing Lord Selkirk's interest with the King, and esteeming as I do his private character, I wished to make him the happy instrument of alleviating the horrors of hopeless captivity, when the brave are overpowered and made prisoners of war.

"It was, perhaps, fortunate for you Madam, that he was from home; for it was my intention to have taken him on board the Ranger, and to have detained him, until, through his means, a general and fair exchange of prisoners, as well in Europe as in America, had been effected. When I was informed by some men whom I met at landing, that his lordship was absent, I walked back to my boat, determined to leave the island. By the way, however, some officers who were with me could not forbear expressing their discontent, observing that, in America, no delicacy was shown by the English, who took away all sorts of moveable property, setting fire not only to towns, and to the houses of the rich without distinction, but not even sparing the wretched hamlets and milch-cows of the poor and helpless at the approach of an inclement winter. That party had been with me the same morning at Whitehaven, some complaisance therefore was their due. I had but a moment to think how I might gratify them, and at the same time do your ladyship the least injury. I charged the two officers to permit none of the seamen to enter the house, or to hurt any thing about it; to treat you, Madam, with the utmost respect; to accept of the plate which was offered, and to come away without making a search, or demanding any thing else.

"I am induced to believe that I was punctually obeyed, since I am informed that the plate which they brought away is far short of the quantity expressed in the inventory which accompanied it. I have gratified my men; and when the plate is sold, I shall become the purchaser, and will gratify my own feelings by restoring it to you, by such conveyance as you shall please to direct.

"Had the Earl been on board the Ranger the following evening, he would have seen the awful pomp and dreadful carnage of a sea-engagement; both affording ample subject for the pencil, as well as melancholy reflection for the contemplative mind. Humanity starts back from such scenes of horror, and cannot sufficiently execrate the vile promoters of this detestable war.

> 'For they, 'twas they, unsheath'd the ruthless blade,
> And Heaven shall ask the havock it has made.'

"The British ship of war Drake, mounting twenty guns, with more than her full complement of officers and men, was our opponent. The ships met, and the advantage was disputed with great fortitude on each side, for an hour and four minutes, when the gallant commander of the Drake fell, and victory declared in favour of the Ranger. The amiable lieutenant lay mortally wounded, —a melancholy demonstration of the uncertainty of human prospects, and of the sad reverse of fortune which an hour can produce. I buried them in a spacious grave, with the honours due to the memory of the brave.

"Though I have drawn my sword in the present generous struggle for the rights of men, yet I am not in arms as an American, nor am I in pursuit of riches. My fortune is liberal enough, having no wife or family, and having lived long enough to know that riches cannot ensure happiness. I profess myself a citizen of the world, totally unfettered by the little mean distinctions of climate or of country, which diminish the benevolence of the heart and set bounds to philanthropy. Before this war began, I had at the early time of life withdrawn from the sea service, in favour of 'calm contemplation and poetic ease.' I have sacrificed not only my favourite scheme of life, but the softer affections of my heart, and my prospects of domestic happiness, and I am ready to sacrifice my life also with cheerfulness, if that forfeiture could restore peace and good-will among mankind.

"As the feelings of your gentle bosom cannot but be congenial with mine, let me entreat you, Madam, to use your persuasive art with your husband, to endeavour to stop this cruel and destructive war, in which Britain can never succeed. Heaven can never countenance the barbarous and unmanly practice of the Britons in America, which savages would blush at, and which, if not discontinued, will soon be retaliated on Britain by a justly enraged people. Should you fail in this, (for I am persuaded that you will undertake it: and who can resist the power of such an advocate?) your endeavours to effect a general exchange of prisoners will be an act of humanity, which will afford you golden feelings on a death-bed

"I hope this cruel contest will soon be closed; but should it continue, I wage no war with the fair. I acknowledge their force, and bend before it with submission. Let not, therefore, the amiable Countess of Selkirk regard me as an enemy; I am ambitious of her esteem and friendship, and would do any thing, consistent with my duty, to merit it.

"The honour of a line from your hand, in answer to this, will lay me under a singular obligation; and if I can render you any acceptable service in France or elsewhere, I hope you see into my character so far as to command me without the least grain of reserve.

"I wish to know exactly the behaviour of my people, as I am determined to punish them if they have exceeded their liberty. I have the honour to be, with much esteem and with profound respect, Madam, &c. &c.

"JOHN PAUL JONES."
"To the Countess of Selkirk."

This gallant epistle received no reply for some months, when Lord Selkirk wrote to say, that if the plate was restored by the order of Congress, or of some public body, he would accept it, and endeavour to make suitable returns for the favour; but if its restitution were to be an act of private generosity, he could by no means accept it. Accordingly, in March 1780, Jones addressed another letter to the Countess, stating, that Congress had given order for the restoration of the plate to its owners, and informing her in whose hands it then lay, waiting her directions for its removal.

Such was Paul Jones's style of warfare; but though his splendid achievements obtained for him unbounded applause, both in America and France, he was exposed to much difficulty and annoyance from not receiving timely and sufficient supplies of money. At one time, very shortly after his feats in the Channel, he was thrown entirely upon his own resources, for the support and clothing of his crew, the maintenance of two hundred prisoners of war, the healing of the sick and wounded, and the refitting of his shattered vessel. Of this he complained bitterly, not so much on his own private account, but because of the discredit it necessarily brought on the cause in which he was engaged, for his limited means could not be kept secret. He suffered much also from the jealousy of the officers of the French navy, who harboured a rancorous envy of his superiority, without any desire to emulate it. He remained for some time in compulsory inactivity, having been refused even the favor of accompanying Count d'Orvilliers as a volunteer, which he was desirous of doing, for the sake of increasing his nautical knowledge and experience. At last, finding all other efforts ineffectual, he addressed a long letter to the King of France, in consequence of which it was determined to appoint Jones to the command of the Duras, forty guns, with unlimited orders. In compliment to Dr. Franklin, he obtained permission to alter the name from Duras to Bon Homme Richard, referring to " Poor Richard's Almanack" published by Dr. Franklin. To the Bon Homme Richard were added the Alliance, thirty-six guns; Pallas, thirty guns; Cerf, eighteen guns; and the Vengeance, twelve guns, and Jones was made Commodore of the squadron. Le Fayette was to accompany him with seven hundred military; but he was retained to assist in the operations of a projected general invasion of England! The squadron, therefore, sailed without him, on the 19th of April 1779. Nothing of importance occurred during the first three months of the cruise, except that the Alliance, Captain Landais, ran foul of the Bon Homme Richard one night in a very suspicious manner. This Captain Landais was a captious, ill-tempered, narrow-minded, envious man, who looked with no friendly eyes on Paul Jones, did all he could to show that he considered himself independent of the Commodore, paid no attention to signals, disobeyed orders, and ultimately parted company. Jones subsequently took two prizes from the Firth of Edinburgh, from which he learned that a king's ship and two or three cutters were lying at anchor in Leith Road, " in a state of indolent security." He intended to surprise them, but was prevented in part by the hesitation of the French officers of the Pallas and Vengeance, and partly by a storm: in short, the squadron, to the bitter mortification of Jones, was very near returning, though not empty-handed, yet without acquiring any new glory: but early on the morning of the 22nd of September, Jones perceived a fleet steering towards him: it, soon, however, retreated, on which he made signal for a pilot. The pilot imagining the Bon Homme to be an English ship, communicated all the information Jones wanted, telling even their private signal. Jones then endeavoured to decoy the ships out of port by the use of the signal, but as the tide was adverse, they declined moving. The entrance to the Humber is exceedingly dangerous, and the Pallas not being in sight, Jones stood off to Flamborough-head, where he expected to meet the Pallas. In the course of the night he chased two vessels, and about three in the morning, being close upon them, he made the private American signal: not receiving any answer, he continued the chase, and at daybreak discovered they were the

Alliance and Pallas. Insulting as this conduct was, and often as it was repeated on the part of Landais, Jones uniformly maintained a dignified moderation, which compels us to recognise in him a rare and noble magnanimity of soul.

On the morning of the 23rd, a fleet of forty-one sail appeared off Flamborough head, and Jones hoisted the signal for a general chase. The merchantmen, observing the American squadron bearing down upon them, made directly for the shore; the two convoys steered for the open sea, and prepared for battle. These two were the Serapis, and the Countess of Scarborough. The Alliance paid no attention to the signals from the Bon Homme, and Jones could not come up with the Serapis till seven in the evening, when commenced one of the fiercest naval engagements which history has recorded. The Serapis was a new ship, of forty-four guns; her crew picked men; and her commander Captain Richard Pearson, celebrated for skill and courage. Except as regarded her captain, the Bon Homme was in all respects the very contrary of the Serapis. The vessel was old, the timbers unsound, some of the guns worn out, and the crew a heterogeneous medley of six nations:—Americans, French, English, Maltese, Portuguese, and Malays. Add to which, the Bon Homme had not her full complement of men, two boats' crews having been lost on the coast of Ireland, and a third boat's crew Jones had sent away to seize a brigantine. The decided superiority of the Serapis over the Bon Homme was evident to all on board the latter. Jones felt that every thing depended on himself, and wonderfully did he approve himself equal to the task.

The action commenced, the two vessels being abreast of each other, and the broadsides were almost simultaneous; but their nearness to each other prevented the Serapis from manœuvring to advantage, and in a short time the Bon Homme ran her bows into the stern of the Serapis. Captain Pearson, aware of the vast inferiority of the Bon Homme, deemed this the consequence of her crew's inability to work her, and demanded if she had struck. Jones himself replied that " he had not yet begun to fight." His vessel, however, was already much galled by the broadsides of the Serapis, and was pierced in several places under water. The water was fast rushing in, and she was in manifest danger of sinking. All this time, though the need of support must have been evident, the Bon Homme received no aid from the rest of the squadron; the Pallas was engaged with the Countess of Scarborough, and the other two, the Vengeance and the Alliance, kept aloof, as if in the hope that Paul Jones might be beaten. The Serapis was much more manageable than Jones's ship; but in attempting to separate from the Bon Homme, her bowsprit ran in over the Bon Homme poop by the mizen-mast. Jones instantly grappled, the action of the wind brought her stern round to the Bon Homme's bows; by this means the ships lay close alongside of each other, their guns touching, and their yards entangled. This was a bold way of saving a sinking ship, and preventing the effect of eighteen pounders under water.

The battle, to use Jones's own words, was fought with unremitting fury. The rammers were run into the respective ships to enable the men to load. The Serapis now fought with the actual view of sinking the enemy, and her broadsides were incessant. But for the two ships being lashed together the Bon Homme must have struck or sunk, or both. The battery of twelve pounders, on which Jones had placed his chief dependance, which was commanded by his only lieutenant, and manned by Americans, was entirely silenced and abandoned. Most of the six old eighteen-pounders that formed the battery of the lower gun-deck, burst, and killed nearly all the men who worked them. At the same time, Colonel Chamillard, who commanded a party of twenty French volunteers on the poop, abandoned his station, having lost nearly all his band. There were only two nine-pounders on the quarter-deck that were not silenced. The purser who commanded the party that worked these guns was shot through the head; and Jones was compelled to fill his place, though his presence was needed in every part of the ship. With great difficulty he rallied a few men, and shifted over one of the lee-quarter-deck guns; these three nine-pounders played well, but not one of the heavier cannon of the Bon Homme was fired during the rest of the action. Notwithstanding this, and the certainty that sooner or later the Bon Homme must sink, Paul Jones fought as if assured of victory, and apparently quite insensible to the superior force of his enemy; and the increasing peril of his situation served only to augment the fury of his attack. One of the three guns above mentioned he kept in constant play upon the mainmast of the Serapis; with the other two he endeavoured to clear her decks, which he effectually accomplished, for in a very short time not a man was to be seen above board. Jones's topmen kept up so well aimed a fire, that if any of the enemy ventured on deck, it was at the expense of his life. Captain Pearson therefore ordered all that remained to keep below; but a disaster rendered them as insecure here as above; their powder monkeys, finding no one to receive the eighteen-pound cartridges, threw them down, and returned for more: some hand-grenades from the Bon Homme set fire to these, and the explosion caused the death of several of the English. Captain Pearson afterwards acknowledged that at this period he felt that to continue the fight would be but uselessly sacrificing the lives of his men, and was about to surrender, when some of Jones's valiant officers, believing, in like manner, there was no hope for them, cried for "quarter!" Delighted at the prospect of saving his own honour, Pearson himself enquired of Jones, if he meant to surrender. "No!" thundered Jones, and the action recommenced with twofold fury. But though Jones managed to keep the decks of the Serapis clear, his ship suffered dreadfully from her lower battery of eighteen-pounders, and he was more than once compelled (for the ship was on fire in many places,) to draw his men from the fight to check the flames, and keep the fire from the magazine. In fact, both vessels were on fire! but the Bon Homme was in by far the more imminent danger, for her hold was filling with water. The moment was fast approaching, in which the Bon Homme Richard must sink, and Jones was in the very rage of despair, when the Alliance drew near. He breathed again —now victory was sure—was his; but, to his utter astonishment and dismay, the treacherous Landais poured a broadside full into the Bon Homme's stern. The crew cried aloud "For God's sake, don't fire into the Bon Homme Richard!" but he continued his firing, and passed onwards. He could not by any possibility mistake the ships, for not only were their construction and appearance different, but the sides of the Serapis were yellow, and those of the Bon Homme black. Signals even had no effect, but she worked round and sent her shot into the Bon Homme's side and head, killed several men, and wounded a valuable officer. "My situation,' says Jones, "was now really deplorable." The Alliance now sheered off, but not without giving the Bon Homme several shots under water. The pumps were of no avail to keep the water under, and some of Jones's bravest officers advised him to strike. Whilst he was delaying a reply to his officer, his master-at-arms set free all the prisoners, to the number of nearly five hundred, telling them to save themselves, as the ship was sinking. But notwithstanding all this, notwithstanding that the rudder was off, the stern-frame and transoms almost wholly cut away, the timbers everywhere torn to pieces, and the vessel itself actually filling with water, Jones would not yield. He saw the mainmast of the Serapis shake, and his attentive ear discerned that the enemy's firing decreased;

whereupon he instantly increased that of the Bon Homme, and at half-past ten, in the sight of thousands, the flag of England, which had been nailed to the mast of the Serapis, was struck by Captain Pearson's own hand. Her mainmast at the same time went overboard; nor was there time to do more than remove the wounded before the Bon Homme sank! The Countess of Scarborough had already struck to the Pallas.

The glory of this victory must be conceded entirely to Paul Jones; but for the exercise of his authority as captain, the Bon Homme had long before struck. The result was wholly owing to his determined and cool intrepidity. The effect on the public mind in France and England exhibited itself in the two extremes of rapture and mortification. These fast succeeding and irresistible irruptions of the American captain spread terror through every part of England, especially on the coasts, and, as is usual when such excitement prevails, every occurrence not expected, or not at once understood, was magnified into a cause of immediate alarm: every sea-port, every town on or near the coast, tremblingly expected to be the object of Paul Jones's next attack; every strange sail in the offing was looked upon as the van of an everwhelming fleet, then bearing down upon that coast; in fact, the whole vocabulary of terror-inspiring words was condensed into two short monosyllables—Paul Jones! Man, woman and child turned pale at the very sound of his name.

In the mean time, the attention of this redoubted captain was engrossed by the disabled remainder of the two crews now his prisoners; nor was the remnant of his own or the crew of the Pallas in a better condition. Contrary winds drove him into the Texel, a Dutch island with a good harbour, the usual station of the Dutch navy, where Jones obtained permission from the States-General to establish a hospital. The English immediately, through their ambassador, claimed from their High Mightinesses the restitution of the English ships, and the delivery into their hands " of a certain Paul Jones, a subject of the king, who, according to treaties and the laws of war, could only be considered as a rebel and a pirate." For some time the States-General refused to interfere, but at length, in December, they sent Jones an order to depart from the Texel, which the English looked upon as an equivalent to their first demand; for they had surrounded the " rebel" with so close a blockade, that his escape appeared impossible. This, however, he effected, and so little apprehensive was he of danger, or so confident in his own resources, that, as it would seem, he was employed at the time in inditing some complimentary stanzas to a lady who had favoured him in a similar way whilst at the Texel, and they were sent to her immediately after escaping out of the Texel from the blockade of the British fleet.

During the course of Paul Jones's stay at the Texel, he addressed the following

Letters to the Dutch Admiral Baron, Vandér Capellen.

ON BOARD THE SERAPIS AT THE TEXEL,
Ocт. 19, 1779.

" My Lord,— Human nature, and America, are under very singular obligations to you for your patriotism and friendship; and I feel every grateful sentiment for your generous and polite letter.

" Agreeable to your request, I have the honour to enclose a copy of my letter to his excellency Dr. Franklin containing a particular account of my late expedition on the coast of Britain and Ireland; by which you will see that I have already been praised more than I deserved. But I must, at the same time, beg leave to observe, that, by the other papers which I take the liberty to enclose, (particularly my letter to the Countess of Selkirk, dated the day of my arrival at Brest from the Irish sea) I hope you will be convinced that in the British prints I have been censured unjustly. I was indeed born in Britain, but I do not inherit the degenerate spirit of that fallen nation, which I at once lament and despise. It is far beneath me to reply to their hireling invectives; they are strangers to the inward approbation that greatly animates and rewards the man who draws his sword only in support of the dignity of freedom.

" America has been the country of my fond selection from the age of thirteen, when I first saw it. I had the honour to hoist, with my own hands, the flag of freedom the first time it was displayed on the Delaware; and I have attended it with veneration ever since on the ocean. I see it respected even here in spite of the pitiful Sir Joseph, (York) and I ardently wish and hope very soon to exchange a salute with the flag of this republic. Let but the two republics join hands and they will give peace to the world.

" Highly ambitious to render myself worthy of your friendship, I have the honour to be, my Lord, your very obliged and most humble servant.

- (Signed,) PAUL JONES

ON BOARD THE ALLIANCE AT THE TEXEL,
Nov. 29, 1779.

"My Lord,—Since I had the honour to receive your second esteemed letter, I have unexpectedly had occasion to revisit Amsterdam; and having changed ships since my return to the Texel, I have, by some accident or neglect, lost or mislaid your letter. I remember, however, the questions it contained, viz., 1st. Whether I ever had any obligation to Lord Selkirk? 2nd. Whether he accepted my offer? 3rd. Whether I have a French commission? I answer, I never had any obligation to Lord Selkirk, except for his good opinion; nor does he know me or mine, except by character. Lord Selkirk wrote me an answer to my letter to the Countess, but the ministry detained it in the general post-office in London for a long time, and then returned it to the author, who afterwards wrote to a friend of his, (Mr. Alexander) an acquaintance of Dr. Franklin's, then at Paris, giving him an account of the fate of his letters to me, and desiring him to acquaint his Excellency and myself, that, "if the plate was restored by Congress or any public body, he would accept it, but that he could not think of accepting it from my private generosity." The plate has, however, been bought, agreeable to my letter to the Countess, and now lays in France at her disposal. As to the third article, I never bore, nor acted under any other commission than what I have received from the Congress of the United States of America.

"I am much obliged to you, my Lord, for the honour you do me by proposing to publish the papers I sent you in my last; but it is an honour which I must decline, because I cannot publish my letter to that lady without asking and obtaining the lady's consent, and because I have a very modest opinion of my writings, being conscious that they are not of sufficient value to claim the notice of the public. I assure you, my Lord, it has given me much concern to see an extract of my rough journal in print, and that too, under the disadvantage of a translation. That mistaken kindness of a friend will make me cautious how I communicate my papers. I have the honour to be, my Lord, with great esteem and respect, &c. &c. (Signed,) PAUL JONES.

One of the chief points which the English ambassador had urged upon the Dutch government was the asserted non-possession by Jones and his squadron of proper commissions. To recognize the commission of Congress would have implied a recognition of the independence of the United States in America; and Holland wished to maintain her neutrality, or rather, was not prepared to declare open hostility to England. To avoid this difficulty, therefore, the King of France, who had supplied the vessels and furnished the means of the cruise, sent an order to Jones to deliver up to the French ambassador all his prisoners, with the Serapis and the Countess of Scarborough, for with the exception of the Alliance, the remainder of the squadron was the property of his most Christian Majesty, and the French ambassador had in consequence the right to dispose of them. They had, accordingly, to the great annoyance of the English government, quitted the Texel, under the convoy of the Dutch fleet. Disappointed in the recovery of their ships, they determined to be revenged on Paul Jones, who of course did not accompany the squadron, but, as has been seen, escaped them. The Bon Homme having sunk, and Landais, on account of his misconduct, having been deposed from his command, our hero was appointed to the Alliance, which, as Paul Jones's vessel, and consequently in the service of Congress, the Dutch government could not openly protect; it was therefore left to its fate, which proved happier than had been anticipated.

The good fortune of Paul Jones did not, however, protect him from the common fate of mankind. The glory he had acquired was supereminent, and his fame was deservedly wide spread; but envy, jealousy, and malicious detraction, compelled him more than once to demonstrate the integrity of his motives, and defend the justness of his actions. To compensate for these mortifications, he was, while at Paris, overwhelmed with applause and distinctions, courted by the great, admired by the fair, and honoured by the particular favour of the King, every painful emotion was quickly dispelled, and he soon showed himself as great an admirer of the rumbling of carriages, as of the roar of musketry, quite as delighted with the glances of killing eyes as with the flashes of slaughtering eighteen-pounders, and much more willing to surrender his heart to the first ruby lips that demanded it, than yield, in his frigate, to the largest three-decker that ever sailed on the ocean. Indeed he proved himself as ardent a worshipper of Venus as ever he had been of the God of war; and so singularly zealous was he in his new service, that he at last found himself in the ecstatic condition, at the same time rather awkward predicament, of being in love with every woman in Paris. But Jones's love was by no means of a common kind; he possessed a deep-rooted, ineradicable admiration for the whole sex, and manifested the sentiment to each individual.

But to render complete the satisfaction he must have derived from the gratulations he received on all hands, Louis testified his warm admiration of his bravery and skill by presenting him with a most splendid sword, inscribed with these words,

" Vindicati Maris
Ludovicus XVI. Remunerator
Strenuo Vindici."

In addition to which was conferred on him the cross of military merit, an honour never before bestowed on one who had not actually served in the army or navy of the kingdom.

To return to the ladies; it must not be supposed Jones's heart issued such prodigious streams of love without exciting reciprocity, and of equal intensity. One lady was so strenuous an admirer of him, and sympathised so completely with all his feelings, was so quick to perceive, and so ready to relieve him in all his perplexities, that when she heard that his crew were kept out of their prize-money, she offered her diamonds and effects of all kinds to be converted into money, that he might be delivered from so galling a mortification. She would sit before his portrait for hours, bathed in tears, possibly for lack of the original; and when he departed for America, rather than not be near him, " she would willingly be the lowest of his crew!" Another, skilled in the art of painting, could find no subject so suited to her taste as the countenance of Paul Jones. This lady was a countess, a married flirt; and Commodore Jones, in genuine sincerity and pure simplicity of heart, in order to lessen the pains of absence, wrote, when he sailed for America, to the Countess, told her he was deeply afflicted by having cause to fear that she was less happy than he wished her to be, than he was sure she deserved to be, and, as the most soothing consolation he could offer, enclosed a cipher for a key to their future correspondence, so that she would be able to write to him " very freely and without risk." Moreover, he sent her a lock of his hair, shorter, unfortunately, by eighteen inches, than three months back, and would have sent, " *if he could*," his " *heart itself.*"

Now when Jones was in Paris he was, as may be supposed, the lion of the day, and it was the fashion to admire nothing else, to talk of nothing else: the Countess was a lady of fashion, therefore she very much admired Paul Jones; the Countess was also a flirt, therefore she laid siege to Jones's heart; the Count, too, was in the provinces, therefore she had a good opportunity of gratifying her ambition to see this mighty man-of-war subdued by the powers

of her charms. But fashions change, and flirts change, and the
Countess changed: in fact she was "astonished at his audacity,"
supposed "that his packet was misdirected," and begged to introduce to him the Count her husband: he was passing through
L'Orient, and she should "be obliged to Jones to pay him every
civility." Jones returned a most dexterous reply, and completely
extricated himself from the dilemma, declaring the cipher to have
been intended for political purposes, to prevent his communications
from being understood, should they fall into the enemy's hands,
expressing his desire to become acquainted and associated with
the Count, and, by stating that he had supposed her philosopher
enough to understand that friendship was nothing to do with sex,
threw all the blame on the Countess for misinterpreting his innocent words.

Paul Jones returned to America, with a powerful commendatory
letter from the French Minister to the American President. His
passage, however, was not made in the Alliance, to which he had
been appointed, but in the Ariel, which was to accompany the
Alliance. For Landais, who, though a Frenchman, was an
American subject, and had received his commission from Congress,
had with consummate impudence, entered the Alliance before Jones
had embarked, and persuaded the men that Jones had been the
chief cause of the detention both of their pay and prize-money,
(which was utterly false,) and that as his command had not been
taken from him by the power from which he received it, he was
still their proper captain, and in that capacity expected from them
implicit obedience. It is some satisfaction to the mind goaded by
disappointment, to be aware of the source to which it may be attributed. This pleasure, derived from ascertaining the cause of
their sufferings, led the men to give credence to Landais statement;
and even that part of the crew which formerly belonged to the Bon
Homme, suddenly admitted suspicions of Jones quite inconsistent
with their experience of his character. Landais was hailed as
their captain, and at his command the vessel immediately worked
out of port, and sailed for America, where, in order to invest the
just charges which Jones might prefer against him with the appearance of mere recriminations, he made allegations respecting
Jones, in consequence of which our hero was, as soon as he arrived,
presented with an order from Congress to answer forty-seven interrogatories, relating to occurrences in Europe.

Jones delivered the French Minister's letter, and had the gratification of seeing the two following resolutions passed, without waiting for his reply to the interrogatories.

"*In Congress, February,* 1781.

"Resolved, That the Congress entertain a high sense of the distinguished bravery and military conduct of John Paul Jones, Esq, Captain in the Navy of the United States, and particularly in his victory over the British ship Serapis, on the coast of England, which was attended with circumstances so brilliant as to excite general applause and approbation.

"Resolved, That the Minister Plenipotentiary of the United States of the Court of Versailles, communicate to His Most Christian Majesty the high satisfaction Congress have received from the conduct and gallant behaviour of Captain Paul Jones having merited the attention and approbation of His Most Christian Majesty, and that His Majesty's offer of investing Captain Jones with a Cross of Military Merit is highly acceptable to Congress."

Jones was very shortly after unanimously elected by Congress to the command of their first seventy-four, the America, then building in the dock-yard of the United States. But this command he never enjoyed, for the Magnifique, a seventy-four, of the French fleet, was lost during the Autumn of 1782, in the harbour of Boston, and Congress, being desirous of testifying to the French King the sense they entertained " of his generous exertions in behalf of the United States," presented him with the America, then just off the stocks. The acknowledgment by England of the American Independence took place before any suitable employment could be found for Jones; but in 1783 he revisited France, in the capacity of Agent of America for European prize-money. In the accomplishment of his diplomatic purposes he was unremitting in exertion, ingenious in the selection of means, and especially skilful in their use.

The ardour of Paul Jones's desire for the eminence of the Americans as a nation, excited his fertile mind to constant activity, and his attention was ever directed to the improvements possible to be effected. So many and of so great importance were the services which his intellect, superadded to those already conferred by his intrepid valour, had achieved, that in 1787, the American Minister in France was ordered by Congress to have a gold medal, with proper divices, struck and presented to Jones, "in commemoration of his valour and brilliant services." A letter was prepared to recommend to the continued favour of His Most Christian Majesty, and another to Jones himself, declaratory of the esteem and honour in which he was held by the nation.

In March 1788, he went to Denmark, to settle a question respecting some prize-money claimed by America. His fame secured him " a very polite and distinguished reception" by the Royal Family and all the court. His health, however, was in a declining state, and he suffered much from fatigue and excessive cold on the road, so that he was obliged to keep his bed for several days, and was not inapprehensive of danger. Unfortunately, it was found that his want of plenipotentiary powers from Congress was a " natural and invincible obstacle" to the business being discussed definitively with him, so that his was not compassed; but he had the happiness to be the means, though at his own expense, and, as he writes, even at the peril of his life—for his constitution was materially injured by the journey—of renewing the negociations between that country and the United States. Whilst at Copenhagen, he received an invitation to Petersburgh from the Empress Catherine, who offered him, if he would enter her service, the rank of Rear-Admiral. Jones accepted the invitation, but assured Mr. Jefferson that he had not " forsaken a country that had had many disinterested and difficult proofs" of his steady affection: and that he could never renounce the glorious title of a " citizen of the United States."

His journey to St. Petersburgh was quite in accordance with the rest of his life, and very much unlike what any one else would have done. He passed through Sweden; the season was too far advanced to permit his return to Paris; the distance would have been too long through Germany, and the English had thrown difficulties in the way of his passage by the Baltic; the Gulf of Bothnia he found barred with ice, and after making several fruitless attempts to cross it in an open boat, about thirty feet long, he compelled the Swedish peasants to steer for the Gulf of Finland. After about four or five hundred miles navigation he landed at Revel, and having paid the men to their satisfaction, he provided them with a good pilot and provisions, and sent them home again. This voyage was looked upon as a kind of miracle, for it had never been attempted before, except in large vessels. His reception, to use his own words, was the most flattering that perhaps any stranger could boast of on entering the Russian service. Her Majesty immediately conferred on him the grade of Rear-admiral. After a fortnight's continued feasting at the court, and in the first society, he was appointed to the command of a division of the fleet serving against the Turks in the Leman sea. The cause of his being assigned this station, was the refusal of the English officers, then in the Empress's service, to act under the command of an enemy of their country. Catherine was adminished by some of her cabinet of the impolicy of offending, for one individual, so large a number of valuable officers; but the Empress was too well acquainted with Jones's value to be persuaded to recall her invitation, and to obviate the difficulty, she assigned to Jones the abovenamed command, and distributed the English officers in the Croustadt fleet under Admiral Greig.

Jones, by timely interference, saved from destruction a flotilla under Prince Nassau, the Admiral, for which he received the Cross of St. Anne; and afterwards when his division was attacked by the Turkish fleet, gained a complete victory, in consequence of the enemy's ships running aground. The royal Admiral, however, before many of the Turkish vessels could be taken possession of, instead of seizing the prizes, to the utter astonishment of Jones, burnt them; nor was his state of astonishment at all diminished, when reading the report of the engagement in the Imperial Gazette, he saw it described as a brilliant victory gained by the Russian fleet under Prince Nassau. He forthwith despatched a violent letter on the subject, which was answered by an order to repair to Petersburgh, and an appointment to the command of the Northern fleet, an office which is the Chiltern Hundreds of the Russian service. Nevertheless, Jones remained for a long time at Petersburgh, in much esteem at Court. But at last the intrigues of the partisans of England drove him form St. Petersburgh in disgust, and the calumnious reports circulated by his enemies, constrained his friend Count de Segur to insert the following check to slander all the public prints, and particularly in the Gazette of France.

" St. Petersburgh, 21st July, 1789.—The Vice Admiral Paul Jones being on the point of returning to France, where private affairs required his presence, had the honour to take leave of the Empress the 7th of this month, and to be admitted to kiss the hand of her Imperial Majesty,* who confided to him the command of her vessels of war stationed on the Leman, during the campaign of 1788. As a mark of favour for his conduct during

---

* This general officer, so celebrated by his brilliant actions during the course of the American war, was called, in 1787, to the service of her Imperial Majesty.

this campaign, the Empress has decorated him with the insignia of the order of St. Anne; and her Imperial Majesty, satisfied with his services, only grants him permission to absent himself for a limited time, and still preserves for him his emoluments and his rank"

" The COUNT DE SEGUR."

The disgust with which Admiral Jones quitted the Russian service did not operate as an obstacle to his petitioning subsequently for renewed employment. He wrote from Paris in July, 1790, to Prince Potemkin, a long letter setting forth his abilities, his services, his honours, and his wishes; but the situation of Russia at that time not requiring the aid of extraordinary naval talent, no answer was vouchsafed to the epistle. Some months after he wrote to the Empress herself, with similar effect. The injuries he received in Russia affected him deeply, and the neglect which was shown to his letter added to the keenness with which they were felt. Some compensation, however, was afforded him by the unexpected liberality of the King of Denmark, who had spontaneously assigned him an annuity of 1500 crowns, Danish currency, to be paid at Copenhagen, without any retention whatever.

Sickness now began to make serious inroads on Jones's constitution, and the greater part of 1791, was passed at Paris in extreme ill health. Thus he lingered till the beginning of June, 1792, when he breathed his last, in the forty sixth year of his age. The National Assembly honoured him by going into mourning on the occasion, and a deputation of that body accompanied his corpse to the grave.

Paul Jones was of a middle or rather inclining to a short stature, slenderly formed,—with a stern countenance and a swarthy complexion. His manner was authoritative and his air determined.

In reviewing the career of this extraordinary man, we cannot but acknowledge, however much it has hitherto been deemed patriotic to denounce him to the English people, that Paul was in no other sense a pirate than Washington was a traitor. He fought zealously for his adopted country—always acted under commission from the American Republic, and was to all intents and purposes, after the independence of that country had been declared, a citizen of the United States.

We stop not to enquire the motives. for we cannot know them, of his hostility to his own country. One thing is certain, that he could never give such an explanation of his conduct in that particular as would exempt him from the stigma attached to such a charge. The probable solution is, that being unemployed in England—descrying a fair field for his talents in America, and, perhaps, indignant at the oppression exercised by Great Britain, he, in the spirit of an adventurer, engaged his surpassing abilities in the service of the then reputed weaker party.

It has indeed been surmised, that the unworthy conduct of certain individuals with whom he had been connected before he crossed the Atlantic, excited or influenced the enmity he bore to the whole country; but that such feeling should have been generated by such means is an imputation upon his sagacity, good sense, and even good taste, which the whole tenor of his life leads us altogether to reject.

Upon the whole, when we consider that Paul Jones, without even the advantages which the majority of people in his original station of life enjoy—without friends, and, consequently, utterly destitute of influence, became, by his own unassisted exertions, a respectable scholar—at least a perfect master of his own language, which he wrote with great elegance and purity—that he obtained the friendship of the greatest men of his time in America—and that he raised himself to the station of Commander in Chief of the Squadrons of the United States—it cannot be doubted or denied that he was a man of vigorous understanding, of dignified and urbane manners, and of the most consummate skill and judgment as a Naval Commander.

Let us not, under the paltry pretext of patriotism, withhold from a great man that meed of fame which his actions, in whatever light we view them—so it be a *light*—are calculated to extort from us. Let Englishmen, at least, not be slow to render that praise which can always be well spared, and never justly retained. It is no disgrace to England, if it be not indeed her glory, that Paul Jones was one of her own sons.

Some years ago, a large bundle of letters were brought to light in a baker's shop in New York, which proved to be the private correspondence of the celebrated Paul Jones. When he left America for the last time, he committed to the care of his friend, Ross, of Philadelphia, several packages of manuscript papers, consisting of letters, journals, and vouchers of his landed and other property in America. A power of attorney was afterwards sent to Mr. Robert Hyslop, merchant of New York, to receive these packages in trust, for the heirs of Paul Jones. An agent came to this country, and settled the pecuniary affairs; but the papers, on being examined, were allowed to remain in the hands of Mr. Hyslop, in trust, as undivided property, belonging equally to all the heirs of Paul Jones. At length Robert Hyslop died, and the papers then fell into the hands of his executor, John Hyslop, baker, in New York. This is a brief explanation of the somewhat singular circumstance, of papers of this sort having been discovered in a baker's shop. They were valuable, as containing the correspondence of some of the most eminent leaders of the revolution.

Another remark we may add respecting the papers of Paul Jones. By his will he left all his effects to his two sisters, who resided at or near Dumfries, in Scotland, to be divided equally between them and their children, in as many shares as there were individuals in the two families, constituting his two sisters guardians of their respective children during their minority. In 1793, one of the sisters and the husband of the other went to Paris, to recover a debt from the French government to Paul Jones, and took with them to Scotland, among other things, all the papers left by him. A division of the effects and papers was immediately made by a gentleman appointed for the purpose, with a mutual consent of the parties, who bound themselves to abide by his decision; and this gentleman pursued an extraordinary course in regard to the papers. He portioned them out in two parcels, by weight and measure, just as they happened to come in hand, without regard to their value or connexion. The two families resided for some time in Scotland; and when Mr. Duncan prepared the short biographical sketch of Paul Jones, for the Edinburgh Encyclopedia, he appears to have access to all the papers. Since that time a branch of one of the families had removed to America, and brought hither a part of the papers; all, it is presumed, which this branch had in its possession.

A few years ago a niece of Paul Jones, who inherited from her mother the portion of papers that fell to her lot, made an overture to the Historical Society of New York to publish them. The negotiation was not successful; but the manuscripts were sent out to New York for inspection, where they now remain in the hands of an individual in trust for the owner. They are fair copies, collected into four volumes, the three first of which relate chiefly to the part the author took in the American Revolution. The last volume is written in French, and is devoted wholly to his services in Russia. The contents of all his volumes are chiefly letters and official papers, some of which had been published. To the first volume is prefixed a memoir of his life, but by what hand we know not. There is also a short narrative of the transaction in which he was engaged during the American war, but the substance of this is nearly the same as that which he presented to the King of France. It is a mistake however, which some way or other crept into the Edinburgh Encyclopedia, that Paul Jones has left any thing which can be properly called a memoir of his own life by himself. What is to be the destiny of these papers we are not informed, but they are obviously essential to any correct delineation of the life and character of Paul Jones.

MAJOR STEDE BONNET.

Major Bonnet was a gentleman of good reputation in the island of Barbadoes, where he was master of a plentiful fortune, having, besides, the advantage of a liberal education. He had the least temptation of any man to follow such a course of life from the condition of his circumstances; and therefore it was very surprising to every one in the island where he lived, when they heard of his enterprises. As he was generally esteemed and honoured before he broke out into open acts of piracy, so he was afterwards rather pitied than condemned by those that were acquainted with him, who believed that his humour of going a pirating proceeded from a disorder in his mind, which had been but too visible in him some time before this wicked undertaking; and which is said to have been occasioned by some discomforts he met with in a married state. But, be that as it will, the major was ill qualified for the business; for he did not understand maritime affairs.

When he was resolved in his wicked purpose, he fitted out a sloop, with ten guns and seventy men, entirely at his own expense; and in the night-time sailed from Barbadoes. He called this sloop the Revenge, and his first cruise in her was off the Capes of Virginia; where he took several ships, and plundered them of their provisions, clothes, money, ammunition, &c., in particular the Anne, Captain Montgomery, from Glasgow; the Turbet from Barbadoes; which latter for the country's sake, after they had taken out the principal part of the lading, the pirate crew set her on fire. They took also, the Endeavour, Captain Scott, from Bristol, and then Young, from Leith. From hence they went to New York, and off the east-end of Long Island they took a sloop bound for the West Indies; after which they stood in and landed some men at Gardener's Island, but in a peaceful manner; for they bought provisions for the company's use, which they paid justly for, and so went off again without molestation.

Some time after, in the month of August, 1717, Bonnet came off the bar of South Carolina, and took a sloop and a brigantine, inward-bound; the sloop belonged to Barbadoes, Joseph Palmer, master, and was laden with rum, sugar, and negroes; the brigantine came from New England, Thomas Porter, master; her they plundered, and then dismissed. But they sailed away with the sloop, and at an inlet in North Carolina, where, careened by them, they set her on fire.

After the sloop had cleaned, they put to sea, but came to no resolution what course to take, for the crew were divided in their opinions, some being for one thing, and some for another; so that nothing but confusion seemed to attend all their schemes.

The Major was no sailor, as was said before; and therefore, was often obliged to yield to many things that were imposed on him, during their undertaking, for want of a competent knowledge in maritime affairs, till at length he happened to fall in company with Edward Teach, commonly called Black-beard, as we observed in his life. This fellow was a good sailor, but a most cruel hardened villain, bold and daring to the last degree, and would not stick at perpetrating the most abominable wickedness imaginable; for which he was made chief of that execrable gang. It might be said, that this post was not unduly filled, Black-beard being truly the superior in roguery of all the company, as has been related in his life.

To him Bonnet's crew joined in consortship, and Bonnet himself was laid aside, notwithstanding the sloop was his own. The major went aboard Black-beard's ship, not concerning himself with any of their affairs; and continued there till she was lost in Topsail Inlet; and one Richards was appointed captain in his room. The major now saw his folly, but could not help himself, which made him melancholy. He reflected upon his past course of life, and was confounded with shame when he thought upon what he had done. His behaviour was taken notice of by the other pirates, who liked him none the better for it; and he often declared to some of them, that he would gladly leave off that way of living, being perfectly tired of it; but he should be ashamed to see the face of any honest Englishman again; therefore, he said, if he could get to Spain or Portugal, where he might live undiscovered, he would spend the remainder of his days in either of those countries, otherwise he must continue with them as long as he lived.

When Black-beard lost his sloop at Topsail Inlet, and surrendered to the King's Proclamation, Bonnet re-assumed the command of his own sloop; the Revenge went directly away to Bath Town, in North Carolina, surrendered likewise to the King's pardon, and received a certificate. The war was now broke out between the Triple Allies and Spain; so Major Bonnet got a clearance for his sloop at North Carolina, and went to the island of St. Thomas, with a design, at least as he pretended, to get the Emperor's commission to go a privateering upon the Spaniards. When Bonnet came back to Topsail Inlet, he found that Teach and his gang were gone, and that they had taken all the money, small arms, and effects of value, out of the great ship, and set ashore seventeen men on a small sandy island, above a league from the main, no doubt with a design they should perish, for there was no inhabitant or provisions to subsist withal, nor any boat, or materials to build, or make any kind of launch or vessel, to escape from that desolate place. They had remained there two nights and a day, without subsistence, or the least prospect of any, expecting nothing else but a lingering death; when, to their inexpressible comfort, they saw redemption at hand. Major Bonnet, happening to get intelligence of their being there by two of the pirates who had escaped from Teach's cruelty, and had got to a poor little village at the upper end of the harbour, sent his boat to make discovery of the truth of the matter, which the poor wretches seeing, they made a signal to them, and were all brought on board Bonnet's sloop.

Major Bonnet told all his company, that he would take a commission to go against the Spaniards, and would sail to St. Thomas's; therefore, he said, if they would go with him, they should be welcome, and they consented; but as the sloop was preparing to sail, a bomb-boat, which brought cider and apples to sell to the sloop's men, informed them, that Captain Teach lay at Ornicock Inlet, with only eighteen or twenty hands. Bonnet, who bore him a mortal hatred for some insults offered him, went immediately in pursuit of Black-beard, but it happened too late, for he missed him there. They cruised after him four days, when hearing no farther news of him, they steered their course towards Virginia.

In the month of July these adventurers came off the Capes, and meeting a pink with a stock of provisions on board, which they happened to be in want of, they took out of her ten or twelve barrels of pork, and about four hundred weight of bread; they would not, however, have this set down to the account of piracy, and therefore gave them eight or ten casks of rice and an old cable, in lieu thereof.

Two days afterwards they chased a sloop of sixty tons, and about two leagues off Cape Henry they took her. They were so happy here as to get a supply of liquor to their victuals, for they brought from her two hogsheads of rum, and as many of molasses; which it seems they had need of, though they had no ready money to purchase them. What security they intended to give, I cannot tell; but Bonnet sent eight men to take care of the prize sloop, who, perhaps, not caring to make use of those accustomed freedoms, took the first opportunity to go off with her, and Bonnet (who was now pleased to have himself called Captain Thomas,) saw them no more.

After this the major threw off all restraint, and though he had just before received his majesty's mercy in the name of Stede Bonnet, he relapsed in good earnest into his old vocation by the name of Captain Thomas, and re-commenced a downright pirate, by taking and plundering all the vessels he met with. He took off Cape Henry two ships from Virginia, bound to Glasgow, which. furnished them with but very little besides one hundred weight of Tobacco. The next day they took a small sloop bound from Virginia to Bermudas, which supplied them with twenty barrels of pork, and some bacon; they gave her in return two barrels of rice, and one hogshead of molasses; out of this sloop two men entered voluntarily into their service. The next they took was another Virginiaman, bound to Glasgow, out of which they had nothing of value, save only a few combs, pins, and needles, instead of which they gave her a barrel of pork, and two barrels of bread.

From Virginia they sailed to Philadelphia, and in lat. 38 N. they took a schooner coming from North Carolina and bound to Boston; they deprived her only of two dozen of calf skins to make covers for guns, and two of her hands, but they detained her some days. All this was but small game, and seemed as if they designed only to make provision for their sloop against they arrived at St. Thomas's; for they hitherto had dealt favourably with all that fell into their hands; but those that were so unhappy as to come after fared not so well: for in lat. 32, off Delaware river, near Philadelphia, they took two snows bound to Bristol, out of which they got some money, besides goods to the value of £150. At the same time they took a sloop of sixty tons, bound from Philadelphia to Barbadoes, which, after taking some goods out, they dismissed along with the snows.

The 29th of July, Captain Thomas took a sloop of fifty tons, six or seven leagues off Delaware bay, bound from Philadelphia to Barbadoes, Thomas Read, master; she was loaded with provisions, which they kept, and put four or five of their hands on board her. Two days after, they took another vessel of sixty tons, commanded by Peter Manwaring, bound from Antigua to Philadelphia which they likewise kept with all the cargo, consisting chiefly of rum, molasses, sugar, cotton, indigo, and about 25*l.* in money, valued in all at 500*l.*; and the same day our rovers, with the vessels last taken, left Delaware bay, and sailed to Cape Fear river, where they stayed too long for their safety; for the pirate sloop, which they now new-named the Royal James, proved very leaky, so that they were obliged to remain here almost two months in order to repair their vessel. They took in this river a small shallop, which they ripped up to mend their sloop. By these means the prosecution of their voyage, as before mentioned, was deferred till the news came to Carolina of a pirate's sloop being there to careen, with her prizes.

Upon this information the council of South Carolina was alarmed, apprehending they should receive another visit from them speedily; to prevent which, Colonel William Rhet, of the same province, waited on the Governor and generously offered himself to go with two sloops and attack the pirate. The Governor readily accepted his offer, and accordingly gave the colonel a commission, and full power to fit out such vessels as he thought proper for the design.

In a few days two sloops were equipped and manned—the Henry with eight guns and seventy men, commanded by Captain Masters, and the sea Nymph, with eight guns and sixty men, commanded by Captain Fayrer Hall, both under the entire direction of Colonel Rhet; who, on the 14th of September, went on board the Henry, and with the other sloop sailed from Charlestown to Swillivant's island, to put themselves in order for the cruise. Just then a small ship arrived from Antigua, one Cock, master, with an account that, in sight of the bar, he was taken and plundered by one Charles Vane, a pirate, in a brigantine of twelve guns and ninety men, who, they said, had also taken two other vessels bound in there; one a small sloop, from Barbadoes, Captain Dill, master, the other a brigantine from Guinea, Captain Thompson, master, with ninety odd negroes, which they took out of the vessel and put on board another sloop, then under the command of one Yeats, his consort, with twenty-one men. This proved fortunate to the owners of the Guineaman, for Yeats having often before attempted to quit this course of life, took an opportunity in the night to leave Vane, and ran into North Edisto river, to the southward of Charlestown, where he surrendered to His Majesty's pardon. Thus the owners got their negroes, and Yeats and his men had certificates given them from the government.

Vane cruised some time off the bar in hopes to catch Yeats, and unfortunately for them took two ships coming out, bound to London. While the crews of these were prisoners aboard, some of the pirates gave out that they designed to go into one of the rivers to the southward. All this they told Colonel Rhet, who, upon hearing it, sailed over the bar the 15th of September, with the two sloops before mentioned; and having the wind northerly, went after Vane, scouring all the rivers and inlets to the southward; however, not meeting with him, he tacked about and stood for Cape Fear river, in prosecution of his first design. On the 26th following, in the evening, the colonel with his small squadron entered the river, and saw over a point of land three sloops at an anchor, which were Major Bonnet and his two prizes. It happened that in going up the river the pilot ran the colonel's sloop aground, and it was dark before they were afloat, which hindered their getting up that night. The pirates soon discovered the sloops; but not knowing who they were, or upon what design they came into that river, they manned three canoes, and sent them down to make prizes of them: but they quickly found their mistake, and returned to the sloop with the unwelcome news. Major Bonnet made preparations that night for engaging, and took all the men out of the prizes. He shewed Captain Manwaring, one of his prisoners, a letter he had just written, which he declared he would send to the Governor of Carolina; the contents were to this effect,—"That if the sloops, which then appeared, were sent out against him by the said governor, and he should happen to get clear off, he would afterwards burn and destroy all ships or vessels going in or coming out of South Carolina." The next morning they got under sail and came down the river, designing only a running fight. Colonel Rhet's sloops got likewise under sail and stood for him, getting upon each quarter of the pirate with intent to board him; which Bonnet perceiving, he edged in towards the shore, and being warmly engaged ran his sloop aground. The Carolina sloops being in the same shoal water, were in the same circumstances; the Henry, in which Colonel Rhet was, grounded within pistol-shot of the pirate, and on his bow; the other sloop grounded right a-head of him and almost out of gun-shot, which made her of little service to the colonel while they lay aground.

At this time the pirates had a considerable advantage; for their sloop, after she was aground, listed from Colonel Rhet's, by which means they were all covered; and the Colonel's sloop listing the same way, his men were as much exposed; notwithstanding which they kept a brisk fire the whole time they lay thus aground, which was near five hours. The pirates made a whiff in their bloody flag, and beckoned several times with their hats, in derision to the colonel's men to come on board, which they answered with cheerful huzzas, and said "That they would speak with them by-and-bye." This accordingly happened: for, the colonel's sloop being first afloat, he got into deeper water, and after mending the rigging, which was much shattered in the engagement, they stood for the pirate to give the finishing stroke, designing to go directly on board him. Bonnet, however prevented this by sending a flag of truce; and after some capitulating, his whole crew surrendered themselves prisoners. The colonel took possession of the sloop, and was extremely pleased to find that Captain Thomas, who commanded her, was the individual person of Major Stede Bonnet, who had done them the honour several times to visit their coast of Carolina.

The Henry had ten men killed, and fourteen wounded; the Nymph two killed and four wounded The officers and sailors in both sloops behaved themselves with the greatest bravery, and had they not so unluckily run aground, they had taken the pirate with much less loss of men; but as he endeavoured to sail by them and so make a running fight, the Carolina sloops were obliged to keep near him to prevent his getting away. Of the pirates, there were seven killed and five wounded; two of which latter died soon after of their wounds. Colonel Rhet weighed the 30th of September, from Cape Fear river, and arrived at Charlestown, on the 3rd of October, to the great joy of the whole province of Carolina.

Bonnet and his crew, two days after, were put on shore, and there not being a public prison, they were kept at the watch-house under a guard of militia; but Major Bonnet was committed into the custody of the marshal, at his own house. In a few days after, David Harriot, the master, and Ignatius Pell, the boatswain, who were removed from the rest of the company to the said marshal's house, and every night two sentinels were set about the said house, whether it was through corruption, or want of care in guarding the prisoners, we cannot say; but so it was, that on the 24th October, the major and Harriot made their escape, the boatswain refusing to go along with them. This made a great noise in the province, and people were open in their resentments, often reflecting publicly on the governor, and others on the magistracy, as though they had been bribed for conniving at their getting off. These invectives arose from their fears that Bonnet would be capable of raising another company, and of prosecuting his revenge against their country for what he had lately, though justly suffered. But they were in a short time made easy in those respects; for as soon as the governor had the account of Bonnet's escape, he issued out a proclamation, and promised a reward of 700*l.* to any that would take him; sending, besides, several boats with armed men both to the northward and southward, in pursuit of him.

Bonnet stood to the northward in a small vessel, but wanting necessaries, and the weather being bad, he was forced back, and so returned with his canoe to Swillivant's Island, near Charlestown to fetch supplies; there being now some information given to the governor, he sent for Colonel Rhet, and desired him to go in pursuit of Bonnet, and accordingly gave him a commission for that purpose. Hereupon, the Colonel, with a great deal of craft, and some men, went away that night for Swillivant's Island, where, after a diligent search, he discovered Bonnet and Harriot together. The Colonel's men fired upon them, killed Harriot upon the spot, and wounded one Negro and an Indian. Bonnet submitted and surrendered himself; and the next morning, being November the 6th, was brought back by Colonel Rhet to Charlestown, and, by the governor's warrant, committed there into safe custody, in order for being brought to his trial.

The king's commission to Judge Trot being read, and a grand jury sworn for the finding of the several bills, a learned charge was given them by the said judge, wherein he first shewed, that the sea was given by God, for the use of man, and therefore is subject to dominion and property, as well as the land. Secondly, he particularly remarked to them, the supreme sovereignty of the King of England over the British seas. Thirdly, he observed, that as commerce and navigation could not be carried on without laws, so there have been always particular laws, for the better ordering and regulating marine affairs; to this he added, an historical account of those laws and their origin. Fourthly, he proceeded to shew, that there had been particular courts and judges appointed, to whose jurisdiction maritime causes properly belong; and that in matters most civil and criminal. And then, Fifthly, he particularly shewed them, the constitution of the present Court of Admiralty Sessions. And lastly, the crimes that were cognizable therein; here he particularly enlarged upon the crime of piracy, which was now to be brought before them.

The indictment being found, a petit jury was sworn, and Stede Bonnet, *alias* Edwards, *alias* Thomas, late of Barbadoes, mariner together with thirty-two of his companions, were arraigned, tried, and found guilty of the indictments exhibited against them, and received sentence of death accordingly.

The judge made a very grave and moving speech to them, setting forth the enormity of their crimes, the condition they were in, and the nature and necessity of an unfeigned repentence: he then recommended them to the ministers of the province, for more ample directions to fit them for eternity. "For," said he, "the priests' lips shall keep knowledge, and you shall seek the law at their mouths; for they are the messengers of the Lord, and the ambassadors of Christ; and unto them is committed the word of reconciliation." After this he pronounced sentence of death upon them, and they were executed on Saturday, the 8th of November, 1788.

As for the captain, his escape protracted his fate, and spun out his life a few days longer; for he was not tried till the 10th of November, when being found guilty, received sentence in like manner as the former, and was accordingly executed.

Printed by WALTER SCOTT, "*The Kenilworth Press,*" *Felling, Newcastle.*

www.ingramcontent.com/pod-product-compliance
Lightning Source LLC
Chambersburg PA
CBHW032008300426
44117CB00008B/944